• Skirmish • Red, White and Blue

The History of the 7th U.S. Cavalry (1945-1953)

TURNER PUBLISHING COMPANY

Publisher's Editor: Robert J. Martin
Writer: Edward L. Daily
Designer: Luke A. Henry

Copyright © 1992
Turner Publishing Company

This book or any part thereof may not be reproduced without written consent of the publisher.

Library of Congress Catalog Card No. 92-060620

ISBN: 978-1-68162-128-9

Extra copies available from the publisher.

Strategic withdrawal south of Seoul on January 3, 1951. (U.S. Army Photo)

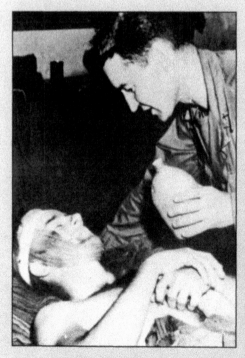

Chaplain helping a wounded trooper. (U.S. Army Photo)

Republic of Korea soldiers. They were tough and determined fighters. (U.S. Army Photo)

A typical Korean village prior to the Korean War. 1950.

1st Cavalry Division troopers looking at where two bullet holes almost went through the same hole in his helmet. (U.S. Army Photo)

TABLE OF CONTENTS

Preface 4
Introduction 5
The GARRYOWEN 6
The Author 7
Legacy of the 7th Cavalry 8
General George A. Custer 9
From the Commanders 10
The Commanders 11
Esprit de Corps to the GARRYOWEN 15
Chapter I OCCUPATION DUTY 18
Chapter II JOURNEY INTO WAR 25
Chapter III PUSAN PERIMETER 33
Chapter IV THE BREAKOUT 46
Chapter V CROSSING THE 38TH PARALLEL 58
Chapter VI CHINESE INTERVENTION 65
Chapter VII ADVANCE TO THE REAR 73
Chapter VIII COUNTERATTACK 79
Chapter IX CHINESE SPRING OFFENSIVE 101
Chapter X IRON TRIANGLE 106
Campaigns 117
Medal of Honor 118
Charts 119
Extracts 120
Glossary 122
Roster 124
Acknowledgments 127
Sources 128
Friends & Remembrances 128

PREFACE

Much about the Korean War still is hidden and much will long remain hidden. Nevertheless, an attempt was made by the author to give a historical account of the 7th Cavalry Regiment's activities during Occupation Duty in Japan after World War II and combat actions within the Korean War. This was accomplished by exploring all known official existing records in the National Military Archives, which have been quoted freely and very often verbatim to give a truthful view of events as they existed at that particular time.

Throughout the years, the original records of the 7th Cavalry Regiment have suffered from many disasters. On March 30, 1952, a fire destroyed the regimental headquarters in Japan, and everything was burned except the regimental colors. To further complicate the matter, but to comply with orders, many valuable records were destroyed to accomplish what they thought was "cleaning out useless files." What this actually caused or created was the existence of incomplete and often inaccurate records.

Perhaps this book will have an eye-opening effect for the reader and will stir memories and answer questions that still prevail or persist. For those who were there, survived the many struggles and hardships, and turned the tide of defeat to victory, I salute all of you. I apologize and ask forgiveness for any errors or omissions that annoy all of those who dare to analyze the confusion, the chaos of battle, to a smartly phrased story.

Edward L. Daily
Author

INTRODUCTION

L to R: Attorney General J. Howard McGrath, President Harry Truman and Defense Secretary Louis Johnson, walk to the White House to discuss first Korean crisis on June 27, 1950. (Wide World)

L to R: Korean Ambassador John Chang and Secretary General Trygve Lie, confirm that it is war against the United Nations. (Acme-UPI)

The Korean War began on June 25, 1950, and ended when an Armistice Agreement was signed on July 27, 1953. The first 17 months the war raged up and down and across the peninsula of that country. Both North Korea and South Korea were devastated. After the war, machines of the United Nations Command, both North and South Korea and the Chinese Communist Forces had chewed up the country, spitting out waste, much had been lost and very little had been gained by either side. The fight to gain land, for one side or the other, ended almost exactly where it began, along the 38th Parallel.

Although great masses of land were taken and lost again by both sides during the first 17 months of the Korean War, the beginning peace talks saw the war stagnate following a last major engagement in late 1951, which was called the Punchbowl. The war stagnated with combatants on both sides living in trenches. The war was a matter of fierce firefights with small arms, reconnaissance and combat patrols and a matter of howitzers and mortars fired discriminately and indiscriminately.

Numerous books detail the history of early Korean War battles, or engagements, both large and small, of men and machines of war, of the way and manner and fighting abilities of all concerned with the war, especially during the first 17 months of the Korean War.

Very few books have been written of the months that followed from October 1951 until the end in July 1953. In those 21 months, many men died in the trench warfare that existed. A warfare likened to that of World War I, but which was fought in a more modern manner. Although still a shooting war, a dying war, the Korean war came virtually to a standstill, degenerating in 1951 into dreary and seemingly endless battles for the same hills. Even though the war came somewhat to a halt, the men fighting it did not.

The many struggles and hardships of combat that were experienced by the 7th Cavalry Regiment, 1st Cavalry Division,

probably were no worse than any other infantry regiment that fought in the Korean War. Justifiably so, nevertheless, the regiment experienced continuous combat and under every possible condition, during the first 17 months of the Korean War. The regiment did their fair share within the United Nations Command in helping to restore peace in South Korea.

But the price of victory did not come cheap. The regiments' desperate battles, fought amid the stinking rice paddies and barren wind-swept frozen hills of Korea, cost the regiment more than 600 killed, 3,500 wounded and 300 missing in action. Also during this same time span, the 1st Cavalry Division suffered 16,498 soldiers killed or wounded in action. The Korean War cost the United States 54,246 killed in action, 103,284 wounded and 8,177 missing in action. A grim reminder of the precious price that is paid for freedom.

And history has a way of making fools of all who would second-guess a verdict, and the Korean War is a particular case in point. The accepted wisdom has been that the war in Korea would be recorded as a wasted effort, a stalemate in the struggle against communism that was best ignored and forgotten.

Recent world events, however, have called that premature evaluation into question. Korea might turn out to be the most decisive conflict waged during the entire 20th century - the war that spelled the death knell of Communism itself.

Within the past two years, we have seen the failure of communism throughout the world. Individual freedom has prevailed in large measure because of the United States stand during the Korean War.

As President Calvin Coolidge once said, *"No man was ever honored for what he received. Honor has been the reward for what he gave."* All Korean War veterans should feel extremely proud because they gave much courage and self-sacrifice to preserve the freedom and democracy in South Korea. I salute all of you . . .

Edward L. Daily
Author

THE GARRYOWEN

BLAZON OF THE REGIMENTAL INSIGNIA
OF THE 7TH U.S. CAVALRY, USA

A cavalry horseshoe, or, heels upward, with crease, sabre and seven nail heads, white. Above and joining the heels of the shoe, a scroll, azure, bearing the words, "GARRYOWEN," or . . .

At the base and emerging from sinister side of the shoe, a dexter arm embowed, vested azure, the hand in the buckskin gauntlet, proper, grasping an old style U.S. Army sabre, or hilted, or blade extending to center or scroll gripe, sabre threaded or . . .

Explanation of Design

The horseshoe is symbolic of the Cavalry. Its color, gold (yellow in heraldic tincture), is the color of the old uniform facings of the United States Cavalry, in existence when the Regiment was organized and still is retained as the color of the Cavalry Arm.

The words, "GARRYOWEN," are the title of an old Scottish (sic) war song known and used as the Regimental song since the days of General Custer. Its rollicking air symbolizes the esprit de corps for which the Regiment is noted.

The arm, taken from the crest of the Regimental Coat of Arms, symbolizes the spirit of the Cavalry Charge. At the time of the organization of the Regiment, this position of the arm and sabre was known as "Raise Sabre" and was taken at the command, "Charge." The sabre itself is of the old Cavalry type used in the Indian campaigns. The gauntlet also is symbolic of those times. The blue of the sleeve is the blue of the old Army uniform. The twisted emblem at toe of shoe is symbolic of Indian days.

For many years, the Regimental song was accepted as being of Scottish origin; however, it has been definitely established that the song is of Irish origin. It had been used by several Irish regiments as their quick march; the Fifth Royal Irish Lancers stationed in the suburb of Limerick called "GARRYOWEN," (the Gaelic word, meaning "Owen's Garden") used it as their drinking song. the words hardly can be called elevating, but depict the rollicking nature of the Lancers while in town on pay day in search of their peculiar style of "camaraderie."

Authority: Boosey: London: (no date, presumably about 1800) "Songs of Ireland."

THE SONG OF GARRYOWEN

It was an Irish quick marching or drinking song adopted by the 7th Cavalry Regiment in 1867. Its first introduction to war was at the Battle of Washita, on Nov. 17, 1868. After that, all 7th Cavalry troopers were known as GARRYOWENs.

We are the pride of the Army and a Regiment of great renown
Our names in the pages of history from 66 on down
If you think we stop or falter while into the fray we're goin'
Just watch our step, with our heads erect when our band plays "GARRYOWEN"

THE AUTHOR

Edward L. Daily

Edward L. Daily enlisted directly into the 1st Cavalry Division in 1948. After completing Armored-Infantry basic training at Fort Knox, Ky., he was sent immediately to the Far East Command in Japan. Arriving in Tokyo, Japan, in February 1949, he was assigned to Company H, 2nd Battalion, 7th Cavalry Regiment.

He soon found himself learning his new trade as a machine gunner in the 1st Platoon. But, at that particular time, most of their training consisted of occupation duty that existed within the Eighth Army. A major influence soon appeared in his life and military career, which came from his company commander, Capt. Melbourne C. Chandler. Chandler attempted to instill in every trooper a dedicated effort to become a better soldier, and he further emphasized the strict guidelines of the heritage and traditions of the famous GARRYOWEN regiment.

When the Korean War started, the 7th Cavalry Regiment departed from Japan in July 1950, to fight against communist aggression from the North Korean Army. Fighting a savage enemy, the 2nd Battalion experienced many battle casualties during the early stages of combat. This created a very serious condition because there was a shortage of replacements and, in some instances, there were none at all! Because of this desperate situation, promotions within the ranks came to those capable survivors. From the recommendations of Lt. Robert M. Carroll, Capt. Mel Chandler and Maj. Omar Hitchner, Commander, 2nd Battalion, he received a battlefield commission to temporary 2nd Lieutenant on Aug. 10, 1950.

Assuming leadership of the same 1st Platoon, it was a very proud time in his life and military career. However, two days later, on Aug. 12, 1950, during a vicious battle on the Naktong River, the forward elements of his platoon were overrun, and he could not evade capture.

With the grace of God, he managed to escape from the enemy on Sept. 12, 1950, and was held captive only 32 days. Receiving the appropriate medical treatment, he volunteered to return to his previous unit and active duty on Sept. 23, 1950. This time, conditions had changed greatly in favor of the United Nations Forces, because the United States Marines and the 7th Infantry Division previously had made an amphibious landing at Inchon, South Korea, thus cutting off the entire supply line of the North Korean Army.

Nonetheless, he would face many struggles and hardships as he remained in combat with the 7th Cavalry Regiment. On May 10, 1951, he returned to the United States. He was honorably discharged from the Army on May 27, 1952.

Among the medals awarded to him were: the Distinguished Service Cross; Silver Star Medal; Bronze Star Medal (V); Purple Heart w/2 Oak-leaf Clusters; Army Commendation Medal; Korean Campaign Medal w/5 Bronze Battle Stars; South Korean Presidential Unit Citation and the Combat Infantryman Badge. In June 1988, he was awarded the American Ex-Prisoner of War Medal by the Department of Defense.

He is a life member of the 1st Cavalry Division Association and the 7th U.S. Cavalry Association; and over the years, he has remained loyal and dedicated to both organizations. Currently, he is a member of the Board of Governors of the 1st Cavalry Division Association. The 1st Cavalry Division is stationed at Fort Hood, Texas. He is currently president of the 7th U.S. Cavalry Association.

LEGACY OF THE 7TH CAVALRY

The westward surge of the American migration to the Great Plains in the 1850s symbolized the restless urge that gripped the entire nation. Spurred on by the pretending clouds of the Civil War between the States, the land-hungry hordes ignored the mounting unrest of the Indians. Marked with savageness, the Indians rose to block the ongoing tide that flooded their territories. The Indian warriors struck with impunity and remounted their attacks in blood-drenched orgies.

With this westward expansion and massive migration of settlers, the need for more soldiers to protect them soon developed. Under the Congress Act of July 28, 1866 (General Order 92), came the birth of the newly authorized 7th Cavalry Regiment and the beginning of a new chapter in the history of the Army.

The 7th Cavalry Regiment was organized at Fort Riley, Kan., and its ranks were filled with a hard-bitten crew of trappers, veterans from the Civil War and frontiersmen. Its prime field officers were Col. Andrew J. Smith, Lt. Col. (Brevet Maj. Gen.) George Armstrong Custer and Maj. Alfred Gibbs.

Also, the influx of Irish immigrants contributed a great share of the troopers within the Regiment, and the brawling, hot-tempered Irishmen found a ready outlet for their exuberant spirits in the campaigns against the Cheyennes. The influence of the Irish on the Regiment is noted particularly in the famous drinking song "GARRYOWEN," which the Regiment has adopted as its own.

When Custer organized the Regimental Band in 1867, he adopted the "GARRYOWEN" as the official song of the 7th Cavalry. On Nov. 17, 1868, at the Battle of Washita, Custer had the Regimental Band play the "GARRYOWEN" as the 7th Cavalry engaged the village of Black Kettle to inspire his command during this battle. The scattered remnants of the Cheyennes were decisively defeated.

Until 1872, the Regiment rode out against the Sioux and Apaches. In 1874, the Regiment moved to the Black Hills of Dakota to afford protection for construction parties of the Northern Pacific Railroad. Hard on the heels of the newly laid tracks came hordes of gold seekers and farmers, and this influx brought about new troubles with the Sioux. As the migration continued, the savageness of the Indians increased until 1876; the 7th Cavalry and its dashing, spectacular leader, Lt. Col. (Brevet Maj. Gen.) George Armstrong Custer, joined other Army units in a concerted drive to break once and for all the power of the Sioux tribes.

Fate was to pick the proud 7th Cavalry to play the leading role in a portrayal of devotion to duty, loyalty to country and honor to self that exemplifies the word "courage." Scouting patrols of Custer's forces were the first to locate the Sioux. Custer had never before faced such an opportunity for delivering a crushing defeat.

With a camp swarming with wives and children and their entire wealth, the Sioux warriors could not scatter and pick their battle ground. The slightest delay might mean the escape of the foe. Fulfilling his command responsibility, Custer made his decision. He split the Regiment into three units, sending two of them to his left under Maj. Reno and Capt. Benteen with the mission of attacking the camp on line with the third unit under his own command. The soundness of this plan is, even today, the subject of heated discussion among military men.

Whether it could have succeeded will never be known, for Reno and Benteen met opposition to their progress, and the full might of an estimated 5,000 Sioux plunged head-on into the five companies under Custer. The determined stand of the valiant officers and men has been immortalized in story, song and picture. Fighting to the last man, they finally were overwhelmed by the masses of charging Indians. The next day when the delayed forces of Reno and Benteen reached the scene, there remained only a Cavalry charger named "Commanche," alive on the battlefield. It was Capt. Keogh's horse!

In 1877, the Regiment returned to action against the wiliest of all Indian generals, Chief Joseph of the Nez Perces. During the bloody four-day battle, the might of the great chief was broken, and the defeated Indians were returned to their reservation.

By 1906, the Regiment had served two tours of duty in the Philippines and in 1916 joined the Mexican Punitive Expedition. It returned to Fort Bliss, Texas, and remained there until it was assigned to the 1st Cavalry Division in 1921.

In February 1943, and within the early stages of World War II, the Regiment was converted from horses to vehicles, which was an exit of an era in military lore. It was passing of an age of chivalry in that had grown from the days of Knighthood and reached its peak in the great Cavalry charges of the Civil War.

The Regiment departed Camp Stoneman, Calif., in July 1943, to their new home in Australia. At a location 15 miles north of Brisbane, the Regiment - for the next six months - would engage itself in jungle and amphibious training. This specialized infantry preparation was for Gen. MacArthur's strategic forces in the South Pacific. Even though it now was an infantry unit, Army standard operating procedures and sentiment of the 7th Cavalry Regiment, it was permitted to keep its old name and that was all.

The Regiment found itself fighting in several different Island Campaigns and eventually defeated the Japanese Imperial Army in the Philippines. These vicious, bloody battles fought in the extreme heat of the South Pacific jungles were won at a cost to the Regiment of more than 300 killed and 1,000 wounded.

On Aug. 13, 1945, the 1st Cavalry Division - which included the Regiment - was selected by the Supreme Commander, Gen. Douglas MacArthur, to accompany him to Tokyo, Japan, and be part of the Eighth Army Occupation Forces. In the early morning of Sept. 8, 1945, the 7th Cavalry Regiment entered Tokyo, and from that date until it sailed for Korea, it performed occupation duty in Japan.

The Regiment suffered drastically during the post-war demobilization of combat units throughout the entire Army. Performing its occupation duties effectively, it had difficulty, however, maintaining a combat readiness and capability. On June 25, 1950, the North Korean People's Army invaded the Republic of Korea, South Korea, with hordes of Communist soldiers. Being poorly prepared for combat, the 7th Cavalry Regiment was thrown into South Korea as an American infantry unit to temporarily halt the Communist tide.

During the Korean War, the Regiment fought many desperate battles within the Pusan Perimeter and throughout the endless mountains of South and North Korea. Amid the hot, stinking rice paddies to the sub-zero frozen hills of Korea, the Regiment experienced some of the bloodiest fighting in its long history. By the time that the Armistice Agreement was signed on July 27, 1953, ending the Korean War, the 7th Cavalry Regiment had suffered more than 600 killed, 3,500 wounded and 300 missing in action.

In a few short years to come, the 7th Cavalry would meet the call to an old, yet new conflict, the Vietnam War. A new concept in warfare and tactical doctrines in the use of helicopters opened the way to a bold, new role in combat for the Regiment.

These crack "Skytroopers," as a new Cavalry with an old spirit - but young at heart - would fight heroically with determination to destroy the Communist enemy in Vietnam. Many bitter and vicious battles were hard fought and won, creating another new chapter in the history of the 7th Cavalry Regiment and the United States Army.

Then, in August 1990, the 7th Cavalry was alerted for quick deployment to Saudi Arabia for Operation Desert Shield. Again answering the call of their nation, it was a period of intense activity to meet their new task. This time to stop the oppressive enemy army of Saddam Hussein, and restore freedom to the country of Kuwait.

It was a new generation of American soldiers who were highly trained and skilled to do their jobs efficiently, with the best military weaponry in the world. In Operation Desert Storm, the 7th Cavalry used tactics by probing and jabbing with fast, lightly armored Bradley and Cobra vehicles against enemy positions in Iraq. This would make way and guide the M1A1 tanks of the First Cavalry Division into battle.

The Persian Gulf War was soon over and the freedom of a small country preserved. Once again, it showed the world that aggression will not be tolerated. Within the Army organization, the 7th Cavalry exemplified that it will always be ready to fight, anytime, anywhere, and win. Furthermore, our nation demands it and our freedom depends on it..... GARRYOWEN!

GENERAL GEORGE A. CUSTER

Born: Dec. 5, 1839
Birthplace: New Rumley, Ohio
Father: Emanuel Custer

Emanuel Custer had five children by his second marriage. They were: George Armstrong Custer, Dec. 5, 1839; Nevin Johnson Custer, July 29, 1842; Thomas Ward Custer, March 15, 1845; Boston Custer, Oct. 31, 1848; and Margaret Emma Custer, Jan. 5, 1852. His father was born in Cryssoptown, Md., in 1806. Leaving there, he settled in New Rumley, Ohio, where he married Matilda Viers at the age of 22. She died six years later, leaving him with three children.

In the early 1850s they moved out of New Rumley a few miles into Harrison County to live in a log cabin. They attended the Creal School a mile and a half north of Scio.

When George was 10 years old, his half-sister (by his father's first marriage), Lydia Custer, married David Reed of Monroe, Mich., some 200 miles from their home in New Rumley, Ohio. At the age of 16, he taught school in Harrison County, Ohio, at Beech Point, and later Locust Grove, and he attended McNeely Formal School (Hopedale College) in between school terms.

In March 1861, his father, Emanuel, purchased 120 acres of land in Wood County before moving to Monroe, Mich., several years later. George earned $26 a month plus board for teaching schools.

In the summer of 1857 he landed on the wharf of West Point, and he would be one of 68 Plebes to be admitted there in July. At the time Custer went to West Point, you were supposed to graduate in five years, but this was changed in April 1861 to four years because of the Civil War. Custer was to have graduated that year in July, but in early June while on duty as Duty Officer he failed to stop a fight and was brought up on charges for failing to stop a riot. On July 15th, he was brought to trial by court martial. He was found guilty and sentenced to be reprimanded in Orders.

In the meantime, some of his friends who had graduated in April went to Washington on his behalf. He was summoned to Washington and thereby was given his first assignment. He was assigned to G Company, 2nd Cavalry. His first battle was at Bullrun, which turned into a defeat for the North.

Early in the fall of 1861, Custer left his outfit and was attached to Gen. Stoneman's outfit. He was sent home on sick leave, staying in Monroe, Mich., from October 1861 to February 1862. He then was assigned to the 5th Cavalry (Army of the Potomac). In May of 1862, he was promoted to captain and became Gen. McClellans' "Aide-de-Camp" (temporary rank).

He took command of A Company 4th Michigan Infantry. Most of these men were from Monroe, Mich., and many had gone to school with him at Stebbins Academy when he lived with his half-sister.

About two weeks later, he was promoted to 1st Lieutenant in the 5th Cavalry. On Nov. 7th, McClellans was put on waiting orders, so Custer went home to Monroe, Mich. While there he met his wife-to-be, Elizabeth Libby Bacon.

In April of 1863, Custer was ordered to join his company opposite Fredericksburgh, Va. Once again, Custer was a lieutenant and in June found himself as a captain and "aide-de-camp" to Gen. Pleasonton. On June 29th, Custer was promoted to the rank of Brigadier General and took command of the Michigan Cavalry Brigade and joined them in Hanover, Penn.

Custer and Elizabeth Libby Bacon were married on Feb. 9, 1864, in the Presbyterian Church in Monroe, Mich.

In October 1864, he was promoted to major general of the volunteers and placed in command of the 3rd Division, which included his crack Michigan Brigade. On Oct. 6, they were told to withdraw. Tom Custer was awarded the Medal of Honor twice. He was the only person in any branch of their service so honored. In May of 1865, the Civil War was over, and Custer was ordered to Texas. In the early spring of 1866, he was ordered back to Washington. The same month, he was mustered out as a major general of the volunteers and automatically reverted to his regular Army rank of captain. He was paid $8,000 a year as a major general and $2,000 a year as a captain. At this time, Custer was 27 years of age and returned to Monroe, Mich., for a much-earned rest.

In July, he received his appointment at lieutenant colonel of the newly formed 7th Cavalry. In October, he joined the 7th Cavalry at Ft. Riley, Kan. His brother, Tom, was appointed as a first lieutenant in the regular Army on July 28, 1866. On Aug. 27, 1867, General Grant ordered a general court martial at Ft. Levenworth, trying Custer for: 1) Absenting himself from his command without authority. 2) Using ambulances for personal business. 3) Ordering his officers to shoot deserters without a trial, among other things. The court convened on Sept. 15, 1867, meeting for four weeks before reaching the verdict of guilty. He was sentenced to a suspension of rank and command and forfeiture of pay for one year.

Custer returned to Ft. Hayes, Kan., on Sept. 30, 1868. In 1871, Custer took part of the Regiment to Elizabethtown, Ky. The rest of the Regiment was sent to South Carolina to break up the Klu Klux Klan and to hunt down moonshiners.

In 1873, Custer and the 7th Regiment were assigned to Ft. Abraham Lincoln at Yankton, Dakota Territory. Margaret Custer, the general's only sister, married Lt. James Calhoun in 1871. He was killed at the battle of Little Bighorn.

At the age of 35, Custer was 5'10" tall. He weighed 165 lbs., had clear blue eyes, and short, wavy, golden-tint hair. Custer and his wife would spend his leave time whenever possible in Monroe, Mich. Custer also was a great lover of literature. On June 27, 1876, Lt. Bradley and his scouting party returned with first-hand information that Custer and all of his 225 officers and men were dead. There were no human survivors, but the horse, Comanche, belonging to Capt. Myles Keough was found alive but severely wounded. He was tenderly taken care of and nursed back to health.

Relatives of Custer who died with him at the battle of Little Bighorn were: Brothers Capt. Tom W. Custer, age 31; Forager Boston Custer, age 25; brother-in-law Lt. James Calhoun; and nephew Harry Armstrong Reed from Monroe, Mich., age 18.

Comanche the horse was retired from all duty until his death at the age of 29 in 1891.

Things found out after Custer's death: 1) There were about three times the number of Indians that the agent had reported. 2) The Indians had been supplied with Winchester repeating rifles and an abundance of ammunition for the purpose of hunting buffalo, while Custer and his men had single-shot Springfield rifles.

General Custer adopted the song GARRYOWEN as a fighting song in 1867.

FROM THE COMMANDERS

A salute to "Old Glory" as it is raised above the American Embassy in Tokyo, Japan, Sept. 8, 1945. L to R: Maj. Gen. Will C. Chase C/G 1st Cav. Div.; Admiral William Halsey; Lt. Gen. Robert L. Eichelberger and General of the Army Douglas MacArthur. (U.S. Army Photo)

During the Korean War, the 1st Battalion along with the other Battalions of the 7th Cavalry Regiment, added another chapter to its glorious past.

It was an honor and privilege to Command the 1st Battalion, 7th Cavalry Regiment, during the first 10 months of the Korean War. Many missions were executed with precision and valor, by brave officers and troopers within the battalion. Their heroic deeds and outstanding combat performances to accomplish the objectives, have always been an inspiration to me, throughout the years. This historical book of the 7th Cavalry Regiment during the Korean War, is a true source of pride for everyone.

> Colonel Peter D. Clainos, U.S.A. (retired)
> Former Battalion Commander
> 1st Battalion, 7th Cavalry regiment
> 1st Cavalry Division, Korea 1950-1951

Congratulations on your achievement of a very important work - the history of the Seventh Cavalry Regiment in Korea.

It is important in itself because it is the story of the brave men who faced the Communist enemy in Korea. But it may be even more significant and timely as an illustration of the consequences of minimizing our military preparedness in the dangerous world which we face in the coming years.

My hope would be that those who are shaping our forces for the future might know the story of the early days of the Korean War, with its warning of the dangers of an ill-considered approach to force reduction. This volume should help in that understanding.

> Brig. Gen. James H. Lynch, U.S.A. (retired)
> Former Battalion Commander
> 3rd Battalion, 7th Cavalry Regiment
> 1st Cavalry Division, Korea 1950

As I look back over my thirty-six years in the Army, none is more meaningful to me than my Command of the 2nd Battalion of the 7th Cavalry Regiment, during the first year of the Korean War. These gallant officers and men demonstrated a courage and bravery of the highest order.

Their motto was <u>Duty, Honor and Country</u>; they gave their utmost to accomplish every mission assigned. It is my hope that the history revealed in this book, will reflect the accomplishments and sacrifices made by these brave men against enormous odds.

> Colonel John. W. Callaway, U.S.A. (retired)
> Former Battalion Commander
> 2nd Battalion, 7th Cavalry Regiment
> 1st Cavalry Division, Korea 1950-1951

To the men who served in the 7th Cavalry Regiment, it was a place called home. His comrades in arms took the place of family, and a deep family relationship started to exist for what reason, maybe, Love of Country, and Personal Pride as well as a desire to not let their comrades down under any condition.

This intense loyalty, generated as it did, close ties among the men of the Battalion and Division to do many of the outstanding accomplishments during the war with Honor and Pride.

It is with humble appreciation that I give them Thanks. Commanding the 3rd Battalion, 7th Cavalry Regiment was an Honor and a Privilege.

> Lt. Colonel Charles H. Hallden, U.S.A. (retired)
> Former Battalion Commander (after Lynch)
> 3rd Battalion Commander, 7th Cavalry Regiment
> 1st Cavalry Division, Korea 1950-1951

THE COMMANDERS

General Douglas MacArthur, Commander-in-Chief, United Nations Command, July 24, 1950 - April 11, 1951. (U.S. Army Photo)

General Matthew Ridgway, Commander-in-Chief, United Nations Command, April 11, 1951 - May 12, 1951. (U.S. Army Photo)

Major General Hobart Gay, 1st Cavalry Division Commander, Sept. 24, 1959 - Feb. 4, 1951. (U.S. Army Photo)

Major General Charles D. Palmer, 1st Cavalry Division Commander, Feb. 5, 1951 - July 16, 1951. (U.S. Army Photo)

Major General Thomas Harrold, 1st Cavalry Division Commander, July 16, 1951 - March 1952. (U.S. Army Photo)

Colonel George A. Millener, Regimental Commander, 7th Cavalry, June 21, 1949 - May 15, 1950. (U.S. Army Photo)

Colonel Cecil W. Nist, Regimental Commander, 7th Cavalry, May 25, 1950 - Sept. 21, 1950. (U.S. Army Photo)

Colonel William A. Harris, Regimental Commander, 7th Cavalry, Sept. 22, 1950 - April 24, 1951. (U.S. Army Photo)

Colonel Dan Gilmer, Regimental Commander, 7th Cavalry, April 25, 1951 - Nov. 26, 1951. (U.S. Army Photo)

Colonel Frank J. Culley, Regimental Commander, 7th Cavalry, Feb. 4 1952 - May 7, 1952; May 13, 1952 - June 2, 1952; June 7, 1952 - Sept. 20, 1952. (U.S. Army Photo)

Colonel Herbert H. Andrae, Regimental Commander, 7th Cavalry, Sept. 21, 1952 - Nov. 21, 1952; Nov. 26, 1952 - Dec. 10, 1952; Dec. 16, 1952 - June 9, 1953; June 16, 1953 - Nov. 6, 1953. (U.S. Army Photo)

Lt. Colonel Peter D. (Pete) Clainos, Commander, 1st Battalion, 7th Cavalry Regiment 1950 -1951. (U.S. Army Photo)

Colonel John W. Callaway, Commander, 2nd Battalion, 7th Cavalry Regiment, Sept. 6, 1950 - July 1951. (U.S. Army Photo)

Colonel James H. Lynch, Commander, 3rd Battalion, 7th Cavalry, 1950. Note his award of the Distinguished Service Cross. (U.S. Army Photo)

THE C.O. OF SKIRMISH BLUE
LT. COL. C. H. 'CHUCK' HALLDEN

Lt. Colonel Charles H. Hallden, Commander (after Lynch) 3rd Battalion, 7th Cavalry, 1950 - 1951. (Courtesy of Lt. Col. Hallden)

Lt. Colonel Melbourne C. Chandler, Executive Officer, 2nd Battalion, 7th Cavalry, 1950 - 1951; Commanding Officer of Company H, 1949 - 1950; 2nd Battalion Commander, July - Sept. 1951. (U.S. Army Photo)

ESPRIT de CORPS TO THE GARRYOWEN

To somewhat clarify the existence or absence of esprit de corps in a military unit, one must perhaps focus on traditions and heritages of an organization and its historical past. To better understand esprit, it is necessary to look beyond the immediate unit and consider the men, events, incidents and battles that are connected to its history as a whole.

The term "Cavalry" has been synonymous with esprit de corps in the military profession throughout the ages. Such terms as Dragoons, Lancers, Hussars, Horse Guards and Cavalry suggest a colorful mounted soldier dashing toward his enemy with sword raised at the charge. And from the earliest times, every battle has had its lessons and has left its mark on the particular unit involved. Weapons and tactics change, but the men who fight the battles and the principles for which they are fought remain much the same. However, a unit enriched with a glorious past history could so imbue an officer or soldier to feel duty-bound to maintain the unit's high reputation in the face of overwhelming odds.

In the case of the GARRYOWEN, 7th U.S. Cavalry Regiment and its modern Army units, the continuance existence of this indefinable enthusiasm, inspiration and spirit cannot be attributed to any single event or individual in the history of the regiment. A combination of legends and traditions have kindled this esprit.

The adoption of the regimental song "GARRYOWEN" in 1867 by Gen. George Armstrong Custer, did much to enhance the prestige of the 7th Cavalry among its sister regiments serving within the frontier. The Battle of the Little Big Horn, publicized out of all proportion to its military importance, has served to focus worldwide attraction on the 7th Cavalry Regiment.

GARRYOWEN troopers always have been and are today, the custodians of a personal pride in self and unit that is exceeded by no other unit in the Armies of the World. This blood bond to the glories of the past, coupled with the heroism and devotion to duty exemplified by deeds in World War II, Korea, Vietnam and Iraq campaigns, have given 7th Cavalry troopers a stubborn determination to endure to the utmost. An example of such esprit was demonstrated in the Korean War, by Sgt. Charles E. Anderson.

Sgt. Anderson first joined the 7th Cavalry at Fort Bliss, Texas in 1942 and accompanied the regiment as a medical aid man attached to Troop B through the Philippine Island campaigns. He was discharged from the service after the war, re-enlisted in October 1948, and rejoined the regiment in Tokyo. He accompanied the regiment to Korea, and again whenever the fighting was heaviest he could be found giving medical attention to the front line trooper without regard for his own personal safety. Sgt. Anderson was evacuated from Korea on Jan. 22, 1951, as a result of an earlier unfortunate incident. On Hill 464 near Weagwan, Korea on Sept. 3, 1950, while attempting to reach a fallen trooper in the front of the lines to administer first aid, he was trapped by an enemy force and could not return to friendly lines. In order to avoid capture, he rolled down a hill and in the process of doing so, lost his upper denture. This device was specially made to correct his con-genital deformity and was impossible to replace in Korea. Rather than report this incident, for what he termed a minor inconvenience, he remained on duty until January. By that time, he had lost so much weight due to his inability to eat solid foods that his condition was noticed by the regimental commander, and he was ordered evacuated. By this time, plastic surgery was necessary to restore his denture, and he was evacuated further to the United States for treatment. Upon his discharge from the hospital in June 1951, he wrote the former regimental commander - Col. William A. Harris then on duty in the United States - requesting assistance in obtaining reassignment in the regiment in Korea. The following are excerpts of that letter:

"I would like very much to return to the 7th Cavalry Regiment in Korea. To you, this desire probably seems like I am attempting to be ridiculous or that I am nourishing a type of adolescent fancy but it is quite the contrary; believe me, Col. Harris. The famed 7th Cavalry Regiment has always stood as a symbol of the entire United States Army. I must confess that I'm rather a sentimental 'old fool' about tradition and as far as my personal opinion, there's no better unit with which one can serve than the ole GARRYOWEN.

Seldom, if ever, have I yet to make a practice of imposing upon an officer for a favor or advice; but this time is an exception, believe me, Sir. All of my inquiries as to the possibilities of getting reassigned to the Regiment have been met with vague answers and the usual Army 'red tape,' if you get what I mean. No reflection upon the service, I assure you, Col. Harris; just my crude method of expressing myself. You must believe me when I say that I am truly willing to sacrifice my life in the present conflict so long as I can get back to the Regiment. I assure you that I will help many of my wounded fellowmen, however, before I do give my life if such should be my fate. If I cannot get back to the unit as an aid man, then I will gladly have my MOS changed from 3666 to that of a rifleman or anything; even to being reduced to the grade of Private if need be."

Sgt. Anderson finally did get authority to return to his regiment in Korea. Upon reviewing his record (he had been awarded three Silver Stars, two Bronze Stars and the Purple Heart during his service with the regiment), the regimental commander assigned Sgt. Anderson as an instructor to teach the inexperienced aid men. However, during the heavy fighting in the fall of 1951, the regiment suffered extremely high casualties, and casualties among medical aid men were in direct proportion. Seeing the need for medical care on the battlefield, Sgt. Anderson voluntarily went forward again as a company aid man and was killed in action on Sept. 25, 1951, while attempting to reach a wounded trooper.

The aforementioned are but a few examples of various incidents ingrained in the history of the regiment that make for the famous GARRYOWEN Esprit - an intrinsic part of the reputation of the regiment. Of the other old historic regiments in the Army, the GARRYOWEN Esprit stands very unique and distinctive, and has won the admiration of soldiers throughout the world.

L to R Corporal Ernie Aguilar and 1st Lt. John "Jack" Haskell, 545th M.P. Company, with an attached "hobby horse" on the hood of their jeep. (Courtesy of Ed Daily)

Chinese soldier who surrendered. (Courtesy of Bob Mauger)

Enemy soldier who died with his boots on. (Courtesy of Bob Mauger)

Chinese prisoners of war waiting for interrogation. (Courtesy of Bob Mauger)

1st Lt. Herschel "Ug" Fuson who was a great West Point football player and brave officer in battle. The Korean War cost him his life. (Courtesy of Ed Daily)

7th Cavalry 2-1/2 ton truck crossing a partially constructed bridge, near Uijongbu. (U.S. Army Photo)

A Chinese soldier stands on top of a knocked out American M-26 tank of the 70th Tank Battalion, 1st Cavalry Division at the battle of Unsan. This particular tank (B-23 of Company B) was supporting elements of the 8th Cavalry Regiment, during November 1-4, 1950. (Eastfoto)

Lt. Col. John W. Callaway, Commander, 2nd Battalion, 7th Cavalry, discusses with Gen. of the Army Douglas MacArthur, about the tactical situation north of Chipyong, Korea, March 1951. Gen. MacArthur's signature at top center of photo. (U.S. Army Photo, courtesy of Col. Callaway)

CHAPTER I
OCCUPATION DUTY

1945

As the Pacific Theater of World War II was coming to a close, the First Cavalry Division began training for a mission that promised to be bloodier than anything they had yet seen. In "Operation Olympic," scheduled for Nov. 1, 1945, they were to be among the first American soldiers to hit the beaches of Imperial Japan itself. However, the war came to a startling conclusion after massive mushroom clouds rose above Hiroshima and Nagasaki.

On Aug. 13th, a warning order was received from Gen. MacArthur's headquarters stating that the First Cavalry Division had been selected to accompany the Supreme Commander into Tokyo and be a part of the Eighth Army in the occupation of Japan. On Aug. 22nd, the regiment boarded the USS "Duel" and sailed with the Division from Batangas Bay on Aug. 25th. The following day, a typhoon warning forced the convoy to make an overnight halt in Subic Bay, but on Aug. 27th the convoy headed out again, steaming northward through the China Sea toward the Japanese homeland. On Sept. 2nd, the long convoy steamed into Yokohama Harbor, past the big battleship, the USS "Missouri," where a little while later, Gen. MacArthur received the Japanese surrender party.

At 1100 hours on Sept. 2nd, the regiment made an assault landing on the beaches of Yokohama with other elements of the Division. The big difference in this assault landing and the others of the past two years was the fact that there was no pre-invasion bombardment and that no resistance was encountered. The following day, the regiment moved to the Zama Military Academy nearby.

At 0800 hours on Sept. 8th, a history-making motor convoy left the Yokohama area for Tokyo. Headed by Maj. Gen. William C. Chase, Commanding General of the First Cavalry Division, the party included a veteran from each troop in the Division so that all units would be represented in this historic climax of the war. Passing through Hachioju, Fuchu and Chofu, the convoy halted briefly at the Tokyo city limits. Gen. Chase stepped across the line thereby putting the American Army officially in Tokyo and added another "First" to the record of the "First Team."

Also on Sept. 8th, Gen. MacArthur made his official entry into the city escorted by the 2nd Squadron, 7th Cavalry Regiment, under the command of Maj. William W. West, III; the 302nd Reconnaissance Troop; the Division Band; and an impressive array of the Division and Regimental colors and troop guidons. At the American Embassy, Gen. MacArthur gave the following instructions to Lt. Gen. Robert L. Eichelberger, Commanding General of the Eighth Army:

"Have our country's flag unfurled and in the Tokyo sun, let it wave in its full glory as a symbol of hope for the oppressed and as a harbinger of victory for the right."

While veteran cavalrymen raised the flag atop the American Embassy building, their comrades stood at attention as the Division Band played the National Anthem. The flag was the one that had been flying over the nation's Capitol in Washington, D.C., on Pearl Harbor Day and had flown over the Battleship "Missouri" while the surrender documents were being signed. The Flag of Liberation was also the first American flag to be flown over Rome, Italy, at the conclusion of hostilities with that country and over Berlin after VE-Day.

This flag is now in the national Capitol and was delivered to Sen. Vandenberg and House Speaker Martin on April 6th, 1948, by Maj. Gen. Hobart R. Gay, then commanding the First Cavalry Division.

On this same morning, the remainder of the regiment moved to the Yoyogi drill field located in the Meiji Inner Shrine in Tokyo.

The Division's first mission in Tokyo was to assume control of the central portion of the city. Troops of the 7th Cavalry guarded the American Embassy where Gen. MacArthur had taken up residence, and the Meiji Shrine, one of the most sacred areas in Japan according to Japanese belief. Daily patrols began the long task of locating, investigating and reporting all Japanese installations that had contributed to the nation's war effort. All arsenals, factories, barracks, and storage grounds had to be examined and reports made of their contents. In addition, the Division was concerned with the status of demobilization of the Japanese armed forces.

An important project during the early days of the occupation was to find adequate housing facilities for the troops. Although September was not a particularly cold month in Japan, the tent camp at Yoyogi proved unsuitable as winter quarters for troopers whose blood had been thinned by two years in the tropics. A typhoon, which damaged the camp on Sept. 16th, emphasized the need for more permanent billets. By Sept. 25th, the entire regiment had moved into the Merchant Marine School in Tokyo.

On Sept. 25th, a great turnover of personnel began in the regiment, which continued for the next several months and added considerably to the difficulties of carrying out the occupation mission. Men with high adjusted service rating scores were transferred to the 43rd Infantry Division for shipment home and discharge. Later, as other units were inactivated or returned to the United States, many low point men were transferred to the regiment to complete their tours of duty; however, these additions and the few replacements that came over directly from the States did not equal the losses through redeployment, and by the end of the year, the regiment had been reduced to 109 officers and 1,765 enlisted men.

The remainder of the year was spent in occupation duties, including the seizing and disposing of munitions, inventorying precious items captured by the Japanese, and conduction patrols in search of hidden Japanese implements of war.

Holiday greeting in 1947 from Sg. 1/c Vallie Stump, Motor Sergeant of the 4.2 Heavy Mortar Company, 7th Cavalry Regiment. (Courtesy of Valley Stump)

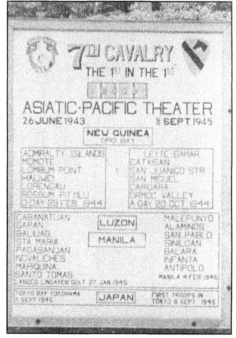

Sign at entrance to 7th Cavalry Regimental Headquarters in Tsukishima, Japan 1947. (Courtesy of Bob "Snuffy" Gray)

L to R: 2nd Lt. Robert H. Voelker, Platoon Leader; Captain Melbourne C. Chandler, Commander 1st Lt., Herman K. Vester, Executive Officer; Sgt. First Class Robert L. Earley, Platoon Sergeant; Company H, 1946. (Courtesy Ed Daily)

L to R: P.F.C. Tom Dover; Sgt. First Class Clifford Fletcher; Sergeant Millard Gray: Company H, 1949. (Courtesy of Ed Daily)

1946

Members of the regiment welcomed the arrival of 1946 - the dawning of a new era - a time when the days of privation, hardship, suffering and death had ceased for the first time since that morning on March 4th, 1944, when elements of the 2nd Squadron landed at Hyane Harbor in the Admiralties.

During the month of January, the regiment engaged in the Herculean task of rendering Japan powerless to wage wars of aggression as vast supplies of weapons, aircraft, ammunition and similar instruments of death and destruction were destroyed.

On March 9th, a ceremony and review were held by elements of the regiment with other units of the Division at the east gate of the Imperial Palace grounds in Tokyo. Lt. Gen. Robert L. Eichelberger, Eighth Army Commander, honored units by presenting them with battle streamers for the Luzon, Leyte-Samar, New Guinea and Bismarck Archipelago campaigns of World War II.

On April 30th, increased unrest among Japanese labor groups and signs of possible disturbances in the metropolitan area necessitated placing the regiment on an alert status until May 2nd.

A show of additional Allied strength was made in Tokyo during early May with the arrival of a battalion of the British Commonwealth Occupation Forces. The battalion, a unit of the 34th Australian Brigade, was attached to the 2nd Cavalry Brigade and billeted at the former Japanese Naval Technical Institute. Guard responsibility at four installations was assumed by the Australians and guard posts at the Imperial Palace grounds were mounted jointly with troopers of the 7th Cavalry Regiment.

On May 12th, members of the regiment participated in a Division review in Tokyo in honor of General of the Army Dwight D. Eisenhower, the Chief of Staff.

The regiment participated in the Fourth of July ceremony in Tokyo with other elements of the First Cavalry Division. All separate squadrons, troops and regiments of the Division were represented and formed in a line of the new colors and unit flags to the respective commanding officers by the commanding general of the Division.

Except for the bomb-scarred sections of To-

kyo - now almost covered with weeds - little evidence remained of the war. For the members remaining in the regiment who had "sweat out" D-Day the previous year, this August in Japan bore little resemblance to the vast military machine they had conquered piece-meal on their island-hopping campaigns of the Pacific. One year of occupation in Japan by the First Cavalry Division had proved a success.

On Aug. 14th, elements of the Division conducted a review at the Imperial Palace Plaza in Tokyo where once the proud armies of Japan were reviewed by the Emperor. This ceremony of commemoration was reviewed by Maj. Gen. Charles W. Ryder, Commanding General of IX Corps.

The critical losses of personnel to the regiment continued to hamper occupation duties during the latter part of the year. Demilitarization of war plants and factories and the seizure of illegally held weapons and war-making implements continued on a lesser scale. Very few caches of arms were found and nearly all war plants were engaged in necessary peace-time pursuits. The huge 1st Tokyo Military Arsenal finally was cleared of all arms and ordinance supplies during the last week of October.

The year came to a close with a few replacements arriving in the regiment during the month of December. They had received some basic training, which varied from three weeks to completion of the basic course and immediately were integrated into the regiment's military training program.

1947

The regiment began the year in continuation of the occupation mission in the heart and nerve center of the Japanese Empire. Its hard-riding motor patrols fanned out from metropolitan Tokyo and Yokohama, the center of all industry, government and occupation policy.

Although there was no change in occupational policy or area of occupation, there had been an almost complete turnover among the troopers. Except for the few remaining combat veterans, the regiment had been replaced almost entirely by new arrivals from the States - young, eager and anxious to learn the ways of the Army. Their time

was devoted to guard duty, patrolling, specialist assignments, and the ever-necessary basic training program.

The month of February began with the regiment being alerted during a threatened Japanese general strike but quickly ended by the noon on the 1st.

Throughout the year, troops of the regiment rotated between Tokyo and Camp Palmer, located about 20 miles south of Tokyo in the Chiba Peninsula, to conduct marksmanship training. Other occupation duties included guarding the 71st Quartermaster Depot at Shinagawa.

Feb. 3rd was proclaimed "Manila Day," a memorable occasion to the few old-timers remaining with the regiment who had been in combat in the Philippines. It was on this day two years before that the famous "Flying Column" entered Manila, liberating the internees at Santo Tomas. The largest review ever conducted in Tokyo up until this time was conducted in commemoration of this day when Maj. Gen. Charles W. Ryder, IX Corps Commander, reviewed the troops.

On June 21st, the 4th New Zealand Composite Guard Battalion was replaced by the 2nd Battalion, 5th Royal Gurkha Rifles as part of the Imperial Palace Plaza.

Highlighting the activities of the regiment was the colorful Independence Day review and parade at Tokyo. Weeks of planning by the Division and other higher headquarters had gone into this event. More than 15,000 troops were aligned on the Imperial Palace Plaza, comprising in addition to the First Cavalry Division, elements of the 11th Airborne Division, the 24th Infantry Division and the 25th Infantry Division. Beginning on the white graveled plaza in front of the main gate of the Emperor's Palace where the troops were presented by the Eighth Army Commander, Lt. Gen. Robert L. Eichelberger, the long line formed into a column and marched past the bunting-draped reviewing stand where General of the Army Douglas MacArthur received the honors. With Gen. MacArthur on the reviewing stand, before a backdrop of allied flags, were distinguished members of the Allied Council, representing all countries with missions in Japan.

Other occupation duties engaged in by the

S.S. GARRYOWEN, docked in Tokyo harbor in 1947. Vessel was used as Red Cross Canteen. (It was dedicated to Mrs. MacArthur and Major General William C. Chase) (Courtesy of Vallie Stump)

Self propelled 105mm (M-7) of old Cannon Troop in 1947. Firing at Camp Weir, Japan. (Courtesy of Vallie Stump)

regiment during the month of July included the surveillance of mass meeting of Japanese labor and political groups in Tokyo. This was to be a never-ending job for troops of the regiment. No difficulties or violence were reported, and the meetings were orderly and well-regulated.

On Sept. 15th, typhoon "Kathleen" made its debut in the area of Central Japan, bringing with it rains and winds that eventually caused the inundation of large parts of the Kanto plain and adjacent areas, including the metropolis of Tokyo itself. The total destruction of the storm and its effects upon the farms, cities and people probably will never be known, but sufficient to say that more than 150,000 acres of land were flooded, 200,000 houses inundated, more than 100 people killed, 700 were missing and more than 400,000

L to R, Sgt. 1/c Robert C. Gray and Sgt. 1/c Dale J. Wright of Co. F, 2nd Bn., 7th Cavalry Regiment, standing on the Imperial Palace Grounds in Tokyo, Japan on June 5, 1947. (Courtesy of Bob "Snuffy" Gray)

individuals evacuated from the flooded areas. Rescue and flood relief operations were accomplished by the untiring efforts of all troopers of the regiment, along with the other elements of the Division who rendered aid to the entire Japanese population.

At the close of the year, the regiment again was plagued with a shortage of personnel and reached its lowest strength since immediately prior to World War II - 52 officers and 848 enlisted men. The 1st Squadron was inactivated because of the personnel shortage, and troops were forced to perform double duty in order to accomplish the numerous occupational duties assigned to the remaining understrength units. However, the regiment could look back with pride at the accomplishments of the successful occupation under the guidance of the Supreme Commander for the Allied Powers - for the Japanese action had been converted into a peaceful nation incapable of waging war, with the framework of a government under its new constitution that would make for a lasting democracy.

1948

During the month of January, the regiment's strength fell to its lowest point in history - 48 officers and 298 enlisted men. This once precisioned fighting regiment - like other proud units throughout the Army - had been reduced almost to ineffectiveness by political decisions. While the United States - the war's victor - lost prestige in an occupied country, the American citizen was lulled into a false economy by an ill-advised reduction of the armed forces. It was next to impossible to muster a sufficient number of troops to man the patrols and sentry posts and keep integral units intact. Except for the cooperation of the Japanese government and the people of Japan, this foolish reduction in our armed forces at such a critical period could have been disastrous, and all of the bloodshed to bring peace to this once warlike nation would have been in vain.

As a result of this reduced strength, maximum consolidation was necessary at the old Japanese Merchant Marine School in Tokyo - the home of the regiment - which, only a few months before had been filled, as well as those at the Fisheries School and the Japanese Cavalry School at Camp Palmer. On many mornings when a troop fell out for training, those present included only the company commander, the first sergeant and the guidon bearer - all other members of the troop were performing guard duty, on patrol or special detail.

Training reached its lowest ebb during the month of January; however, minimum requirements were met in spite of personnel shortages in all ranks. In order to perform necessary occupational assignments and carry out other essential military functions of safeguard and custody, troopers frequently worked around the clock.

On May 1st, the regiment along with all other elements of the First Cavalry Division, was placed on an alert status in preparation for a possible outbreak of violence expected as a result of May Day festivities and the Korean elections. The alert status remained in effect from May 1st to 12th and surveillance patrols kept a vigilance in all areas of responsibility. This, no doubt, accounted for the fact that no outbreaks of a subversive nature occurred in the First Cavalry Division area of responsibility.

On July 28th, the regiment celebrated organization day. Included among the ceremonies of the day was a review and parade at which time Lt. Col. Brice C. W. Custer, grand-nephew of General George Armstrong Custer, was decorated with the Croix de Guerre by Lt. Gen. Zinovi Pechkoff, French Ambassador and Chief of the French Mission in Japan. Notwithstanding the fact that the understrength regiment included mostly recruits and inexperienced non-commissioned officers, the French Ambassador was impressed by the regiment's appearance and typical GARRYOWEN esprit on the occasion of this presentation ceremony as indicated in the following letter:

July 28, 1948

Dear Colonel Chase:

"It gave me much pleasure to decorate Lt. Colonel Custer this afternoon in front of the 7th Cavalry Regiment. Let me express my heartiest congratulations on the perfect appearance of your men.

These new recruits have struck me by their soldierly bearing for which I wish them to be warmly congratulated in my name.

With much appreciation for having been associated in such manner with the celebration of the 82nd Anniversary of your distinguished Regiment, I am,"

Yours sincerely,
/s/ GENERAL Z. PECHKOFF
/t/ GENERAL Z. PECHKOFF
Ambassadeur de France
Chief of the French Mission in Japan

On Sept. 9th and 10th, all units of the regiment participated in a Division command post exercise.

During October, the regiment received the largest group of replacements received to date - six officers and 519 enlisted men. While there still remained a shortage of good non-commissioned officers for squad leaders and company grade line officers, this increase in strength permitted the 1st Squadron to be reactivated on Oct. 5th. On the following day, the 1st Squadron consisting of a cadre of 45 men under command of Lt. Col. John R. Riley moved from Judd Barracks in Tokyo to Camp Drake. On Nov. 15th, a 13-week training cycle began when Troop D joined Troops A, B and C. By the end of the year, the regiment had reached a strength of 76 officers and 2,083 enlisted men.

Due to the improved personnel situation, the regiment was able to increase its training, and the troops conducted rifle marksmanship training at Camp Palmer during November and December.

The regimental football team - the "GARRYOWENS" - won the Division championship and met the 13th Air Force team in the Bamboo Bowl in Manila on New Year's Day. The team was coached by 1st Lieutenant Meade Wildrick.

On Dec. 22nd, the regiment participated in a division review before Lt. Gen. Walton H. Walker on the Imperial Palace Grounds in Tokyo.

1949

During the year, the regiment continued its combined mission of occupation duties and training. The latter increased in momentum with a corresponding reduction in occupational responsibilities as the year progressed.

On Jan. 1st, the Cannon Troop was inactivated, and the troops were assigned to the Provisional and 2nd Squadrons. However, the troop was again activated on March 22nd and redesignated the Heavy Mortar Company.

On Jan. 19th, the regiment assumed patrol duty on the Imperial Hunting Grounds south of Tokyo, which was continued until March 5th. Troop F performed guard duties at the 71st Quartermaster Depot during the period Jan. 3rd until March 30th, at which time it was replaced by Troop E, which remained there until July 5th.

The most important organizational change in the history of the regiment took place on March 25th, when the long-established and traditional Cavalry arm was abolished throughout the Army and the regiment was organized as an Infantry Regiment. Concurrent with this action, the last remaining square division in the Army was eliminated, and the brigade organizations in the First Cavalry Division were abolished. Troops became companies and squadrons became battalions in accordance with Tables of Organization and Equipment (TOE) 7-11N dated 21 April 1948. Not withstanding this reorganization, all units remained designated as "Cavalry" with Infantry in parentheses after the unit designation. The 3rd Battalion and Tank Company were reconstituted and designated as Regular Army Units but remained inactive.

The first phase of the Mobilization Training Program Tests was taken by all units prior to April 30th. Training prior to field maneuvers was greatly accelerated and consisted of basic military subjects, communications, intelligence and reconnaissance, participation in Division command post exercises, and field firing of crew served weapons was emphasized. During June, the training emphasized the rocket launcher, combat formations, bayonet, combat orders, techniques of fire and squad tactics.

On May 3rd, the regiment was relieved of guard duty at the Imperial Palace and assumed responsibility for guarding the 22nd Ordinance Center, Bank of Chosen, Takashiba Pier, the Tokyo Quartermaster Base Depot and furnished escort guards for the Sugamo prison, where the Japanese war criminals were being held. These duties continued until July 5th.

On May 16th, the GARRYOWEN Service Club Number 31 was officially opened with an appropriate ceremony at which time Brig. Gen. Thomas Herren and Pvt. Ralph Marksberry crashed the gates with sabers. For entertainment as well as for avocational purposes, the troops were offered variety shows, kendo and judo, exhibitions of tea and wedding ceremonies, card tournaments, bingo, dances, quiz programs, pool, ping-pong, and craft-shop facilities.

On. July 4th, the entire regiment participated in a parade and review on the Imperial Palace Plaza for the Supreme Commander of Allied Powers, and immediately thereafter began packing weapons and equipment in preparation for the move to the maneuver area at Camp McNair located at the base of Mt. Fujiama - approximately 100 miles southwest of Tokyo. During the period July 7th to Sept. 3rd, squad, platoon and company tactics tests were conducted for all units of the regiment.

On Aug. 5th, Brig. Gen. Henry I. Hodes, Acting Division Commander, reviewed the troops and on Aug. 11th, Lt. Gen. Walton H. Walker, Commanding General, Eighth Army, inspected training. On Aug. 26th, the 1st Battalion held a field exercise using ball ammunition in the attack, for the benefit of Maj. Gen. Leland S. Hobbs, Commanding General of the IX Corps.

Prior to movement back to permanent barracks in Tokyo on Sept. 1st, all battalions had completed a defensive exercise using ball ammunition.

Upon arrival at their respective barracks on Sept. 3rd, all troops spent a few days cleaning equipment as well as repairing barracks and facilities damaged by typhoon "Kitty," which struck the islands during the absence of the troops. Occupational guard duties then were resumed at the Bank of Japan, and Sugamo Prison. Companies A and G were assigned duty at the Tokyo Quartermaster Depot, while Company H was assigned responsibility for guarding the Bank of Japan. These duties continued until Dec. 1st.

On Sept. 5th, a regimental review and retreat parade was held honoring the Regimental Rifle Team that won first place in the Far East Command Small Arms Tournament. Representatives of the team were Sgt. Joseph Lang, Cpl. Ernest Terry and Pfc. Efland Carlson of Company F; Pvt. Thomas Bubanich and Pvt. Donald West of Company A; Sgt. First Class Armin Hilly of Company C; and 2nd Lt. Reuben D. Kvidt of Headquarters and Headquarters Company.

By early September this year, black-market activities had assumed major proportions because of the thriving black-market activities throughout the Tokyo area. Efforts to curtail these illegal operations were constantly and relentlessly pursued; however, no noticeable results were ascertained until the month of September at which time a provisional security platoon was formed and became operational. Patrols in addition to the usual mobile patrols, became active in the vicinity of the regimental area and raids and seizures were conducted on black-market establishments.

Pfc. Alvin Parker, Company E, was entered in the First Cavalry Division Boxing Tournament and won the Division Heavyweight Championship on Sept. 20th, but he was defeated in the final bout in the All Japan Finals. For his outstanding performance, he received a trophy and a 21-jewel Elgin wrist watch.

On Oct. 11th, the regiment participated in a Division parade and review on the Imperial Plaza for Gen. J. Lawton Collins, Chief of Staff, United States Army; and in a similar parade for the House Appropriations Committee on Nov.18th.

The regimental football squad, coached by 1st Lt. Herschel Fuson ended the season with a record of three wins, one tie, and six defeats, which was in considerable contrast to the previous season that ended with the team winning the

Old Cannon Troop in Tokyo, 1947. C/O Captain Bill Holland; First Sergeant Alfred Ruhnke; Platoon Sergeant Earl Early, Mess Sergeant Bill McKown; Motor Sergeant Vallie Stump. (Courtesy of Vallie Stump)

Division championship and participating in the annual Bamboo Bowl game at Manila's Stotsenberg football field on New Year's Day.

A Christmas party was held for 550 Japanese children from the adjacent school. The children were escorted by troopers to the theater and sang Christmas carols, saw a Mickey Mouse movie, and were entertained by Santa Claus, who distributed gifts. This is but one of many occasions during the occupation in which the regiment, the units of the regiment, or individual troopers provided entertainment for Japanese children in an effort to impress the new Japanese generation with American democratic ideals.

The regiment celebrated its 83rd anniversary on Dec. 22nd. The day was declared a holiday, and all clubs held "open house." Climaxing the day's festivities was the first showing in the regimental theater of the film "She Wore a Yellow Ribbon," which portrayed the part of the regiment in the Indian wars.

Throughout the latter part of the year, the organization became more conscious of training responsibilities and greater effort was exerted to attain a state of 100 percent combat readiness. The Heavy Mortar Company ranked first in the Division and the IX Corps Test conducted on Nov. 4th.

By the end of the year, 95 percent of all men had fired their individual weapons, and more than 300 men had attended specialist schools conducted by the First Cavalry Division and the Eighth Army. It is impossible to estimate the number of lives this increased training activity saved during the coming months. Sgt. 1st Class Vallie Stump, motor sergeant for the Heavy Motor Company, remembers:

"I was the Motor Sergeant for the Heavy Motor Company of the 7th Cavalry Regiment, and on Nov. 4, 1949, we were ranked No. 1 within the First Cavalry Division and IX Corps, from the Inspection and Tests that were conducted on that day. Indeed, it was a very proud day, not only for me, but to every officer and trooper in the Company.

To obtain this great achievement, it took many hours of hard work and dedication from everyone. Also, overall operations within the Division and Eighth Army were rapidly changing to a better effort to educate and properly train the soldiers. All of my mechanics were sent to specialist schools that were available. All drivers of vehicles were constantly instructed on how to properly maintain their equipment. And many were assigned to work along with the mechanics. Our weekly vehicle maintenance was scheduled every Friday, and there was

an everyday motor stable for one half hour in the morning and one half hour in the afternoon. This helped to keep all vehicles in excellent shape for the every Saturday morning Motor Pool inspection.

All this gave me a greater ability to enforce a stricter work habit and the men with increased education and training had the capacity to do a better job. This persistent education and training would prove to be extremely valuable in the coming months ahead in Korea."

An additional statement from Sgt. 1st Class Vallie Stump:

"Too little is said in recognition of the fact that the maintenance of vehicles in direct support to the front-line units and companies, is of the most difficult task. It is a vital part of the operation. Because of the swiftly changing circumstances involved with combat conditions, many temporary repairs must be attempted or made to avoid the possible loss of a vehicle. In front-line duty, there is no such thing as parts availability to repair vehicles. You beg, borrow and steal or make good with what you have in case of an emergency to keep those vehicles rolling for officers and troopers who are doing the actual fighting."

Camp McNair training base for the 1st Cavalry Division, 1949. Note Mt. Fuji in the background. (Courtesy of Ed Daily)

Squad tents at Camp McNair. Note Mt. Fuji in the background. (Courtesy of Ed Daily)

"Pup" tents at Camp McNair. Note Mt. Fuji in the background. (Courtesy of Ed Daily)

Mt. Fuji as seen from Lake Kawaguchi, Japan. (Courtesy of Ed Daily)

Parade and Review for the Supreme Commander of Allied Powers on the Imperial Palace Plaza Grounds, July 4, 1949. (Courtesy of Ed Daily)

The GARRYOWEN Pipe and Drum Band. (Courtesy of Ed Daily)

The GARRYOWEN Drum and Bugle Corps. (Courtesy of Ed Daily)

M-24 Light Tanks of the 16th Recon Company, in Parade for the Supreme Commander of Allied Powers, July 4, 1949. (Courtesy of Ed Daily)

7th Cavalry in Parade for the Supreme Commander of Allied Powers on the Imperial Palace Plaza Grounds, July 4, 1949. (Courtesy of Ed Daily)

2nd Battalion, 7th Cavalry, in Parade for the Supreme Commander of Allied Powers on the Imperial Palace Plaza Grounds, July 4, 1949. (Courtesy of Ed Daily)

Top left: Geisha and Maiko kimonos of Japan. Top right: Diabutsu at Kamakura, Japan. Center: Twin Bridge, Imperial Palace, Tokyo. Bottom left: "Honey Buckets" of Japan. Bottom right: General Headquarters (GHQ) in Tokyo. Dai-Ichi building (SCAP & FEC). (Photos courtesy of Ed Daily)

CHAPTER II
JOURNEY INTO WAR

1950

During the early part of the year, the regiment increased the tempo of its training. All companies alternated training periods at Camp Palmer and emphasized individual and crew-sized weapons training. All units were relieved of occupation duties that heretofore had prevented the reduced strength organizations from concentrating on training.

While battalion and regimental training exercises had not been included in the training during the early part of the year, squad, platoon, and company problems were emphasized. Additionally, the regiment began a series of alert exercises designed to maintain all units in a high state of combat readiness. When these alert exercises were held - at any hour of the day or night - the entire organization loaded all TOE equipment, three days' ration, and a basic load of ammunition in organic transportation and moved to a designated assembly area. The objective of the exercise was to move the entire organization from the barracks to the assembly area, fully combat loaded, in the shortest possible time. Twenty minutes from the time the alert notice was received until the unit was ready to move was considered the optimum. Upon arrival in the assembly area, a short command post exercise usually was held, and all vehicles, basic loads, equipment and weapons were inspected before returning to the barracks. This training was to pay off many times over later in the year.

During the period Feb. 22nd to 24th, the 2nd Battalion participated in an air-transportability exercise. The entire battalion moved all personnel, equipment, 1/4-ton vehicles, three days' rations, and a basic load of ammunition by shuttling with six C-54 aircraft from Tokyo's Tachikawa airport to Sendai, Japan. Upon arrival at Sendai, the battalion conducted a short overnight defensive exercise and returned by shuttle movement in the same aircraft. Although this exercise was short, the training received in air transportability also served this battalion well in later months in Korea.

At this time, the regimental organization was identical to a typical infantry regiment except that it lacked one battalion and a tank company. Actually, it was a two-battalion regiment with a 20 percent personnel shortage in all units - basic riflemen particularly were short.

In the early morning hours of June 25th, the North Koreans launched their powerful offensive across the 38th parallel against the Republic of Korea, and the attention of the entire world suddenly was focused upon that little, mountainous Asian nation. Since the Republic of Korea was not a member of the United Nations, the United States government immediately brought the aggression to the attention of the United Nations Security Council, branding the assault across the 38th parallel by the hostile forces as a breach of the peace, an act of aggression, and a clear threat to international peace and security.

The attacking Communist divisions drove swiftly toward Seoul, 50 miles to the south, and by June 28th, three days after the beginning of the North Korean invasion, the capitol had fallen into enemy hands. The element of tactical surprise and the North Koreans' overwhelming superiority in weapons crushed organized Republic of Korea resistance in the vicinity of the parallel. North Korean tank columns ground forward unscathed against the poorly equipped, ineffective, Republic of Korea (ROK) forces that lacked tanks and adequate anti-tank weapons. As the Communist offensive swelled in power, masses of South Koreans, soldiers and civilians alike, moved south across the wide Han River seeking whatever protection that natural obstacle might provide. The wild exodus of refugees from Seoul swelled the population of the town of Suwon, a few miles below the capitol, to almost 500,000.

On June 27th, the president announced the United States' decision to send air and sea forces "to give the Korean Government troops cover and support," and on June 30th, he announced that he had authorized the use of the United States ground troops against the North Korean invaders.

Initially, there was little reaction to this Korean incident among the members of the 7th Cavalry. The regiment was placed on a routine alert, passes were restricted, and all units were directed to submit emergency requisitions to fill their shortages of TOE equipment and weapons.

While understrength units of the Far East Command were being readied for commitment in Korea, combat elements of the 24th Infantry Division were being flown into Korea as fast as air space was available in order to stem the Communist avalanche, and the remainder of the 24th Infantry Division began moving to Korea by water.

In June 1950, GHQ, FEC, located in Tokyo, Japan, with offices in the Dai Ichi Building, had Maj. Gen. Edward M. Almond as Chief of Staff and Maj. Gen. Doyle O. Hickey as Deputy Chief of Staff. The Eighth Army was commanded by Lt. Gen. Walton H. Walker and Far East Air Forces (FEAF), came under Lt. Gen. George E. Stratemeyer. The FEAF headquarters were separate from GHQ, FEC.

Levels of supplies on hand in the FEC by mid-1950 amounted to a 60-day depot level, plus 30-day levels in station stocks. Both supply sources were out of balance in quantity and quality. Some weapons such as medium tanks, 4.2-inch mortars and recoilless rifles hardly could be found in the command. Units deactivated in the command had turned in large quantities of equipment, but most of this was unserviceable. Eighth Army was authorized 226 recoilless rifles, but had only 21. Of 18,000 1/4-ton jeeps within stock of the Eighth Army, only 8,000 were serviceable and of 13,780 2-1/2-ton trucks, only 4,441 were in running condition.

Total ammunition resources amounted to only 45 days' supply in the depots and a basic load of training ammunition in hands of units. The level of perishable food supplies also was 45 days in depot stocks and operating levels at various stations. Petroleum products on hand included a level of 180 days' packaged and 75 days' bulk at depots, station levels of 15 days each of packaged and bulk and 15 days with units.

Soon young cavalrymen would face massive battles without Congressional declarations of war, without maximum efforts to supply enough men and material to the front lines and without the complete support of the American people. They would engage in a "limited war" to fight against a totally new foe: communism.

Returning now to the activities in the 7th Cavalry Regiment, on June 25th the 1st Battalion departed Camp Drake - located about 15 miles north of Tokyo, Japan - for the Tachikawa Air Force Base for Air Transportability Training. However, upon their arrival, they found that planes were not available because of the Korean situation. The 2nd Battalion had just returned from Mount Fuji where squad and platoon firing tests were conducted, and the battalion had made detailed plans to move from McKnight Barracks in Tokyo to Camp King, located 18 miles northeast of Camp Drake; however, this move was canceled.

The 24th Division - being readied for immediate shipment to Korea - needed squad leaders and platoon sergeants for their understrength rifle and weapons platoons, and on July 1st, the 7th Cavalry Regiment lost 168 key non-commissioned officers by transfer to the 24th Division, leaving only master sergeants and first sergeants in the regiment. This loss was a serious blow to the heart and soul of the regiment as many of these trained non-commissioned officers had been with their units for several months.

On July 2nd, the regiment received some training in cargo net climbing and on debarking from LCVPs. However, the training was a hurried affair and of little value.

MacArthur had decided on an amphibious operation against the enemy even before the first clash between American and North Korean soldiers at Osan, South Korea. On July 2nd, he asked Washington for a Marine RCT. On the next day, he ordered 1,200 specially trained operators for amphibious landing craft. He asked on July 5th for an engineer special brigade trained in amphibious operations and on the same day called for an airborne RCT "to participate in planned operations from July 20th to Aug. 10th." (The Draft Plan, Operation Bluehearts, JSPOG, GHQ, FEC, July 1950, copy in files.) Joint Strategic Plans and Operations Group (JSPOG); General Headquarters (GHQ); Far East Command (FEC).

MacArthur had conceived these "planned operations" a few days after the North Koreans struck. MacArthur then believed that he could land an assault force from the First Cavalry Division and the Marine RCT against the enemy's rear at Inch'on as early as July 22nd. This force would envelop Seoul and seize the high ground to the north. At the same time, all forces available to Gen. Dean would attack to drive the North Koreans back against the Han River. Maj. Gen. Edwin K. Wright's planning group, JSPOG, worked out the details of this early plan. They assigned to it the code name "Operation Bluehearts."

Gen. MacArthur, on July 6th, called Maj. Gen. Hobart R. Gay, commander of the First Cavalry Division, to Tokyo and told him of the plan. Some of MacArthur's staff held high hopes for the operation. Gen. Willoughby, MacArthur's G-2, admonished Gay to step lively or be left behind.

"You must expedite preparations to the utmost," Willoughby warned, *"because if your landing is delayed, all that the First Cavalry Division will hit when it lands will be the tail-end of the 24th Infantry Division as it passes north through Seoul."*

Operation Bluehearts died a-borning. The failure of the weak American and weaker ROK forces to halt the enemy and forced commitment of the First Cavalry Division before July 22nd made the operation, in July or even in August, quite infeasible. It was canceled on July 10th.

On July 8th, the regiment was alerted for amphibious operations in Korea and planning began for the operation. The regiment was to have four ships (USNS Shanks, USNS Ainsworth, one LST and a Japanese freighter) for the movement. Lack of information as to the capacity of the ships seriously hampered planning. The Yokohama port personnel stated that 2-1/2-ton vehicles could not be loaded on the Shanks and Ainsworth. Therefore, these type vehicles had to be placed on the Japanese-operated LST and the Japanese freighter. Lt. Col. Gilman A. Huff, with the regimental S-3, and eight other officers (three from each battalion and two from special units) worked as embarkation officers. The S-3 established the vehicle priority list and Lt. Col. Huff and the embarkation officers planned the loading.

By July 10th, the regiment began receiving equipment shortages, chemical first, followed by engineer, ordnance and quartermaster items. The weapons were in poor condition even though their status had been reported to higher headquarters. Mortars, 75mm recoilless rifles and few machine-guns were considered combat serviceable. Vehicle maintenance had been stressed constantly during the occupation; however, the vehicles were in very poor condition because of their age, and in fact many of them had been with the regiment through the Pacific campaigns in World War II. It was the opinion of the motor officer that 75 percent of the vehicles would not prove combat serviceable. Endeavors to get ammunition for rocket launchers met with no avail as did efforts to obtain 57mm recoilless rifles. In short, the regiment was ill-prepared for combat due to shortages of personnel and equipment - the result of penny-pinching, which reduced the Army following World War II, but nevertheless a practice that has followed every war throughout American history.

Loading of vehicles on the LST and the Japanese freighter "Shinshi" began early on the 14th. On the freighter 40 2-1/2-ton trucks and trailers, seven jeeps, and one trailer, and a 3/4-ton maintenance vehicle were loaded. The drivers and three officers, Capt. O.P. Smith, Lt. Ralph Crider, and Warrant Officer Martin, went aboard the ship with 14 days' supply of rations and water to stay with the vehicles until their arrival in Korea. The "Shinshi" was loaded with 10 2-1/2-ton trucks with trailers, and Lt. George Nelson was placed in command of the 10 drivers and one interpreter aboard this ship.

The LST and the "Shinshi" sailed on the 15th, and the loading of TOE vehicles, except 2-1/2-ton vehicles, got under way in Yokohama where the USNS Shanks and Ainsworth were docked. On this day, items of PC&S property were turned in for storage.

The Shanks was loaded with vehicles and equipment by 0130 hours on the 16th, and the Ainsworth by 0500, and the regiment was aboard by 1445 hours on July 17th as the Ainsworth and Shanks pulled away from the pier at 1720 and 1730 hours respectively. Both ships anchored in the bay until 2000 at which time the convoy consisting of the Patrick, Ainsworth, Shanks and a Navy Corvette took a southerly route for Korea. The Corvette led the convoy with the other ships in the order listed above.

On July 18th and 19th, instructions were held aboard ship on communications pertaining to use and care of sets. Each company was oriented by either the S-3 or S-2 on the Korean situation and was given pointers on combat - what to expect and how to react. The situation as presented called for the 5th and 8th Cavalry Regiments to make an amphibious landing at Pohangdong on the 18th. The 7th Cavalry Regiment was to land two days later as the Division reserve. The mission of the 5th and 8th Cavalry Regiments was to secure the beach and high ground north and west of the beach and city, and to prevent enemy artillery from falling on the beach area. The 1st Battalion, 7th Cavalry was to land and move to Yongdok and relieve elements of the 27th Infantry Regiment. Typhoons "Gracie" and "Flossie" created rough seas and a slow journey, and July 20th found the regiment still en route to Korea on the southerly route off the coast of Kyushu.

Preliminary planning indicated that either LCMs or LSUs would be available for debarking, and groups were divided into 100 men each. Duffle bags were stacked on "B" deck, and each supply sergeant was designated as guard to remain behind and see that the bags got ashore. Drivers were notified that they would stand by at the top of the hatch to handle their vehicle once it was hoisted up to them. Lt. Col. Huff was designated to handle the unloading the supplied with a small detail. The following day, the regiment received definite information from the Assistant Division Commander - Brig. Gen. Frank Allen who was aboard the USNS Patrick - as to the number and types of landing craft available for unloading. He also stated that three officers and 100 enlisted men would remain on each ship until unloading was completed.

At 1730 hours, July 22nd, the convoy anchored in the vicinity of the make-shift harbor facilities of Pohangdong and debarking began as planned. By 2230, all troops had debarked and moved to a bivouac area four to six miles out of the town. Even though many of the men were happy to be back on solid ground, they were curious and apprehensive as to what the future held. As the men haphazardly dug in for the night, the regimental commander and S-3 left for a conference with Gen. Allen. The 1st Battalion, plus one platoon of the Heavy Mortar Company and one Medical Platoon relieved the 1st Battalion, 35th Infantry Regiment, and was given the mission of defending Pohangdong from the north. On the following day, the regiment made plans to move from the site of the original bivouac near Pohangdong to the Taegu-Kumchon sector, a distance of 100 miles where the Division was assembling. The move was made by truck and rail in three serials, as follows: rail-transported troops, under the command of Lt. Col. Herbert B. Heyer, included 20 officers and 71 enlisted men from Headquarters and Headquarters Company, four officers and 25 enlisted men from Medical Company, two officers and 50 enlisted men from Service Company, plus the entire 2nd Battalion. While plans called for departure from Pohangdong around 1300, the actual move did not begin until 1830 due to the lack of rail transportation.

No such delay was encountered by the truck-transported troops, who began their departure with the Regimental Intelligence and Reconnaissance Platoon in the lead at 1030 hours. Col. Cecil B. Nist and his S-2 and S-3 staff officers accompanied this group. By 1100 hours,

Captured American soldiers during the first few days of fighting in Korea, 1950. Many were from the 24th Infantry Division. (Eastfoto)

An infantry squad captures and burns Korean village. (U.S. Army Photo)

all remaining troops who did not go by rail moved out in the second seial under the command of Maj. Lucian Croft, regimental S-4.

During the early morning hours prior to the move, a messenger from one of the outposts came into the bivouac area and requested an interpreter. He had presented the regiment with a problem that was to be repeated many times during the 7th Cavalry's operations in Korea. He had 11 Korean civilians near his outpost who apparently had not been informed of the danger of remaining in the vicinity of troops after nightfall and could not communicate with them.

The order of formation for the Division in the Kumchon area - the destination - was given as follows:

5th Cavalry, 8th Cavalry, Division Artillery and the 7th Cavalry less the 1st Battalion.

After the 1st Battalion arrived at its sector on the front lines in the Kumchon-Pohangdong area and had been assigned its mission of holding a first or second defensive position as the situation might arise, another problem that was to be repeated many times confronted the battalion. Refugees and friendly Korean troops entered our defensive positions in their march rearward and were fired upon by our own troops because they were unable to establish their identity. Minor enemy skirmishes developed. However, artillery and naval fire support in this sector played the major role.

On July 24th, the 1st Battalion's command post moved forward to Changsa-dong, north of Pohangdong. The enemy attacked during the early morning hours but were repelled quickly. During the greater part of the day, the enemy was steadily hammered by 4.2-inch and 81mm mortar fire, field artillery and naval gunfire, plus air strikes by the Fifth Air Force. The enemy was forced to retreat for a distance of approximately 2,000 yards. Yongdok was leveled and left ablaze by continuous naval gun fire from warships anchored in the harbor east of the town.

The main serial from Pohangdong arrived at 0005 hours on the 24th and made contact with the command group that had preceded it. The regimental command post was established approximately two and a half miles in rear of the front line occupied by the 5th and 8th Cavalry. Prior to the arrival of the 2nd Battalion, at 1420 hours, the regimental commander was directed to form two

provisional rifle companies from service and headquarters personnel due to a serious breakthrough on the right flank. Arrival of the train at 1420 hours with the 2nd Battalion eliminated the requirement for the two provisional rifle companies, and the 2nd Battalion was alerted for combat within 20 minutes after arrival.

The 2nd Battalion then went into position in the immediate vicinity of the regimental command post where it remained for the remainder of the night. During the night, numerous enemy groups attempted to infiltrate their positions. This caused continuous firing throughout the night by the inexperienced troops in their first night in combat. During one engagement with a small enemy force in the Company E area, 2nd Lt. Alan F. Plummer was killed and Pvt. Willie C. Sanderlin wounded. Thus, the regiment suffered its first losses in the Korean War.

At 0005 hours on July 25th, the 1st Battalion reported that a group of ROK soldiers had attempted to bring a group of Korean civilians through a road block in the Company A area. When challenged to halt, the Koreans dispersed and fled in panic. Not knowing who they were, our troops fired a volley of small arms and machine-gun fire into the scattered group. Second Lt. Francis J. Maloney, Jr. of Company D, with a small group of his men, formed a patrol and went forward to contact the scattered Koreans who still were believed to be enemy. Maloney dispersed his men, warning them not to fire until a verbal command was given by him, and then moved forward alone to make contact. Upon discovering that the Koreans were friendly, the ROK troops and civilians were collected easily, brought through our lines and held until daylight for release.

The 1st Battalion was relieved in place by the 1st Battalion, 21st Infantry, 24th Division at 2000 hours and departed by motor convoy at 2135 hours for Pohangdong, where rail transportation was waiting to take them to the Yongdong sector to join the remainder of the regiment.

Back in the regimental command post, a meeting of unit commanders was held to review the situation, and the 2nd Battalion was alerted to pull in their outposts in preparation for a move to the vicinity of Eido. During the morning of the 25th, Mr. Jamieson, Australian delegate to the UN Commission and Col. Nayar, Indian delegate

to the UN Commission, visited the regimental command post for an orientation as to the location of the front lines.

Late on the 25th, the first of a series of withdrawals began. These actions, difficult to execute even with trained troops, were particularly costly to the inexperienced undermanned regiment. The first of these withdrawals began under the direction of Capt. Charles E. Perez, commanding officer of the Service Company, when the regimental service and supply trains were moved further to the rear. The 2nd Battalion then moved out toward the front lines at 1850, followed by reorganized groups from Headquarters and Headquarters Company, to relieve the pressure on the hard-pressed 8th Cavalry Regiment's positions. An estimated 2,000 enemy troops were directly in front of these positions with tanks, artillery, mortars and automatic weapons. Enemy patrols continued to harass the flanks and rear, and enemy troops, posing as refugees, became a considerable threat and caused numerous casualties.

Regimental supply personnel had not been idle during this period. Maj. Croft reported that 15 of the vital 3.5-inch rocket launchers had been issued to the regiment. Capt. Perez had organized his kitchen trucks about 300 yards to the rear and prepared a welcomed hot meal for the troops - the first since their arrival in Korea. Of a more somber nature was the necessary removal on this day of all identifying markings on ambulances and other medical vehicles because enemy fire had been intentionally directed against such vehicles evacuating wounded from the front.

The regimental trains with all other regimental vehicles again were withdrawn about 4-1/2 miles to the rear at 2000 hours, as all roads became seriously congested with disorganized groups of vehicles from the 24th Division, combined with masses of refugees and ROK troops.

By midnight of July 25th-26th, the regimental command post had been located at a forward position near Eido, and communication lines established between the Heavy Mortar Company and the forward units of the regiment. An early morning rush of activity began with a telephone call ordering all regimental S-3s to the Division headquarters to receive orders for a general withdrawal. At 0120, the 2nd Battalion reported that the road was clogged with refugees and that an

Sergeant Tom Randell, forward observer, 4.2 Heavy Mortar Company, 7th Cavalry Regiment. (Courtesy of Tom Randell)

A typical command post base as an infantry battalion detrucks near the frontline to assemble for action. (U.S. Army Photo)

Officer on right is Captain John B. Wadsworth, Commander of Co. H, 2nd Bn, 7th Cav. Other two officers unknown. (Courtesy of Ed Daily)

Landing and initial committment - After landing at Pohang-dong on 18 July 1950, the 1st Cavalry quickly took up blocking position near Yongdong. The crushing North Korean offensive, however, forced United Nations defenders to pull back into the Pusan Perimeter, early in August.

enemy tank had passed their command post going toward the rear area. Later a messenger from Heavy Mortar Company reported that refugees, approximately 200 yards from their road entrance, had been stopped and ordered into the adjacent fields to clear the way for vehicular traffic.

A call from Maj. William O. Witherspoon, the regimental S-3 then at Division headquarters, ordered the immediate alert of all personnel for evacuation of their respective positions, as a serious break-through had occurred in the sector to the right of the Division. All elements of the regiment were to begin an immediate withdrawal with the exception of the 2nd Battalion that was under attack.

During the withdrawal that followed, the 2nd Battalion was under continuous attack. The unit became scattered,and out of communication with each other; many platoons did not receive the order to withdraw, and general chaos and confusion resulted as enemy tanks and "refugees" began firing wildly from the road leading to the rear. The road soon became choked with men - elements of the 8th Cavalry, the 24th Division, the 2nd Battalion, 7th Cavalry, "refugees," and enemy troops - and vehicles, both our own and those of the enemy.

The Company H command post was located along the railroad that ran parallel to the troop-filled road. In an effort to separate the troops of the 2nd Battalion from the surging mass in the road, Capt. Melbourne C. Chandler, commander of Company H, took his small company headquarters group to the road in an attempt to separate the friendly troops away from the column on the road and onto the railroad. After collecting approximately 300 troops of the 2nd Battalion, he led them down the railroad toward the position last occupied by the regimental command post. There was no communication by radio with any units at this time, and the location of other friendly units was unknown. After traveling approximately seven miles with this disorganized group, dodging enemy tank fire and avoiding contact with the human mass on the road, the group was met by Maj. William O. Witherspoon who directed them into

an assembly area near the new location of the regimental command post. The exhausted men fell to the ground immediately; however, rest was short-lived as it was imperative that units be regrouped in order to form some semblance of a defensive position and to establish communications.

Much equipment and many weapons were lost during this chaotic withdrawal, and the following morning, small groups went forward to recover as much as possible that was strewn along the road and railroad. Regarding this chaotic withdrawal of July 26th, 2nd Battalion Headquarters reported the following equipment was left behind: one switchboard, one emergency lighting unit, 14 machine-guns, 9 radios, 120 M-1 rifles, 26 carbines, 7 BARs, and six 60mm mortars.

The strenuous climb over mountainous terrain during the withdrawal necessitated the evacuation of five men. Additionally, the regiment suffered one killed, six wounded and 199 missing.

By 0800 hours on the 26th, units of the 2nd Battalion moved astride the road into defensive positions.

Troops of the 1st Battalion arrived at 1200 hours by train just south of the Hwang-gan rail station to rejoin the regiment.

The 2nd Battalion, which was to relieve the 1st Battalion, 5th Cavalry by extending the line to the left, reported that unit in contact with the enemy, and a reconnaissance force was organized immediately and dispatched. Meanwhile, all bridges and trestles forward of the position were destroyed, and mortar fire and patrols engaged enemy guerrilla forces in the nearby villages.

The morning of July 27th found the 5th Cavalry Regiment located to the left and rear, and the 27th Infantry Regiment, 25th Division on the right of the 7th Cavalry Regiment, with the 77th Field Artillery in support. Division reported that there were no friendly troops to the southwest of the regiment's position. The lack of sufficient supporting artillery and the 270⁰ perimeter being

covered by artillery fire, required each piece in the batteries to be laid separately in order to deliver immediate fire on call. When a volume of fire was required, it was necessary to shift the trails of the other pieces in the battery.

Press representative Tom Lambert of the Associated Press, Davis Warner of the Daily Telegraph and London Hearald in Melbourne, Stanley Massey of the Consolidated Press in Sidney, Christopher Buckley of the London Daily Telegraph, Alan Humphrey of the London Daily Mail, Ian Morrison of the London Times and Bill Hudons of the Australian Associated Press, visited the regimental command post during the day.

The day was spent in consolidating positions, extensive patrol activities and skirmishes with small scattered enemy groups and patrols. The regiment lost two killed and four wounded during the day's activities.

With the 2nd Battalion spread to the right and the 1st Battalion to the left, activities for the 28th were marked by efforts to establish rapid communications and liaison with the supporting artillery. By 0615, the snarled communication system had been improved, and a message from the 1st Battalion confirmed enemy flanking movements as well as intensified attacks against the front lines that threatened both the 1st and 2nd Battalion sectors. Messages at this time also revealed that the 1st and 2nd Battalions were in contact with each other but that the 2nd Battalion's right flank had been penetrated by an unknown number of enemy troops. Lt. Col. Peter D. Clainos, commanding the 1st Battalion, reported that an attempted penetration of the right and left flanks of this battalion had been turned back momentarily. The enemy was following a typical pattern of attack by forcing mobs of civilians ahead of their troops into the line of fire.

The regiment was informed of a potential means of emergency withdrawal by Col. Rosenberg, regimental commander, 5th Cavalry, who visited the command post at 0730 to discuss the situation on the right flank. He had utilized bulldozers during the night to prepare a new route of withdrawal.

At 0900, Gen. Frank Allen and his aide, followed by Lt. Col. J.H. Michaelis, commanding officer, 27th Infantry Regiment, arrived at the regimental command post. Gen. Allen presented the following current plan: the 8th Cavalry was to move up, the 7th Cavalry to hold the position while the 2nd Battalion attacked to close the gap between the 27th Infantry and the 7th Cavalry Regiments. The 8th Cavalry was to locate one battalion on the forward ridge and one battalion behind the 27th Infantry to occupy the critical ground on their left flank, while plans were being made to withdraw the 27th Infantry to the rear.

At 0330 hours on July 29th, the 2nd Battalion received orders to withdraw in the following order - Companies F, Headquarters H, G and E. The withdrawal was made down a valley of terraced rice paddies filled with water. Enemy troops occupied the ridges on each side of the valley and were racing parallel to the withdrawing column in an attempt to cut them off. A heavy volume of small arms fire poured in on the column from either side from the closely pursuing enemy while artillery and tank fire furthered hampered movements. The blackness of night was shattered continuously by red, white and green signal flares fired over the heads of our troops by the pursuing enemy.

By 0830 on the 29th, elements of the 1st and 2nd Battalions had passed the Hwang-gan railroad station and had taken up new positions. Extensive patrols to the front and flanks were initiated during the day while refugees steaming to the rear continued to cause the troopers considerable trouble. During the night of July 28th-29th, and during the withdrawal, the regimental casualties were one officer wounded, nine enlisted men wounded, one killed and one missing.

The 1st Battalion, 27th Infantry, pulled back at 2230 that night and was replaced by a battalion of the 5th Cavalry. Later, the 5th Cavalry and the

entire 27th Infantry withdrew, leaving only the 7th and 8th Cavalry Regiments on the front line of defense. The 1st and 2nd Battalions were notified that there would be no friendly troops in front of them the following morning.

During the early hours of July 30th, as the 5th Cavalry began withdrawing from their position, enemy tanks appeared in front of the 2nd Battalion. Two tanks were at close range in a draw in front of Company E, and one tank and enemy troops appeared to be massing on the 5th Cavalry's former line. The 8th Cavalry was located on the right flank, to the right of the road, but heavy artillery and mortar fire was causing them to withdraw into the village of Noo Dong.

Although enemy tanks had been reported moving down the road parallel to the 2nd Battalion's front, conflicting reports indicated that the vehicles heard in the early morning darkness were friendly engineer troops with bulldozers.

At 0400, Company H began receiving heavy tank and mortar fire. The first positions hit were the 81mm platoon. A tree burst from a tank round instantly killed the mortar platoon leader - Lt. Robert Wood - and within minutes the entire mortar platoon of Company H either had been killed or wounded. Enemy mortar and tank rounds fell in the Company H command post area killing or wounding several in the area.

To understand an incident that occurred at this time, it is necessary to digress from the events as they occurred on this day. During the period Company H spent at Camp Palmer, Japan, on the firing range and while undergoing company and platoon tests at Camp McNair during the previous year, the company commander had insisted that all mess, administrative and supply personnel not only qualify with their individual arms, but also on at least one crew-served weapon. All mess personnel, including the mess sergeant - Sgt. 1st Class William Brown - became proficient machine gun-

ners. Upon arrival in Korea all company field mess equipment was sent to the rear with the regimental trains, and due to personnel shortages in the machine gun platoon, all mess personnel were assigned as machine gunners. Within 10 days after Company H first entered combat, the mess sergeant and all but one cook had become casualties while distinguishing themselves in combat. The following action on the morning of July 30th involved Brown, for which he was awarded the Silver Star.

The enemy tanks reported moving down the road were thought to be engineers working on the right flank of the battalion's position. Front line personnel did not realize that the 5th Cavalry had pulled back during the night. When Company H began receiving direct tank fire, an enemy infantry attack also was launched on the left flank of their position. Attached to Company E, left of Company H, was a section of heavy machine guns from Company H, one gun being manned by Sgt. 1st Class William Brown and Pvt. George E. Vernon. After two waves of the enemy had been repulsed, and as the third wave began forming, the two machine gunners ran out of ammunition. The gunners picked up their individual weapons, fixed bayonets, and, screaming at the top of their lungs, charged down the hill at the enemy. The enemy was so surprised that they dropped their weapons and fled. After running out of ammunition, Brown and Vernon picked up enemy hand grenades and threw them at the fleeing enemy, killing 12 and wounding an estimated 25. Among those killed was an enemy officer who was armed with a new, civilian model, U.S. Colt .45 automatic pistol, probably taken from an overrun U.S. unit early in the battles of Korea.

By midmorning, the enemy had pulled back, and small arms fire became sporadic. Capt. Melbourne C. Chandler, commander of Company H, directed the evacuation of the dead and

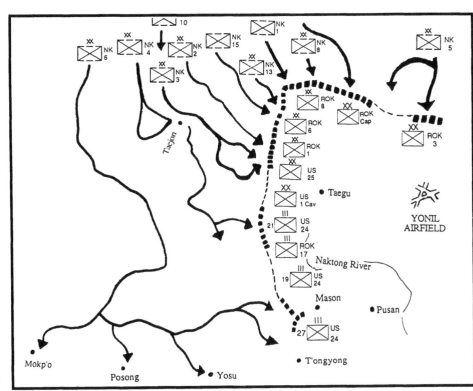

The front moves South, July 14 - August 1950

Sgt. 1/c Harold Blanc, Communications Sergeant Company H, 2nd Bn., 7th Cavalry. Heading for Korea on the USNS Shanks, July 1950. (Photo courtesy of Ed Daily)

wounded from the Company H area. He then remained with the one telephone left in his area, and from an exposed position directed artillery and mortar fire on five enemy tanks and small groups of personnel. Although slightly wounded and subject to heavy enemy fire, he remained in this position until late in the afternoon, destroying four of the tanks and approximately 50 enemy troops. By later afternoon, the fire fight had ceased, and engineer troops moved up the road immediately to the front of the 2nd Battalion to implant mine fields and perform other demolition work. The remaining heavy weapons crews were shifted along the front lines, and rocket launcher teams were placed in more advantageous positions to cover the draws, roads and mine fields. Enemy troops appeared to be massing in front of the 7th and 8th Cavalry fronts in preparation for new attacks during the forthcoming night. Warning orders were issued, and around 2100 hours, units of the 8th Cavalry followed by the 7th Cavalry began the next planned withdrawal to delaying positions to the rear.

During the day, the regiment had lost one officer killed and one wounded; three enlisted killed and 28 wounded; and three enlisted men missing in action.

The regimental command post executed a quick withdrawal during the early morning hours of July 31st and had established their new location in the town of Kiwan-ni by 0400 hours. The withdrawal was made with scant margin for error, for by 0100 hours, the old command post position was under heavy mortar and artillery fire. The enemy continued sending strong patrols against the entire front and frequently became engaged with the rear guard troops and the engineers covering the withdrawal.

The 2nd Battalion came under heavy artillery fire during the early morning hours, and just prior to daybreak, the enemy launched an attack on each flank of the battalion's positions. This was definitely the most severe attack that had been launched against the 7th Cavalry up until this time. The main attack was centered on the road and the right flank of the 2nd Battalion, as an enemy company attempted to roll up the battalion's left flank. Enemy mortar fire was extremely heavy and the battalion suffered a number of casualties. Urgent requests for ambulance jeeps, mortar and machine gun ammunition were received as the battalion directed heavy fire against the determined enemy. The attack finally was broken, and the enemy again withdrew into the town of Noo Dong, after suffering heavy losses against the 2nd Battalion's lines.

During this action, many acts of heroism were performed by various members of the command. Included among these were: Capt. James T. Milam, commander of Company E, who, after accounting for 34 enemy dead, including an enemy captain in front of his positions, personally led a patrol forward and destroying an enemy machine gun and killing seven more of the enemy in the immediate vicinity of his company sector. Chaplain (Capt.) Emanuel Carlsen remained with the battalion and took charge of the evacuation of the wounded while exposed to heavy shell fire. Lt. John C. Lippincott and his platoon from Company F,

who determinedly held their ground along the road leading into the battalion sector while subjected to intense enemy machine gun with mortar fire. Lt. John O. Potts of Company F rendered aid to a wounded soldier while under heavy fire, and Pvt. Willis Monington, also of Company F, did an outstanding job of maintaining communications by repairing broken wire throughout the entire action. Cpl. Chester L. Hart, of Headquarters Company, 2nd Battalion, went to the rescue of a seriously wounded soldier, completely disregarding the hail of rifle and machine-gun bullets.

At 0400 on Aug. 1st, the regiment again withdrew to defensive positions approximately five miles south in order to take advantage of more defensive terrain. The enemy did not follow this withdrawal, and there was no enemy contact during the day.

At 1400 hours on Aug. 2nd, the regiment began a retrograde movement from the Kumchon area to a point four miles north of Waegwan and then to Taegu. The regiment was assigned the mission of protecting the withdrawal of the entire First Cavalry Division. Company E with Company A, 8th Cavalry, protected the withdrawal of the regiment from Kumchon. An account of this action follows:

Company E, commanded by Capt. James T. Milam, reinforced by a heavy machine gun squad from Company H, 8th Cavalry, with Company A, 8th Cavalry, took positions along the high ground astride the road running north and south through Kumchon. Company E was in position to defend the main withdrawal from a possible enemy flank attack. Shortly after going into position, enemy troops estimated to be of regimental strength were sighted moving toward the Company E front.

The enemy, sensing contact, began dispersing to the hills and was fired on by Company A, 8th Cavalry. The enemy responded by destroying a heavy machine gun attached to Company A. The 60mm mortars of Company E went into action and destroyed four enemy automatic weapons and caused the enemy to change their positions. Small arms fire was exchanged with the enemy being held in check. When a radio message from Company A revealed that the last elements of the Division had cleared the crossroads seven miles to the south in the vicinity of Waegwan, Company E dispatched a message to Company A to hold until Company E could withdraw to a hill to the right rear of Company A in order to protect their withdrawal. Company E fell back slowly under cover of the natural terrain features while receiving increasing small arms and automatic weapons fire as the enemy realized that contact was being broken.

Company A, 8th Cavalry, had been unable to hold the enemy any longer and was entrucking on the side road, while Company E still was more than 900 yards away from their entrucking point and separated from this point by open rice fields. Company E then covered its own withdrawal by firing and falling back through ravines, rice paddy levees and irregular ground until it reached the river. Here the company dispersed, crossed the Naktong River and succeeded in reaching the protective cover the far bank while under intense hostile small arms and

mortar fire. Company E personnel aided in the evacuation of Company A's wounded and then entrucked in blazing Kumchon to rejoin their battalion the following morning at 0100 hours.

In order to protect the withdrawal of the Division, the 1st Battalion went into position prior to darkness on the crossroads facing south, and the 2nd Battalion assumed positions of the Kumchon-Waegwan road four miles north of Waegwan.

During this withdrawal, Company A, 7th Cavalry was ordered to remain in a defensive position to protect the troops of the 1st Battalion as it withdrew to a new defensive position. The withdrawal of troops was made in an orderly fashion with no enemy activity encountered by the main forces of the battalion. Eight minutes prior to the designated time Company A was to withdraw, 2nd Lt. Charles F. McGee, platoon leader of the 3rd Platoon, saw enemy troops approaching their position on the company's left flank. The enemy approach was obscured by heavy foliage, and word was passed along the line to hold fire until the enemy came closer and into view. The enemy kept moving up from left to right in front of the company's position to where Sgt. 1st Class Walter B. Wilson with the 2nd and 4th Squads of the 3rd Platoon was protecting the right flank. The enemy - garbed in well-fitting uniforms - came closer, moving in an orderly fashion in command of a young North Korean officer. As the enemy advanced, knowing that our troops were in the vicinity, some of them attempted to camouflage themselves by moving small uprooted pine trees in front of them. Wilson made contact with the company by field telephone and had 60mm mortar fire directed to an area where he saw about 15 enemy troops congregating. This caused the enemy to flee in panic, but they were reassembled quickly by orders shouted from their leaders. They then formed in the draw on Wilson's right flank as Cpl. Ramey's 2nd Squad and Cpl. Lowrey's 4th Squad opened up with rifle and automatic small arms fire, wounding approximately 25 enemy troops. The enemy withdrew and regrouped, but this action had permitted the remainder of Company A, minus this 3rd Platoon, to withdraw and rejoin the battalion.

The enemy then attempted to penetrate the draw through the center of the 3rd Platoon - the last troops remaining to cover the withdrawal. Sgt. Wilson, upon discovering the enemy's new thrust, took his two squads and moved to a knoll where they had excellent observation.

In the meantime, Cpl. Young's 1st Squad situated on a crest opposite the draw, brought heavy fire upon the enemy's column, killing at least 35. Sgt. Wilson sent one squad down one side of the draw to outflank the enemy and as this squad moved to their position, Sergeant Wilson's men rained heavy small arms fire on the enemy. The remaining enemy - too few and well-concealed - caused Lt. McGee to withdraw his troops rather than pursue them further, and the 3rd Platoon rejoined the company. As a result of the well-directed actions of Company A's 3rd Platoon under the able leadership of Lt. McGee and Sgt. Wilson, not a single casualty was suffered, while an estimated 155 enemy troops were killed in this skirmish.

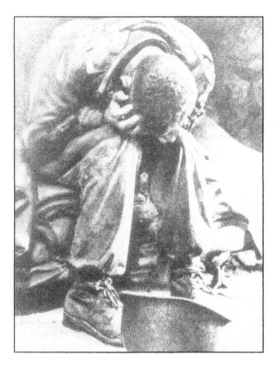
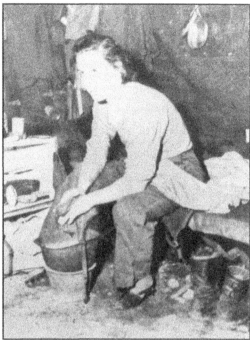

Top left: The tragedy of combat - some would breakdown. (UPI) Top right: Army nurse taking a breather - they had to work under very deplorable conditions. Middle left: The Decisive Factor, the Air Force, bombing a North Korean railroad yard. (USAF, VIA-Wide World) Middle right: Destruction of the Kum River Bridge, July 1950. (U.S. Army Photo) Bottom left: A platoon leader hurls hand grenade at the enemy. (U.S. Army Photo) Bottom middle: Papa-san in South Korea, 1950. They were highly respected for their age. (U.S. Army Photo) Bottom right: 1st Cavalry Division troopers loading into Landing Craft at Pohang-dong, July 18, 1950. (U.S. Army Photo)

31

North Korean People's Army moved South to cross the 38th Parallel, 1950. (Eastfoto)

President Truman conferring with General MacArthur over Korean War situation in 1950. (U.S. Army Photo)

General Walker, Eighth Army Commander, conferring with fire support officers July 16, 1950. (World Wide Photo)

The North Korean soldier was tough, disciplined and experienced. (Eastfoto)

Artillery Support from 105-mm Howitzers. (Courtesy of Bob Mauger)

1st Cavalry Division Troopers riding their future meal. (Courtesy of Bob Mauger)

CHAPTER III
PUSAN PERIMETER

In preparation for the final withdrawal to positions along the Naktong River - the main defensive line of the Pusan perimeter - Maj. William O. Witherspoon and Capt. William Cochrane with the Regimental I&R Platoon and Communications Section, departed at 0900 hours on Aug. 3rd for Taegu. The regiment followed the 8th Cavalry in the move to the Naktong River sector. Due to heavy traffic and the clouds of dust, progress was very slow, and the regiment did not arrive in Taegu until 1600 hours. The 1st Battalion was placed in Division reserve and went into an assembly area two miles north of Taegu. The 2nd Battalion, along with other elements of the regiment, moved 13 miles southwest of Taegu and went into a defensive position overlooking the Naktong River.

During the next few days, the regiment enjoyed a relatively quiet period. Defensive positions were prepared along the 30,000-yard regimental frontage facing the Naktong River, while the North Korean hordes regrouped in preparation for their assault against the thinly held Pusan perimeter in an attempt to drive the UN troops from Korea. It should be borne in mind that while the regiment had been assigned a frontage of 30,000 yards, only the 2nd Battalion was available to the regiment to defend the sector. The 1st Battalion remained in Division reserve and constituted the only reserve force readily available for counterattack in the entire Division sector; therefore, the regimental sector was defended by only one battalion. Under conditions of such wide frontages, the sector assigned the regiment was in reality a strong outpost position with company and platoon strong points organized for defense. Every available trooper and weapon in the regiment (less the 1st Battalion) was employed in these defensive positions. The area between the strong points was patrolled both day and night. In order to protect the most critical terrain - including a partially destroyed bridge - and to provide maximum heavy weapons support along the entire front, even the heavy weapons company (Company H) occupied front line positions and was assigned approximately 3,000 yards of the front to defend. Day and night patrols were dispatched across the Naktong River in front of the regiment's positions in order to maintain contact with the enemy massing for the impending attack. During the day, the unending line of refugees streamed through the area. At night, listening posts were established along the entire river line.

On Aug. 8th, the 16th Reconnaissance Company was attached to the regiment and was placed on the left flank to make contact with the 3rd Engineers, 24th Division. Information was received that approximately 280 North Koreans had infiltrated through the 24th Division, which presented a threat to the regiment's left rear.

On Aug. 9th, the 1st Battalion was committed to action by the Division and moved out of their bivouac area located two miles west of Taegu at 0840 hours. Company A, 71st Tank Battalion, was attached to the battalion and by 0940 both units were engaged with the enemy,

which had penetrated the 5th Cavalry positions to a point two miles southeast of Waegwan. This was the first of these vicious attacks that were to continue daily in the First Cavalry Division zone for the next 33 days. The following is an account of the 1st Battalion's action on Aug. 9th and 10th:

The 1st Battalion's mission was to counterattack astride the Taegu-Waegwan road, surround and annihilate an estimated enemy company located on "Triangle Hill," and restore the positions in the 5th Cavalry sector within one hour. The battalion detrucked and went into an attack formation about 2,000 yards from the enemy positions. The entire battalion moved forward with companies deployed as follows: Headquarters Company and elements of Company D on the right with a platoon from Company A, Company B in the center, Company C to the left and Company A in reserve.

On a mountain known as "Observation Hill," strong enemy machine gun, mortar and small arms fire was encountered. Company B, the center company, became involved in a fierce fire fight but continued to advance until reaching the hill; however, they were thrown back immediately by the savage enemy counterattack. As fighting continued, it became apparent that the hill could not be secured during the daylight hours and the battalion was ordered to consolidate its positions and hold for the night.

During the afternoon, enemy artillery and mortar fire constantly raked the battalion command post, causing six casualties. Among these was Maj. F.A. Daubin Jr., battalion executive officer, seriously wounded by an artillery round. His driver, Pfc. Edward Curry, was killed by the same round.

Positions occupied during the night were in the shape of a semi-circle around the base of the mountain covering the north, northeast, east and southeast approaches. The only escape for the enemy was through the 5th Cavalry adjacent to the river. There was little enemy activity during the night except for the frequent exchanges of hand grenades and mortar fire.

The attack on the enemy resumed at 0600 hours on Aug. 10th. The 3rd Platoon of Company A met with strong enemy machine gun fire, and the platoon leader - Lt. Charles F. McGee - was killed by a burst of machine gun fire at 0700 hours.

The enemy was too well dug in on the surrounding hills to dislodge by infantry attacks, and the entire battalion was pulled back to permit the artillery and mortars to fire on the entrenched enemy. The Air Force also was called into action to bomb and strafe the enemy positions.

After a short-lived rest, Headquarters Company Platoon and the Pioneer and Ammunition Platoon proceeded forward with the artillery observers to occupy two hills about 1,000 yards in front of the battalion command post. On "Triangle Hill" and the smaller hill in front and to the left, a number of enemy troops still occupied their battered dug-in positions. Three M-24 tanks moved down the road until they came to an open stretch where they had full view of both hills and opened up with machine gun and tank fire. Also aiding Companies A and B who began their attack was Company D's 81mm mortars, set up along the north side of a railroad embankment. In the face of this combined fire power, the North Korean Communist troops began leaving their positions on the

hills and ran down into the rice paddies where they were annihilated as Company A's troops came around the right of the hill and Company B came around the left slopes. Thus, the mission was accomplished - "Triangle Hill" was captured - and the position restored.

Enemy dead was 300 to 400 as a result of this action, which revealed that an enemy battalion opposed our troops rather than an estimated company. During this action many of the enemy, after firing their last round of ammunition, would surrender with a United Nations safe conduct pass that had been dropped from airplanes earlier in the Korean action.

The Division Commander, Maj. Gen. Hobart Gay, called Lt. Col. Clainos the following day and complimented him on the fine job performed by the 1st Battalion.

The 1st Battalion's losses during this two-day engagement were 15 killed, 48 wounded, and one missing in action. Other losses in the regiment amounted to four killed and two wounded as a result of patrol actions along the front.

Enemy troop concentrations continued to build up along the entire front. From positions overlooking the Naktong River, the 7th U.S. Cavalry waited for the enemy onslaught, which was anticipated momentarily, and on Aug. 12th, the first of three major thrusts was made across the Naktong River toward the key city of Taegu. At 0530 hours on Aug. 12th, movement was heard along the Naktong River to the direct front, and the listening posts along the river were driven in by small arms fire.

At 0605, Company H suffered the brunt of this first attack by an overwhelmingly superior force. The initial crossing of the river was made by approximately 1,000 troops of the 10th North Korean Division in the vicinity of the destroyed bridge to the left front of the company's positions. Although the river was unfordable, an entire enemy regiment with all equipment, including four heavy Russian-made machine guns, had crossed the river by using underwater ropes and had outflanked the company positions. Many enemy troops reached the high ground in rear of the company positions and launched simultaneous attacks from the rear as other groups attacked to the front. The enemy attacked in waves, the first wave consisting of white-clad civilians impressed into service and armed only with crude spears or captured weapons. The second wave consisted of the well-trained, well-armed North Korean troops. As many as six waves were included in each attack formation with every other wave formed by trained enemy troops.

The first Company H positions to be overrun were the 81mm mortar observation post and the forward heavy machine gun positions. The enemy, using automatic weapons and hand grenades, was determined to secure the high ground (Hill 209) commanding the destroyed bridge, which could be repaired and provide a back entrance into Taegu.

At the time the mortar observation post was overrun, the forward observer - Sgt. Millard G. Gray - was talking by field telephone with his company commander, Capt. Melbourne C. Chandler, stating that he could hear the enemy approaching in the predawn darkness and was requesting instruction when an enemy grenade was thrown into his position, severely wounding him and the telephone operator, Pfc. Harry Shappell. (Sgt. Millard Gray was one of the few non-commissioned officers assigned to the regiment who also had fought with the 7th Cavalry Regiment in World War II.) Sgt. Millard G. Gray remembers:

"I will begin my brief story in the early evening and morning darkness of Aug. 11-12, 1950, when we had alerted our command post that the enemy was possibly building up forces for an attack directly in front of our positions and near the destroyed steel-concrete bridge that previously spanned the Naktong River.

Actually, our position was the most forward outpost, which enabled us to keep in contact with the riflemen who were assigned to the listening posts on the edge of the Naktong River. Also, this position gave us a commanding view of the river itself and the destroyed steel-concrete bridge. The road from that destroyed bridge went directly to the back door of Taegu, where the Eighth Army Headquarters were located. A distance of only 14 miles away.

I was the Forward Observer for the 81mm mortar platoon, which was the 3rd Platoon of Company H, and 2nd Lt. Ed Daily was the 1st Platoon Leader of the same company, and our telephone operator was Pfc. Harry Shappell. Lt. Daily had established machine gun positions to the front and flanks in preparation of a possible massive enemy attack. We had been notified of a 100 percent alert earlier in the evening. Company F was to our left flank and Company G was to the right flank. Also, to our immediate right was a 75mm recoilless rifle team from the 2nd Platoon of Company H.

One must understand some of the conditions that existed within the Army and the 7th Cavalry Regiment at this particular time. Our 81mm mortar ammo was packaged during World War II (1944), which was old, and it was hard to observe, due to going-off prior to arriving at the target. And to make the situation even worse, there was a very serious shortage of all types of ammunition.

In the predawn darkness of Aug. 12th, the listening posts along the river were being driven back by enemy small arms fire. I asked for rounds to be fired from the 3rd Platoon and received only two. However, it was enough for me to see a large enemy movement directly to my front. I reported by field phone to Capt. Melbourne C. Chandler, Commander, Company H, on what I had seen. I asked for more rounds to be dropped 1,000 feet and fire for effect. They fired only four more rounds because it was too close to our forward positions and the critical shortage of ammo.

Earlier by field phone, Lt. Daily had requested a volley of 105mm howitzer rounds to be fired from Battery B, 77th Field Artillery. His request was denied because he couldn't give them an estimated strength of the enemy and further, the critical shortage of 105mm ammo.

At this time, Lt. Daily left the outpost to check the line and alert all machine gun positions to prepare for a massive enemy attack. Then shouting and screaming from the enemy began at approximately 0600 hours, which was the start of the vicious battle. The enemy was all around us by sheer numbers alone and soon all positions were overrun. I quickly called by field phone and asked for rounds to be fired directly on our outpost position. This was denied.

Suddenly, an enemy hand grenade landed next to Pfc. Harry Shappell, and I shouted, "Grenade, throw it!" As Shappell attempted to throw the grenade, it exploded simultaneously, blowing off his right hand and wounding me with eleven pieces of steel slivers, from my one ankle up to my shoulder.

Within a minute, Lt. Daily returned to the outpost and began to shout, "Medic! Medic!" He quickly attempted to administer medical treatment to Shappell and me. By now, Shappell was becoming delirious from shock and pain. Very soon to arrive was the combat aidman who then used his professional medical experience to treat our wounds. By late afternoon, the superb medical evacuation team had me at the 49th General Hospital in Tokyo, Japan.

I eventually recovered from my wounds and volunteered to return to my previous unit. Lt. Ed Daily was captured during this vicious battle and somehow managed to escape from the enemy. He also volunteered to return to his previous unit. We both continued to fight in combat with the 7th Cavalry Regiment until we were rotated out of Korea in the late spring of 1951." GARRYOWEN!

Although Pvts. First Class Norman Tinkler and Raymond Scarberry and Pvt. J.P. Smith were severely wounded by the first wave of attacking troops, they stayed in their forward machine gun position, firing their weapons to the front and to the rear, until their ammunition was exhausted or their weapons rendered inoperative by enemy fire. Due to this volume of fire placed upon the enemy, the first waves of attacking troops were forced to withdraw up the mountain where they regrouped and then attacked the 81mm mortar positions and the company command post. Extremely heavy casualties were suffered during the first hour of fighting, and all company positions - machine gun, 75mm recoilless rifle and 81mm mortar - were overrun.

Seeing that the enemy was receiving reinforcements from the reverse side of the mountain to the rear of the company position and that the company would be cut in half, Capt. Chandler decided to attack the enemy to the rear of his company position where an estimated force of about 125 was located on the high ground. Approximately 25 of the slightly wounded who were awaiting evacuation near the company command post, the company clerk, supply personnel, cooks and drivers were assembled and as Capt. Chandler yelled, "GARRYOWEN!", he led the force up the rugged mountainside. The attacking force made their way about three-fourths of the distance to the mountain top when their ammunition supply was completely exhausted, and they were pinned down by heavy automatic weapons fire and hand grenades from enemy positions as close as 10 feet away. Lt. Robert M. Carroll, wounded earlier in the fight, had been left at the bottom of

North Korean soldiers not so lucky defending their positions. (Courtesy of Bob Mauger)

North Korean prisoners of war being taken to clearing station. (Courtesy of Bob Mauger)

the hill to direct into position any reinforcements that might arrive. Instead, he gathered three stragglers in the area and led a charge into the enemy until he was severely wounded by a hand grenade.

Unable to progress any further up the mountain, Cpl. Harry Straitman was dispatched to the company command post for additional ammunition, while Capt. Chandler and Pvt. Thomas L. Palmer returned to the overrun 81mm mortar positions, turned one mortar around 180 degrees and brought fire upon the enemy. By taking all powder charges from the rounds and elevating the tubes to a vertical position, 81mm mortar fire was brought upon the enemy at ranges as close as 100 yards, and the pinned-down troopers of Company H were able to disengage from the enemy, return to their original position at the bottom of the hill, and replenish their ammunition supply. This bold attack had stopped the enemy in rear of Company H.

A force of 242 South Korean police (temporarily attached to the regiment) under command of Maj. Charles G. King, and the Regimental Intelligence and Reconnaissance Platoon under command of Lt. Crawford Buchanan, along with 15 truck drivers, cooks and supply personnel from the Regimental Service Company arrived to assist the beleaguered force of Company H. Assisted by this force, Company G on the extreme right flank and Company F on the extreme left flank, the tide of battle was turned, and the enemy retreated through the rice paddies toward the river. Artillery barrages and air strikes were brought to bear upon the fleeing enemy, killing hundreds before they could cross the river.

Two platoons of Company F had been sent from the left flank to aid Company H. Lt. John C. Lippincott with a rifle platoon reached the high ground in support of Lt. Thomas H. Stone's platoon in time to see Lt. Stone exchanging hand grenades with the enemy. Lt. Lippincott stated that grenades filled the air as thick as blackbirds, and he hesitated a moment or two in trying to determine where to fire.

As a result of the day's action, 237 enemy were known killed in rear of Company H's positions and scores of others probably killed. A tabulation of enemy killed in the front of Company H by other elements of the regiment, including the Air Force and the 77th Field Artillery, could not be determined accurately; however, it is known that an enemy battalion was annihilated and 35 prisoners taken. The regiment lost 15 killed and 60 wounded, mostly from Company H. While directing reinforcements into the area, Capt. Chandler was wounded by a grenade thrown at close range and was evacuated. Thus, all but one officer - Lt. William Kaluf - and more than 70 percent of the enlisted men of Company H became casualties during the day.

As a result of the heroic defense by Company H, recommendations were submitted for one Distinguished Service Cross, five Silver Stars and seven Bronze Stars for members of the company.

The 1st Battalion was released to the regiment at 0200 hours from Division reserve and elements of the battalion reached Hill 344 around 1800 hours. A patrol from Company A did not reach the town of Nyonpung as they were stopped by machine gun fire and small arms fire approximately half way to their objective.

During the early evening hours of Aug. 12th, Lt. Frank Earle, of Company D, with a motorized

North Korean soldiers captured by elements of the 7th Cavalry Regiment, in September 1950, are being processed by a clearing station of the 545th Military Police Company. (Photo courtesy of Reuben Kvidt)

patrol started out in a northwestern direction from the village of Noi-Dong and turned left in a southwesterly direction to the village of Yong P'o along the banks of the Naktong River. The patrol stopped after proceeding along the road from the village of Yong P'o for a little more than two miles. The point of the motorized patrol was sent out into the village of Chung-Dong, passing and making contact with a 57mm Recoilless Rifle Squad from Company F, where guides were to be contacted to direct Lt. Earle's platoon to their designated position.

Finding no guides, the motorized patrol returned. Lt. Earle, with a dismounted patrol, then went forward on the road and proceeded to the outskirts of Sach'on in an attempt to make contact with troops of the 1st Battalion. Fearing the possibilities of being ambushed as the patrol had moved too far forward, he returned, and the patrol moved back and bivouacked for the night with Company F.

Second Lt. James W. Mann, a forward observer of the 77th Field Artillery Battalion and Lt. Col. William A. Harris, commanding officer, 77th Field Artillery Battalion, proceeded to Ridge 344 with a Company B patrol. The patrol returned, but both Lt. Mann and Col. Harris remained in enemy territory and from a vantage point directed artillery fire on enemy positions until dark.

At 0555 hours on Aug. 13th, an enemy machine gun began firing at close range on Company C, followed by a general attack of infantry, supported by machine gun and automatic weapons. This attack lasted for four hours; however, the enemy failed to dislodge the 3rd Platoon of Company C from its position. By continuous infiltration, the North Koreans had occupied the high ground on the right flank of the 1st Battalion along Ridge 344. Company C's 60mm mortar section was outstanding in keeping them at bay until Company B could be called for assistance to dislodge this enemy group from the battalion's sector.

Company B immediately proceeded by the route taken by the 1st Battalion on the previous day, and then south to clear the western slope of Hill mass 344. When Company B arrived in the vicinity of Na Dong, elements of the company were pinned down by machine gun fire coming from the high ground on the eastern slope of Hill mass 344. Company B's machine guns and Company C's 60mm mortar fire finally forced the enemy machine gun to move its position; however, during this action Lt. Eugene E. Fels, commanding officer, Company B, was wounded by a burst of enemy machine gun fire and his radio operator, Pfc. Victor Baker was killed. Lt. William Chappell assumed command of Company B.

Lt. Gamble and Sgt. Steward, 2nd Platoon, Company C, with 18 men, including the artillery forward observer, were covering a part of Ridge 360 to observe the forward area when they received orders to proceed to Ridge 344 where Company C was located. When they arrived at the top of Hill 360, they came face to face with 25 to 35 North Koreans. They drove the enemy from the high ground toward the river through Company D's position. However, Lt. Gamble was wounded by sniper fire, and Sgt. Steward took command of the platoon and remained on Hill 360 for approximately 1 1/2 hours until artillery fire forced him to move to another position.

Meanwhile during this action on Aug. 13th, Lt. Earle's platoon, which had bivouacked with Company F the preceding evening, made radio contact with Companies A and C, which were engaged with the enemy. Lt. Earle brought his 81mm mortars and 75mm recoilless rifles into action to give these companies some support. Small arms and automatic enemy fire started to rain down on the 75mm recoilless rifle team and the mortar platoon. As Master Sgt. Nauwieler fired his 75mm recoilless rifle from an open position at point-blank range, the enemy turned their

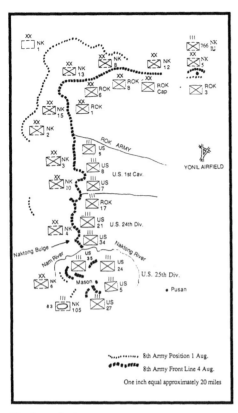

The Pusan Perimeter.

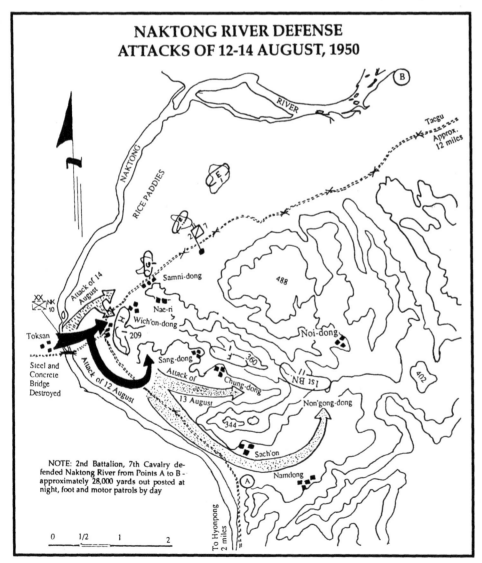

NAKTONG RIVER DEFENSE
ATTACKS OF 12-14 AUGUST, 1950

NOTE: 2nd Battalion, 7th Cavalry defended Naktong River from Points A to B - approximately 28,000 yards out posted at night, foot and motor patrols by day

attention to that position, and Sgt. Nauwieler was hit four different times before leaving his position. Pfc. Alexander Stuart, realizing the plight of Sgt. Nauwieler, rushed to his position and poured fire on the enemy until the sergeant could be removed.

The 81mm mortar platoon also had been hotly engaged and was sorely in need of ammunition. Cpl. Swing, under heavy small arms fire, rushed down into the draw in plain view of the enemy and threw ammunition from the trailers into the waiting arms of the mortar crew. During this operation, two rounds of mortar ammunition were struck by enemy small arms fire, causing the powder increments to be set off. Disregarding this danger, Swing continued unloading ammunition until he was wounded by shell fragments from enemy artillery and mortar fire that began falling in the area.

In a last desperate effort before the enemy was forced to withdraw from their positions due to the heavy concentration of fire, they rushed Lt. Earle's platoon. The mortar crew kept elevating their tubes until they were firing at the enemy 200 yards away. The remainder of Earle's platoon rushed to the left flank of their position to stem this fanatical attack, which lasted for 30 minutes. Enemy fire then became sporadic, and as Sgt. Steven's platoon approached from the northeast corner of Hill 360, the enemy fled in panic.

Earle's command was under continuous attack from 0800 to 1500 hours, and only when the attack ended were the wounded evacuated with the aid of troopers from Company F nearby. All of Earle's platoon vehicles had been practically destroyed by enemy small arms fire, and all mortar increments and the propellant charges on seven rounds of 75mm recoilless rifle ammunition were set off. Why the warheads didn't explode still remains a mystery.

With Company D's battered vehicles that were still in an operational condition, including ones with flat tires, the platoon returned to the road from whence they came the preceding evening. In the village of Samni-Dong, they were attacked again by enemy small arms fire but received no casualties.

Now to return once again to where the greater part of the 1st Battalion received the brunt of the second major attack toward Taegu at the crack of dawn on Aug. 13th. Shortly after the enemy crossed the Naktong River and started their attack, they split their forces and proceeded through the valley on the battalion's right flank. Sporadic enemy fire began from all directions as Companies A and D outposts, consisting of 18 men, held off the enemy attack until mortar and artillery fire could be delivered into the entrance of the valley. The enemy then moved from right to left on the road to the front, taking cover in rice paddies and under a small bridge. One enemy column proceeded up the road in a southerly direction, while another group occupied the high ground in front of the battalion's positions. The battle raged throughout most of the day, and at 1515 hours, the artillery, in close support with the Air Force, shelled, rocketed and strafed Pakkok-Tong, Samni-Dong, and Sach'on.

The supply of ammunition, food and water was very low, and the battalion requested priority be given to the supply of the front lines by airdropping ammunition. At approximately 1700 hours, L-5 liaison planes dropped ammunition on the forward slopes in front of the battalion positions. However, this method of supply did not prove successful, as the M-1 ball ammunition was damaged and scattered over a large area. The mortar ammunition was not damaged but created a problem in recovery as it rolled down the steep slopes of the hill and into ravines that were covered under a dense growth of foliage. Some ammunition was recovered, and with the 1st Battalion's troop sorely needed ammunition replenished, they started once again to drive the enemy back across the Naktong River. The difficult supply problem was solved partially by using native bearers to pack ammunition, water, rations and other supplies to the forward positions, although the difficult terrain made this method very slow. The engineers, with three bulldozers, cut a road through rice paddies, around ravines and up and down hillsides in record time. One such road was built from a rear point approximately 1,500 yards beyond the village of Noi-Dong, which cut the time for a round-trip by pack and litter personnel from four and a half to two hours.

Enemy activity ceased for the remainder of the evening, and casualties for Aug. 13th for the 1st Battalion amounted to 15 killed and 21 wounded. The remainder of the regiment lost 10 killed and 18 wounded.

On Aug. 14th, the 7th Cavalry Regiment was composed of the 2nd Battalion on the front line with Company E on the right, Company G in the center, Company H and Company F on the extreme left flank. The Heavy Mortar Company and the 77th Field Artillery Battalion were in support and the 1st Battalion was on the left of Company F; however, the regiment's extreme left flank was open since physical contact with the 24th Division had not been established. Also, one platoon of the 71st Tank Company; Company A, 8th Engineer Battalion; and one squad of Company B, 8th Engineer Battalion were in support of the regiment. On the right was the 8th Cavalry. The 16th Reconnaissance Company made their appearance later during the day.

The third attack to seize Taegu began during the hours of early morning darkness on Aug. 14th, when a heavy infiltration movement was detected by Company G's listening posts along the Naktong River. The veteran troopers crouched low awaiting the first glow of daybreak, and the North Korean troops began their expected attack at 0531 hours. By sheer weight of numbers, they soon succeeded in driving Company G's outer perimeter defense to the rear. Approximately 700 enemy troops attacked the scattered defensive positions of Companies G and H. Again, the enemy was determined to secure the high ground, which would cover a suitable river crossing and protect the road, affording him a back entrance into Taegu.

By 0620 hours, the enemy had penetrated as far as Yong P'o with an estimated 400 to 500 troops. At 0630, the 16th Reconnaissance Company was committed to action in an attempt to flank the enemy and by 0635, the enemy penetration had reached Wichon-Dong, and fighting in the understrength Company H and a portion of Company G's area had reached the hand-to-hand stage.

One machine gun team of Company G earned a recommendation for award by their company commander, Capt. Herman L. West, when the light machine gun manned by Pvt. Theodore Hickman went out of comission with a ruptured cartridge at a time when his company's position was in imminent danger of being overrun. The assistant gunner Pfc. Arthur Hunter succeeded in holding off several of the enemy with his rifle while Pvt. Hickman dashed for the company command post and returned with an extractor for his fouled weapon.

According to eye witnesses at the time, Pfc. Hunter's voice could be heard, over the sound of his firing, singing out, "GARRYOWEN! Yahoo! Look at 'em! I got one!"

Several enemy dead were found in front of the position later.

Perhaps the closest call of the attack came to Pfc. Robert D. Roberts, Company G, who at the time of the attack was manning a machine gun on the southwestern slope of the hill adjacent to the company command post. At 0700 on the morning of the attack, his helmet was pierced by an enemy bullet that entered through the front a scant half-inch over his head and passed through the helmet liner and on through the back of the helmet without touching his head. One-half hour later, another bullet entered the front of his helmet in almost exactly the same spot, grazed his scalp and passed through the rear of his helmet. Both bullets had torn through several letters and photographs he had been keeping in the half-inch space above his scalp in the helmet liner. At the time of the second shot, he also was wounded in the back

Destroyed bridge that spanned the Naktong River. Site of the 10th North Korean Division crossing and major battles of August 12-14, 1950. (Courtesy of Bob Mauger)

by shrapnel but after receiving medical attention returned to the fight four hours later.

During this attack, Company G's command post, located in a dugout, was overrun. While the company commander, Capt. Herman L. West, was reporting the situation by telephone to the 2nd Battalion Commander, Lt. Col. Gilman A. Huff, he abruptly stopped his conversation. A few minutes later, he calmly resumed his conversation, and in his typical slow southern drawl said, "Excuse me, sir, I had to shoot a couple of Gooks that stuck their head in my CP." Although the area was overrun, Capt. West and his headquarters personnel remained at their dugout company command post position in an apple orchard throughout the action. Enemy troops also were in Yong P'o and Wichon-Dong with the furthest penetration at Naeri.

A secondary attack had begun in the 1st Battalion's sector at about the same time. At 0637 hours, the 1st Battalion was ordered to send patrols to the road south to contact elements of he 24th Division, south of Hyongpong. A tank platoon was sent to the vicinity of Samni-Dong to eliminate the enemy pocket estimated to be about 400. At 0750, it was reported that the enemy held Hill 360 and that Company B was in the process of attacking this position. The enemy continued to cross the river near the bridge as Companies F and G closed in on the enemy on the right front of the 1st Battalion. Company H began receiving enemy tank and artillery fire from across the river and numerous air strikes were made on the road and rice paddies from Yong P'o toward the destroyed bridge.

By 0918, the enemy pocket had been eliminated in the Yong P'o and Samni-Dong areas; however, many enemy still remained in the rice paddies to the front. Mopping up continued to be a tedious job for the remainder of that day and the

following, as North Korean troops, pretending to be dead, would throw grenades when the cavalrymen came within range.

The 1st Battalion reported that Company B had secured Hill 360 and that one platoon was moving down the hill to the rice paddies in order to assist Company C in sweeping north toward the road. Company C ambushed and killed seven enemy near Hill 360 while Company B moved to the northwest in order to sweep the rice paddies and contact Company F. One patrol ran into a mine field en route to Hyongpong, and one man was killed and one wounded. The patrol continued to this town and made contact with elements of the 24th Infantry Division at 1628 hours.

By midmorning on the 14th, the Air-Ground Liaison Officer reported that aircraft had located three barges loaded with enemy personnel near the destroyed bridge. The barges were strafed, and the pilots reported that the "river ran red" at this point. Around noon the Air-Ground Liaison Officer reported that pilots could see nothing but enemy dead on the west side of the river.

At 1350 hours, the Division chief of staff notified the regiment that the 1st Battalion would again revert to Division reserve before dark. An estimated enemy battalion was engaged in the fight during the day, and more than 1,000 of them were annihilated, 150 of them in Company G's position alone, while 20 prisoners had been captured. Company G lost two men killed and three wounded during the day's action, and the 1st Battalion lost two killed and two wounded.

The 1st Battalion returned to Camp McGee two miles north of Taegu and reverted to Division reserve at 2300 hours. Elsewhere in the regimental area, the front remained calm, as the major enemy thrust toward Taegu had been broken by the heroic troops of the 7th Cavalry during the period Aug. 10th to 14th.

North Korean soldiers captured by elements of the 7th Cavalry Regiment. Many were wearing the civilian clothing of South Korea, which made it difficult to distinguish them as the enemy. (Photo courtesy of Reuben Kvidt)

During the attacks of Aug. 12th to 14th, the 10th North Korean Division suffered a severe blow to their 25th and 27th Regiments, with an estimated loss of 2,500 to 3,000 soldiers. This caused much panic and confusion within their ranks. Their attack was scheduled previously to coincide with that of the 3rd North Korean Division on Aug. 9th, but something went wrong, and they did not jump off until Aug. 12th. These three days gave Hap Gay time to redeploy Clainos' Clouters.

The historian further wrote: *"The battered 10th North Korean Division withdrew to Koryong and then to Songju, where they were headquartered. They eventually buried their artillery and retreated northwest through the hills toward Taejon."* He stated: *"They were saddled with inept leadership and either through misunderstanding or ineptitude of its command, it did not move again to fight in the perimeter. It is one of the great mysteries of the Korean War."*

From the book, "The Forgotten War," author Clay Blair wrote: *"When the 10th Division crossed the Naktong River, it confronted first Gil Huff, next Billy Harris and then Pete Clainos, who came up with his Clouters on Aug.14. These three tough, canny leaders inflicted yet another terrible slaughter on the NKPA. In its baptism of fire, the 10th Division suffered 2,500 casualties. Its survivors were apparently so demoralized - or so ineptly led - that the division could not be used again in the attacks on Taegu. It would remain in defensive positions at Koryong. However, they were headquartered in Songju, which was south of the Waegwan-Taejon highway."*

Patrol activity increased along the regimental front during the period Aug. 15th to 29th at which time the entire regiment moved to positions approximately five miles east of Waegwan. During the period of patrolling, the regiment lost eight killed, 15 wounded and one missing in action.

On Aug. 19th, Company C, 70th Tank Company, was attached to the regiment. This company became an integral part of the regiment during the remainder of the Korean operations and shared in the glory and hardships of the GARRYOWENs.

On Aug. 20th, news correspondents Hal Boyle (AP), Kenneth Inouye (Telenews), Hal Gamble (Stars and Stripes) and Frank Emery (INS) visited the 1st Battalion and interviewed officers and men who had taken part in previous battles along the Naktong River front.

On Aug. 2nd, Gen. J. Lawton Collins, Chief of Staff; Gen. Walton H. Walker, Commanding General, Eighth Army; and Gen. Hobart Gay, Commanding General of the First Cavalry Division, visited the regimental command post. When they inquired as to what the regiment needed most, the reply was more men and ammunition.

During the latter part of August, ammunition of all types was in extremely short supply. Artillery units were rationed to 50 rounds per gun per day except for an emergency. 4.2-inch mortars were limited to 10 rounds per gun per day, and 81mm mortar units were limited to 15 rounds. These amounts could be exceeded only upon Division authority, when the unit was under attack or when exceptional targets were presented.

At 2000 hours on Aug. 26th, the 2nd Battalion, 30th Infantry, 3rd Division, arrived in Taegu to become the 3rd Battalion of the 7th U.S. Cavalry. This much needed 3rd Battalion was activated Jan. 25th, 1949, at Fort Benning, Ga., had completed basic and advanced training and had taken part in exercise PORTREX - an amphibious training exercise in the Caribbean Sea. The battalion lost approximately 500 men as replacements for other units upon the outbreak of the Korean War, was alerted for over-

seas movement on July 20th, received replacements on July 23rd, arrived at Camp Stoneman, Calif., on Aug. 8th, and arrived in Taegu on Aug. 26th. The completely equipped battalion consisted of 685 enlisted men, 33 officers and five warrant officers and was a welcomed addition to the understrength battle-weary 7th Cavalry Regiment.

On Aug. 28th, three British officers - Capt. Brown, 1st Battalion, Argyll and Sutherland Highlanders; Capt. Hodge and Capt. Shipton of the 1st Battalion, Middlesex Regiment - held an interview with Lt. Col. Peter D. Clainos, commanding officer of the 1st Battalion, 7th Cavalry. The interview was recorded for use in Australia.

The regiment, as part of the First Cavalry Division, then was given the mission of pushing the enemy back across the Naktong River where they had penetrated the area east of Waegwan in the sector held by the Republic of Korea forces.

At 1900 hours on the 28th, elements of the 3rd Battalion, 23rd Infantry, 2nd Division, began relieving the 2nd Battalion, 7th Cavalry, along the Naktong River as the latter unit withdrew into an assembly area preparatory to moving early the next morning.

At 0547 on the 29th, the 1st Battalion was released to control of the regiment and began moving into the area east of Waegwan dominated by Hill mass 518. The 2nd Battalion began moving to the same area at approximately 0800, and the 3rd Battalion moved into their sector at approximately 1300. The remainder of the day was spent getting into position and preparing for the attack on Hill 518 believed to be lightly held by the enemy.

On Aug. 30th, Company B dispatched a patrol to Hill 518 and made excellent progress. Company A reinforced this patrol and the 1st Battalion was told to hold Hill 518 if the patrol secured it. The 1st Battalion reinforced the patrol with Company A and the remainder of Company B. Intense automatic weapons, small arms and mortar fire was received when the force was within 200 yards of the summit. The companies withdrew and secured positions for the night on the slope of the mountain, having lost 10 killed and 36 wounded.

Throughout the day of Aug. 31st, harassing artillery and heavy mortar fire was placed on Hills 518 and 346. An air strike also was placed on the north side of Hill 518. By midmorning, Company C contacted the 8th Cavalry by patrol and began organizing positions in order to close the gap between the 1st Battalion and the 8th Cavalry on the right. The tank company changed positions because of intense enemy artillery fire, and the road behind the 1st and 2nd Battalion sectors received frequent rounds of extremely accurate enemy mortar and artillery fire.

The 1st and 2nd Battalions continued to patrol to the front in order to maintain contact with the enemy, while the 3rd Battalion dispatched patrols to the rear in order to check the area and to receive training. The regiment suffered six wounded during the day as a result of patrol skirmishes.

By Sept. 1st, the regiment's front line units began to suspect that they were faced by an enemy force of something greater than a "reinforced company" on Hill mass 518. As the first week wore on, enemy artillery and mortar fire increased in intensity and accuracy. Patrols sent out by all three battalions on the line were met with increasing resistance, and considerable enemy activity could be observed across the Naktong River during the day and could be heard at night.

Within the vicinity of Hill 518 on Sept. 2nd, Company E of the 2nd Battalion had been alerted to check all positions for a possible enemy attack. It was a beautiful day, the sun was shining bright and the morning air was calm. There was no action with the enemy at the time. Pfc. Marvin C. Daniel, a rifleman in Company E remembers that particular day and his brief story is as follows:

"Lt. Otis Lane and Sgt. John Jano walked on past me to approximately 25 feet further on down the hill. They were going to inspect the positions of the 1st Platoon when suddenly there was an artillery or heavy mortar round that landed very near both of them. There was dust, dirt, shrapnel and rocks thrown through the air, and I couldn't see who was possibly hit. When the air began to clear, I could see Capt. James T. Milam, Commander of Company E and 1st Sgt. Homer Leacock exit the command post tent. Capt. Milam shouted for me to rush over to them to see if I could give the troopers some help. As I approached Lt. Lane, he was attempting to stand up. He was riddled from his neck down, and his one leg was almost blown off. He looked at me eye to eye and from his voice he said: "Don't bother with me, I'm dead!" He then fell to the ground and died a few minutes later. Sgt. Jano was shouting, "Come to Jano, Come to Jano!"

Sgt. Jano was evacuated from the hill with very serious wounds. I went back to my position and began to read the 23rd Psalm in my Bible, which gave me comfort after this one very tragic combat experience. And Capt. James Milam was killed in action a few days after this happened. Strangely, every day since, my thoughts have gone back to that mountain and the tragedy that occurred in combat on that day."

On the morning of Sept. 3rd, the first organized enemy attack was launched against the forward units. It was then found that the high ground in rear of the regiment's main battle positions was occupied by an unknown number of enemy troops and with each attack against our front lines, more enemy troops infiltrated through to the high ground to the rear of our positions. This high ground was to have been the next rearward defensive position of the regiment in the event a withdrawal was ordered; however, the regiment soon found itself between two enemy lines.

To indicate to the reader the furious actions that took place throughout the regimental sector during the first week of September, the paragraphs that follow are chronological extracts from battle reports and describe the relentless pressure exerted by the enemy during this period.

At 1110 hours on Sept. 1st, the 2nd Battalion reported a nine-man enemy patrol crossing the river. Enemy artillery continued to fall in each battalion sector during the day, causing the 1st and 2nd Battalions to move their command posts. Supporting artillery destroyed an enemy mortar position 400 yards northeast of Hill 518, and detailed plans were made to seize Hill 518 the following day.

The assault on Hill 518 began at 0900 hours on Sept. 2nd with an air strike of four flights of F51s dropping 24 napalm bombs and strafing targets on the ridge and the north side of the hill.

Pilots reported bombs were "on target" and effective, and tanks of Task Force Blue began firing to the right front in support of the attack. At 1022 hours, Company F, on the left flank, began firing their machine guns in support of the 1st Battalion.

At 1029 hours, the 1st Battalion reported that their attack and the supporting artillery fire had been stopped by four F80 jet planes making an unscheduled attack on Hill 518. The unscheduled air attacks on Hill 518 were shifted to Hill 346 and other targets, and the 1st Battalion resumed the attack.

Harassing enemy artillery fire fell in Company I's sector at 1101 hours, simultaneous with the movement of approximately 35 enemy troops across the company front, who were taken under fire. About 40 enemy and three field pieces spotted on Hill 346 by a 3rd Battalion outpost were hit with good results by an attack from four F80s that struck the position at 1132 hours.

One of the 2nd Battalion's supporting tanks from Company C, 70th Tank Battalion, was hit by an enemy 120mm mortar round at 1210, killing one crew member and wounding two more.

At 1240 hours, the Regimental Intelligence and Reconnaissance Platoon reported that an air attack had caused explosions with black smoke at a village in front of the 2nd Battalion. Enemy tank activity later was reported as burning furiously at 1300 hours following an air strike by F51s and F80s.

At 1320 hours, the 1st Battalion reported that they were held up by intense machine gun and mortar fire. At 1410 hours, they reported that their attack was being held up by fire from prepared enemy positions on Hill 490 and requested permission to shift Company A around to attack from the north and northwest, while two additional companies were placed in the frontal attack. The shift of Company A was granted, but the battalion was informed that the 3rd Battalion would push their attack from Company I's position in a northwesterly direction from Hill 490 later that afternoon. At 1615, the 1st Battalion withdrew to regroup and resumed the attack at 1700 hours.

At 1715 hours, after firing white phosphorous and smoke shells on the hills to the left front, the 3rd Battalion attacked through Company I's positions northwest toward Hill 490, as planned. This allowed the 1st Battalion to resume their assault against Hill 518 from a westerly direction approximately 15 minutes later. The 1st Battalion began its advance on Hill 518 as the 3rd Battalion advanced to the base of Hill 490.

At 1830 hours, the 3rd Battalion's advance was halted by heavy machine gun fire as they neared the summit of Hill 490 on the northeast side of Hill 518. A report was received from the 3rd Battalion that Hills 490 and 518 would be assaulted simultaneously at 1850. However, at 1920 hours, two enemy machine guns from Hill 490 began firing on the battalion, necessitating counter fire from our heavy machine guns before the advance could continue. By 1930, the 3rd Battalion was on Hill 490 and within 200 yards of Hill 518; however, small arms, automatic weapons an mortar fire increased in intensity and forced them to withdraw and regroup.

The 1st and 3rd Battalions were notified to establish contact when Hill 518 was taken, with the boundary to be in the large draw leading northwest from Hill 518. The 2nd and 3rd Battalions were to establish contact with each other while the 1st Battalion was to contact elements of the 8th Cavalry on the right flank of the regimental sector.

Move up that 3.5 Rocket Team (Bazooka) for support. Note enemy automatic rifle laying in foreground. (U.S. Army Photo)

Badly wounded trooper receiving blood plasma at Aid Station. (U.S. Army Photo)

Boots of a trooper who was killed on a patrol. (U.S. Army Photo)

Lt. Talbert's Marauders were sent on a raid against the small villages along the Naktong River during the hours of darkness.

Heavy harassing fire from enemy artillery and 120mm mortars fell over the entire regimental sector, with 150 rounds falling in the vicinity of the tanks alone. The Regimental Intelligence and Reconnaissance (I&R) Platoon was forced off of the regimental outpost by artillery fire, and each battalion reported heavy artillery fire, with an estimated 200 rounds striking the 2nd Battalion sector. Heavy fire was received from 2000 to 2115 hours, and all communication lines were broken. The forward collection station was forced to withdraw because of enemy artillery. Small enemy groups crossing the Naktong River were reported by Companies F and G, and several enemy artillery pieces, mortars, tanks and vehicles across the Naktong River along the entire regimental front were reported by observers.

By 0100 hours on Sept. 3rd, the 3rd Battalion again succeeded in advancing to within 200 yards of the summit of Hill 518. The 1st Battalion had been stopped near the top of Hill 490, while the 2nd Battalion reported that all remained quiet in front of their positions. At 0356 hours, heavy tank and artillery fire struck the 2nd Battalion's positions, and Company E received and repulsed a probing attack. Lt. Talbert's Marauders returned to their original positions at 0110 hours. The regiment's I&R Platoon reported one large and one small enemy artillery piece across the river, which were directing fire in the vicinity of along the forward slopes and on the crest of Hill 464 - directly in the rear of the 2nd Battalion's positions, while the battalion received sporadic tank and artillery fire in their positions.

Company F received a heavy, artillery-supported attack on their sector's right flank at 0515 hours, which forced them to fall back from their forward positions, and by 0640 hours on the morning of the 3rd, Company F had been driven off Hill 300, thus exposing the 2nd Battalion's right flank. Artillery fire was placed on the hill to prevent the enemy from reinforcing this penetration. At 0725 hours, the 1st Battalion reported

that an unknown number of the enemy had penetrated through Company F to the bridge on the main supply route and requested that the I&R Platoon engage the enemy in that vicinity. By 0820 hours, Company F had counterattacked and again occupied Hill 300.

At 0633 hours, elements of the Security Platoon of Headquarters Company, under the command of Lt. John C. Lippincott, were ordered to intercept and destroy the enemy groups, which had penetrated the forward positions and were proceeding up the mountains in the rear of the 2nd Battalion's positions (Hills 464 and 380). The platoon started up the connecting trail, into the saddle between Hills 464 and 380, to clear the ridges of enemy groups. By 0849 hours, Lt. Homer C. McNamara, I&R Platoon leader, reported that he could see Lt. Lippincott's group and that they were under heavy fire from an estimated 25 enemy on Hill 464. Later, Lt. Lippincott reported that his men were receiving mortar and automatic fire from Hill 464 and that the enemy had a radio and an 82mm mortar on the hill. He deployed his men to approach the hill from the south side and requested that a patrol from the 3rd Battalion approach Hill 464 from the west. At 1135 hours, the 2nd Battalion was ordered to send a combat patrol toward Hill 464. At 1306 hours, Lt. Lippincott reported that his patrol had flushed the enemy from their positions and that they were in pursuit. At 1340 hours, the 8th Cavalry was notified that the enemy force was being driven to the southwest on the trail from Hill 464 to Changa-Dong and south through the draw, and was requested to send a combat patrol to intercept this force. At 1403 hours, Lt. Lippincott requested litter bearers for five men seriously wounded.

Meanwhile, at 0844 hours on Sept. 3rd, the 1st Battalion again was attempting to seize Hill 518, and at 0926 hours the 3rd Battalion began their attack on the hill. The 3rd Battalion reported that progress was slow but that they were continuing their attack. At 1040 hours, the 8th Cavalry Regiment reported an enemy penetration between the 1st and 3rd Battalions on Hill 518, and at the same time Lt. Talbert reported an enemy force had penetrated to Songok-Tong - a village between the 1st and 2nd Battalions. At 1159 hours, Talbert's Marauders had withdrawn to Hill 400 and reported that the draw leading from the northwest of Hill 400 was teaming with enemy troops.

At 1240 hours, a tank platoon and two infantry squads were organized in the 3rd Battalion rear area and ordered to attack toward the 8th Cavalry in order to clear the main supply route of small enemy groups that had infiltered to the rear of the 3rd Battalion.

At 1330 hours, the 1st Battalion reported that the enemy occupied Hill 326 and Hill 400 in strength and that Talbert's Marauders virtually were cut off; however, by 1435 hours, Talbert's Marauders had been reorganized on Hill 400.

At 1450 hours, the 1st Battalion reported that Company A was at a point approximately 500 yards from the top of Hill 518.

At 1800 hours, the 2nd Battalion requested a concentration of artillery fire be placed on 100 to 150 enemy troops crossing the Naktong River to their front.

The 1st Battalion launched another attack at 2228 hours on Hill 518 with four platoons moving from the north. The leading platoon launched a frontal assault from this direction while the other platoons attempted to infiltrate around the flanks in an attempt to capture Hill 518. Later reports revealed that the attack was continuing, but that all platoons were engaged in hand-to-hand combat.

During the early morning hours of Sept. 4th, the tempo of enemy activity increased. A number of small probing attacks were launched along the entire regimental front, many small enemy group infiltrated in, between and behind all battalion positions, and contact with enemy groups was reported from almost every point on the compass. However, the 1st Battalion's advance toward the top of Hill 518 continued to progress satisfactorily, while the I&R outpost on Hill 464 (in rear of the 2nd Battalion's positions) reported that they were receiving heavy small arms fire from Hill 300 (about 400 yards west) and artillery fire from the broad valley across the Naktong River.

At 0130 hours on the 4th, the 2nd Battalion reported receiving tank fire on their right and small arms fire in the center of their positions. Two enemy tanks and 20 to 40 enemy troops were located in the draw between their left flank positions and the 5th Cavalry Regiment.

At 0520 hours, the 3rd Battalion reported enemy in unknown strength within 100 yards of their command post. At 0650 hours, the 3rd Battalion reported enemy to the front and rear of their positions.

At around 0600 hours, the I&R Platoon reported that the enemy was attacking their position on Hill 464, and contact with Lt. McNamara on the I&R outpost on Hill 464 was broken. At 0722 hours, Lt. McNamara reported to the command post and stated that he had to destroy his radio and light machine gun to keep them from falling into enemy hands and that the enemy now held Hill 464.

At 1301 hours, the 1st Battalion reported that the enemy was well fortified on Hill 518 and that they still were trying to gain the top of the hill. At 1307 hours, artillery fire was placed on the enemy side of Hill 464, and the 3rd Battalion was ordered to dispatch Company L to take the hill.

At 1439 hours, Lt. Ralph Terrell, regimental son officer to Division, returned from a road reconnaissance to report that the 8th Cavalry had committed tanks and engineers to replace its 2nd Battalion (on the right flank of the 7th Cavalry's 3rd Battalion), which had been hit hard, and that the enemy now had firmly established a road block in rear of the 8th Cavalry positions.

Although continuous efforts to capture Hill 518 were made throughout the day by the 1st and 3rd Battalions, little ground was gained due to the strong, well-fortified enemy positions and heavy automatic weapons fire.

At 2037 hours, the 1st Battalion reported that contact had been made with the 1st Battalion, 8th Cavalry on their right flank, and that all avenues of approach were covered between the two battalions. The 1st Battalion also reported that Talbert's Marauders were attacking Hill 400 again.

At 2242 hours, an outpost on hill 400 reported receiving enemy mortar and automatic weapons fire and were instructed to withdraw from the hill. The 3rd Battalion reported that the enemy occupied Hill 464 and were well-entrenched and that their troops were within 500 yards of the top of the hill.

The 2nd Battalion reported that many enemy vehicles and personnel were assembling to their front and that they were taking the enemy under artillery fire.

At 0300 hours on Sept. 5th, enemy harassing small arms fire was reported by Sgt. Brooks, Security Platoon, from his post on Hill 400.

At 0405 hours, the 2nd Battalion reported three enemy tanks in the draw between them and the 5th Cavalry Regiment on the left and that a 3.5-inch rocket launcher team had been dispatched to destroy the tanks. Enemy infiltration through the draw between the 2nd Battalion and the 5th Cavalry was observed as pressure built up against Hill 303 (in the 5th Cavalry sector) and the 2nd Battalion was directed to dispatch a reinforced platoon to seize the hill and organize it for defense.

The enemy became more active from the northwest slope of Hill 490 and launched a counterattack against the 3rd Battalion at 0915. At 1350 hours, the 3rd Battalion reported the enemy had penetrated their positions, and by 1345 hours, the 1st Battalion received a sharp attack from the northwest side of Hill 518.

The Security Platoon Leader Lt. Lippincott was dispatched to attack an enemy patrol near the regimental command post, and an estimated 20 enemy troops were dispersed as a result of the fire fight.

Taegu was again in the grip of crisis and evacuation seemed almost a certainty. As a precaution, Walker ordered the Eighth Army Staff and a few other elements to withdraw to Pusan. However, his "tactical staff" did not abandon the city. Gen. Walker told one American division commander (probably Gay) defiantly: *"You will not withdraw your division beyond terrain from which it can cover Taegu. If the enemy gets into Taegu, you will find me resisting him in the streets, and I'll have some of my trusted people with me. And you had better be prepared to do the same. Now get back to your division and fight it."* The Army historian further wrote that Walker told another general that *"he did not want to see him back from the front again unless it was in a coffin."*

Maj. William O. Witherspoon, regimental S-3, dispatched a liaison officer to each battalion at 1500 hours with a warning order for a probable withdrawal during the night of Sept. 5th-6th. An urgent message was dispatched to the 2nd Battalion stating that it was absolutely essential that they secure Hill 464 prior to dark; however, at 1800 hours Hill 464 remained in enemy hands.

At 1835 hours, the regimental command post moved to a new location to the rear, and officers were dispatched to each battalion with directions for the impending withdrawal while the regimental executive officer went forward to coordinate the movement.

At 0105 on Sept. 6th, a withdrawal was ordered for all regimental units, and the 3rd Battalion reported that their command post was under attack. Communications were broken with all battalions for the remainder of the night, and fragmentary reports indicated that the situation was critical. Two tanks were abandoned, one because of mechanical failure and the other because of its inability to operate through the mud. The 2nd Battalion fought its way out while under continuous fanatical charges from a strong enemy force supported by tanks and artillery.

The 3rd Battalion marched down the road to the west behind the 5th Cavalry's former positions. Rain and muddy roads caused additional problems during the withdrawal.

The 2nd Battalion withdrew southward toward what was to be the new front lines of the regiment. Company G, with elements of Companies F and H, withdrew toward Hill 464. The 2nd Battalion Headquarters and Headquarters Company, with elements of Companies E and H, and the remainder of Company F, withdrew toward Hill 380. Company E, with the remainder of Company H, also withdrew toward Hill 380; however, since this group held the left flank of the battalion's front line positions and was the last to disengage from the enemy, they were diverted in a southwesterly direction and did not join the main battalion group on the long ridge leading to Hill 380. Instead, Company E, with elements of Company H, turned west toward the 5th Cavalry's former positions and engaged scattered enemy groups in minor skirmished along the way. It was during one of these skirmishes that Capt. James T. Milan, former commander of Company E, and at the time 2nd Battalion S-3, was killed while personally covering the withdrawal of the last elements of Company E.

The main battalion group started up the long steep slope leading southward to Hill 380. Maj. Omar Hitchner, in command of the battalion, sent out a point under command of Lt. Pennel JH. Hickey. Enemy contact was not made until the group was within 50 yards of the crest of Hill 380 where heavy automatic weapons fire was received from the well dug-in and concealed enemy on the peak of the hill. The group was pinned down, could not move and could not see the enemy troops. After several minutes delay, Maj. Hitchner directed a machine gun be brought forward and set up to fire on the hidden enemy troops. After the machine gun was in position, he directed the gunner to cover him while he moved forward in an attempt to locate the enemy, but as he moved forward, he was killed by an enemy anti-tank rifle. Capt. Melbourne C. Chandler, then battalion executive office, assumed command of the group during the remainder of the withdrawal. The only operational radio with the group was the one carried by Capt. Albert B. Cassidy, 77th Field Artillery Battalion Liaison Officer with the 2nd Battalion. At approximately 1130 hours, contact was established with Company G on Hill 464. However, the enemy on Hill 380 had the 2nd Battalion group so well covered, that movement was impossible, and after losing three more men in an attempt to move from the position, the plan was abandoned.

The 2nd Battalion finally contacted the regiment by radio and informed it of the situation and that an attempt would be made to go around Hill 380 during the hours of darkness; attack from the opposite side at daylight; and, that further contact by radio would not be attempted since the batteries were getting weak.

As darkness fell, the battalion group began their march west for approximately 1,500 yards and then eastward for approximately 1,200 yards around Hill 380. The march, led by Capt. Chandler and Lt. John B. Wadsworth, was made over extremely rough terrain, down almost vertical rocky slopes and through dense underbrush. As the crest of the ridge line was reached, an enemy patrol was heard immediately in front of the group and the column waited until the patrol passed. From this point looking northward, the

Light .30 caliber machine gun position. (U.S. Army Photo)

entire valley across the Naktong River appeared to be filled with green flashes from the enemy artillery firing toward Taegu. At approximately 0400 hours, the exhausted group reached a point some 900 yards south of Hill 380 - 1,500 yards south of their position on the previous day. During this time, the group had no water or food, and the ammunition supply was extremely low. At daybreak, the regimental headquarters again was contacted, advised of the situation and informed that the group planned to attack Hill 380. The battalion was informed that Capt. Fred DePalma with a group of replacements had been dispatched to assist and that 100 native carriers were being dispatched with ammunition, rations and water.

At 0710 hours, contact was made with Capt. DePalma's group, and Lt. John B. Wadsworth with two enlisted men were dispatched to contact the group of carriers and lead them to the battalion position. The attack on Hill 380 was successful. Approximately 50 enemy troops were killed and considerable equipment captured, including radios and telescopes, which had been used to direct the accurate mortar and artillery fire on the regimental positions during the past three days.

At 1300 hours, radio communications were opened again with the regiment at which time the 2nd Battalion group was advised that the carriers could not get through, that the 2nd Battalion group appeared to be surrounded, and to withdraw to friendly lines by any route possible. (Note: The nearest friendly lines known to the group at that time were those of the 5th Cavalry, approximately 3,000 yards to the southwest.) The only map sheet carried by the group did not extend further south or west than Hill 380; therefore, the group could only withdraw in a general southwesterly direction.

The scattered groups were gathered, formed into a column, and the remaining ammunition equally distributed - this consisted of about two clips of M-1 or carbine ammunition per man, one box of machine gun ammunition for each of the three light machine guns, and seven 60mm mortar rounds for the two mortars. The column started their march toward what they hoped would be friendly lines. After bypassing several small en-

emy groups, the tired, hungry column halted at about 1600 hours for a rest. During the halt, the forward scouts reported that they could see troops around the former 5th Cavalry regimental command post. Capt. Chandler borrowed the Artillery Liaison Officer's field glasses and went forward. Someone could be seen emerging from a dugout who motioned and shouted, "Hey, G.I. - this way." Upon adjusting the field glasses, the figure was recognized as a North Korean officer. Closer observation revealed many enemy troops racing along the small ridge north and parallel to the column to get back to their run positions. Capt. Chandler immediately turned the column south and led them as quickly as possible across water-filled rice paddies to cover. By the time the enemy could get their guns into action, the major portion of the column was safely out of range. Mortar fire and approximately 40 enemy troops closely pursued the disorganized group across the rice paddies. At that time, a friendly artillery liaison plane appeared overhead and directed artillery fire on the enemy troops, thus permitting the 2nd Battalion group to reach the 5th Cavalry lines approximately 1,000 yards further south.

From the time the withdrawal began during the early morning hours of Sept. 6th, this group had been without sleep, food or water; their ammunition was exhausted; and for the most part they were out of communication with friendly forces. From the time the withdrawal began until friendly lines were reached late in the afternoon of Sept. 7th, they had suffered one officer killed, three enlisted men killed, and nine wounded. During the withdrawal across the rice paddies, Capt. Chandler had the heel shot from his boot and discarded his boots. When he led the column into the command post of the 2nd Battalion, 5th Cavalry, he was barefoot, wet, covered with mud and had some difficulty in establishing his identity as a battalion commander.

The 2nd Battalion group was provided transportation back to Camp McGee where they rejoined the other elements of the battalion and the regiment.

The following is an account of Company G

and the elements of Companies F and H, which withdrew toward Hill 464.

When the 2nd Battalion was ordered to withdraw from its positions along the Naktong River to positions on high ground to their immediate rear, Company G was given the mission of attacking and seizing Hill 464 while the remaining units of the battalion moved by a different route to attack and seize Hill 380. This operation was unique in that the battalion had to disengage from enemy contact, attack to their rear, and seize and occupy a new main line of resistance. Elements of the regiment had attacked Hill 464 on three previous days without success.

At 0300 hours on Sept. 6th, Company G withdrew from close contact with the enemy and began movement toward their objective. During this time, the company was subjected to sporadic enemy tank and artillery fire but continued to withdraw. Rain and the muddy terrain made the withdrawal even more difficult.

At 0800 hours, Company G was near the top of Hill 464 when three enemy soldiers were seen and killed quickly. The company continued under heavy automatic fire, which caused the troopers to disperse and seek cover. At this time, it was discovered that Hill 464 had a double peak. One platoon under Lt. Richard Tobin was employed around the right flank of the first peak, while another platoon under Lt. Lawrence Ogden placed heavy fire on the enemy positions. Tobin worked his platoon up to within 50 feet of the first peak when they came under heavy crossfire from both peaks and were pinned down. The third platoon then was employed further around the rugged mountain and subjected the enemy to such a volume of fire that Tobin was able to withdraw his platoon. Company mortars were employed with good effect; however, the determined enemy refused to be ejected from the key terrain features.

Contact was made with the remainder of the 2nd Battalion, and information was received that the battalion was pinned down by heavy fire from Hill 380 and from the reverse slope of Hill 464. At 1600 hours, the battalion commander ordered the company to withdraw under cover of darkness to the southeast side of Hill 464 and to take up positions in rear of the hill in order to make contact with the 1st Battalion thought to be on the right.

During the hours of darkness, the company moved out. Litters were constructed from tree branches and ponchos to transport the wounded. The withdrawal route led down a shale slide, which made footing difficult under normal conditions - not to mention the rain, darkness and the enemy troops in close pursuit. Progress was extremely slow, and the journey required several hours. Lt. Tobin was placed in charge of the point. Half-way down the mountain, the company was subjected to artillery barrages that fell within ten yards of Capt. Herman L. West, the company commander, and 1st Sgt. Bill Williams. The first sergeant was killed instantly and Capt. West was injured.

At this time, the column became scattered, and the point separated from the main body. Even though injured, Capt. West reorganized his company and in his slow southern drawl he remarked, "No damn Gook is going to take my men prisoners." He told every man to move as quietly as possible and not to fire under any circumstances as the closely pursuing enemy could be heard in very

Officer on left is Lt. Colonel John W. Callaway, Commander of the 2nd Battalion, 7th Cavalry. Officer on right is unknown. (Courtesy of Ed Daily)

1st Lt. John "Jack" Lippincott in front of jeep that belonged to Colonel William "Wild Bill" Harris, Commander 7th Cavalry Regiment. Note saddle on hood. (Courtesy of Ed Daily)

direction. "By moving without firing in the darkness, the enemy probably will think we are one of them, and I am going to lead all of you out of here." Capt. West led the entire group to the base of the hill mass; however, upon reaching this point, it became necessary to halt so that the litter bearers could rest. Here, the unit again came under artillery fire, and Capt. West quickly led the column up a draw to the east in an effort to locate a friendly unit. After failing to find friendly forces and unable to contact anyone by radio, the company was placed in a defensive position for the remainder of the night.

As dawn approached on Sept. 7th, four figures were observed coming down the trail toward the company. They were identified as enemy troops and killed, but this firing brought the surrounding hills to life, and lead came flying from every direction. Lt. Tobin, with a part of the company, was ordered to attack an enemy position located on a small hill to the right of the company, and 13 enemy troops were killed. A briefcase with much valuable information was found, a 120mm mortar and two prisoners were captured. At this time, friendly planes above were preparing to attack the company. A hasty signal was improvised with paper, branches and rocks, which read "SOS-GI." This apparently satisfied the airmen as they disappeared. Later, it was learned that a strafing and bombing mission had been planned on the hill where the company was located; however, quick thinking and a field expedient saved the day.

At this point, contact was made with a patrol from the 1st Battalion on the right, and two platoons of Company G were dispatched to that area. The company commander remained in the immediate area and waited for the remainder of his company, which was delayed by the litter cases. A runner reported that the litter bearers were exhausted and could not proceed any further. Artillery began falling between the two company groups; however, Capt. West quickly moved through the artillery barrage to his men and led the entire group through the artillery fire to safety.

The achievements of this company were outstanding in that all wounded were evacuated over treacherous terrain; all equipment was brought out in spite of enemy automatic weapons, artillery and mortar fire. The company had disengaged from close contact with the enemy, fought its way through enemy troops, killed many to include an enemy regimental commander and two staff officers, and captured important documents, and had been without food and sleep for two days and nights. Capt. West was awarded the Distinguished Service Cross for his heroic actions during this engagement.

Later, it was learned from prisoners that Hill 464 was an enemy assembly point and had been utilized for several nights for that purpose in the enemy's drive toward Taegu.

During the withdrawal on Sept. 6th, the 1st Battalion occupied their new positions extending from the base of Hill 464 eastward to Hill 620 with relatively little enemy contact.

At 0415 on Sept. 7th, the 1st Battalion reported hearing North Koreans on their left flank in the vicinity of Company A. Shortly afterwards, a sharp fire fight developed in this area, and a call from the Heavy Mortar Company revealed that personnel from Company A and the 1st Battalion's

supply personnel had withdrawn from their positions. The opposing enemy force - estimated at 150 - conducted five attacks during the early morning hours against the 1st Battalion. Two platoon of the Heavy Mortar Company supporting the 1st Battalion were pinned down by the enemy machine gun fire and displaced to the rear with their mortars, taking the enemy under fire with good results. Sgt. Eddie L. Fletcher, Heavy Mortar Company, was outstanding in directing

his platoon in the fire fight and in the evacuation of eight wounded men.

Elements of Company F, which had been with Company G, reported to the 77th Field Artillery Battalion on the 7th at 110 hours, and promptly were clothed and fed. In return for the hospitality Company F remained with the 77th Field Artillery Battalion for the remainder of the day in order to furnish protection to them during their forthcoming withdrawal.

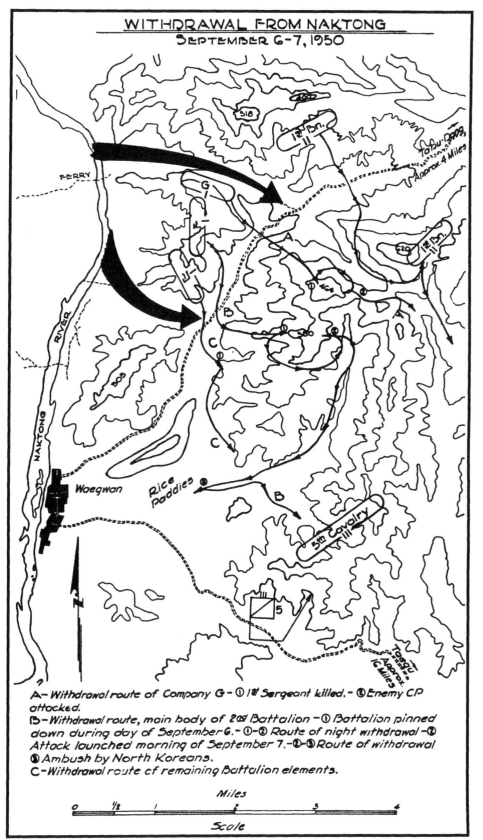

WITHDRAWAL FROM NAKTONG
SEPTEMBER 6-7, 1950

A - Withdrawal route of Company G - ① 1st Sergeant killed. - ② Enemy CP attacked.
B - Withdrawal route, main body of 2nd Battalion - ① Battalion pinned down during day of September 6. - ①-② Route of night withdrawal - ② Attack launched morning of September 7. - ②-③ Route of withdrawal ① Ambush by North Koreans.
C - Withdrawal route of remaining Battalion elements.

Miles

0   ½   1   3   4

Scale

During the afternoon of Sept. 7th, the disorganized regiment was placed in Division reserve in the vicinity of Camp McGee, and the scattered units began assembling at that point. The 1st Battalion in coordination with the 1st Battalion, 8th Cavalry, began their withdrawal at 1600 hours and came under operational control of the 5th Cavalry Regiment upon reaching their assigned defensive positions. The last units of the regiment reached Camp McGee at 0200 hours, Sept. 8th. The 2nd Battalion was re-clothed and reorganized under its new commander, Maj. John W. Callaway. The 3rd Battalion was bivouacked in the rest area but remained alerted with its staff on reconnaissance, while the 1st Battalion was on the line between the 5th and 8th Cavalry Regiments under control of the 5th Cavalry.

At 1500 hours on Sept. 8th, the following information was given to the 3rd Battalion: "One of the missions of the Division in the withdrawal was to attack to the rear and clean out enemy pockets which had infiltrated. This has been done except on Hill 343 in the 8th Cavalry sector. The 8th Cavalry is attacking Hill 343 from the north. One platoon of the 71st Tank Battalion is attacking from the south. Little is known of the progress of the attack. One possible mission of the 3rd Battalion may be to attack Hill 343 from the southwest on September 9th. Contact should be made with the 8th Cavalry, and a reconnaissance of the area should be made. The 3rd Battalion probably will be attached to the 8th Cavalry for the operation."

Company C on Hill 345 was attacked during the night of Sept. 8th-9th and lost three 60mm mortars and one 57mm recoilless rifle during the operation. However, the company recaptured its lost position and recovered the weapons the following morning, but due to enemy mortar barrages, the company later was forced to withdraw to Hill 174. Company A remained on Hill 203. Company B was driven off their positions on Hill 392 while suffering four killed and 18 wounded, but recaptured the hill on the morning of the 9th.

The 2nd Battalion was alerted at 0700 on Sept. 10th with the mission of capturing Hill 660, while the 3rd Battalion remained in the 8th Cavalry area awaiting further orders.

The 1st Battalion was subjected to heavy mortar fire during the day on the 10th, and the enemy continued their attacks during the hours of darkness. Company A occupied positions on the left front of the battalion sector; Company B was pinned down on the rear of Hill 174; and Company C was on the line of the right of Company A. Company B suffered three killed and 16 wounded during the early morning hours from mortar fire.

Sgt. H.P. Flerchinger, platoon sergeant with Company B, distinguished himself in hand-to-hand combat in taking an objective during this action. When the platoon leader was wounded, the company commander directed Flerchinger to reorganize the platoon and to re-take the high ground that the platoon had lost. The attack was launched and the hill secured except for occasional sniper fire. When two of the sergeant's men were wounded from sniper action, he decided to go sniper hunting himself. A machine gun was placed in position to cover his advance around a rocky ledge. After advancing a few yards, he suddenly came face to face with six North Koreans who dispersed when he tossed a grenade in their midst. He continued to move forward in pursuit of the snipers when he came across four more North Koreans group together. This happened so suddenly that he did not have time to use his pistol or his remaining three grenades. He took off his helmet and threw it at the North Korean. Three of them attempted to grab their rifles but Flerchinger jumped in the middle of them, and they ran off. Then it was a knock-down and drag-out affair with the other one. The sergeant managed to place his feet in the enemy's stomach and held him high in the air in hopes that his men would fire. Finally, he threw the enemy soldier over the ledge where a machine gun killed him, and no more sniper fire was received that night in the Company B area.

The early morning hours of Sept. 11 were typical of the past several mornings in the 1st Battalion area, in that they received repeated attacks. However, before being relieved by elements of the 5th Cavalry Regiment, the 1st Battalion recaptured Hill 174 after making four attempts during the day.

At 0650 hours on Sept. 12th, the 2nd Battalion departed the bivouac area. By 0830 hours, Company F had departed a forward assembly area for positions on Hill 660 where they were to relieve elements of the 1st ROK Division, and by 1210 hours, Company F had organized their positions, Company G was enroute to their positions, and Company E was moving toward Hill 516.

The enemy continued to pour southward across the Naktong River toward Taegu. Hill mass 314 - a key terrain feature - was occupied by a large enemy force. On three previous occasions, other elements of the First Cavalry Division had attempted to secure this hill mass, which commanded a strategic position in the enemy's fanatical drive toward Taegu.

Recuperating from its engagement near Waegwan during the withdrawal, the 3rd Battalion was given the mission of capturing Hill 314 and was told that this hill mass was the key to the defense of Taegu and had to be taken and held at all cost. While going into position for the attack, the 3rd Battalion passed other friendly units who spoke discouragingly of the hill because of their encounter with it previously and expressed the view that it could not be taken with less than a full-scale regimental attack.

The 3rd Battalion, commanded by Lt. Col. James Lynch, began their attack at 1100 hours on Sept. 12th, after an air strike, but without the usual artillery preparation due to the critical shortage of ammunition. The enemy fired a 120mm mortar concentration on the line of departure and the reserve company assembly area. The battalion's advance continued for 500 yards under sporadic machine gun and rifle fire. At this point, the entire battalion was pinned down by intense rifle and mortar fire, and observed about 400 enemy to their left front preparing for a counterattack. An air strike was requested but was delayed. However, the counterattack was repulsed by infantry and mortar fire.

It was at this point that 1st Lt. Joseph A. Fields, commanding Company I, displayed outstanding leadership as he reorganized his company under the intense mortar fire without regard for his own safety, after his company had suffered 25 percent casualties. At 1400 hours, an effective air strike was placed on the top of the ridge and on the north slope, and the order was given to assault the hill mass with Company I on the right and Company L on the left. The troopers surged up a measure 60 degrees slope for a distance of 1,000 yards against well-employed enemy machine guns and riflemen who poured a heavy volume of fire into the assaulting troops. The top was reached, but intense mortar fire and the lack of cover caused the troopers to withdraw. The hill was assaulted a second time, and again they were driven back by the intense mortar and machine gun fire. Company L, led by Capt. Robert W Walker, and troopers of Company I came back fighting madly for the third time. As Capt. Walker reached the top, he shouted, "Come on up here where you can see them. There are lots of them and you can kill them!" The men responded instantly, yelling madly, and shouting, "Kill them," and reached the top after fierce hand-to-hand combat with grenades, rifle butts and bayonets. They overran the enemy positions and charged down the opposite slope in pursuit of the enemy until ordered to halt for reorganization and defense of the hill. The charge so demoralized the enemy that they ran screaming to the rear, abandoning their weapons, as effective artillery fire was placed on them.

Prisoners revealed that more than 700 enemy troops had been on the hill. Counted enemy dead exceeded 250, and prisoners captured at a later date stated that practically all of the remaining 450 either were wounded or missing. The enemy's defenses consisted of caves with machine guns covered by snipers in rock crevices and ravines. Mortar fire from 60mm, 82mm, and 120mm was intense and precisely registered on the key points over which the battalion was required to advance. Losses to the battalion were 28 killed and 248 wounded. The regimental commander dispatched a message to Lt. Col. Lynch which read: "Congratulations - Your capture of Hill mass 314 today adds another page to the glorious history of 'GARRYOWEN'"

The capture of this strongly defended and physically difficult objective was completed in 4-1/2 hours despite heavy casualties and indicates the outstanding courage, devotion to duty and esprit de corps of the regiment at this time. The battalion's conduct in the attack was in keeping with the finest traditions of the 7th U.S. Cavalry. The 3rd Battalion, 7th Cavalry, was awarded the Presidential Unit Citation for this action.

At 1400 hours on Sept. 13, Lt. Gen. Walton H. Walker, Eighth Army Commander, addressed the officers and enlisted personnel at the regimental command post regarding future offensive operations. He stated that an amphibious operation would be made on the west coast within the next few days and that the North Koreans probably knew this already. He mentioned briefly the history of this regiment and said Gen. MacArthur had stated that the 1st Cavalry Division was the most ferocious outfit he had ever seen; that Gen. Chase, the Division's former commanding general, was the most ferocious commander he had known. Gen. Walker expressed the hope that when this regiment started forward we would have only one thought in mind and that was to KILL. He further stated that he hoped we would be the equal of the killers in the 7th Cavalry's history who served in the regiment when Gen. Custer commanded it.

North Korean tank member who attempted to escape from his burning Russian T-34 tank as Task Force Lynch fought northward through enemy held territory. (U.S. Army Photo)

North Koreans captured by elements of the 1st Bn., 7th Cavalry, September 1950. Many were stripped of their uniforms due to concealment of weapons and hand grenades. (Photo courtesy of Reuben Kvidt)

Atrocities committed by North Korean soldiers, in September 1950. (Courtesy of Reuben Kvidt)

Atrocities committed by North Korean soldiers September 1950. (Courtesy of Reuben Kvidt)

Dead North Korean officer waiting for burial. (U.S. Army photo)

North Korean soldier attempts to escape from fox hole, but is burned beyond recognition by napalm bomb. (Courtesy of Bob Mauger)

CHAPTER IV
THE BREAKOUT

At 1100 hours the following day, the G-3 Eighth Army visited the command post and discussed the situation in general. It was revealed that the First Cavalry Division was part of the I Corps now and that an amphibious landing was scheduled by the X Army Corps for Sept. 15. Shortly thereafter, I Corps was to be on the offensive with the scheme of maneuver on D-Day, H-Hour: the 5th Cavalry on the left, 8th Cavalry to the right, and the 7th Cavalry to follow. The Division was to make a sweeping movement from its present positions toward the Naktong River and Waegwan.

At 1100 hours on Sept. 16th, the 2nd Battalion was directed to move to the vicinity of Hill 246 in preparation for an attack along the Taegu-Waeguan road. Two companies of the ROK Special Training Battalion relieved the 2nd Battalion on Hill 660. At 1426 hours, the 2nd Battalion was attached to the 5th Cavalry Regiment for operational control, which marked the beginning of the breakout from the Pusan Perimeter and the historic drive northward to within 30 miles of the Yalu River on the Manchurian border.

Upon arrival in the assembly area, the 2nd Battalion issued orders and prepared for the assault the following morning. The battalion objective was Hill mass 300, which dominated the Taegu-Waegwan road - essential to the successful breakout from the Pusan Perimeter. This hill mass had been unsuccessfully assaulted during the previous three days by other elements of the Division.

At 0700 hours on Sept. 17th, the battalion attack began as Company E moved across the line of departure toward the forward slope of Hill 188 to protect the movement of Company G crossing the wide valley. Company F moved southwest of Hill 188 to protect the battalion's south flank and drew heavy enemy fire from Hill 184. The battalion received orders to leave enough troops at Hill 184 to contain the enemy and to move the remainder of the battalion around the hill across the road to the battalion objective - Hill 300. Company G moved toward Hill 105, Company E occupied Hill 100, and the battalion commander and a small staff displaced forward to Hill 100. Company G received mortar and sniper fire, and the artillery observer with Company F was wounded. Company G was on Hill 105 at 1330 hours but receiving heavy enemy fire. Company F was ordered to contact Company G, and both companies were ordered to push northeastward to the road.

Company E was ordered to attack Hill 184 at 1400 hours; however, stiff resistance was encountered, and the hill was not taken. Companies F and G made contact and continued their movement toward the road.

At 1800 hours, the 5th Cavalry's 2nd Battalion attacked from the southeast and assisted Company E in taking Hill 184 as this was the key terrain feature delaying the advance to the final objective. Companies F and G assaulted the high ground immediately across the road, and the enemy withdrew to the higher ground to their rear. The companies overran and destroyed several enemy mortars but met exceptionally strong resistance as the enemy was pursued to the higher ground north of the road. Capt. Fred P. DePalma, commanding Company G, was killed during this assault, and the two companies became somewhat disorganized and pulled back to the south side of the road for the remainder of the night.

The 2nd Battalion resumed their attack on the morning of Sept. 18th, with Company E attacking southwest of Hill 184 and then northwest to the high ground across the road. Company E received all types of fire but continued to move slowly. Company F was committed at 1300 hours in conjunction with friendly tanks. Both companies crossed the road at 1700 but continued to receive heavy volumes of enemy fire. Company G moved to the ridge east of Company E in order to secure the battalion objective but was pinned down by enemy fire from south of road and withdrew slowly to the high ground north of the road. Company F (now consisting of 45 men) remained in the vicinity of the tanks near the road. Companies E and G then were consolidated (totaling 120 men) and attacked to within 200 yards of the summit of Hill mass 300 by 2200 hours and dug in for the night.

The attack continued at daylight on Sept. 19th, with Company F moving up the slope toward the battalion objective. Company E also attacked following an artillery preparation but was forced to withdraw because of heavy automatic fire. By 0800, a lengthy column of friendly vehicles began moving down the Taegu-Waegwan road toward Waegwan - the breakthrough had begun.

At 0830, Company F was in position for the final assault against the enemy positions on the objective and by 0900 occupied the southern tip of Hill 300 after fierce hand-to-hand combat. Companies E and G supported the attack by fire but could not move forward. Within 30 minutes the enemy counterattacked, causing Company F to withdraw 100 yards. Capt. William L. Webb, commanding Company F, was wounded while individually attacking an enemy machine gun position, and Lt. Christensen assumed command.

At 1000, all companies were ordered to make a coordinated assault on Hill 300. After a short artillery preparation (due to the shortage of ammunition, only the center guns of each battery fired), Company F advanced as the attack began; however, the other companies again were stopped by heavy automatic fire. Company F failed to hold the terrain, recovered and again was forced to withdraw. Heavy mortar and artillery fire again were placed on the objective, and an air strike was requested on the reverse slopes.

The requested air strike arrived at 1530, and again the objective was assaulted after an artillery preparation. Company F made some progress but was repulsed by the enemy. Lt. Radcliff, commanding Company E, was wounded as he led Companies E and G in the assault. At 1630, enemy troops were observed running from the objective, and artillery fire was placed on them.

One of the finest hours as General Douglas MacArthur watches the invasion of Inchon from the bridge of the USS Mount McKinley. He is flanked by (from left) Vice Admiral A.D. Struble, Major General E.K. Wright, and Major General Edward M. Almond, X Corps Commander. September 15, 1950. (U.S. Navy Photo)

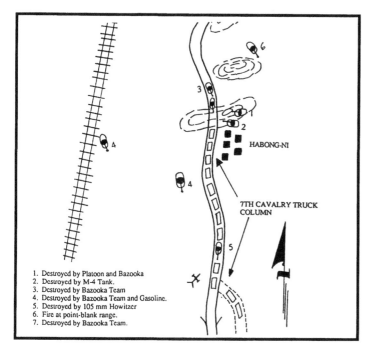

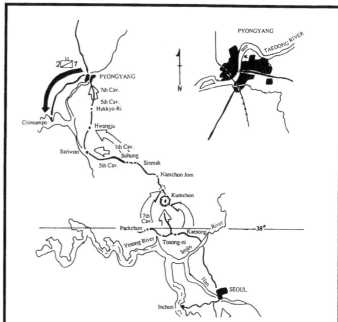

Tank fight at Habong-Ni September 26, 1950.

Above the parallel.

1. Destroyed by Platoon and Bazooka
2. Destroyed by M-4 Tank.
3. Destroyed by Bazooka Team
4. Destroyed by Bazooka Team and Gasoline.
5. Destroyed by 105 mm Howitzer
6. Fire at point-blank range.
7. Destroyed by Bazooka Team.

At 1815, all companies were ordered to assault the objective simultaneously. The 1st Battalion, 5th Cavalry, moved to the right of Company E, and the hill mass was secured against light opposition, and all counterattacks were repulsed during the night.

After two days of continuous fighting, the 2nd Battalion had seized an objective 300 meters in height, which completely controlled the Taegu-Waegwan road, and made possible the breakthrough along the Taegu-Waegwan road, which had occurred on the morning of Sept. 19th. The 2nd Battalion had defeated a strong enemy force in dug-in position and emplacements, supported by at least twelve 120mm and 82mm mortars, tanks and other flat trajectory weapons. The attack had been made over a distance of 8,000 yards across rice paddies and open terrain, and without roads to support the attack. One hundred and fifty Korean porters were used as ammunition bearers and litter carriers.

The battalion objective had provided superior observation in all directions for the enemy. Enemy positions were found to be dug into solid rock, while other positions were located in deep holes with overhead cover from which the enemy used periscopes for their observation. It is estimated that the enemy suffered more than 400 casualties with approximately 200 killed. This estimate is based on the number of enemy dead observed on Hills 184 and 300. At least eight enemy mortars were destroyed or captured, and the number of enemy tanks and flat trajectory weapons destroyed by the tank platoon supporting the battalion is not known.

This victory did not come cheap, for the 2nd Battalion suffered 28 killed, 202 wounded and four missing in action, in addition to six killed, 27 wounded and one missing in action among the South Korean troops assigned to the battalion. Among the American casualties were three company commanders and one company executive officer wounded and one company commander killed.

The following is an account of the action of

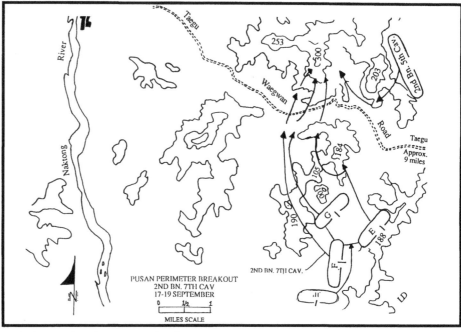

the Naktong River Breakout during Sept. 17th-19th, from Col. (then Maj.) John W. Callaway, Battalion Commander, 2nd Battalion, 7th Cavalry Regiment. Col. Callaway was the 2nd Battalion Commander from Sept. 6, 1950, to July 1951.

"As the old saying goes, blind people have different ideas of how an elephant looks. The same is true in war. The battalion commander, company commanders and front line troops see a battle differently. The battle I shall attempt to describe is my best recollection of my actions and thoughts almost 40 years after the event.

To lead up to this battle, let me begin on Sept. 6, 1950. After three days of heavy fighting, the North Koreans had forced the 5th Cavalry Regiment of which I was a member to withdraw some four miles south of the Naktong River. At the time, I was a major and executive officer of the 2nd Battalion of the 5th Cavalry Regiment. I had arrived in Korea some three weeks before as a casual officer. As we were preparing our defen-

sive positions, word came for me to report to the 7th Cavalry Regimental Headquarters and assume command of the 2nd Battalion of that regiment. The Regimental Commander explained to me that the battalion had been overrun and the battalion commander killed. He further advised that stragglers would be walking south along a dry stream bed about a mile from his headquarters. These men were members of the 2nd Battalion.

Not long after reaching this position, stragglers began to appear with their individual weapons and little more. They were sorted out by companies and advised to take it easy. By nightfall, most of the stragglers had shown up. The next day or so, in a reserve position, the battalion began to receive additional stragglers, replacements and equipment since all equipment that could not be carried by a fighting soldier on foot had been lost.

The battalion spent the next week reorganiz-

The courtesy speaks for itself. From "Of GARRYOWEN In Glory"

"Skirmish" Command Post, 7th Cavalry Regimental Commander Colonel "Wild Bill" Harris, in 1950. (Courtesy of Ed Daily)

Surrender of Senior Colonel Lee Hak Ku, Chief of Staff, 13th North Korean Division, Sept. 21, 1950. (U.S. Army Photo)

ing and re-equipping. This, of course, was a major undertaking since there had been considerable casualties, both officer and enlisted.

On the afternoon of Sept. 16th, orders were received to go by convoy to an assembly area on the Waegwan-Taegu Road south of Hill 188. The battalion arrived in position around 1600 hours and dismounted in an assembly area waiting further orders. The Division Commander, Gen. Hap Gay, appeared on the scene and was furious that the battalion was not attacking to the North. Unfortunately, communications had broken down between his headquarters and mine. I convinced him that we could do a better job by attacking the following morning. Reluctantly, he approved.

The 2nd Battalion, 7th Cavalry had been attached to the 5th Cavalry Regiment and would make the main attack from the south along the Taegu-Waegwan Road with the objective, Hill 300, which dominated the Taegu-Waegwan Road and the crossing of the Naktong River at Waegwan.

In studying the terrain, it became obvious that the key hill other than 300 was Hill 184, which dominated the rice paddies over which our troops must pass. The first order of business was to seize Hill 184 and then bypass to the south of it. Company E was assigned the mission of seizing Hill 184 and supporting the attack of Companies F and G toward Hill 300. I also decided to send a platoon that evening to reconnoiter Hill

184 to see if the enemy occupied it. If not, [the] platoon was to remain there until E Comp[any] arrived. By 2300 hours, the reconnaissance [pla]toon reported that it was on Hill 184 and that t[here] was no enemy. This knowledge gave me s[ome] relief, so I slept soundly.

By daylight, the battalion was getting bre[ak]fast and moving toward the line of departure. [For] some, this would be their last meal; for oth[ers,] their last battle; and for all members of the batt[al]ion, the most important battle they would fight [in] Korea. This battalion had been selected to ope[n] the hole for the breakout of the Naktong Perimeter and the final destruction of the North Korean forces.

As the companies started in an approach march formation across the one and one-half miles of open rice paddies, heavy enemy 4.2 mortar fire began to rain on them. From my observation post, I began to search with my binoculars for the platoon that was supposedly on Hill 184. Unfortunately, the platoon had gone to another hill one-half mile southwest of Hill 184. Convinced that Hill 184 was the enemy OP, I ordered our artillery to take the hill under fire. In the meantime, Company E continued to move toward Hill 184. The enemy fire continued, and Company E met stiff resistance as it attempted to seize Hill 184. Companies F and G were ordered to bypass Hill 184 and cross the Taegu-Waegwan Road toward Hill 300, the final objective.

By evening, Hill 184 had been seized, but Companies F and G had run into heavy enemy resistance on the high ground across the road. Enemy mortars and machine guns as well as several tanks had been overrun; however, the enemy resistance became stronger. As a result, the companies withdrew south of the road for the remainder of the night.

The following day, the battalion began its attack toward Hill 300, which was about a mile from the road. The going was rough as the enemy defended every foot from dominating terrain. Despite the enemy's stubborn resistance, the gallant men of the 2nd Battalion seized their objective and opened the hole for the breakthrough to the North. It was a great thrill to sit on top of Hill 300 and watch the miles of US 2-1/2-ton trucks and jeeps wind their way to the north.

The enemy had suffered more than 400 casualties with approximately 200 killed. At least eight enemy mortars had been captured, and a number of tanks and flat trajectory weapons had been destroyed.

This victory was costly to the 2nd Battalion with 28 killed, 202 wounded and four missing in action. In addition, six South Korean troops assigned to the battalion were killed, 27 wounded and one missing.

In my view, this was the most significant battle the 2nd Battalion fought during the year I served in Korea. Unfortunately, because the battalion was attached to another regiment, very little has been said or written about this great event. Those who were there know of the outstanding victory that was achieved and the great sacrifices that were made by those brave soldiers of the 2nd Battalion, 7th Cavalry Regiment" GARRYOWEN!

Most experiences in combat are not pleasant; however, occasionally an amusing incident does occur. One that I have always enjoyed hap-

d after our battalion opened the hole in the
h Korean defenses along the Naktong River
pt. 19, 1950. Because of our severe casual-
ve were ordered to quiet sector along the
ong River where we relieved the 27th British
hanized Brigade, which went north with the
t Cavalry Division. During the relief, the Bri-
Commander advised me of his policy regard-
he North Koreans, which was to "live and let
." I accepted his advice, and other than send-
a night patrol along our side of the river to
scue a British Landrover vehicle and two jeeps
that we needed desperately, both sides remained
quiet. By this time, we had reverted to the command of Headquarters Eighth Army Rear since
most other major combat headquarters had gone
through the hole to link up with x Corps units 160
miles away, just south of Seoul. The G-2 staff of
Eighth Army came up with an idea of sending a 2-
1/2-ton sound truck with a person who could speak
the Korean language to one of our line companies
to advise the North Korean troops across the river
that they had lost the battle and should surrender.

While I was not happy with the idea, I saw no
harm since our front line company was well dug in
and would probably suffer no casualties. My front
line company commander was not so optimistic, so
I had to insist that he go along with the idea.

The 2-1/2-ton truck arrived shortly after dark
with its blackout lights. I instructed the driver to
continue up the road about 600 yards, and our
front line company commander would show him
where to set up. I remained beside the road to see
the action.

The loud speaker sounded off for about 30
seconds when I heard the enemy mortar shells
beginning to land in the area. It was quite a
concentration of mortar fire. I next heard a vehicle
coming down the road from the front line company. It was traveling about 20 miles per hour with
only its blackout lights. I tried to stop the truck but
to no avail.

I called the company commander, and he
assured me that there were no casualties. We had
a good laugh since it was apparent that the North
Korean troops across the river had not heard that
they had lost the war.

Several days later I received a call from the
Eighth Army G-2 Section asking what had happened to their sound truck and troops they had sent
up. I told them about the truck passing me headed
south about 20 miles per hour and would not stop.
I suggested that they try looking down around
Pusan, the US supply seaport, about 80 miles to
the south."

The following is an account of the action of
the Naktong River Breakout during Sept. 17th-
19th, by Capt. John C. Rourke, Battalion Surgeon
for the 2nd Battalion, 7th Cavalry Regiment. Capt.
Rourke served as the 2nd Battalion Surgeon from
the end of July 1950, to February 10, 1951.

"At the time, I had been assigned with the
medical unit of the 2nd Battalion for approximately six weeks. I was well-supported by the
recent appointment of Maj. Richton who was a
medical service administration officer. He was
assigned recently to replace the previous assistant surgeon who had been wounded.

From my outstanding recollections, this was
the first true attack in which the 2nd Battalion had
been engaged in since my assignment to the medical unit. Secondly, it was an extremely difficult

and bloody battle because the troops had to fight
on foot across 8,000 yards of open rice paddies
and rough terrain.

Their first objective was to secure three
small hills just south of the Taegu-Waegwan
road. The road actually crossed between the line
of battle, and the final objective was to secure
several larger hills just north of the road. One
objective was Hill 300, which was strongly dug-
in and heavily defended by the North Korean
soldiers. It was solid rock at the top of the hill, and
the enemy took advantage of this to build shelters
over top of their positions. They were supported
heavily by machine guns, mortars and artillery.

The forward medical-aid station was established at the line of departure for the attack, and
it was commanded by Maj. Richton. He had the
difficult task of directly supervising the arduous
job to the litter teams. They followed the troops
into battle, but once a trooper was wounded, it
required them to carry and walk that wounded
trooper a long distance back to a point where they
could be safely carried further to the rear.

Maj. Richton, and the little teams under his
command, performed bravely and diligently during the extremely difficult conditions of battle.
The line was long in getting the wounded back to
safety.

After the wounded were brought back to a
transport point, they were either moved to my aid
station or some went to the bypass medical aid
station of the 5th Cavalry Regiment, which was
located a short distance to our rear. At this
particular time, our 2nd Battalion was attached
to the 5th Cavalry Regiment during this phase of
battle operation.

With the large number of casualties, we ran
out of supplies, particularly, litter bearers and
the Thomas Leg Splints, which were used to
transport wounded with broken thighs. It because
extremely difficult to draw medical resupplies
from the 5th Cavalry Regiment sources. This was
due to their own shortages of medical supplies,
because they had suffered heavy casualties themselves.

There may have been some misunderstanding on the part of the 5th Cavalry unit, which we
had been ordered to draw medical supplies from.
It left me with the impression that when a fighting
unit is attached to another organization, and in
spite of the plans and intentions, they can still find
themselves in the status of an orphan.

One time during the final day, the backup
supplies became so critical that I personally
journeyed back to the supporting 5th Cavalry
medical unit. There I found that they also were

2nd Lt., Edward Daily, 1st Platoon Leader, Co. H, 2nd
Battalion, 7th Cavalry. (Courtesy of Ed Daily)

Captain John R. Flynn, Commander Co. K, 3rd Battalion, 7th Cavalry. (Courtesy of Ed Daily)

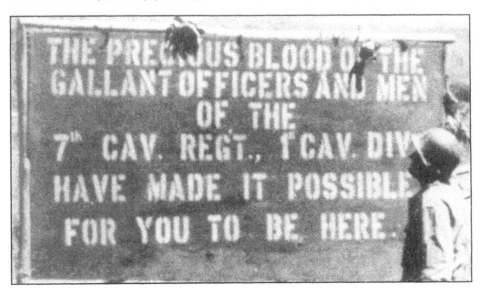

THE PRECIOUS BLOOD OF THE
GALLANT OFFICERS AND MEN
OF THE
7TH CAV. REGT., 1 CAV. DIV.
HAVE MADE IT POSSIBLE
FOR YOU TO BE HERE.

Compliments of the GARRYOWEN Regiment. (U.S. Army Photo)

lacking in medical supplies and were unable to help. Then I journeyed several miles further to the rear to the Medical Company of the 7th Cavalry Regiment. However, they were all loaded up and ready to move and support the attacking elements to the north. This was the actual start of the historical attack and drive through enemy-held territory to eventually link up with the 31st Infantry Regiment, 7th Infantry Division. It was better known as Task Force "777," which actually covered a long distance of 196 road miles and marked the longest drive in the history of the American Army through enemy-held territory.

They were unable to help me, which was somewhat of a disappointment. Not knowing what to do, I sought out the assistance from Capt. McCullough, who was the Catholic Chaplain in the 2nd Battalion. He had become a close friend during the long days of battle in the Naktong River Defense and Perimeter.

I said, "Father sir, your old friends in the 2nd Battalion are bleeding badly and need help." He listened and then quickly set off on his own plan of relief to help the situation. Within 30 minutes after my arrival back at the aid station, he came forward with large amounts of supplies that I had requested. He definitely was a true friend in need.

I remember this period very vividly. I must say that I never did have the opportunity to observe or visualize the actual field of action. My location was just south of the battle where a close view could not be obtained. Capt. Mel Chandler, our 2nd Battalion Executive Officer, kept in close contact with what was going on within the battle.

In Mel Chandler's book, "Of GARRYOWEN In Glory," he states that during this particular battle and within the 2nd Battalion, there were 28 killed, 202 wounded and four missing in action. However, I do know that the number of killed in action increased somewhat because of the subsequent death of some of the wounded after they were taken from the battle area.

I would like to recall three separate individuals of these particular wounded that I know

subsequently died. The first was a young rifleman, whose name I do not remember, who was about 20 years old. He was brought into my aid station in a state of irreversible shock, and he was remarkably elusive. However, he could relate clearly what actually happened to him. Two days prior to his arrival at my aid station, he had been wounded in the thigh and was immobilized on the ground. This was during an attack and then a quick withdrawal, which caused him to be left behind and without proper medical treatment.

The North Koreans had retaken the same area and an enemy patrol had discovered him laying there quietly on the ground. One of the enemy soldiers walked up to where he lay and stood over him with a Russian Burp gun in his hands. At that time, the enemy soldier took the automatic weapon and sprayed the chest and abdomen of the wounded American soldier. He had approximately eight or nine small caliber wounds in both of those particular areas.

He was so clear and coherent in explaining or recalling what the North Korean soldier had done to him. He was so eager to relate his personal feelings of outrage concerning the conduct of the enemy soldier. I'm positive that this young soldier did not survive his wounds even after he arrived at the MASH (Mobile Army Surgical Hospital), which was located in the town of Taegu.

Another wounded individual that I remember was Capt. Herschel "Ug" Fuson, who was a very colorful officer. "Ug" as he was known to all of his men, was somewhat of a celebrity because he was a tall and heavy ex-football player. He had been a star performer at West Point while attending the United States Military Academy. Also, he had played football during the glory days of 1944-45. Further, he had been a lineman who played with such legendaries as Doc Blanchard (Mr. Inside), and Glenn Davis (Mr. Outside).

"Ug" was a pleasant and quiet person. We talked in brief statements after he was brought into my aid station. He had a bullet wound that went through his right armpit and into the area

where the neck and shoulder join. He didn't seem to be too uncomfortable, only that he was very hungry. His enormous appetite was one of his remarkable attributes.

He was oozing blood from the wounded area, which was difficult to control because of the many important blood vessels that were damaged. I can remember taking a tight wadded bandage and jamming it up into the armpit and then bring his right arm down against the side of his chest. I attempted to bind the arm there to keep the pressure on the breathing points.

All during this time, "Ug" was not particularly attentive to what I was doing, but was surveying the situation. Suddenly he spotted, by accident, a young soldier from one of the mess halls walking around with a large carton of donuts. These donuts were being distributed to wounded personnel who needed food.

"Ug" called the donut giver over to him and with his large left hand open, he reached into the carton of donuts. Somehow he managed to grasp seven or eight donuts, which he then proceeded to heavily consume with his enormous appetite. In view of a very serious wound, I was amazed at how quickly the donuts disappeared. Needless to say, those who knew "Ug" said that was the way he was.

About one month later, I received the most unfortunate word that "Ug" had died in a hospital in Tokyo from delayed complications of his particular wound. However, I would learn many years later from a newspaper article that "Ug" had died the following year in June 1951, from complications that were attributed to a heart ailment.

My third memory of a wounded individual is that of Lt. Radcliff, who was the Commanding Officer of Company E. He was wounded seriously the last day of battle. Also, the 2nd Battalion troopers had almost completed their objective in securing Hill 300.

I got to know Lt. Radcliff prior to his serious wound when I treated him for minor scratches and scrapes. I had joked with him at that time that

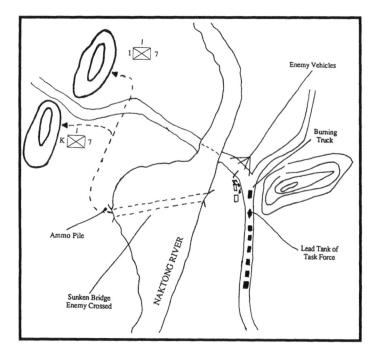

Task Force 777 September 22, 1950

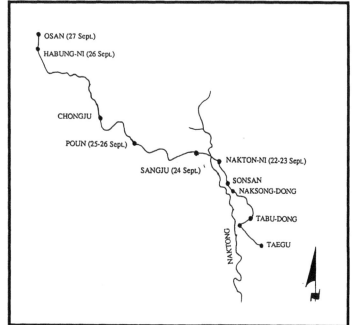

Task Force 777 September 22-27, 1950

Corporal Richard D. LaRue, 31st Infantry Regiment, 7th Infantry Division and Private First Class James M. Dye, 7th Cavalry Regiment, shake hands and exchange division patches, when (Task Force Lynch) 1st Cavalry Division, from the south and 7th Infantry Division from the north met at Yongjon-ni, September 27, 1950. (U.S. Army Photo)

2nd Battalion, 7th Cavalry Command Post in Korean school house near Naktong River, August 1950. (L. to R.) 1st Lt. Herman K. Vester, HQS. Company, 2nd Bn.; Lt. Col. James H. Lynch, Commander 3rd Bn.; Lt. Col. Gilman A. Huff, Commander 2nd Bn.; Capt. Robert S. McBride, S-3, 3rd Bn., discussing the situation at Tuksong-dong. (U.S. Army photo)

he was like a cat with nine lives. It seemed that in the midst of serious wounded personnel he had received only a few minor scratches. However, this time he was very seriously wounded with multiple bullet wounds of the abdomen.

Arrangements were made immediately to send him to the MASH unit located to the rear. This Mobile Army Surgical Hospital was established in a school house within the town of Taegu. Also, the Eighth Army Headquarters was located in this town. I was able to visit him there two days later, and I'll never forget the scene that I saw.

The incoming unit for the wounded was established in a huge wide open area that looked like the combination assembly area and cafeteria of the school. Every square foot of space was utilized and occupied with cots. Many wounded were being treated for shock, and every effort was put forth to keep them stabilized. This was to prepare them for emergency surgery that was being performed by five separate teams on a 24-hour basis. This was due to the large influx of casualties.

When I visited Lt. Radcliff, I discovered that he was extremely ill. Although he was sedated heavily, he did arouse enough to recognize me and say a few words. It was at this particular time that he gave me his report. His comments were, "Doc, they were looking down our throats!" This was in reference to the difficulty of fighting a battle up hill and against a heavily armed and entrenched enemy. Unfortunately, Lt. Radcliff died one week later at the MASH unit from direct results of his wounds.

This visit to the MASH unit to see Lt. Radcliff has always remained in my memory. It gave me the opportunity to see the grim determination and dedicated effort of the very talented medical personnel, performing under the most difficult circumstances. They attempted to provide the best possible treatment to the very large number of casualties. It was not, however, a happy or laughing situation as portrayed on the television series, MASH. I have always resented this particular television program for its casual, trivial and demeaning presentation of a very serious and important aspect of the wounded soldier during the Korean War.

We veterans of the Korean War remember the many deeds and sacrifices of the combat soldier as they were. Unfortunately, I think the television series, MASH, has contributed to an overly casual and easily forgotten attitude of the younger generation toward the Korean War."

The following is an account of the assault action on Sept. 19, 1950, from 1st Lt. Pennel "Joe" Hickey, 3rd Platoon Leader, Company F, 2nd Battalion, 7th Cavalry Regiment.

"As I recall, we jumped off at 0800 hours to attack up one finger of the ridge with Company F. Company G was to advance up another finger of the ridge, with the two companies in a coordinated assault when we neared the enemy-held ridge line.

My platoon led the attack, but we didn't encounter any enemy as we secured over one-half of the finger of the ridge. Suddenly, we started to encounter enemy foxholes and bunkers. One of the B.A.R. men, Cpl. James Dady from Texas, did himself proud. The first three or four foxholes we encountered he made a one-man dash up the finger of the ridge and fired a burst into the foxholes and then ran back to our lead elements and flopped down. There were no enemy in those foxholes, but that takes nothing away from the courage that Cpl. Dady displayed.

The enemy obviously had pulled back to position higher up the ridge. About this time, we started receiving small arms and automatic weapons fire. It must have been between 1000-1100 hours, as Cpl. Dady made one more dash up the finger of the ridge blasting everything in sight with his automatic rifle. Upon his return, he fell to the ground to my left, which was about 10 yards away. I moved over to him, and as I got up in a prone position to tell him a "good job" on his behalf, a shot rang out and took a nip out of the top edge of his right ear. Cpl. Dady turned white as a ghost, but he wasn't really hurt.

Feeling that Dady was putting us all to shame, I decided to rush the next foxhole. I ran up about 20 yards with carbine in my hands and set on full automatic, with a banana clip. I stood over the foxhole and pulled the trigger, when suddenly the carbine fell into two pieces in my hands. (I hadn't set a retaining clip). I couldn't help but

laugh to myself at the foolishness of the situation, so I high-tailed it back to our troops in a hurry.

Shortly after this, Capt. William L. Webb, commanding Company F, was wounded while individually attacking an enemy machine gun position. He got shot through his leg a little above the knee. He gave me his map and told me to take command and continue the attack. I envied him somewhat as he fell back down the hill with a "great" wound.

We kept advancing against increasingly heavy fire, and shortly thereafter we were pinned down again. Talking by radio with the battalion, we found the situation was the same with Company G. We stayed in position because the ground provided good cover from direct fire. Now we attempted to regroup and count noses. Surprisingly, we could find only 35 of our platoon and attachments. The others were far down below us.

After 30-90 minutes in this position, word was received from the battalion that both Companies F and G would continue the attack. We jumped off together for the so-called "one-inch movement." We had progressed only 10 yards when we were pinned down again. Hill 300 definitely was defended heavily by the enemy. To move forward any further would have been difficult because of the open and exposed ridge line. Actually, we moved back to where we had been before and eventually we got relieved by a unit from the 8th Cavalry Regiment at approximately 1600 hours."

Once again "Seoul City Sue" referred to the 2nd Battalion, 7th Cavalry, as the "Ghost Battalion." The battalion originally had been referred to as the "Ghost Battalion" during the retrograde movements north of Kumchon and Kwan-ni in late July, presumably because after each attack, despite heavy casualties, the 2nd Battalion would appear in a new location to fight again like demons.

Meanwhile, the rest of the regiment had been preparing for the forthcoming offensive.

Operational control of the 3rd Battalion passed to the 8th Cavalry during the early morning hours of the 19th, while the 2nd Battalion remained under 5th Cavalry control. The 1st Battalion was ordered to attack, supported by

Looking from the front seat of a jeep at Russian T-34 tanks waiting in ambush. Task Force Lynch (777), September 1950. (courtesy of Vallie Stump)

Jeep was destroyed by enemy mortar round and sitting in what's left of "38th or bust," is 7th Cavalry Regimental Motor Sergeant, Annis. (Courtesy of Vallie Stump)

tanks, to secure the initial objective on the high ground on Hill mass 328 and thence generally north on a series of phase lines toward Hill 300 and Waegwan.

At 0730 hours on the 19th, Company A moved out from its position for its object on Hill 300. Companies B and C moved down the Waegwan road at 0730 hours to support Company A and the attached tanks.

At 1043 hours, the regiment was notified that the primary mission was now to take Hill 464 before nightfall and to coordinate the attack closely with the 5th Regimental Combat Team on the left, which would attack Hill 300 in conjunction with the regimental attack.

At 1115 hours, the regiment was notified that the 2nd Battalion would be moved as soon as they could be assembled to relieve the 27th British Brigade south of Taegu prior to darkness.

On Sept. 20th, the 1st Battalion continued its attack but began receiving intermittent mortar fire from the vicinity of Hill 303 (just east of Waegwan) at 1200 hours, and by 1405 hours Company A had secured Hill 168 south of Waegwan. At 1650 hours, Company C advanced without opposition, followed by tanks and mine-sweepers, and by 2010 hours, the entire 1st Battalion had overcome all resistance and was advancing to the northeast.

Lt. Col. William A. Harris from the 77th Field Artillery Battalion assumed command of the 7th Cavalry Regiment at 2300 hours on the 20th, and assembled staff personnel for a meeting with attached unit representatives plus battalion commanders to plan for the forthcoming operation. The operations plan called for the 3rd Battalion plus the I&R Platoon and two platoons of Company C, 70th Tank Battalion, to advance along the route of the 1st Battalion at 0600 hours on Sept. 21st. In the event the 3rd Battalion overtook the 1st Battalion, the 1st Battalion was to halt in place, and the 3rd Battalion was to attack through them to Tabu-Dong. In the event the 3rd Battalion did not overtake the 1st Battalion, they were to go into an assembly area and establish necessary defensive positions to secure the route. Whichever element reached Tabu-Dong was to turn south and contact the 8th Cavalry and establish the necessary defensive positions to secure the road - to be accomplished by dark on the 21st.

During the advance toward Tabu-Dong on Sept. 21st, Lt. Col. Clainos was wounded when his jeep hit a mine, and Lt. Frank Maloney suffered severe injury to his eyes as a result of this explosion. Lt. Col. Harris led the 3rd Battalion en route behind the 1st Battalion, which continued its advanced.

By 1100 hours on the 21st, the head of the 1st Battalion column received small arms, machine gun and artillery fire, but an hour later the column still was advancing and was within 1,000 yards of their objective. The battalion by-passed the attached tanks as they were delayed by mine fields.

The 1st Battalion was notified at 1315 hours of a change in mission - to take and secure Tabu-Dong and then send probing patrols south to contact the 8th Cavalry. The 3rd Battalion was notified of the change in mission and informed to pass through the 1st Battalion and to send reconnaissance elements north on the blacktop road and to be prepared to attack in that direction.

As the day ended, the 1st Battalion reported Tabu-Dong cleared of enemy. Maj.William O. Witherspoon assumed command of the 1st Battalion at 1700 hours as Lt. Col. Clainos was evacuated due to injuries received when the mine exploded under his jeep earlier in the day.

At 1850 hours, contact was made with the 8th Cavalry. Sgt. First Class Robert P. Goodrow, Company C, was the first man to shake hands with a member of the 8th Cavalry. Thus, a flanking movement from left to right (Waegwan to Tabu-Dong) completely across the fronts of the 5th and 8th Cavalry Regiments had been accomplished. Remnants of two enemy division were encircled, and their supply and communication lines were cut. The 7th Cavalry had once again accomplished one of the outstanding feats of the war and stood ready for the onslaught into Central Korea. Lt. Col. James H. Lynch, Commander of the 3rd Battalion, gave the following full report of the subsequent drive northward:

"At 1700, on the night of 20 Sept. 1950, in the vicinity of Tabu-Dong, 13 miles north of Taegu, Korea, Lt. Col. William A. Harris, Commanding Officer, 7th Cavalry Regiment, issued a warning order that, as soon as the 1st Battalion, 7th Cavalry, had taken Tabu-Dong and joined with the 8th Cavalry Regiment two miles to the south, I would organize "Task Force Lynch" and

proceed by motorized column to seize and secure the river crossing located on the Naktong at Sonsan, some 25 miles to the northeast. The territory to be penetrated was held by elements of the 1st and 3rd North Korean Divisions, which had been mauled badly by the 1st Cavalry Division and the 1st ROK Division, in the preceding 10 days of fighting around Waegwan, Tabu-Dong and the Walled City of 'Kasan.'

The enemy appeared on the point of collapsing and the breakthrough contemplated a pursuit to the Naktong.

To constitute my task force, the 3rd Battalion, 7th Cavalry Regiment, was to be reinforced by two tank platoons totaling seven M-4 tanks, the Regimental I&R Platoon, an Engineer Company with a dozer, a 4.2-inch chemical mortar platoon, the 77th Field Artillery Battalion less a Battery, and an air-control party to provide air cover.

After receiving this order, I moved the battalion into a perimeter defense for the night of the 20th, just west of Tabu-Dong, closing by 2200 hours.

The 1st Battalion had seized Tabu-Dong and joined the 8th Cavalry to the south by 1900 hours, so my staff proceeded to plan the Task Force organization, to execute the assigned mission at 0600 on the 21st. At 0200 on the 21st, Col. Harris and his staff arrived at my CP and confirmed his warning order with an executed time of 0630, 21st Sept. Planning for the mission was completed by 0330, and a meeting of all commanders concerned was arranged for the first light at 0530.

At 0400, the group of 2,000 North Koreans trapped between the 7th and 8th Cavalry Regiment attempted a breakthrough to escape to the north, using my battalion for their escape route. During the next two hours confusion reigned. Repeated "Banzai" attacks into my CP and the surrounding area were repelled, and the North Korean escape route shifted to the west. I concluded that it would be impossible to organize the Task Force under fire and with the approval of my Regimental Commander delayed my commanders meeting until the situation was clarified. The meeting was finally held at 0600, and the time for the movement of the Task Force was set for 0800. At 0800, the I&R Platoon moved out on the assigned route, to be followed in order by the two tank platoons, the engineer company, my command group, Company L, Company K, Battalion Headquarters Company, Company M, Company I and the Field Artillery Battalion (-). We proceeded without incident for five miles through a scene of devastation and destruction. The Air Force had done a complete job of destruction of enemy weapons, tanks and ammunition.

About five miles out, the point came under sporadic small arms fire and deployed to return fire. I moved forward and got them back in their vehicles with instructions to push on through anything except determined resistance. Several miles further down the road, the point was again halted by hand grenading from the rice paddies to the right of the road. With the assistance of my Division Commander, Gen. Gay, and Assistant Division Commander, Gen. Allen, this brief resistance was eliminated, and the column proceeded. The pursuit had been so immediate and aggressive that the enemy had no time to mine the road. The column continued rapidly and proceeded with little resistance. After the hand grenade fight, I decided that the tanks should lead the column and had the I&R Platoon follow them.

Throughout the move, the air patrol was attacking the fleeing enemy column five to 10 miles ahead of us on the road with good effect.

As the tanks rounded a bend of the road at Naksong-Dong, the lead tank was hit by fire from two anti-tank guns concealed by the road at a range of 200 yards. In this fight, Gen. Gay and Gen. Allen narrowly escaped being hit by several shells falling just to my rear. On order, the tanks pushed forward and eliminated the two anti-tank guns, allowing the column to proceed.

At this point, I received an air-dropped message from G-3, 1st Cavalry Division, but unsigned and unauthenticated, changing my objective to the Ferry Crossing at Naktong-ni, some 10 miles beyond the assigned objective. After conferring with Gen. Gay, who did not know of this change, I decided to proceed to the original objective and to verify the change as we moved. I felt that the verification would come before arrival at that objective.

Several miles further down the road, the I&R Platoon became involved in a grenade fight with a squad of North Koreans hidden in a culvert beside the road. It was most peculiar and amusing to watch. As I came up to them, I observed the

I&R men dash up to the ditch and drop a grenade and dash back. Immediately several "gook" grenades came out of the culvert and the I&R Platoon scattered. One I&R jeep was stalled in the road above the culvert. In his attempt to place a close one in the culvert, one scout missed and landed his grenade under his own jeep, which caught fire and burned merrily. After 10 minutes of the fight, the culvert was quiet, and the column proceeded.

At 1530, I arrived in sight of our original objective on the Naktong, still without verification of our change in mission. An I&R scout came running back to report a large enemy counterattack coming across the river. I dismounted L Company and started forward with them to block. On arriving at the head of the column, I could find no resistance but did find a rather shame-faced I&R Lieutenant, who explained that his message must have been garbled.

My immediate concern now was security for the night. It was 1600; I had no verification of the change in orders; I was 25 miles into enemy territory; I did not know the situation except in my immediate area; and I had permission of the Division Commander to hold up for the night on my original objective until the change was verified. I proceeded to pull in my two-hour long column and organize a perimeter. This had just been completed at 1800 when the verification came through with orders to proceed immediately to Naktong-ni, 10 miles north and to secure the river crossing at that point. The delay was not wasted as we spent our time flushing out some 50 North Koreans hiding in the rice paddies and in the surrounding hills.

At 1900, just as the sun went down, the lead tank with infantry riding moved out, and the column pushed on. A bright three-quarter moon alleviated the vision problem, and the move progressed smoothly. About five miles down, we commenced to pass burning villages, and soon we were into the rear of the retreating North Korean column.

We followed a novel procedure here; instead of firing, we merely kicked the gooks in the pants and started them to the rear with their hands on their head and with no guards.

After proceeding through several miles of this, the head of the column halted. I went forward to learn the situation. As I arrived near the head of the column on a bluff overlooking the

river crossing, a tank fired and a tremendous fire started in front of the lead tank. Within a minute, all hell broke loose. An enemy ammunition truck loaded with heavy stuff had been hit and commenced to blow up. By the light of the fire was revealed a column of 400 enemy foot troops crossing the river on the sunken bridge below us to our left. The tanks commenced firing, but shortly word spread to the foot soldiers that the loud explosions from the ammunition truck were enemy infantry grenading us from the bluff above us on the right. I sent a platoon up on the bluff to stop the rumor and secured my flank and then concentrated on the fight that went on for another 10 minutes. By this time, the ammunition truck had set fire to several others and shells, grenades and small arms ammunition were bursting and popping all over the place. One shell came in the middle of my forward CP, wounding one tanker, so we immediately backed the column off about 100 yards. Reconnaissance of the fire revealed a large number of enemy field pieces, trucks and several tanks, all abandoned, which we had caught trying to cross the river. At this stage, a quick estimate revealed:

1) It was 2300 hours;

2) I had a sizable fire block to reduce before I could proceed;

3) I still had to secure the far bank of the river to fulfill my mission;

4) I could only guess at the continuation of the road on the far bank to determine my objective for a river crossing; and

5) My assault boats at the rear of the column probably could not be brought forward on the narrow, jammed road.

The Engineers, less the dozer that had broken through a bridge at the rear of the column, and the tanks went to work on the block and got the six burning vehicles and guns off the road before the fire spread further. This involved many individual acts of heroism, considering the explosive situation and the intense heat, and required several hours. At the same time, the undamaged enemy equipment ahead was pulled out of the road and revealed a bag of about 50 usable trucks of varying size, many still bearing the unit of an American division (equipment lost during the July withdrawal - 20 field artillery pieces and two tanks). Two other tanks had been abandoned further to the rear.

This clearing went on for the rest of the

Destroyed Russian tank T34/85, vicinity of Waegwan, South Korea, September 1950. (U.S. Army Photo)

Destroyed Russian tank with SU-76mm self propelled gun, vicinity of Waegwan, South Korea, September 1950. (U.S. Army Photo)

night. At the same time, I sent across the river an Engineer Reconnaissance party to investigate the crossing and an I&R squad to reconnoiter the far bank. I collected my commanders and at 0200 had issued a tentative order for crossing in column on the sunken bridge at 0430 with Company K in the lead, Company I to follow and Company L to secure the high ground on the near bank. This was necessary as POWs reported over a battalion had dispersed to the hills on the near bank upon our arrival, and I knew that an unknown number might come up on our rear using the crossing as an escape route.

I moved my mortars, and the tanks took position on the bluff to support by fire. The machine gun sections were attached to the crossing companies, and the 75mm Platoon took up blocking positions on the rear bank on the road to the north.

At 0300, the reconnaissance patrol returned and verified that the underwater bridge could be crossed, waist deep, and reported the location of the road on the far side. They could not report the extension of the road through the mountain on the far side, so I took a guess on where the road should go and assigned objectives to I and K Companies, and the attack was confirmed for 0430. At 0400, the attack companies picked up their forward observers from the mortars and artillery, their guides from I&R, and their wire teams from the Battalion Communication Platoon. At 0430, the lead elements of Company I entered the icy water on the sunken bridge.

The current was swift and the underfooting tricky. Men lost their footing in the river and had to be pulled out. And then, just as the lead company entered the river, another of the long list of incidents took place. An ammunition pile placed exactly at the exit of the sunken bridge from the river on the far side started to burn and explode. What caused it, I do not know. It may have been smoldering from our fire fight and suddenly been fanned into flames, or it may have been set by North Korean soldiers for just the purpose it served. The entire exit area was lighted up, and all secrecy of the crossing destroyed. It was a weird sight to view the troops swarming out of the river and ducking around the exploding ammunition pile. By 0530, as dawn broke, the two companies were across and moving to their objective.

As it grew brighter, I studied the terrain from my OP and to my dismay, saw the road veered to the right from where I had placed it in my original moonlight estimate. I immediately called my company commanders on the radio and changed their objectives. About one-half hour later, in full daylight when the mist raised and I had a good view, I definitely located the road and found it right where my original guess had placed it. A second radio call got my Companies back on the right track, and at 0730 I radioed the Regimental Commander 'Mission Accomplished.'

The Task Force had penetrated 36 miles into enemy territory in 23 hours, captured five tanks, 20 field pieces, 50 trucks, made a night river crossing, secured a Division bridge site and killed or captured more than 500 enemy.

On 23 Sept., the 1st Battalion, 7th Cavalry, passed through the 3rd Battalion, crossed the river and occupied Sangju, 10 miles to the north. On the night of the 23rd, my Task Force marched

Support artillery firing their 105-mm Howitzers almost point blank into North Korean positions (Courtesy of Bob Mauger)

north to Sangju closing by 0600, 24 September. At 1100, 24 September, Company K, commanded by Capt. John Flynn, with Company M attachments and a platoon of tanks, pushed forward to Poun, 30 miles northwest, and secured the town by 1730 with only minor opposition. On the 25th, the rest of the Task Force moved up to Poun and reconnoitered roads to the north. We found them impassable and returned to Poun on the night of the 25th.

At 1000 hours 26th Sept., I received orders that my Task Force would proceed north immediately to effect a junction with the 7th Division at Osan, 55 air miles, 102 road miles distant. At 1130, the head of the column, one I&R squad and three M-4 tanks moved out. We proceeded for miles north without opposition, being greeted by cheering crowds of liberated South Koreans. At 1730 hours, the column was forced to halt temporarily. The tank element had consumed their gas supply and the refuel tank supposed to be in the column had failed to join. We proceeded to collect all gas cans from the trucks in the column and had enough to fill three of our six tanks when a fortunate thing happened. A North Korean maintenance convoy of three trucks going south bumped into the head of our column, the drivers bailed out, and we examined the contents. Aboard was sufficient gas to refuel our other three tanks, so we silently thanked the thoughtful gooks and proceeded on our way.

My Regimental Commander Col. Bill Harris, who was with me, had a bold idea and authorized me to proceed with lights at my discretion. I so ordered and also instructed my three lead tanks to move aggressively to Osan and thence north to Suwon if the 7th Division was not at Osan. The three lead tanks were followed by the I&R Squad, the Engineers platoon, my command group, I Company, L Company, M Company, Headquarters Company, the FA Battery and K Company. The remaining three tanks joined the tail of the column after refueling.

The moon had risen, but a cloudy night obscured vision. Behind me were miles of vehicle lights winding their way through enemy-held territory - a weird sight to behold. Shortly after dark, I could see by the lights that my three lead tanks were proceeding at a faster clip than my truck

column could maintain, and all efforts to pull them down by 300 radio failed. After riding "Point" for several miles, we began to see groups of 15 or 20 North Korean soldiers in the villages we passed - apparently just as surprised to see us as we were them. As the vehicle behind me was some distance away, I decided that discretion rather than valor seemed in order and held fire.

Here, a quick mental review of FM 7-20 revealed no situation where the battalion command group is suggested as point for a column in enemy territory, so I pulled over and put out a platoon of infantry in trucks with a 3.5-inch rocket launcher and a .50 caliber MG on the ring mount as point.

We took up the march again and along the way shot up a truckload of North Korean soldiers who refused to surrender. We were not 10 miles from Osan and continuing to encounter isolated groups of enemy whom we fired upon and killed or dispersed. Some distance ahead I heard tank or artillery fire and could see sporadic small arms tracer fire. At this point, I decided the party was over and turned off lights. Just short of Habang-ni, we by-passed a bridge and continued through the village. To the right of us, 20 yards off the road, I noticed an enemy tank with its tube pointed right across the road. I ducked under the line of fire and made some jesting remark to my S-3, Capt. Cecil Curles, about the tank, thinking it to be like others we had passed that the Air Force had destroyed.

Just as we passed the tank, the solemn voice of Capt. Johnston, commanding the Regimental Mortar Company, came over the radio, "Don't look now, but to our right is a T-Three Four." Almost simultaneously, the tank opened up with machine gun and cannon fire. I pulled over and hit the ditch as did the rest of the column. The tank, with it's brother also in ambush, continued to fire up and down the road over our heads and in all directions.

This went on for several minutes while I said my prayers and took stock of the situation. My S-2, Lt. John Hill, pushed ahead and pulled back the point: my platoon of infantry and their precious 3.5-inch rocket launcher. We could not determine, but felt sure the tanks' infantry were with them so Hill and Lt. Nicholas, the FA Liaison Officer (Note: FM7-20 says nothing about this for FA Liaison Officers or S-2s), organized an attack on the tank area with the platoon and the bazooks team.

Meantime my S-3, Capt. Cecil Curles, was attempting to contact the Regimental Commander, or S-3, or anybody, on the 608 without success. The tank was continuing to fire down the road and across the fields but missed my S-3. Capt. Curles and I worked our way across the road as the tank hunters moved toward their target. As they moved up, the enemy tanks started their motor and gunned them but did not move out. The bazooka team knocked out one tank, but before they could get the other, it moved out and started down the column. After running over several of my vehicles, it went to the right into the rice paddies several hundred yards where it commenced to fire on the column. Maj. Hallden, my Executive Officer, had organized the antitank action in the middle of the column. A 75mm RR returned the fire, and the tank was halted but continued to fire. A bazooka team with Capt. James Webel, Regimental S-3 and Lt. Woodside, commanding Company L, closed with the tank and destroyed it. Capt. Webel administered the coup de grace with a can of gasoline into the engine. The gas exploded and blew him off the tank, but he suffered only minor burns.

While this was going on, the situation still was confused at the head of the column. The village and several of my trucks were burning, casting a weird light over the whole scene. At this juncture, we could hear coming from the north the roar of tank motors and the clank of tank tracks. Being an optimistic soul, my first thought was that they were my three point tanks that had gotten away from me earlier in the evening. Then the clank of the tracks became clearer as the tanks came over the hill 800 yards away, and I began to doubt my optimism. I told Cpl. Howard, my driver, to get up quickly and throw the lead 2-1/2-ton truck across the road to block it. He dashed out and jockeyed the truck into position. The brakes failed to hold, so Howard deliberately stayed with it until he had it accurately placed, with the North Korean tanks coming down on him less than 100 yards away. Finally the tanks, two of them, pulled up less than 10 yards from the truck (Howard having bailed out by this time) and the commander inquired in Korean the equivalent of "What the hell goes on here." This settled all doubt in the minds of the American bystanders (an inaccurate term - we were still low in the ditch) and we opened rifle fire to make the tanks button up. The reaction was immediate and positive. Machine-guns and cannons opened up, and the truck burst into flames. This was most fortunate for us as it delayed the tanks for 10 minutes, while my three remaining tanks moved up and engaged in battle and my bazooka teams down the column were organizing.

Then followed a strange and fascinating sight. My three M-4s moved up in column into the firelit battle area, and the enemy tanks and mine exchanged shots. Finally, they had closed to a range of 18 yards and were still fighting. And then it became obvious the M-4s were being defeated after accounting for one T-34. The enemy tanks moved ahead and started down my column and into the rice paddies on the flank. By this time, there were 10 enemy tanks.

One of those tanks carefully picked its way down the column after running over several jeeps and fired bursts of machine gun fire into the vehicle radiators.

At this point, Capt. Robert B. McBride, my Headquarters Commandant, not fully understanding the situation and thinking the tank to be "friendly," got out in the road and proceeded to give the tanker hell for overrunning his jeep and admonished him for not being careful. The answer was a burst of MG fire that creased Capt. McBride and resulted in his being awarded the "Order of the Purple Pants" at a ceremony on the following day. Capt. McBride gave up directing traffic, and the tank proceeded.

A 105mm howitzer of C Battery, 77th FA, commanded by Capt. Wardlow, which had gone into hasty position, blew the turret off the tank at a range of 30 yards.

From the head of the column, I moved back to rejoin my lead company and to find Colonel Harris. I located them and found that the tank fighters were active. The bazookas went after tanks for the next hour and under the personal direction of Capt. James Webel, Regimental S-3, Lt. William Woodside, commanding Company L, Lt. Hill, my S-3, and Lt. Nicholas, FA liaison with the battalion, the tanks were finished off. Tank fighters stopped them with 3.5-inch launchers and finished them with grenades and gasoline. Here, the Regimental Commander, Col. Harris, decided that we had better hold up on a position and reorganize before proceeding from there. Using my officer staff, my driver, Cpl. Howard, and my orderly, Cpl. Brooks, I rounded up the scattered groups of riflemen in the dark, got my company commanders together, organized a perimeter defense and took stock of the damage on both sides. On the enemy side, we had destroyed seven T-34 tanks. Three had withdrawn. On our side, we had lost two tanks, about 15 vehicles, two men killed and 26 wounded. The battle had lasted about two hours.

By 0200, 27 Sept., the position was secured. I sent out a tank-killer reconnaissance patrol to look of the enemy tanks. They reported back at 0530 with no success.

At 0700, 27 Sept., the battalion was organized for a foot approach march to Osan, four miles distance. Just as Company L, the advance guard company, was leaving its position, a burp gun opened up from within its area. Without hesitation, under the leadership of Lt. Woodside, the nearest platoon closed in with marching fire, and the gun was silent within two minutes.

The column organized and moved out. Again we could hear tank motors just over the hill, and tank cannon fire fell to our right. The point, armed with a 3.5-inch closed in on the tank and accounted for number eight.

The rest of the march went without incident, and we joined with the 31st Infantry of the 7th Division at Osan at 0830, 27 Sept.

In 21 hours, the Task Force had covered 120 road miles, destroyed or overrun 13 tanks and killed or captured 200 enemy.

We had split the enemy in the middle and effected a solid juncture between I Corps and X Corps troops."

The above accurate description of Task Force Lynch covers only a part of the regiment's activities. At 0830 hours on Sept. 26th, during a regimental commanders' meeting in Sangju, Lt. Col. Harris, commander of the 7th Cavalry Regiment, had received the "go ahead" signal to move forward and contact elements of the 7th Infantry Division in the vicinity of Osan, and had organized the regiment and attached units into Task Force 777. (So named because it consisted of the 7th Cavalry Regiment, the 77th Field Artillery Battalion, and Company C, 70th Tank Battalion.) Task Force 777 was organized as follows:

TASK FORCE LYNCH (3rd Battalion) commanded by Lt. Col. James H. Lynch, comprising: 3rd Battalion, 7th Cavalry; Battery C, 77th Field Artillery Battalion; 2nd and 3rd Platoons, Company C, 70th Tank Battalion; 3rd Platoon Heavy Mortar Company; Regimental I&R Platoon; 2nd Platoon, Company B, 8th Engineers; Medical Platoon, Collecting Company; Forward Observer Party, 77th Field Artillery Battalion; Tactical Air

This ferry crossing site on the Naktong River was captured from the North Koreans by elements of the 1st Battalion, 7th Cavalry Regiment and put to their own use in late September 1950. The enemy used this ferry operation to transport their wounded, supplies and equipment. (Photo courtesy of Reuben Kvidt)

Control Party; SCR 399 Radio Team from the 13th Signal Company; Regimental Command Group.

TASK FORCE WITHERSPOON (1st Battalion) commanded by Maj. William O. Witherspoon, comprising: 1st Battalion, 7th Cavalry; 77th Field Artillery Battalion (less Battery C); Company C, 70th Tank Battalion (minus); Company B, 8th Engineers (minus); 1st Platoon, Heavy Mortar Company; Medical Platoon, Collecting Company.

(The 2nd Battalion plus the 2nd Platoon, Heavy Mortar Company, remained in Eighth Army reserve southwest of Taegu where it engaged in daily patrols and skirmishes with scattered die-hard enemy groups that had been cut off in their retreat northward.)

At 1130 hours on the 26th, Task Force Lynch followed by the Regimental Command Group departed the assembly area and by 1700 hours, had passed through Chongju via Kuryong-san, Naebung-myon, Ponghwang-ni, Miwon-ni, Namil-myon. No enemy resistance was encountered. After passing through Toam-ni, Poknyon-ni, Wangsong-ni, Kumon-ni and Ipchon-ni, the Task Force halted while the vehicles were refueled.

Task Force Witherspoon had been notified to advance at 1530 and disregard phase lines. A local priest from the village of Poun volunteered to guide the Task Force as no guides had been provided by the regiment.

The 10 tanks encountered by the leading elements of Task Force 777 (Task Force Lynch) about eight miles short of their objective near Osan, held up the column about two hours. Seven enemy tanks were destroyed, one by friendly tanks, one by direct artillery fire and the remaining five by infantrymen who used bazookas, grenades, gasoline and recoilless rifles.

One enemy tank, backing out of the village, ran over two jeeps, crashed into some 2-1/2-ton trucks and moved on into a rice paddy. As it moved across the rice paddy, the infantrymen fired with both 57mm and 75mm recoilless rifles. The tank stopped, but the motor continued to run. Sgt. William H. Hopkins jumped on the tank and threw several grenades into the tank, but the motor continued to operate. As a bazooka team prepared to bring fire on the tank, Capt. James B. Webel, regimental S-3 and 1st Lt. William Woodside, the commanding officer of Company L, approached with a five-gallon can of gasoline. Lt. Woodside poured some gasoline down the hatch, but only a small fire erupted. Capt. Webel then jumped on the T-34 and poured the gas down a hatch. A huge explosion knocked him about 30 feet, and the tank quickly burned - Capt. Webel suffered only minor burns.

The second enemy tank proceeded 200 yards down the column of vehicles and friendly troops, firing as it moved. A 105mm howitzer was hastily thrown into position along the side of the road by Capt. Theodore G. Wardlow, Sgt. Austin L. Monday, Pfc. Andrew J. Desmond and Sgt. Prado, and several rounds were fired by direct fire at the tank. The last round stopped the tank about 30 yards from the muzzle of the gun.

Capt. Webel, Cpl. John R. Muhoberac, Sgt. Thomas C. Hughes, Jr., Sgt. William E. Cox, and Pfc. Billy M. Mixon formed a volunteer bazooka team. Two tanks were knocked out by this group on the far side of the town, while Cpl. Muhoberac

knocked out one more tank on the near side of the town. A friendly tank knocked out another T-34 and a seventh tank was knocked out by a bazooka team formed by Lt. John Hill, S-2, of the 3rd Battalion and Lt. Nicholas, Forward Observer of the 77th Field Artillery Battalion, using a 3.5-inch bazooka. The remaining three enemy tanks withdrew to the north. Reconnaissance patrols pushed forward but could not locate the tanks.

At 0200 hours on the 27th, the attack was halted until daybreak. Reorganization for the following day revealed that Task Force 777 had lost two killed and 28 wounded; two tanks and about 15 other vehicles had been lost in the day's action.

At 0300 hours, Lt. Col. Harris sent a personal message to Maj. Gen. Hobart R. Gay, referring to the Commanding General's earlier officer to provide a bottle of champagne for each tank knocked out by ground forces, as follows: ". . . Fm TF 777 - Send seven bottles of champagne to CO TF 777. Put three more on ice. I'll get them later. Will continue on mission."

Meanwhile, a message was dispatched to the commanding officer of the 8th Cavalry as follows: "7th Cav is eight miles south of objective. Heavily engaged with tanks and infantry. Proceed immediately to assist."

At dawn, the column pushed forward on foot, supported by tanks and followed by tactical transportation. The three remaining enemy tanks were encountered and destroyed by tank and bazooka fire.

At 0826 hours on Sept. 27th, the mission was accomplished. Contact was made with Company H, 31st Infantry Regiment, 7th Infantry Division. A message to the First Cavalry Division from Task Force 777 at 0855 read as follows:

"Mission accomplished. Contact between Company H, 31st Infantry Regiment and forward elements of TF 777 accomplished at 0826 hours. Our contacting unit was Company L. We are jointly reducing enemy positions to east and west of Osan with 7th Division elements under Air Force and Navy fighter strikes. This is unification."

The village of Osan was checked carefully for enemy and secured by Task Force Lynch. Task Force Witherspoon arrived in Osan at 1430 hours.

At 1500 hours on Sept. 27th, the Commanding General and the Assistant Division Commander arrived in Osan and congratulated the Task Force.

The distance from Taegu to Osan is 196 road miles. The last leg of the drive (Poun to Osan) covered a distance of 102 miles.

A large sign erected on the north side of Osan read:

"Osan, Korea."

At 0826 hours, on 27 Sept. 1950, forward elements of Company L, 7th Cavalry, 1st Cavalry Division made first contact with Company H, 31st Infantry, 7th Infantry Division at this location, thereby making a solid United Nations front from Pusan to Seoul.

This drive from Taegu to Osan, a distance of 196 road miles and 116 air miles, marked the longest advance in the history of the American Army through enemy-held territory - GARRYOWEN."

On Sept. 28th, patrols were dispatched and the I&R Platoon moved north to Suwon and reported the road clear except for snipers.

A truck convoy and eight ambulances with casualties departed at 0730 hours; however, an enemy road block 18 miles south in the vicinity of Songhwan caused them to return to Osan.

At 1950 hours, the regimental commander and S-3, and other elements of the regimental headquarters, departed for the road block area. The following is an account of the action:

A mobile command group departed Osan with two platoons of tanks and 3.5-inch rocket launcher teams, after alerting two platoons of infantry to follow, and proceeded 10 miles south, where they met the column of trucks returning to Osan. The drivers were highly excited and gave a report that six enemy tanks with about 500 infantry had attacked the column near Songhwan. Acting upon this information, the command group established a delaying position utilizing a 3.5-inch rocket launcher and two machine guns. A messenger was dispatched to Osan to return with additional infantry from the 3rd Battalion.

Position areas for the two platoons of tanks, which arrived shortly thereafter, were selected. At this time, air reconnaissance reported that the enemy tanks had turned northeast at P'yong-taek. Acting on this information, a trap was set using one platoon of tanks to block at Sojong-ni and the other platoon of tanks to proceed to P'yong-taek to attack the enemy tanks from the rear.

At this time, Capt. John R. Flynn and two platoons of Company K, which were following the command group, arrived on the scene. The attacking platoon of tanks was moved forward with two 3.5-inch rocket launcher teams to establish a road block in the town of P'yong-taek and to protect the advance of the main element. At this point, air reconnaissance reported that two of the enemy tanks had turned around and now were headed southwest toward the town. Capt. Flynn and his force arrived in P'yong-taek, and one platoon reinforced was ordered to protect the northeast of the town, while the other platoon reinforced was to protect the south. While these platoons were moving into position, the two enemy tanks entered from the northeast en route to the center of the village. The two enemy tanks were immediately brought under fire, and a fire fight involving 75mm recoilless rifles, 3.5-inch rocket launchers, and tank fire ensued for a period of 45 minutes, during which time both enemy tanks were destroyed by rocket launcher and tank fire. Nine enemy tank crewmen were killed and the North Korean Lieutenant, tank platoon leader, was captured.

American casualties during this action totaled four; however, Lt. William Bicknell and two enlisted men were killed earlier in the afternoon at the roadblock. During the time this fight was in progress, the Air Force destroyed two additional tanks.

Sgt. Thomas E. Randell, forward observer of the Heavy Motor Company, 7th Cavalry Regiment, remembers the "breakout," and he wrote:

"Actually, the breakout of the Pusan Perimeter was accomplished by the 2nd Battalion, 7th Cavalry Regiment, during Sept. 17-20, 1950. This victory didn't come cheap, and many casualties were experienced, which left the battalion understrength. This prevented them from continuing on northward with Task Force Lynch (777) and the balance of the 7th Cavalry Regiment.

This left the 2nd Battalion as a mop-up unit to the many North Korean soldiers that were bypassed during the breakout and northward thrust of the 7th Cavalry Regiment. Our Heavy Mortar Company was really the only support unit to the 2nd Battalion, because the artillery battery had also moved northward with Task Force Lynch.

Looking through a 20 power scope, I could see many North Korean soldiers crossing rice paddies and disappearing from view behind a nearby hill. I called the battalion on my field telephone to report the sightings and asked for permission to fire on the enemy location.

Shortly, I received a return call from an officer and permission was denied. I had the personal feeling that the North Koreans were preparing to attack, and if I could reach their location with mortar fire, it might abort their plans. Within a few minutes, I received a return call from the officer and permission to fire was granted because some riflemen from the line company had verified my previous report.

Also, we had no Fire Direction Center as they had gone northward with Task Force Lynch. I called my Firing Platoon and gave them the coordinates and soon their first round was on the way. The round fell far short of the target, so more charges were added and each time they failed to reach the location. I was almost ready to give up when Cpl. Funderburk, from Tennessee, came on the field phone and said that he was moving everyone to a safe distance, because he was going to hit that target, 'no matter what!' I told him that the mortar would blow up, and he would be killed. He said not to worry and continued to add more charges.

Finally, one round scored a direct hit on the location, and Cpl. Funderburk kept on firing, which caused a tremendous explosion. Large clouds of dark black smoke rose into the sky as secondary explosions could be heard. Suddenly, North Korean soldiers were fleeing through the rice paddies as they attempted to escape from the fire, smoke and explosions.

A small reconnaissance plane circled overhead and above the fire and smoke, and quickly departed because of small arms fire from the ground. Later in the afternoon, a two-engine bomber came from the south and, after making a dry run over the location, it too received small arms fire from the ground. When it made the turn, it dove straight in, strafing and bombing, and when it pulled up out of the dive, the tail gunner would have his turn, firing from the rear turret.

The officer from the 2nd Battalion called me on the field telephone and wanted a play-by-play description of the action. He further informed me that the small spotter plane had taken some photos and said that he would let me know what kind of a target we had hit as soon as possible.

I looked at my map and after some calculations, estimated that our 4.2 mortar that was recommended to fire safely at 4,400 yards, had actually hit this enemy location at 5,200 yards. GARRYOWEN!

The following day, the officer from the 2nd Battalion informed me that the aerial photographs showed trucks, possibly tanks, artillery weapons, fuel storage and with an estimated kill of 200 North Korean soldiers."

Elements of the regiment conducted aggressive patrolling in and around Osan until Oct. 5th, when orders were received to continue the advance northward.

On Oct. 2nd, the 2nd Battalion was released from Eighth Army reserve near Taegu and the entire battalion was flown from the Taegu airstrip to Suwon where it joined the rest of the regiment. While only a few of the personnel remained with the battalion who had participated in the brief period of airborne training in Japan during the earlier part of the year, this training proved invaluable when this air movement was made.

Upon arrival at Osan, Lt. Col. Gilmon A. Huff, who had returned from the hospital, again assumed command of the 2nd Battalion. The strength of the 2nd Battalion was 825 - the highest since its arrival in Korea.

For their outstanding performance in Task Force Lynch, the 3rd Battalion, 7th Cavalry Regiment, became the only battalion in Army history to win two Presidential Unit Citations within two weeks.

From the book, "The Forgotten War," author Clay Blair wrote: "The mythology of the Korean War was to be called the Eighth Army breakout. It was not, in fact, a breakout but rather the pursuit and exploitation of an enemy force that was compelled to withdraw because Inchon made its position in South Korea untenable. Possibly Eighth Army could have achieved a true breakout without Inchon. It certainly could have achieved one had the Inchon forces been utilized to reinforce the Pusan Perimeter. It probably could have achieved one earlier had the Inchon forces landed at Kunsan.

Whatever the correct terminology, it was indisputably a remarkable achievement. It freed Eighth Army from a demoralizing, costly, positional warfare and instilled it with pride. It 'shattered' or 'destroyed' or 'routed' the NKPA as a viable entity in South Korea. It liberated all of South Korea below the Han River. It achieved a linkup with X Corps.

However, in one important respect the operation had to be marked down: It had failed to 'trap' or 'pound to pieces' the NKPA in South Korea. The trap lines Walker threw across the peninsula were too little, too late, especially the all-important, Waegwan-Taejon line, which was decisively weakened by Walker's last-minute decision to divert the First Cavalry to its celebrated but largely militarily meaningless linkup with X Corps. Nor was the Eighth Army hammer blow on the X Corps anvil ever realized. That colorful metaphor became, in reality, the 7th Cavalry and 31st Infantry trapping a dozen T-34 tanks near Osan in a successful but singularly uncoordinated operation from which most of the NKPA troops escaped.

It was impossible to determine how many NKPA troops escaped from Eighth Army in South Korea. The official Army historian guessed '25,000 to 30,000,' but the total was probably much greater, perhaps as many as 40,000. Whatever the figure, it was a very serious loss, reminiscent of two major Allied blunders in World War II: allowing a comparable number of German troops to escape from Sicily to fight again; then through the Falaise gap in Normandy. Presumably the majority of the NKPA troops who managed to escape were mostly combat-wise veterans, not recent North or South Korean conscripts. The numbers were more than sufficient to provide cadres to rebuild the NKPA, should Moscow be inclined to support such a course."

Homeless Orphans. (Courtesy of Bob Mauger)

The thousands of refugees always presented a problem on the narrow dirt roads. (U.S. Army Photo)

CHAPTER V
CROSSING OF THE 38TH PARALLEL

The 2nd Battalion departed Osan for the new regimental assembly area near Munsan-ni at 0900 on Oct. 5th, and the remainder of the regiment closed in the area the following day.

The regiment had been ordered to cross the Imjin River and seize Kaesong; however, upon arrival there it was ordered to proceed westward and cross the Yesong River and seize Paekchon, and to be prepared to continue further movement to the north and west.

The Division Commander stated that he had grave doubts that the Yesong River could be crossed in the 7th Cavalry Regiment's sector, as the river was unfordable and spanned only by a partially destroyed combination railroad-road bridge.

However, even generals have underestimated the fighting ability of the 7th Cavalry Regiment, and the 1st Battalion was given the mission of leading the attack over the 800-yard-long bridge spanning the Yesong River, heavily defended by a fanatical enemy. Company C spearheaded the attack supported by tank, artillery and mortar fire, and air support. The company began the attack at 1545 hours, and as they proceeded, the enemy sent a withering barrage of anti-tank, mortar, automatic weapons, and small arms fire into the advancing column. Seventeen men were wounded on the bridge; however, due to the aggressiveness of the leaders, both non-commissioned officers and officers alike, the bridge was crossed in 20 minutes. Company D with its mortar fire destroyed an enemy ammunition dump and two 82mm mortars approximately 500 yards on the far side of the bridge. The advanced elements of Company C located two enemy machine guns on the high ground to their right front and quickly destroyed them. During the attack, Company C suffered four killed and 36 wounded. Company B following behind Company C, moved across the bridge slowly and also was pinned down by a murderous barrage of enemy fire. However, the company crossed the bridge - under continuous fire - then attacked to the left of the road and cleared the enemy from the hills. When the company reached a point 30 yards from its objective, a defense line was established until ammunition could be replenished. Upon receiving the sorely needed ammunition, Company B moved forward in the attack and secured its objective. On the bridge, Company B suffered 24 wounded and while attacking the high ground received one killed and one wounded. Company A, followed Company B, raced over the bridge, secured its objective and suffered only minor casualties during the attack.

Battery B, 77th Field Artillery Battalion, displaced forward at 2235 hours in order to support the attack. The 2nd Battalion also moved to the east bank and prepared to cross as the 3rd Battalion followed to protect the east bank. The 1st Battalion suffered 78 casualties in the attack while securing the river crossing.

The 2nd Battalion began crossing at midnight on Oct. 9th-10th and had completed the crossing by 0525 hours. Company B, 8th Engineers, under command of Capt. Merlin W. Anderson repaired the bridge while under fire, as several counterattacks were repulsed by Companies B and C. The 2nd Battalion moved through the 1st Battalion toward Paekchon but met stiff resistance prior to daylight. Prisoners reported an enemy battalion of 410 men in the area. Lt. Col. Huff received a slight wound in the chest while directing the attack near the front and was evacuated, and Maj. John W. Callaway again assumed command of the 2nd Battalion at 0450 hours on Oct. 10th.

By 0600 on the 10th, Company A had moved to the high ground 2,000 yards west of the bridge along the road. Company B was nearing the high ground on the left, which was their objective; Company C had secured the high ground that overlooked the bridge from the east; and Company D remained in position to protect the left flank on the west side of the bridge. Forty-six enemy had been killed and 42 captured by the 1st Battalion during this attack.

The first jeeps began crossing the bridge at 0620 hours while the 1st Battalion continued to receive fire from the north. The 2nd Battalion continued their aggressive drive northward toward Paekchon, broke through the enemy's hasty defense along the road and arrived in Paekchon at 1235 hours. The city was cleared quickly, and the battalion secured the high ground northwest of the town.

When the regiment was given the mission of crossing the Yesong River, Col. Harris dispatched Capt. Arthur H. Westburg to Inchon to contact the Navy in an effort to obtain any landing craft that might be available to assist in the river crossing. Upon his arrival in Inchon at 0200 on the morning of Oct. 10th, Capt. Westburg awoke the naval officer in charge and requested landing craft for the 7th Cavalry to effect a river crossing. This unusual request, at that hour in the morning, for a unit fighting inland somewhat startled the Navy. However, after a few hurried phone calls, and with Capt. Westburg's persistence, the naval craft were obtained, and at 1700 hours, 13 LCMs from Inchon turned into the Yesong River headed for the bridge site. Upon arrival, the LCMs greatly hastened the regiment's crossing of the river, and as Cpl. John L. McCann came marching down the road with 28 prisoners and asked, *"What the heck do I do with these?"* they were promptly put to work unloading the LCMs.

The LCMs also were utilized during the day of Oct. 11th to move tanks across the river. During this operation, the motor on one LCM failed, and because of the high-tide conditions, the LCM with tank and crew drifted down the river toward the sea. The coxswain managed to beach the LCM four miles downstream, but because of enemy mortar fire, he continued down the river to the sea. The LCM drifted to the mouth of the river, then as the tide came in, the craft returned upstream and docked at the unloading site. It was assumed that the entire group with Capt. Charles R. Shaw, commander of Company C, 70th Tank Battalion, was in the middle of the Yellow Sea until their return.

Maj. Lucian C. Croft, regimental S-4, obtained two gasoline engines and placed them on a rail car for use in transporting supplies from the unloading site on the river to Paekchon. This was the first of several GARRYOWEN railroads in Korea.

At 0830 hours on Oct. 11th, the 3rd Battalion was directed to move to Hanpori, secure the bridge there and move immediately southward toward Kumchon.

At 0934 on the 11th, the 3rd Battalion reported that they were 1,000 yards from their objective at Hanpori preparing to attack. The 2nd Battalion departed for the 3rd Battalion area with the regimental command group as the forward elements of the 2nd Battalion, 21st Infantry, arrived to relieve the 1st Battalion, 7th Cavalry at Paekchon. The 3rd Battalion captured Hanpori around noon against light opposition.

Thus, the 7th Cavalry had reached a point some 30 miles behind the enemy with the 5th and 8th Cavalry Regiments driving the elements of the two North Korean Divisions into the 7th Cavalry perimeter at Hanpori. Enemy units and small groups attempting to escape this encirclement of our forces were captured, while others attempted to fight their way out to the north,

Wounded North Korean soldier who was identified as one of those involved in the Naede Murders. The officer to the right is Major Brown of G-2 Intelligence, 1st Cavalry Division. (Courtesy of Fred Herrmann)

attacking or ambushing any of our forces encountered in their path.

During the night of Oct. 12th, Master Sgt. John H. Smith, platoon leader of Company L, saw 11 enemy trucks coming toward his position with their lights on. He let four trucks pass and then had his platoon open fire, killing 50 to 60 North Korean soldiers and capturing a like number. His platoon also captured six trucks; destroyed four and captured two 76mm guns that the trucks were pulling, five 82mm mortars, and destroyed one ammunition truck. Among the prisoners was a North Korean regimental commander who had a document stating that two North Korean Divisions would break out of Kumchon on the night of Oct. 14th.

When Lt. Willie L. Hamblin departed the regimental trains area at Paekchon to contact the regiment at Hanpori on the morning of Oct. 13th, he suddenly came upon an enemy group attempting to escape from the encirclement. After a brisk fire fight, he killed nine and captured 32. Later that morning as the rear command group proceeded from Paekchon to Hanpori with the 1st Battalion and elements of the 77th Field Artillery Battalion, they also were ambushed when the column became separated because of the rough, narrow, winding roads. Tanks were dispatched from the head of the column to the rear; however, a rifle company from the 21st Infantry, 24th Infantry Division, came to the rescue of the bewildered headquarters personnel.

A second ambush took place along this route involving supply personnel returning from Hanpori to Paekchon for supplies. Capt. John Brewer, 2nd Battalion S-4 and 10 enlisted men were captured after running an enemy fire block. The group was placed in a house for the night and as the North Koreans withdrew the following morning, enemy riflemen entered the house, sprayed the room with machine gun fire, and left them for dead. Fortunately, Capt. Brewer and five of the men were not wounded seriously and escaped.

The following is an account of the North Korean atrocities on Oct.. 13th, 1950, from Sgt. First Class Frederick C. Herrmann, Motor Sergeant, Service Company, 2nd Battalion, 7th Cavalry Regiment:

"In the early morning of Oct. 13th, 1950, many of the Service Company truck drivers were tired and exhausted from driving many long hours without getting the proper sleep. So I volunteered to drive a truck in the next supply convoy from our present location in the town of Paekchon to the town of Hanpori. The rifle companies of the 2nd Battalion were located in that vicinity, which was our front line.

However, within our area it was estimated that two North Korean divisions were cut off and might be attempting to flee or escape northward. At this particular time, the 2nd Battalion had the enemy on the run, and it was extremely difficult for our supply trains to keep up with their constant movement. The roads throughout the area were rough, narrow and sometimes very congested due to the large numbers of destroyed enemy vehicles.

Our convoy trip to Hanpori went very well, and all supply trucks arrived on schedule. It didn't take long for the trucks to be unloaded as Capt. John Brewer, 2nd Battalion S-4, ordered us to return to the town of Paekchon.

During the return trip, I had just made a comment to the gunner of the 50-caliber machine gun mounted on our truck, that it didn't seem like a war was going on in the area. Suddenly, enemy mortar rounds started landing on and near the road directly in front of us. Then North Korean soldiers appeared all over the place as we attempted to run the fire block. However, we were very soon forced to stop our trucks and were immediately taken prisoner.

The enemy took our group of 13 men, including Capt. Brewer, to a house for the evening. The enemy seemed to be very apprehensive of the situation. Just prior to dark, they started to talk with each other. I couldn't understand their language, but I would soon learn what they were talking about. They started shooting their automatic weapons as I saw one of my fellow comrades hit and fall near me. I immediately turned and dove under a nearby table for protection. I felt the pain as the bullets ripped through both of

my legs. Many shots were fired as I lay there on the floor praying for my life.

Soon the North Koreans left the house, but I was afraid to say anything as I thought they might hear me and return. Throughout the night I lay on the floor just praying to God to help me get out of this horrible ordeal. The next morning I soon discovered that the North Koreans had withdrawn during the night or early morning. Then I found out that five of us, including Capt.. Brewer, had miraculously survived the enemy atrocities. However, the eight other never survived and lay there in cold blood. Actually, the enemy had left all of us for dead.

We left the house in an attempt to locate friendly lines and seek immediate medical aid. Soon an Army 2-1/2-ton truck arrived and took us to the 8055 Mobile Army Surgical Hospital (MASH). Once there, we received the appropriate medical attention, and soon I was served a delicious hot meal.

Soon an officer from the G-2 Intelligence arrived and his name was Maj. Brown. He debriefed me as I attempted to tell him what actually happened when the North Koreans, for no apparent reason, expressed their brutal and barbaric way of life by shooting all of us. He said he would do everything possible to bring to trial those North Korean officers and soldiers who were responsible for the murders.

I was transferred to the 49th General Hospital in Tokyo, Japan, for further medical treatment. I was contacted several other times by G-2 Intelligence concerning the North Korean atrocities. They further informed me that where the atrocities had taken place was in the village of Naede, which was located near the town of Kaesong and just north of the 38th Parallel. The Army had classified the atrocities as the 'Naede Murders.'

Then I eventually was transferred to Valley Forge Army Hospital for further medical treatment. Due to the medical circumstances, I received a disability retirement from the Army on Dec. 31, 1951.

In 1953, I was notified to appear at a Sub-Committee on Investigation Hearings in Room

House in village of Naede, where North Korean soldiers committed atrocities on October 13, 1950. Later called Naede Murders. (Courtesy of Fred Herrmann)

Corporal Richard Dowell, Company B, 1st Bn., 7th Cavalry Regiment, playing cards at Camp McGee reserve area, on August 11, 1950. This camp was located two miles north of Taegu, South Korea. It was named in honor of Lieutenant Charles F. McGee, who was killed in action on Triangle Hill on August 10, 1950.

318, Senate Office Building, Washington, D.C., on Dec. 2nd-4th, 1953. This was the War Crimes Investigations of the Naede Murders, which brought forth 29 American officers and enlisted men as witnesses. After several days of hearings, the Naede Murders were written off the books. Needless to say, the only thing that the hearings produced was a very disappointed group of witnesses.

I was informed that from the Korean War a total of 216 North Korean war criminals were never convicted and eventually were released."

Enemy groups escaping from the Kumchon trap established many ambushes along the roads as the 5th and 8th Cavalry Regiments drove the enemy from the south into the 7th Cavalry positions. However, 1st Lt. Richard G. Shanks and platoon Sgt. Lester McKee from Company K while on a patrol 1,200 yards south of Hanpori met Capt. Harry A. Buckley with a tank from the 5th Cavalry, thus completing the encirclement of two enemy divisions in the Hanpori-Kumchon area.

At 1015 hours on Oct. 14th, an operations order was issued at Hanpori, assigning the regiment the mission of attacking to the northwest and seizing Pyongyang - the North Korean capital.

The 2nd Battalion departed northwest toward Namchonjon - their objective - en route for Pyongyong and became involved in a fierce fire fight. They pulled back for the night and planned to resume the attack on Namchonjon the following morning.

Immediately following air strikes on Namchonjon, the 2nd Battalion attacked the town from the south at 0730 hours on Oct.. 15th. By 1200 hours, the 2nd Battalion had entered Namchonjon but had received 10 killed and 30 wounded on the south edge of town. At 1250, the town was reported secure and the 2nd Battalion attacked to secure the high ground northwest of town. The 3rd Battalion was ordered to move through Namchonjon as rapidly as possible to be followed by the 1st Battalion and remaining elements of the regiment.

On the following day, the 1st Battalion continued to move rapidly en route for Hwangju after securing Sindang-ni. Enemy elements continued to be overrun, and many prisoners were captured as the regimental column dashed north on a trail lateral to the main route - Sanghwa-ri, Togu-ri and Hwangju.

As the day ended on Oct. 17th, the 1st and 2nd Battalions were on their objective and the 3rd Battalion seven miles south of Hwangju. Snipers molested the column throughout the day, and several vehicles were lost on the mountainous, narrow, winding roads.

The 1st Battalion moved to the west and contacted British units three miles from Hwangju, as the 3rd Battalion moved through the 2nd Battalion for the next jump in the race toward Pyongyang. Resistance was light until the town of Hukkyori was reached where tank fire was received and resistance increased but was eliminated quickly as the 2nd Battalion flanked to the west, seized the high ground and moved toward the town.

This maneuver of the 2nd Battalion has been referred to as an "End Run." The following account of the action as told by Capt. Robert G. Abarr, the 2nd Battalion's S-2.

"The order came down for the 2nd Battalion to outflank the enemy and knock out the strong defenses that were holding up the entire Division's advance. We received the order about 4:00 p.m. on the 18th and were to move by foot during darkness to get in position prior to daylight and launch a coordinated attack. Lt. Col. Huff took Companies E, F and G, but left Company H back due to the rugged terrain.

He called me in and stated that we were to move out just before dark and go across country approximately four miles west, then right approximately four miles, then right again about four miles to the main road leading into Pyongyang to help knock out the enemy and open the road. My job was to lead the way with, as he called it, 'my I&R' and find a gap through the enemy's lines to pass our battalion through. I had only a 20-minute start on the battalion and had never seen the terrain before. The weather was bitter cold, a light snow was on the ground, and creeks and rivers were half frozen.

I started off with my section. We would go to a point, reconnoiter ahead and then leave one man to direct the battalion. Everything went well until we came to a stream that was too deep to ford, and we had to back track for about a mile. Finally, we found a crossing site, and I led the battalion through chest-deep ice water.

Later we found a gap in the enemy lines and marched the entire battalion unnoticed with 30 feet of a Korean unit (Platoon or company size) that was digging in.

The Colonel (Huff) didn't question my route

in the least, but it was sure a calculated risk, and I had a hard time keeping track of where we were on the map. Just before we got to our final objective, we started over a hill, and the enemy took us under light machine gun and automatic weapons fire. We backed off a bit and sent Company G in an attack. This was the time they went running up the hill, screaming "GARRYOWEN!" The attack completely surprised the enemy as we had no casualties, and the enemy took off running.

At this point, we received word that the enemy strong point along the main road had been broken and that we were to stay where we were until daylight - which was in approximately one hour.

I estimate that I led the battalion approximately 12 to 15 miles through enemy-held territory that night, and I'm sure I did not take the most direct route. At times I thought the blind was leading the blind."

Moderate resistance was encountered during the early morning hours of Oct. 19th, and one T-34 enemy tank in excellent condition and 250 drums of gasoline were captured. The 1st Battalion flanked to the right and secured the commanding terrain overlooking Hukkyori. The 3rd Battalion was attached to the 5th Cavalry for operations effective at 1100 hours, and the remainder of the regiment remained in place and watched other elements of the First Cavalry Division drive into Pyongyang after leading the drive all the way from Seoul.

The 7th Cavalry moved from Hukkyori to Pryongyang at 0630 hours on Oct. 21st. Shortly after arriving in an assembly area in Pyongyang, the regiment received the mission to move rapidly to the southwest to seize the port city of Chinnampo. The regiment was organized into Battalion Combat Teams, and movement began at 1400 hours with the 2nd Battalion Combat Team leading. Slight resistance was encountered at Kangso but was overcome rapidly, and movement to the south continued without further opposition. This move was made without prior reconnaissance, and as darkness fell, the entire column turned on their lights and "barreled their way down the road."

The leading elements of the 2nd Battalion Combat Team entered Chinnampo at 0130 hours on Oct. 22nd, and the last elements of the regiment closed in the area at 0555 hours. The entire

Many bridges were destroyed along the Naktong River and within the Pusan Perimeter, 1950. (Courtesy of Bob Mauger)

Floating pontoon bridge over the Naktong River at Waegwan, 1950. (U.S. Army Photo)

Bob Hope and Marilyn Maxwell, doing a show for the Eighth Army troops in the North Korean capital of Pyongyang on Oct. 29, 1950. (Courtesy of Jim Harris, 70th Tank Battalion)

route was lined with cheering civilians waving South Korean flags and seemed happier to see us than any previous group encountered. The only casualty suffered during this move was when Chaplain Francis McCullough was hit in the nose with an apple thrown by enthusiastic Koreans offering presents. The day was spent in searching Chinnampo for enemy stragglers and abandoned enemy installation containing records, supplies or materials.

During the closing days of October, rumors became more frequent that the end of the North Korean War was in sight and that the North Korean forces had ceased resistance.

The regiment was busily engaged in clearing the surrounding area of small enemy groups and Communist sympathizers, and in assisting the Navy to clear the harbor of mines. Plans were made to stage a victory parade down the Imperial Plaza in Tokyo on the forthcoming Armistice Day as the war seemed all but over, and some units even prepared loading plans for the ships that were to return them to Japan.

On Oct. 25th, a congratulatory message from Gen. MacArthur was received concerning the regiment's entry into Pyongyang that read, "Heartiest congratulations to you all. That is certainly hitting the old pill for a home run."

During the stay in Chinnampo, a captured North Korean train - soon named the "GARRYOWEN Express" - made daily supply runs between Chinnampo and Pyongyang. Sgt. First Class Vallie Stump, Motor Sergeant for the Heavy Motor Company, remembers:

"When our 7th Cavalry troops took the port city of Chinnampo, they found a steam railroad engine in a steel plant. Our regimental commander, Col. William 'Wild Bill' Harris, heard about it, and he personally contacted me. He asked me if I thought there was a possibility of getting a railroad in operation. I took a wild guess and assured him that I could, and he immediately ordered me to 'get after it.'

I arrived at the railroad yard and discovered that the steam engine already had been fired-up by a North Korean crew. There were two engineers, two firemen and an oil man who was the Master Mechanic. I couldn't speak Korean, so I tried to speak Japanese, which the old man understood.

We proceeded to put a train together that was made up of flat cars to facilitate the loading and unloading of vehicles. They could drive the vehicles across the flat cars, for the full length of the train.

Actually, we loaded trucks aboard the train at Chinnampo and hauled them to the North Korean capital city of Pyongyang, where we unloaded them. Our first trip was made with a recon jeep that was equipped with a heavy .50-caliber machine gun. Also a few guard troops were positioned within the train, and we arrived at our destination without incident.

After unloading the trucks, they were driven to a supply depot and loaded with supplies. Then they were driven back and reloaded on the railroad flat cars. Then our train returned to Chinnampo.

The roads in the area were in such poor condition, that it was almost impossible to drive

on them. Approximately one-third of our trucks had broken springs, so the best way to get supplies was by our railroad operation. It worked very well, and quickly it was called the 'GARRYOWEN Express.'

Bob Hope brought his show into Pyongyang, and we took our troops from Chinnampo to see the show. Some of the troops rode in the special coach that I had for Col. 'Wild Bill' Harris, and the others rode on the trucks. After the terrific show, we returned to the train and headed back to Chinnampo.

About two miles outside of Pyongyang there was a railroad that ran to the north. Within the area, there was a series of switches to connect the two railroads together. It was all up grade to reach this particular area. When the engine of our train reached the switches, it derailed pulling the tender off with it. The engine rolled down the ties between the rails, and we finally got it stopped.

We sized up the situation and then uncoupled the cars and with the help of the troops, we moved each one by human power. Then we attempted to get the tender and engine onto the rails by forcing them back between the rails. However, we were only able to get part of it back onto the rails because the engine drive wheels started to spin. To avoid damage to the engine, we stopped this procedure.

Then the old man told me about an operating engine several miles up the railroad and toward the north. I borrowed a jeep and driver from a tank unit that was near by and headed for the rail yard. Shortly, my one engineer and I found the steam engine, and then we attempted to find the crew. We didn't have to look very far, because we found them sleeping in a tower. After we woke them up, it was luck in our favor because they had banked the fire, and soon we were heading back to the derailment.

When we approached the derailed engine, luck with us again because the couplings of each tender matched up perfectly. We spiked two frogs to the rails and started to move both engines. Our luck continued as we got the engine back onto the rails, and we were back in operation. Then we backed down and coupled up to the cars, and got the train movement under way.

At this particular time, I discovered that if we had gone a half mile farther and then derailed, it would have been, 'Katie Bar the Door,' because it was all down grade, and our train would have been 'Honking On.' From the time we derailed until we were under way again, the 'GARRYOWEN Express' was delayed a total of four hours, 15 minutes.

Actually, we started out originally with a Manchurian engine; however, it was in poor condition because the boiler was leaking badly. This condition got worse, and there was only two water points, and this made a possibility of blowing up the engine. The old man told me about a Little Pacific engine in the round house at Pyongyang. I went to a military railway company that had moved into Pyongyang and requested to speak to the commanding officer. After a brief discussion, the officer agreed to give me the Little Pacific. Incidentally, the engine was built in Lima, Ohio.

We continued to operate the railroad without any further problems. Then I was instructed to move the train northward. However, a tunnel was blown so I had to remain where I was until the tunnel and track were cleared. During this time, we had two switch engines working in the rail yards in Chinnampo. Things were very busy in the harbor because a port company was clearing dangerous mines from the water. Several units within the 7th Cavalry were assigned and assisted in the harbor clearing project. Also, the United States Navy assisted in the overall operation.

On my last trip, we were returning to Chinnampo and as we came out of the tunnel and rounded the curve, I suddenly noticed near the yard limits an engine heading our way. The yard engine was on the main line and that was the same track that we were on. Everyone seemed to see the yard engine at the same time. The old man shouted to stop, and the brakes were applied to their maximum. Then they attempted to reverse the engine to help slow it down. On the other engine, two men bailed out and took off, instead of trying to help the situation. I began to think, 'Damn, this ain't gonna be my best day.' Luck was with us again as we started to slow down and finally stopped short of the other engine. When the two men returned to their engine, the old man really gave them hell. Once I reached the yard, a major from the port company relieved me of the 'GARRYOWEN Express.'

I immediately reported this to Col. "Wild Bill" Harris. The next day was Thanksgiving Day, and Col. Harris stopped by to see what happened. I explained what took place, and then he went to see the major who was attempting to eat dinner in their mess hall. Col. Harris chewed the major up one side and down the other, and I quickly learned the tougher side of Col. 'Wild Bill.' Then we sat down to have our dinner, and after we finished our meal, we left for Pyongyang.

The Chinese Communist Forces entered the war, and I rejoined the Heavy Motor Company as Motor Sergeant. The last word I had on the train was that it was taken south with hundreds of refugees on it. The 'GARRYOWEN EXPRESS' was still serving its purpose."

During this period, many of the troopers enjoyed the first hot baths and hot food in many months and could get a full night's sleep in relative safety without danger of a surprise attack. However, on the last day of October, this serene life came to a sudden halt as the regiment received unexpected orders to move north without delay.

Fragmentary information received by the regiment indicated that some of the Eighth Army's units farthest north had met with unexpected strong resistance that had halted their advance to the Yalu River. At 0800 on Oct. 31st, the 1st Battalion Combat Team departed for Yongsan-Dong. Thus began another chapter in the history of the GARRYOWEN's part in the Korean War.

A village house made of mud wattle and thatched roof. Once on fire they burned smokily. The vicinity of Taegu, South Korea, 1951. (Courtesy of Paul "Bill" Fleming)

The city of Waegwan was almost completely destroyed. (U.S. Army Photo)

Thousands of North Korean soldiers surrendered near the 38th Parallel, as they attempted to flee northward. By November 3, 1950, over 135,000 enemy soldiers had surrendered. (U.S. Army Photo)

Dead South Korean civilians near Seoul in September 1950. These atrocities were committed by North Korean soldiers. (Courtesy of Ed Daily)

Dead South Korean civilians near Seoul in September 1950. These atrocities were committed by North Korean soldiers. (Courtesy of Ed Daily)

Killed in cold blood during Naede Murders. (Courtesy of Fred Herrmann)

These 7th Cavalry troopers were shot in cold blood during Naede Murders. (Courtesy of Fred Herrmann)

Major Brown of G-2 Intelligence, 1st Cavalry Division, as he investigates the atrocities. (By Fred Herrmann)

Killed in cold blood during Naede Murders. (Courtesy of Fred Herrmann)

Sixty defenseless civilians bludgeoned and shot to death in cold blood. Many times the enemy used civilians to move equipment and supplies and only rewarded them with death. (U.S. Army Photo)

From top to bottom: Captured North Korean steam engine in the port city of Chinnampo, which became the "GARRYOWEN Express." (Courtesy of Vallie Stump) — A United States Fifth Air Force F-51 Mustang (Sexy Sally), drops napalm jellied gasoline tanks on an industrial target in North Korea. (U.S. Air Force Photo) — U.S. Navy FU4 leaving for bombing and strafing mission. At the time, it was a terrific support fighter plane. (U.S. Navy Photo) — L to R: M/Sgt. Monske; M/Sgt. Wright; Sgt. Faust; Cpl. Matthias, of the I&R Platoon, HQ & HQ, 2nd Bn., 7th Cavalry Regiment at Chinnampo Harbor North Korea in October 1950. (Courtesy of Henry Matthias)

CHAPTER VI
CHINESE INTERVENTION

During the first week in November an air of excited expectancy hung over the front line troops. While there had been no official confirmation of contact with the Chinese Communist Forces along the Eighth Army Front, the front line trooper sensed that the enemy he now was facing was something more than the "remaining elements of the badly mauled North Korean Army." Newscasts made frequent reference to Chinese "Volunteer Forces" and during the week, word was received of the 8th Cavalry massacre at Unsan. Frequent alerts, shifting of positions and subsequent withdrawals of the regiment added to the fear that another war - more tiring and vicious than the one supposedly just won - was beginning. This new unknown enemy, the sudden change from the summer heat of South Korea to the beginning of winter in North Korea, the overcast sky, frequent rain and occasional snow flurries with the temperature near freezing, and the absolute lack of winter field clothing all served to add to the discomfort and gloomy atmosphere that prevailed throughout the regiment. The Command Reports for the month of November revealed many confusing activities within the overall operations of the 7th Cavalry Regiment.

On Nov. 1st, the 2nd and 3rd Battalion Combat Teams moved to the vicinity of Ryukyu upon relief at Chinnampo by the 187th Regimental Combat Team. The 1st Battalion Combat Team had departed Chinnampo for Yongsan-Dong on the previous day and was attached to the 5th Cavalry Regimental Combat Team for operations.

At 2000 hours on Nov. 1st, I Corps directed the formation of Task Force Allen - under the command of Brig. Gen. Frank A. Allen - to be composed of the 2nd and 3rd Battalion Combat Teams, 7th Cavalry Regiment, plus attachments, and the 10th Engineer (Combat) group. Task Force Allen had the combined mission of furnishing the rear guard to cover the withdrawal of the First Cavalry Division from the vicinity of Yongsan-Dong and the defense of a zone to the northeast assigned by I Corps.

Reconnaissance parties were sent out in the early morning hours of Nov. 2nd from the 2nd and 3rd Battalion Combat Teams to reconnoiter defensive positions in the area assigned by Gen. Allen. In the later afternoon, orders were received from Maj. Hugh Queenin, Liaison Officer, G-3 Section, First Cavalry Division, to move all combat troops and a command group to the vicinity of Yongsan-Dong, reporting immediately upon arrival to the Commanding General, First Cavalry Division, for instructions. However, prior to the departure of the regimental mobile command group from the vicinity of Ryukyu, at 1715 hours, the 3rd Battalion Combat Team received orders to remain in place. The mobile command group found their route clogged with vehicles of the 24th Division moving in the opposite direction and did not arrive in Yongsan-Dong until approximately 2100 hours.

At Yongsan-Dong, this group came under the command of Brig. Gen. Charles D. Palmer, who was to direct the withdrawal operation. Leading elements of the 2nd Battalion Combat Team did not arrive until 0010 hours on Nov. 3rd, and the remainder of the combat team did not close until 0230 hours because of the traffic congestion. By 0400 hours, the members of this team deployed into assigned positions approximately four miles northeast of Yongsan-Dong.

Meanwhile, information was received at the rear command post at Ryukyu of a serious breakthrough in the Republic of Korea (ROK) II Corps' sector in the vicinity of Kunu-ri to the east. Various reports were received that Kunu-ri was about to fall and security in the Ryukyu area was strengthened immediately. Two platoons of infantry reinforced with tanks were sent up the road for approximately a half mile to establish a road block; however, the expected enemy attack failed to materialize. Republic of Korean soldiers, withdrawing down the road without orders, were stopped at the road block and organized into units.

On Nov. 3rd, the 1st Battalion Combat Team reverted to regimental control. No enemy contact was made in covering the withdrawal of the 5th and 8th Regimental Combat Teams. The 1st Battalion Combat Team, followed by the 2nd Battalion, the regimental mobile command group, and the 16th Reconnaissance Company began a withdrawal through Pakchon and Anju, while the 3rd Battalion Combat Team and regimental service trains remained in the vicinity of Ryukyu.

On the following day, the 1st Battalion moved into the vicinity of the regimental command post at Sapyong-ni, the 2nd Battalion remained in the vicinity of Yongbong-ni, while the 3rd Battalion, the rear command group and the service trains remained in their positions in the vicinity of Ryukyu. The entire Regimental Combat Team was alerted to move on an hour's notice. There was no contact with organized enemy units, but several prisoners were taken as a result of screening "refugees," found to be carrying grenades and drums of submachine gun ammunition in their packs and clothing. The anticipated fall of Junuri still did not materialize.

By Nov. 6th, Task Force Allen was dissolved. The Regimental Combat Team reverted to the control of the First Cavalry Division, and tentative plans were prepared for the defense of a zone located south of the Chongchon River.

At 1900 hours, a report was received that three enlisted men of the 3rd Battalion, 8th Cavalry Regiment, had returned to the 1st Battalion's positions from the vicinity of Unsan where their unit had been cut off on Nov. 2nd. At 2325 hours, 10 additional enlisted men from the 8th Cavalry came into Company B's sector. All of the men were fed, given medical attention, bedded down for the night and evacuated through medical channels the following morning.

On Nov. 7th, the regiment occupied positions along the south bank of the Chongchon River. The 3rd Battalion maintained contact with the 19th Infantry Regiment, on the left, by strong combat patrols as the 19th Infantry attacked during the morning hours.

A patrol from the 3rd Battalion encountered a civilian who stated that on Nov. 6th, a large group of enemy horse cavalry, dressed in blue, entered a town in the area of Sinchon-Dong and then dispersed into the hills in small groups.

Strong combat patrols were sent to the front daily to gain and maintain contact with the enemy. A patrol led by Lt. Ralph D. Terrell, Company B, reported seeing two men wearing blue uniforms with black boots and some type of piping on little blue caps. The patrol also reported Chinese in the village of Sojinbyon and on the south bank of the river.

On Nov. 10th, a patrol from Company G was engaged by an estimated enemy platoon using machine gun and semi-automatic fire from the high ground north of the river. The entire patrol was brought under fire while in an open rice paddy, and after all 57mm ammunition was expended, the gun was destroyed, and the patrol withdrew. Twenty men returned, including one man wounded; however, the officer in charge of the patrol and 17 men failed to return.

Patrols from the 3rd Battalion crossed the river and patrolled northward for approximately three miles; however, this patrol later was ordered to return to investigate signs in the sand along the river observed from an air liaison plane, indicating the presence of American wounded. The patrol returned to this point and searched an area extending 500 yards along the river bank and found signs, but no trace of Americans in the area. The men who had written in the sand were from the Company G patrol and had managed to return without help; however, the 3rd Battalion patrol then came under heavy mortar fire and was forced to withdraw. While crossing the river, they sustained one wounded.

Late on the night of the 10th, orders were received for a general attack across the Chongchon River to begin the following day. Three successive phase lines were to be seized, the last being an east-west line north of the walled city of Yongbyon.

The regimental attack northward began on the morning of Nov. 11th with the 2nd Battalion leading the attack across the river. The three battalions met little resistance, and on the morning of Nov. 14th, Company I, reinforced by two platoons of tanks from Company C, 70th Tank Battalion, entered Yongbyon without opposition and secured the town and its principal approaches.

One vehicle of the I&R platoon, while on a mission to contact the 3rd Battalion, 19th Infantry Regiment, struck a mine of the wooden-box type. Three men, one of whom later died, were injured seriously. The driver of the vehicle was able to walk under his own power, although he was suffering from shock. First Lt. Richard B. Talbert, I&R Platoon leader, displayed exceptional courage and complete disregard for his on safety by entering the mine field and removing the wounded men despite the great danger.

The mission of the regiment for the next few days was consolidating the Yongbyon area and securing of the Division's left flank to permit an advance to the north by the infantry regiments on the east flank.

A 3rd Battalion patrol, consisting of one reinforced platoon supported by two tanks, made a 4,000-yard penetration into enemy territory to rescue three soldiers of the First Cavalry Division reported by civilians on Nov. 16th. These soldiers had escaped from the "Lost Battalion" of the 8th Cavalry Regiment and had been sheltered and fed by a friendly Korean at Ha-Dong but were suffering from exposure. Two of them were wounded

First Chinese Prisoners. Some of them were possible within the attacking enemy forces that brought devastation to the 8th Cavalry Regiment during the Unsan battle on November 1-4, 1950. (U.S. Army Photo)

and were given treatment at the regimental aid station and were evacuated.

During the next few days, contact with the enemy was all but lost. It appeared that the enemy forces had withdrawn toward the Yalu River, and faint hopes were raised that the "Chinese Volunteers" had returned across the Manchurian border - 60 miles to the north.

On Nov. 20th, the Regimental I&R platoon formed a motorized patrol and proceeded to Ipsok and Pyong-Dong, only 45 miles from the Manchurian border. An estimated enemy company was encountered in the hills north of Pyong-Dong, and a fierce fire fight took place that forced the platoon to withdraw. Two men were missing in action, two men were wounded and two jeeps destroyed. The enemy was reported dressed in American field jackets and American steel helmets!

The patrol leader - Lt. Richard B. Talbert - reported that false information was given to the patrol by hostile civilians at Ipsok and Pyong-Dong. He again distinguished himself by remaining as rear guard until the remainder of his patrol had withdrawn. Later reconnaissance by the Air Force revealed approximately 1,500 enemy troops 3,000 yards east of the scene of the fire fight.

At approximately 1945 hours the same day, elements of Company L, supported by mortar fire from Company M were successful in driving off an enemy patrol of unknown strength near their positions. Enemy patrol action forced abandonment of the regimental shower point, and the 2nd Battalion was ordered to send a reinforced patrol to recover and secure the shower point. The patrol encountered some resistance from an estimated enemy squad. Elements of Company H employed light machine guns and 75mm recoilless rifle fire against the enemy who dispersed and fled to the southwest. One rifle squad, reinforced with a section of machine guns and one 75mm recoilless rifle squad, was left to guard the shower point area.

The regiment was ordered to occupy the high ground north of Yongbyon, and movement began at 1300 hours on the 21st. By evening, the 1st and 2nd Battalions had closed in their new positions, and the 3rd Battalion - organized as Task Force Hallden - had closed in its staging area for Operation Nightingale. (This operation was designed to search out the area adjacent to the site of the 8th Cavalry's ambush at Unsan for survivors. The area was by this time several thousand yards deep in enemy-held territory.)

On Nov. 22nd, 27 men, including 19 from the 8th Cavalry Regiment and seven from elements of the 24th Division, came into the 3rd Battalion Headquarters. They received medical treatment and were evacuated through medical channels. The men had been prisoners of the Chinese Communists for approximately 15 days and reported that they had been released as a propaganda gesture and that there were many more American prisoners in the Yalu River area.

All patrols from Task Force Hallden in execution of Operation Nightingale accomplished their missions without incident. No additional American survivors were found, but two South Korean soldiers from the II ROK Corps who had been hiding in the hills were rescued. Two men were wounded in the operation. One patrol later encountered resistance from 120mm and 60mm mortars, small arms, and automatic weapons fire from the high ground north and west of Sangcho-Dong. An estimated two enemy companies were entrenched in this area and were taken under artillery and mortar fire.

A bountiful Thanksgiving meal was enjoyed by all units in the historic walled city of Yongbyon on Nov. 23rd. Col. Harris, the regimental commander, visited each company mess to extend Thanksgiving Day greetings. Later in the day, the relief of the regiment began by elements of the 25th Infantry Division and the regiment assembled in the vicinity of Kunu-ri on Nov. 24th as part of the Eighth Army reserve.

The Army historian wrote: "On the eve of the Eighth Army offensive - Thursday, Nov. 23 - the Americans enjoyed a traditional Thanksgiving Day dinner. They were served shrimp cocktail, stuffed olives, sweet pickles, roast young tom turkey, sage dressing, giblet gravy, cranberry sauce, candied sweet potatoes, mashed potatoes, buttered corn, green peas, fresh baked bread and butter, pumpkin and mince pies, fruitcake, candies, nuts, oranges and apples. Some units also got a ration of whiskey; others were provided hot showers and a change of uniform."

In the rear-area position in Army reserve, Hap Gay took advantage of the holiday to hold regimental parades and to award medals. It was a stirring moment in the First Cavalry. The regimental adjutants read off battle streamers. Makeshift bands played sentimental divisional and regimental songs: "She Wore a Yellow Ribbon" and "GARRYOWEN." It was cold: 15 degrees.

On Nov. 26th, while in Army reserve near Kunu-ri, a regimental review was held for the purpose of awarding decorations of valor and in remembrance of those who had given their lives in Korea. This was the first time since the regiment had landed in Korea that Col. Harris had been provided an opportunity to speak to the entire regiment in one assembly. In a moving address, he paid tribute to the numerous "firsts" that GARRYOWEN had accomplished in the past decade. Col. Harris called attention to the fact that these firsts had been made possible by the teamwork of all concerned. He expressed his appreciation for the exploits of the regiment, and called for a further expression of devotion to duty in the days to come.

The awards were made by Gen. Gay. Chaplain Frank R. Griepp read the 23rd Psalm following 60 seconds of silence for the honored dead. A bugler intoned taps, and Chaplain Francis McCullough read the names of the men receiving posthumous awards. The ceremony concluded with a prayer by Chaplain Emanuel Carlsen.

Immediately following the review, the Regimental Combat Team was ordered to proceed to an assembly area in the vicinity of Kujong-ni, and to be prepared for operations to the north or northeast, and the GARRYOWENs moved quickly from the review field to the battlefield.

Soon after the Regimental Combat Team got into position, plans were made on Nov. 28th to move to Pukchang-ni, secure that area to protect the Eighth Army's east flank, and to cover the reorganization of the II ROK Corps, which had been driven back by continuous heavy enemy attacks. Liaison was established with the II ROK Corps and close liaison maintained with the 6th ROK Division north to the vicinity of Walpo-ri where the ROK Army was reorganizing to establish defensive positions.

During the early morning hours of Nov. 29th, large numbers of ROK troops began withdrawing through the regimental Combat Team's perimeter, hotly pursued by Chinese Communist forces - many dressed in civilian clothing and posing as refugees. The regimental perimeter became involved in the fire fight in the 1st and 2nd Battalion sectors. First Lt. John E. Sheehan, commanding Company E, was killed and five others were wounded by small arms fire as the 2nd Battalion roadblock attempted to stem the tide of refugees and enemy troops.

At 1000 hours, the Regimental Combat Team was ordered to move to Sinchang-ni to secure the vital road net there. This operation was to be executed following the withdrawal of the 6th ROK Division. The movement began at 1200 hours, and the last elements closed into the area as darkness fell over the tired, cold and hungry troops of GARRYOWEN.

After the withdrawal of the ROK II Corps, the entire left flank of the Eighth Army's positions was exposed. A strong Chinese Community Army was rapidly moving southward in an effort to trap the Eighth U.S. Army before it could withdraw further south. The regiment's mission at Sinchang-ni was to stop this enemy force to permit the withdrawal of the Eighth Army. To accomplish this mission, the 2nd Battalion was placed on the left side of the main road leading into Sinchang-ni and the 1st Battalion on the right. The 3rd Battalion - in reserve - and the regimental headquarters were located southwest of the town approximately three miles. Companies F and C joined on the road leading into the town. At 2100 hours on Nov. 29th, these positions were attacked by a Chinese Communist division marching in a column of regiments down the main road. The following is a description of the fierce battle that ensued - the first major engagement between the GARRYOWENs and the Chinese Communist forces.

Using bugle calls and whistles, the enemy struck the right platoon of Company F and the left platoon of Company C with an overwhelming attack. Company F's roadblock was overrun immediately and a column of approximately 150 enemy troops marched single file down the road toward Sinchang-ni. The 2nd Battalion's command post was located in a police headquarters on the outskirts of the town nearest the front line positions. Members of the Headquarters Company, 2nd Battalion, set up three machine guns, including a .50-caliber machine gun and cut the enemy column down like cornstalks. Before enemy reinforcements could reach the area, the command post was moved to a school house further into the town. However, the 2nd Battalion

aid station was filled with wounded and could not be moved. All available personnel were left to guard the aid station while Capt. John C. Rourke, the battalion surgeon, continued to treat and evacuate the wounded as the battle raged in the street outside. The Headquarters Company personnel had stopped the enemy thrust into town, but sporadic small arms fire continued throughout the town for the remainder of the night.

Meanwhile, heavy fighting was taking place in the 1st Battalion area where the brunt of the attack was concentrated. At approximately 2200 hours, Company C became engaged in an intense fire fight and after a short period, the platoon on the left flank commanded by Lt. William Marslander was overrun.

By midnight, the enemy had penetrated the regimental perimeter in force, and the command post of the 1st Battalion was under heavy attack. A fierce fire fight, marked by the use of automatic weapons, head-to-head fighting and hand grenades ensued. The 1st Battalion Headquarters group with elements of Companies C and D withdrew to the southeast approximately 1,000 yards and established a defense line. This group, using automatic weapons, accurate mortar and artillery fire falling within 100 yards of their position, managed to drive off the enemy.

At 2200 hours, the 3rd Battalion, which was in regimental reserve, was informed of the penetration along the main road into Sinchang-ni. Two tanks from Company C, 70th Tank Battalion, and a section of heavy machine guns from Company M were attached to Company L, Lt. Franklin A. Bristol commanding, and ordered to counterattack to restore the lines. The counterattack drove to the perimeter in the vicinity of the former Company F positions despite intense mortar fire. The counterattacking force then was directed to proceed to the 1st Battalion command post area to search for wounded to restore the

front line by morning. At 0200 hours, Company L began its counterattack using marching fire and arrived at the objective after killing many of the enemy. Then, an estimated enemy platoon launched a last desperate attack against the exposed left flank of Company L. A diamond formation with jeep-mounted machine guns from Company M was used to drive off the attack.

At approximately 0300 hours, a trooper from the 1st Battalion made his way into the 2nd Battalion command post and reported that he had escaped encirclement and had heard the enemy blowing bugles and whistles and that he saw them assembling on the main road preparing to withdraw northward. Upon receiving this information, all available artillery fires were placed on the main road leading north from the town.

At daylight, Company L executed a sweeping patrol through the entire area, picking up enemy prisoners and friendly wounded, and by 0700 hours the regimental perimeter was restored.

Known enemy casualties were 350 killed within the Regimental Combat Team perimeter and 1,250 more were believed killed by artillery fire outside the perimeter. The enemy unit that made the deepest penetration was identified as the 374th Regiment, 125th Division, 42nd Chinese Community Army - an elite spearhead group of the Chinese Communist Forces.

Regimental casualties during this action were 38 killed, 107 wounded and 11 missing in action.

Among other incidents that occurred during this action was when Maj. William L. Cochrane, regimental S-2, was dispatched to the rear at about 2200 hours to lead the counterattacking force forward. While enroute to alert the 3rd Battalion, he jeep was hit by an enemy grenade that killed his driver and knocked Maj. Cochrane unconscious. He was found about 0400 the following morning by a passing medical jeep, cold,

Actual enemy photo of the first Chinese Communist Forces crossing the Yalu River in early October 1950. (Photo courtesy of John Cauley)

shaken up and barefooted. The enemy had taken his identification tags and combat boots and had left him for dead.

At the time, the 1st Battalion's command post was overrun, Lt. Charles M. Coin, assistant battalion surgeon, was in his aid station located in a Korean house. Suddenly, five enemy troops burst into the room and a hand-to-hand struggle ensued. One of the enemy sprayed the room with his "burp gun," killing the enemy soldier struggling with Lt. Coin. The lieutenant feigned dead, and as soon as the enemy cleared the area, he rejoined his battalion.

Bugle calls and whistle signals were used throughout this attack. It was reported that the Chinese spoke English when approaching our positions, thereby confusing the front line troops, particularly in the darkness. These tactics were repeated many times later during the Korean War.

Lt. Edward Daily, 1st Platoon Leader, Company H, 2nd Battalion, remembers:

"During Nov. 29th, the refugee problem was merely one of many confronting the 2nd Battalion. It was the coldest day since our arrival in Korea. The temperature had dropped to near zero. Disorganized South Korean soldiers from the 19th Regiment, 6th ROK Division were withdrawing through our defensive positions, and many civilians had mingled in with them. This created a constant threat because of the enemy posing as a refugee could possibly pass through our blocking positions without being noticed. Rumors prevailed that some of the enemy were capable of speaking English.

My company commander, Capt. John B. Wadsworth, had ordered my platoon to assist in establishing blocking positions on the main road to Sinchang-ni and support elements to other units within the 2nd Battalion. To assist in the most forward position, a 57mm recoilless rifle team was provided from Company F by orders of its commander, Capt. Arthur Truxes.

One thing I had noticed was the extreme forward location of the command post tent of Company F. I calmly asked Capt. Truxes if he was going to move and relocate his command post on further down the road and near Sinchang-ni. He quickly answered, 'What in the hell are you talking about, Lieutenant? I'm staying right here

where all the damn action and fighting is going to be!'' Indeed, these were the words of a very brave officer. (I eventually learned that when the Chinese made their initial attack and penetration of the breakthrough, Capt. Truxes was killed in action while defending his position.)

At the command post of Company H, Capt. Wadsworth indicated from reports that a Chinese Communist Division was within our area. Due to the overall crisis in the battalion, I was ordered to keep in close contact with the company. Sgt. 1st Class Harold Blanc, our Communications Sergeant, was ordered to return with me to the main blocking position to double check all wiring.

The captain provided us with a jeep (H-3), which was equipped with an SCR-300 radio. Sgt. Blanc secured from the mess personnel, a thermal container of hot chow to take with us for the troopers on the main blocking position. Prior to departing, we looked at our watches, and it was almost 2100 hours. As the jeep driver proceeded to take us northward, it was not necessary to use the headlights because the moon was extremely bright.

Shortly up the road, we suddenly heard strange sounds of bugles and whistles within the dark night. Then bright purple flares were roar-

ing high in the sky and popping loudly. We stopped the jeep, and I immediately went to the rear of the vehicle to use the radio. My radio contact with Sgt. Simmons was very brief because he quickly informed me that we were under a vicious and massive enemy attack, and they already had penetrated the right flank.

Then, without an incoming sound, a mortar round hit and exploded in the road behind me, which sent whining shrapnel, debris and dirt through the air of the cold winter night. All I remember was a very bright flash, and I found myself laying in a frozen rice paddy. As I attempted to crawl to the road to check on the jeep driver and Sgt. Blanc, I soon realized that all hell had broken loose.

The night was a panoramic view of exploding artillery and mortar rounds, with tracers of pink and green color endlessly searching for their targets. Once on the road, I soon discovered that the jeep driver had been killed from a severe head wound. By the grace of God, Sgt. Blanc managed to escape injury and death. Shrapnel from the mortar round hit the spare tire and ripped it off the support bracket of the jeep. He had been resting his back on the spare tire at the time of the mortar round explosion, and all that

Actual enemy photo of the Chinese Communist Forces attacking the defensive positions of the United Nations Forces. (Photo courtesy of John Cauley)

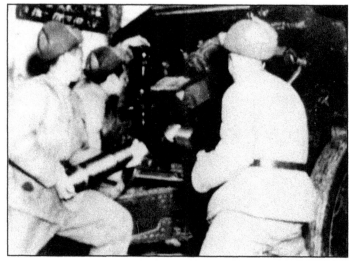

Actual enemy photo of Chinese Communist Forces artillery, firing on positions of the United Nations Forces. (Photo courtesy of John Cauley)

Actual enemy photo of the United Nations Forces attacking a defensive position of the Chinese Communist Forces. Note torn enemy guidon! (Photo courtesy of John Cauley)

Trooper carrying .30 caliber light machine gun during snow storm. (U.S. Army Photo)

Frozen bodies of American Marines in November 1950. The Winter was very severe during their withdrawal. British commandos and South Korean soldiers are gathered for group burial at Koto-ri. (U.S. Marine Corps Photo)

The Marines reclaimed all of their dead on the retreat from Changjin Reservoir. Chinese soldiers stripped clothing from many of the bodies. (U.S. Marine Corps Photo)

Sgt. Blanc received from the ordeal was a sore back and a headache.

I managed to move forward along the edge of the road to possibly come into contact with the troopers of my platoon. Soon I found the position of Cpl. Mack Bentley, a first gunner from my platoon, who was blasting away at the right flank with his .30-caliber machine gun. Then to arrive was 1st Sgt. Bob Earley of Headquarters Company, and he informed us that an attempt would be made to restore our link-up with the 1st Battalion on the right flank. At this location, the 2nd Battalion was holding its position under the most severe conditions of combat.

First Sgt. Bob Earley was an excellent soldier in Japan, and he proved himself to be a very brave individual in a critical situation of combat. He then suggested that I go to the 2nd Battalion aid station, and he would try to help the situation in the 1st Platoon; and he also would notify Capt. Wadsworth of the circumstances. (However, at this location all communications were lost.) By now my wounds were giving me a lot of pain, so I decided to make the journey to the aid station. Sgt. Earley and I wished each other the best as I departed.

Shortly down the road, I couldn't believe what I was seeing. Many Chinese soldiers were laying on both sides of the road like a line of dominoes, head to toe. Their bodies were torn to pieces, and some were still alive as the outcry of pain sometimes carried above the sounds of battle. I couldn't understand where all these dead and wounded enemy soldiers came from. At one point, I thought perhaps I was going in the wrong direction. (I eventually learned that these enemy soldiers made the breakthrough and had marched down the road and were cut down like cornstalks.)

I finally reached the 2nd Battalion aid station, which was a house in the town of Sinchang-ni. A lot of havoc was being caused by sporadic enemy fire from various houses in the town. Inside the aid station, I was processed quickly by Capt. John C. Rourke, 2nd Battalion Surgeon, who was knee-deep in wounded troopers from the GARRYOWEN regiment. Words cannot express the critical situation that existed at this particular time and how admirably Capt. Rourke and his entire medical staff performed throughout this vicious combat ordeal.

Eventually, I was loaded on a 2-1/2-ton truck with many other wounded personnel of the 7th Cavalry and transported to the 121st Evacuation Hospital in Ascom City, South Korea. After five to six weeks of recuperating at a Swedish hospital in Pusan, I volunteered to return to the heroic 7th Cavalry Regiment in early January 1951.

The great success of the 7th Cavalry Regiment in the battle of Sinchang-ni, can be attributed to several reasons. The excellent coordination of artillery support to an infantry unit. Support by the 3rd Battalion to the 1st and 2nd Battalions and their combined fighting Seventh spirit to win the battle. It was the decision and orders of Lt. Col. John W. Callaway, 2nd Battalion Commander, to unload the 105mm ammunition trucks and to use them to transport the critically wounded. This emergency evacuation plan helped to save lives. The dedication and devotion to duty by Capt. John C. Rourke, 2nd Battalion Surgeon, and his entire medical staff and aid men in their attempt to save lives of the wounded troopers, against overwhelming odds. It was a true example of the GARRYOWEN Espirit de Corps.

Capt. John C. Rourke, Battalion Surgeon for the 2nd Battalion, 7th Cavalry Regiment, remembers: "My memory of that night is vivid and enduring. The time element between 2100 hours of Nov. 29 through 0400 hours on Nov. 30 was some of the most intensely busy and frantic hours of my military service as a battalion surgeon.

The Chinese Communists attacked in force at 2100 hours and very quickly proceeded to overrun the 1st Battalion Command Post and Aid Station. My 2nd Battalion Aid Station was located in a small house on the edge of town and very near the enemy assault. It was an actual collecting point for all wounded personnel from both battalions.

Because of the rapid advance of the forward elements of the enemy assault, we were being endangered with the possibility of the enemy overrunning our aid station. We were overwhelmed quickly with a number of wounded, and many of them were very serious. The Chinese attack penetrated to within the edge of town and only yards away from my aid station.

Fortunately, the 2nd Battalion Headquarters Company under the direction of Lt. Col. John W. Callaway, 2nd Battalion Commander, expediently set-up an interior defense line at the edge of the town to repel the attacking enemy forces.

Many personnel were directed to immediately establish defensive positions very near my aid station. A heavy .50-caliber machine gun and two other .30-caliber light machine guns were deployed to stop the advance of the enemy column. The Chinese thrust was stopped, and most of their forward point elements were destroyed. However, intense firing from the interior block by the 2nd Battalion forces continued for many hours. Sporadic small arms fire from within the town of Sinchang-ni could be heard throughout the night.. This indicated that small numbers of the Chinese had actually reached the town.

Immediate organizational plans for operating the aid station was to receive and examine and decide on urgency of treatment of each wounded as he arrived at the front door of the small house. The doors and windows of the house had been covered with Army blankets to black out the inside. There was no furniture, no electric lights or lanterns, so we had to make use of hand-held flashlights. Many numbers of the seriously wounded were treated with control of external bleeding and given morphine for relief of pain as necessary. They then were bundled in blankets on a stretcher to keep them as warm as possible. They immediately were transferred to the back rooms of the house for further processing.

Fortunately, the house was as warm as toast because of its design, where a fire in the ground level of the kitchen had converted hot heat beneath the floor of the house for warmth. This was a very useful thing.

It prevented shock patients from getting worse by chilling. The outside temperature was bitter cold and estimated to be about zero degrees. The night was unusually bright and clear with little wind blowing. There was a very bright moonlight that enabled us to see better than normal at this particular time and hour.

Those wounded who might be called 'walking wounded' or 'ambulatory' with wounds in the extremities or wounds that allowed them to get out on their own, were treated as quickly as possible with appropriate dressings and immobilization of the wounded part. However, it was decided not to give them much for relief of pain in order not to convert an ambulatory soldier into a drugged or sleeping one who would then be incapable of moving on his own accord. The prime reason for this was just in case the aid station was overrun.

As the numbers mounted, my aid station team was divided into an ambulatory group to take the numerous walking-wounded out into a deep frozen ditch, which was located behind the house and ran parallel to the road. This task was done after the necessary treatment was completed by the doctor. This was necessary because there was not enough space in the small house, and we could disburse the wounded in the event of mortar fire. Furthermore, it allowed them the opportunity to take care of themselves in the event we were overwhelmed by the enemy.

One of the biggest problems was the lack of transportation because the aid station was supplied with four jeeps, and each one was equipped with two litters to carry the more seriously wounded to the rear area. These rapidly filled vehicles, sometimes had the ambulatory wounded riding the hood or holding on anyway possible to accompany the seriously wounded for further medical treatment.

It was not known at the time if any enemy roadblocks or patrols existed at the rear where the jeeps had to travel. Our medical clearing station was approximately two or three miles to the rear. The many trips that were required to transport the wounded became extremely long after the first rush. The vehicle shortage became critical, and soon there were no jeeps available from my aid station to transport the seriously wounded.

By midnight, there were 27 or 28 seriously wounded laying on stretchers on the floor of the aid station. Most of them were sleeping because of the morphine, and many were on the verge of surgical shock. There was little or nothing to treat this specific problem. The only intravenous fluids available were two units of plasma. These units consisted of two glass bottles with dry plasma in one and the other contained sterile salt water solution to reconstitute the dry material into usable form. However, both of the liquid containers were frozen solid and could not be thawed, due to the extremely cold weather.

At approximately 0100 hours, we still had the 27 or 28 seriously wounded, but we also had 30 or 40 ambulatory wounded in the large ditch at the rear of the aid station. By this time, I already had received three direct orders to move the aid station out of this forward and dangerous location. However, I could not do so because of the inability to move the wounded personnel.

Finally, between 0100 and 0200 hours, the nearby situation became clarified when Lt. Col. John W. Callaway, 2nd Battalion Commander, stopped by to see me. He recognized the predicament and arranged through other sources to have four or five 2-1/2-ton trucks dispatched immediately from our supporting artillery units. These trucks previously had carried artillery ammunition but were very quickly unloaded and then rushed to our situation to help evacuate the wounded.

Once this was accomplished, and I don't how many trucks were used, but we eventually were able to get all of the stretchers and ambulatory wounded evacuated to the rear area. By 0300 hours, we were then able to move the id station and its personnel further to the rear, which was a school house that was located next to the 2nd Battalion Headquarters. Throughout the early morning, the wounded personnel were continued to be brought in, but nothing like the first hour of battle.

From the book, "Of GARRYOWEN and Glory," by Melbourne C. Chandler, it is recorded that the casualties of Sinchang-ni were, 38 killed in action; 107 wounded in action; and 11 missing in action. Some of the missing turned out to be prisoners of war of the Chinese Communists. Cpl. Carl J. Bafs, a combat aidman from my aid station had been assigned as an outpost guard to the aid station during the battle. The other two were Master Sgt. Earl Early and Sgt. Glen Bumgarner from the Weapons Platoon of Company F.

After daybreak, the area of battle was screened carefully, which revealed more wounded and dead who were brought to the collecting point near the aid station. By midmorning, I was able to accompany Lt. Col.. John W. Callaway, 2nd Battalion Commander, on a reconnaissance back to the roadway north of my aid station and up the road to the open field where the enemy assault was stopped.

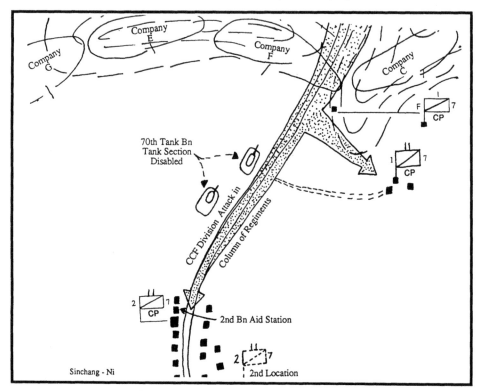

Battle at Sinchang-Ni, Night of November 29-30, 1950.

There were hundreds of dead Chinese laying on the road between the aid station area and the northward perimeter line where Companies C and F were located previously. We did not go further north of this point, but we were informed that beyond the outer perimeter of the 7th Cavalry Regiment, there were more than 1,200 enemy dead. These enemy soldiers had been caught or trapped by our extensive artillery barrages as they attempted to flee northward. This was an example of how valuable the field artillery can be when used effectively.

In summary, the aid station personnel were able to perform well and adequately under very dangerous circumstances. The greatest problem confronting us that very hectic night may be listed as follows: first, the 374th Regiment, 125th Chinese Division of the 42nd Chinese Communist Army, in the desperate attempt to destroy the 7th Cavalry Regiment defenses; second, the extremely cold and below freezing temperatures were seriously injurious to the wounded personnel and immobilized many; thirdly, the difficulties with coordinating the need for transportation to serve the overwhelming flood of wounded during the early part of the battle.

I'm very proud of what the regiment was able to accomplish, and I'm very honored to have been a part of that service. There are many who deserve credit for our victorious outcome that night and early morning battle at Sinchang-ni on Nov. 29th-30th, 1950.

First, of course, was the excellent leadership in the regiment and battalions and their ability to quickly and effectively respond to a very dangerous situation. I commend the many brave troopers who fought bitterly and to those who made the ultimate sacrifice; and finally, I recall the great effort that was put forth by the many aidmen and stretcher bearers who are the very front line of medical care in combat. Many times they are unsung heroes, but are the angels of mercy dressed in khaki."

Col. (then Major) John W. Callaway, 2nd Battalion Commander, 7th Cavalry Regiment, remembers the night of Nov. 29-30, 1950, and the critical situation. His story about the "Unsung Hero of the Battle of Sinchang-ni" is as follows:

"To understand the role of this individual, it is necessary to review his background in Korea up to the time of the battle of Sinchang-ni. Lt. Col. Gilman Huff was Commanding Officer of the 2nd Battalion of the 7th Cavalry Regiment when it was deployed to Korea. After a short period in Korea, Lt. Col. Huff became ill and was evacuated to Japan. His executive officer, Maj. Hitchner, assumed command and was killed on or about 6 Sept. 1950, at which time Maj. John W. Callaway was transferred from the 5th Cavalry Regiment to assume command of the 2nd Battalion of the 7th Cavalry Regiment. Around Oct. 5, Lt. Col. Huff returned to the 2nd Battalion and assumed command. Maj. Callaway became Executive Officer. In the next day or so, the battalion made a river crossing over the Yesong River. During this battle, Lt. Col. Huff suffered a bullet wound through the fleshy part of his chest and was evacuated. Maj. Callaway again took command, and the battalion continued the attack across the river and seized the town of Paekchon, which was across the 38th Parallel and into North Korea. While not a main axis into North Korea, it is believed that the 2nd Battalion was the first unit of the allied forces to enter North Korea.

Several weeks later, Lt. Col. Huff rejoined the Battalion. Due to his wound, his arm was in a sling, and he was somewhat limited in his physical activities. For this reason, he had Maj. Callaway remain with him at the forward command post, and Maj. Chandler continued the duties of the Executive Officer of the Battalion.

On the afternoon of Nov. 29 at Sinchang-ni as the 2nd Battalion Companies were going into their defensive positions, word came over the radio from nearby observation planes that thousands of Chinese soldiers were converging in an area about 10 miles up the valley from the regiment's defensive positions. Request for air strikes could not be approved because all available fighter aircraft were on other priority missions.

Maj. Callaway checked on all the Company positions, while Lt. Col. Huff had the Battalion Artillery Liaison Officer preplan a number of concentration points from in front of the lines out to the maximum effective range of the artillery. These artillery concentration points were primarily in the valley that extended some 15 miles northeast of the regiment's positions.

The enemy struck shortly after dark against the right platoon of F Company and the left company of the 1st Battalion. This was the signal for Lt. Col. Huff to order the artillery fire. The enemy could not be seen, but Lt. Col. Huff's instinct told him that the enemy was concentrated in the valley and was walking toward the 7th Cavalry Regimental positions. He had his artillery liaison officer move the artillery concentrations from in front of the battalion lines as far up the valley as its effective range permitted and then bring it back. Thousands of rounds were expended and VT fuses were used, which meant the rounds would explode about 10 feet in the air and spray the area with deadly shrapnel.

The enemy managed to break through the front lines, and a number of the soldiers began to withdraw. Maj. Callaway gathered up these troops plus members of the battalion headquarters and a tank that had withdrawn. He formed a second line of defense across the valley. Shortly thereafter, a column of men were seen walking down the road. Maj. Callaway ordered one of the soldiers to challenge the column, assuming that the soldier knew the password for that day. The soldier from his prone position shouted: 'Are you GI?' At that instant, an enemy bugle from the column sounded! It was if a command had been given to commence fire. All weapons in the backup line opened fire at once. The enemy column appeared to fade away. After about 15 seconds, Maj. Callaway ordered 'Cease Fire,' and all was quiet. The enemy column had been caught by surprise. The next morning more than 75 enemy dead were counted, having been killed where they were in the column.

Meanwhile, Lt. Col. Huff kept the artillery walking up and down the valley. Maj. Callaway received a call from a member of the regimental staff to counterattack and return about 500 yards to the original positions of F Company. Maj. Callaway objected to this order because he was in a strong position and was tied into a company from the 3rd Battalion, which was in reserve. At that point, Col. Harris, the regimental commander, came on the phone and explained that the regi-

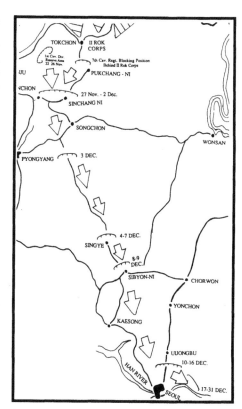

The Chinese Communist Offensive - In response to a limited United Nations Offensive, the Chinese Reds launched their first full-scale attack on 26 November, and quickly shattered the II ROK Corps in the center of the line. United Nations forces then began a series of withdrawals that carried them below the 38th parallel before the end of 1950.

ment had lost contact with the 1st Battalion Command Post and wanted Maj. Callaway to take his reserve troops and counterattack. Sporadic firing of small arms could be heard, but little else except for the artillery blasts beyond the front lines. Maj. Callaway ordered marching fire, and this reserve group of soldiers made their way back to the F Company front lines with no casualties and took up defensive positions. This probably was the first time that U.S. troops had counterattacked the Chinese.

Lt. Col. Huff's continually ordering artillery fire met with some resistance from the artillery command because the numbers of rounds fired depleted their stocks, and the pieces were overheated from the rapidity and large numbers fired. Moreover, due to the darkness, results could not be evaluated. Despite this concern, Lt. Col. Huff prevailed, and the artillery continued until daylight.

This large enemy force had been stopped, and it suffered enormous casualties, primarily because of Lt. Col. Huff's direction of the division artillery on the enemy attempting a move down the valley. More than 350 known enemy casualties were found within the perimeter. The pilots from the observation planes estimated that the number of dead Chinese soldiers outside the perimeter was more than 1,250. Gen. Walker, Commanding General of Eighth Army, later stated that this action by the regiment not only inflicted severe casualties on the enemy, but gained Eighth Army at least four days of valuable time. It was a major factor in preventing the encirclement of United Nations Forces. The 7th Cavalry Regiment suffered 38 killed, 107 wounded and 11 missing in action.

The success of this battle was due primarily to Lt. Col. Huff who knew what the artillery could do and exploited it to the maximum. He is certainly the Unsung Hero of the critical battle of Sinchang-ni!"

From the book, "The Forgotten War," author Clay Blair wrote: *"Billy Harris' 7th Cavalry met the CCF due east of Sunchon, near Sinchang-ni on the night of Nov. 29-30. It was another shock. Harris was tightly buttoned up, with Pete Clainos' 1/7 on the right of the road, John Callaway's 2/7 on the left, James Lynch's 3/7 in reserve. The CCF 125th Division swarmed at the 1/7 and 2/7 about 9 p.m. The fighting was close and fierce and soon hand-to-hand. Both the 1/7 and 2/7 CPs were overrun and forced back.*

In this developing crisis, Billy Harris committed his reserve, Lynch's steady 3/7. Lynch came up with tanks and A/A vehicles blazing. So reinforced, the 1/7 and 2/7 managed to regroup and mount counterattacks, supported by the faithful howitzers of the 77th FAB, now commanded by Ross Lillard. A terrible slaughter ensued. By dawn, the 7th Cavalry's perimeter had been restored. Harris' men counted 350 CCF bodies inside the perimeter and estimated that another 1,250 lay immediately outside. The 7th Cavalry suffered 156 casualties, including 38 dead and 107 wounded."

Col. Frank Griepp, Chaplain, 7th Cavalry Regiment, remembers: *"My very first meeting with Col. "Wild Bill" Harris was at dusk the night of 29 Nov. 1950. I had been visiting some men at their outposts near Sinchang-ni when I ran into him, and we exchanged a few words. It turned out that a few hours later, those positions were attacked viciously by the 125th Chinese Division. By the command leadership of Col. Harris and all of his battalion commanders, and the stubborn*

fighting ability of the whole 7th Cavalry Regiment, those positions were held; thus keeping the main roads open for other Eighth Army units to begin that advance to the rear. I came out of that night with a tremendous respect for the command structure and the combat fighting ability of the GARRYOWEN Regiment."

In the aftermath of this tough fighting, Billy Harris became deeply worried about the health of his able 3/7 commander, James Lynch. *"He was blacking out, and he couldn't rest,"* Harris remembered. *"Both the regimental surgeon and chaplain came to me and suggested he needed relief. He had done a wonderful job, and I hated to lose him; but there was really no choice."* Reluctantly Harris called his old friend, the I Corps chief of staff, Rinaldo Van Brunt, and asked him to request Lynch through channels. Having won two DSCs - and the unprecedented two Presidential Unit Citations in the Pusan Perimeter for the 3/7 within two weeks - Lynch left the 7th Cavalry and joined the I Corps G-3 section. He was to rise to one-star general before retirement.

The Commanding General, Eighth Army, later stated that this action by the regiment not only inflicted severe casualties on the enemy, but gained the Eighth Army at least four days of valuable time and was a major factor in preventing the encirclement of United Nations Forces.

The 3rd Battalion, 8th Cavalry Regiment, and the Argyle and Sutherland Battalion, 27th British Commonwealth Brigade, were attached to the Regimental Combat Team on Dec. 1st, and a plan was initiated to withdraw to positions approximately six miles to the rear. Orders were issued to attack and destroy the enemy on Hill 335 and to prevent enemy movement to the west of an arbitrary north-south line. The first part of this mission was given the 3rd Battalion, 8th Cavalry, and the British Brigade.

The 3rd Battalion, 8th Cavalry, had driven off an estimated enemy platoon and closed in its position by 1845 hours. The British Brigade encountered extremely difficult terrain and did not close in its position during the night. However, the British Brigade patrolled the gap between the 3rd Battalion, 8th Cavalry, on its left and by 2100 hours, the remainder of the units in the Regimental Combat Team were in position.

The British Brigade closed in on their position on Hill 335, and the 3rd Battalion, 8th Cavalry, silenced the small arms fire at approximately 1100 hours on Dec. 2nd while straightening their lines. Two patrols were dispatched on a reconnaissance to determine the strength and location of the enemy; however, neither patrol found any evidence of enemy activity in their immediate area as the enemy had suffered too heavily during the previous engagement to follow the withdrawal of the RCT.

At 1715 hours on the 2nd, the Regimental Combat Team moved out in an attack to secure an eastern route of withdrawal. The 2nd Battalion seized the initial objective by 2030 hours against stubborn enemy resistance. A large enemy concentration massing for a counterattack against this objective was engaged by artillery fire and dispersed by 2130 hours.

At this point, a message was received from the First Cavalry Division stating that strong enemy concentrations had been reported along the eastern route of withdrawal and directing that the RCT withdrawal be made over a western route. The Regimental Combat Team changed its course toward a temporary assembly area at Tungyong-ni, making the 10-mile march by foot in a snow storm and across a half-frozen river. Numerous casualties resulted from frostbite and other foot ailments.

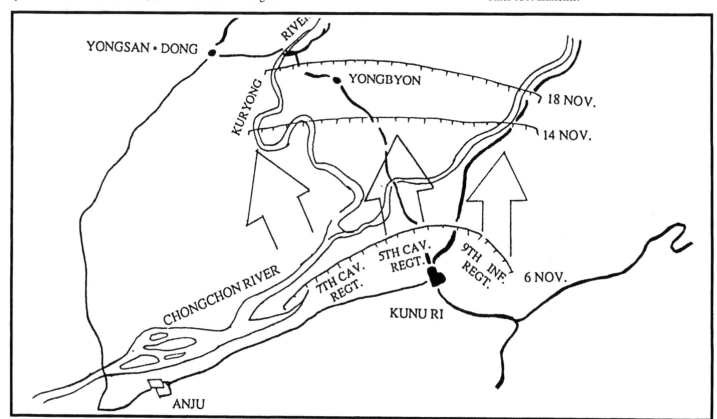

The Chongchon River Line - When the Reds failed to follow up their overwhelming attack against the 8th Cavalry Regiment, the 1st Cavalry Division occupied a defense line behind the Chongchon River. In mid-November, the Division advanced northward as far as Yongbyon meeting very little opposition.

CHAPTER VII
ADVANCE TO THE REAR

Early on Dec. 3rd, orders were received to move the Regimental Combat Team to a blocking position near Chongbong-ni to continue the protection of the east flank of the Eighth Army during its general retrograde movement. The regiment began the 98-mile retrograde movement to Chongbong-ni at 0930 hours on Dec. 4th, and continued throughout that night under extremely difficult conditions, over bad roads and through snow storms; however, on Dec. 5th, the Regimental ·Combat Team was ordered into a new assembly area and closed into Somaktong at 1150 hours.

The following day, the Regimental Combat Team began the long retrograde movement back to Seoul as the covering force for all other Eighth Army elements as far south as Pyongyang. Thereafter, the withdrawal followed the route Miudong - Sibyon-ni - Inchon.

The route back was disheartening to the troopers as they passed familiar landmarks, which only a few weeks earlier had been fought for and won with sweat, blood and lives. Now these same landmarks were being given up without a fight to the Communist hordes, and a long, slow march in the bitter cold weather only added to their despair. Southbound vehicles of every possible description lined the roads, bumper to bumper, as far a the eye could see. The tired, hungry and cold troopers - many had not been issued winter clothing - fell asleep whenever the long convoys stopped and had to be frequently awakened to keep the column moving.

The Regimental Combat Team arrived at 0200, Dec. 12th, at the assembly area near Nakponni - just north of Seoul, and the RCT formation disbanded. On Dec. 16th, the regiment moved east of Seoul, and for the remainder of the month prepared defensive positions, strung barbed wire entanglements, planted mines and generally prepared for the expected enemy onslaught. Patrols were sent out daily to locate and maintain contact with the pursuing Chinese Communist forces while smaller combat patrols combed the rear areas to clear out the guerrilla forces in the regimental zone.

On Dec. 19th, the Greek Expeditionary Force (GEF) was assigned as the 4th Battalion of the Regiment. This battalion - composed of a proud group of Greek combat veterans, just arrived from their native country, were assigned as a part of the United Nations Forces in Korea - was located south of Suwon. Members of the regimental staff departed on this date to welcome the battalion and to arrange for an orientation in operational and supply, and maintenance teams were sent to the 4th Battalion (GEF) to provide instructions in the operation and maintenance of U.S. equipment.

The 4th Battalion (GEF) - commanded by Lt. Col. D. Arbouzis, a veteran of more than 13 years combat experience - was a valuable addition to the combat strength of the United Nations Forces, and the GARRYOWENs welcomed them as part of the regiment.

On Dec. 23rd, Gen. Walker's jeep, siren screaming, had been speeding up the icy northbound lane of a highway that was jammed bumper

Colonel Frank Griepp, Regimental Chaplain, 7th Cavalry Regiment, in front of his office tent. (Courtesy of Col. Frank Griepp)

to bumper in the southbound lane with vehicles. A weapons carrier from the ROK 6th Division suddenly pulled out of the jammed-up southbound lane, directly into the path of Walker's jeep. Walker's driver, Master Sgt. George Belton, could not avoid a collision. Walker; his aide, Lt. Col. Layton C. Tynor; his bodyguard, Sgt. Francis S. Reenan; and Belton were thrown into a ditch. All four badly injured men were taken immediately to the nearby 8055th MASH unit. Walker was dead on arrival; the others survived and eventually were evacuated to hospitals in Japan.

Young Sam Walker was designated to escort his father's body back to the States. He did not return to the 19th Infantry. Posthumously promoted to four stars, Johnnie Walker was buried in Arlington National Cemetery. Sam, who later commanded a brigade in Vietnam and won further decorations, likewise rose to four stars, and upon retirement in 1978, he was appointed superintendent of VMI.

The news of Gen. Walker's death had reached MacArthur within minutes, and he in turn telephoned Joe Collins in Washington. The historian wrote: *"As had previously agreed between MacArthur and Collins, should anything happen to Walker, Lt. Gen. Matthew Bunker Ridgway was to succeed him as Eighth Army commander."*

Gen. Walker's death occurred at a turning point in the Korean War: the Chinese Communist Forces invasion of South Korea and the X Corps withdrawal from North Korea and consolidation into Eighth Army. Henceforth, the war to assume a more conventional shape, with opposing forces massed along a single conventional front.

Walker made many mistakes, especially in the early days of the war. However, Walker's insistence to Joe Collins that X Corps be brought around from Hungnam and incorporated into Eighth Army set the stage for Eighth Army's ultimate victory over the Chinese Communist Forces.

In Korea, Ridgway would prove to be an

Colonel Frank Griepp, Regimental Chaplain, 7th Cavalry Regiment, giving services on Jan. 30, 1951. (Courtesy of Col. Frank Griepp)

exception. His brilliant, driving, uncompromising leadership would turn the tide of battle like no other generals in our military history.

A hot dinner was served to all troops on Christmas Day and Col. William A. Harris - promoted to full colonel the previous day - visited all companies throughout the regiment to extend his personal holiday greetings.

On Dec. 30th, the 4th Battalion (GEF) took its place on the line with the regiment and its valiant deeds and heroic actions from this day forward in the Korean War area described in later actions.

The historian wrote: *"Cavalry morale in the 7th Cavalry had improved substantially, especially in the regimental CP. One reason was that Billy Harris now wore brand-new bird colonel insignia. Another reason was that the 7th Cavalry was reinforced substantially on Dec. 19. On*

1st Lt. Albert R. Moses, Commander, Company G, 2nd Bn., 7th Cavalry Regiment, January 1951. (Courtesy of Bob "Snuffy" Gray)

First Sergeant Walter T. Raisner, Company E, 2nd Bn., 7th Cavalry Regiment, February 1951. (Courtesy of Bob "Snuffy" Gray)

that day, the Greek Battalion became, in effect, a permanent 'fourth battalion. ' " The 7th Cavalry warmly embraced the Greeks in both body and spirit. The Greeks would remain permanently attached, giving the 7th Cavalry substantial added manpower and firepower. *"It was a superior outfit,"* Col. Clainos remembered. *"The Greeks were good fighters, . . . the officers were exceptional leaders."*

As the year drew to a close, the regiment was alerted for a possible counterattack against what appeared to be an imminent attack by the Chinese Communist Forces. The GARRYOWENs looked back on a year as eventful as any other single period in the regiment's history. It had been filled with the bloody battles along the Naktong River, Hills 518, 380, 314 and 300. It also was marked with success as the GARRYOWENs led the Eighth Army's drive into North Korea - the longest drive in the shortest period of time in the history of the American Army. These actions had not been accomplished without their toll - for less than one-half of the original number who had departed Japan six months earlier still remained with the regiment.

1951

The Chinese Communists ushered in the new year with a mass suicidal attack against the Republic of Korean (ROK) 2nd Infantry Division and the U.S. 24th Infantry Division deployed along the 38th Parallel. As the Chinese launched

their long awaited offensive, some units of the First Cavalry Division were withdrawn south of the Han River on New Year's Day. The 7th Cavalry Regiment was given the mission of covering all Eighth Army elements out of Seoul and was alerted to go to the aid of the hard-pressed 24th Infantry division - fighting desperately to slow the enemy's drive.

On Jan. 2nd-3rd, a couple of interesting articles appeared in the Stars and Stripes newspaper. One was by Virginia MacPherson who was the United Press Hollywood Correspondent. Her story was highlighted by: Fighting 7th Cavalry Picks "Sweetheart," and she wrote:

"Not even a tough war can make GIs in Korea forget about 'cheesecake.' The 7th Cavalry Regiment is battling it out with the Chinese Communists now, but they're mixing bullets with ballots to pick their official 'sweetheart.'

And the young lady who gets the title is a curvy 20-year-old redhead named Polly Bergen, who measures an eye-popping 38-24-36.

She's not very famous in Hollywood yet, but she hopes to be. And as far as the 7th Cavalry's concerned, she's their baby because her first big movie, Nat Holt's 'Warpath,' is all about the beginning of the regiment.

Col. W. A. Harris, commanding officer of the GARRYOWEN regiment, wrote from Korea that this selection was no small matter or no empty thing. 'Before the luscious Miss Bergen was accepted,' he said, 'her pictures were shown

to selected combat veterans, both officers and enlisted.' The Colonel hinted that it was the best scenery they've had to look at since they landed a Pohang-dong on July 22.

The Colonel said that the combat-weary veterans had to pick the official photograph by eyeing Miss Bergen's chassis in brief shorts and a tight sweater. And Polly wasn't wearing the GARRYOWEN insignia on her sweater. However, Col. Harris hastened to add, 'it wasn't the outside of the sweater that mattered.' "

The other Stars and Stripes article was headlined "Ridgway Visits First Cavalry." It emphasized what the new Eighth Army Commander said during his first visit to the battle-tested division. Lt. Gen. Matthew B. Ridgway said:

"We are here to determine whether the ultimate war will be fought in the United States or elsewhere. Every soldier must be made to know that we are not here just to save a small muddy village. This division had fought magnificently. You have written a chapter in American military history that will live forever."

During the first three days of Jan. 3rd-4th, preparations were made to evacuate the remaining elements of the Eighth Army south of the Han River. The regiment continued its rearguard mission as the last elements of the 24th Division withdrew from Seoul. At approximately 0400 hours, word was received that the last battalion, 5th Regimental Combat Team, was about to entruck, and the 7th Cavalry Regiment's 2nd

Battalion, 4th Battalion (GEF) and 1st Battalion were ordered to move by motor by way of Seoul bridge. The 3rd Battalion was to withdraw on foot by way of the Inchon bridge. By 0747 hours, all elements had cleared the Han River and were moving toward their assembly area in the vicinity of Konjuam-ni. The movement continued under extremely crowded road conditions and continued throughout the night of Jan. 4th.

The 4th Battalion (GEF) received its first casualty of the Korean War when a communications man froze to death during the night of Jan. 4th-5th. An appropriate ceremony was held and attended by Col. Harris, Gen. Allen, Maj. Gen. Frank Lowe, and representatives from all regimental units., Sgt. Thomas E. Randell, forward observer of the Heavy Motor Company, 7th Cavalry Regiment, remembers that bitter cold night, and he wrote:

"It was extremely difficult to dig in the frozen ground to build fortifications for a defensive position, which was approximately 12 miles southeast of Seoul. We kept busy filling sand bags and erecting bunkers deep enough to withstand an expected enemy artillery bombardment. Barbed wire had been placed in front of us to slow the human waves of Chinese that were expected to hit this section of the front-line.

A unit of the Greek Battalion were dug in here, and the hill was honeycombed with slit trenches and fox holes to provide cover from the bitter cold and impending Chinese onslaught. We were reasonably comfortable during our long night vigil because we had down-filled sleeping bags. However, the Greeks were trying to survive under the same miserable weather conditions with only Army blankets to fend off the zero temperature.

On our way off the hill in the morning for chow, we would rouse these Greek soldiers because their mess tent was located very near to ours. This particular morning, I was going through the same routine, and I called to wake up a Greek soldier in a slit trench, and he failed to respond. I crawled down and put my hand on his body to shake him awake. Needless to say, I soon discovered that he had frozen to death during the bitter cold night. I talked to one of their sergeants, and he attempted to tell me that the soldier had complained the previous day about stomach pains."

With the exception of necessary security measures, maximum effort was directed toward rest and rehabilitation for the next few days after nearly 70 hours of continuous movement.

On Jan. 7th, the 3rd Battalion was moved to the vicinity of Toesowon and Yobanae, and given the mission of refuge control in the Division zone. The thousands of refugees streaming southward to escape the Chinese Communist hordes constituted a traffic hazard and hampered tactical operations. The Taejon railroad was established as the main refugee artery route.

On the afternoon of the 9th, the battalion commanders and members of the regimental and battalion staffs conducted a reconnaissance for counterattack routes in planning for the regiment's counterattack mission as the IX Corps Reserve.

Logistics operations for the first 10 days of January were complicated by the bitter cold, the lack of supply routes, dense traffic and the narrow, icy, mountain roads. The ration and clothing supply points were located 78 miles from regimental headquarters and required six hours for trucks to travel each way. The ammunition supply point was located 70 miles from regimental headquarters and required four hours for trucks to travel each way.

The reconnaissance of the new positions and construction of a road into the 1st Battalion area continued despite 18° below zero temperatures, which froze two bulldozers. Counterattack plans were prepared and training and patrolling were conducted.

At 0900 hours on Jan. 24th, the regiment was formed into a RCT and moved to an initial assembly area near Changhowan-ni on the main line of resistance. Units began movement at 1900 hours from the initial assembly area to a tactical assembly area in the vicinity of Pabalmak and all units, with the exception of the 77th Field Artillery Battalion and the 3rd Battalion, 7th Cavalry Regiment, had closed prior to midnight. This operation - designed to conceal the concentration of the Regimental Combat Team below the line of departure - was characterized by extreme difficulties in getting transportation off the road due to the icy conditions. The road into the area ran over a built-up dike with few turn-offs. This condition, coupled with the fact that security permitted only limited daylight reconnaissance, combined to delay the concentration of the Regimental Combat Team. Although this concentration took place approximately 12 miles in front of the main line of resistance, there was no enemy contact; however, the 2nd Battalion, 5th Infantry Regiment, which was screening the area with patrols, sighted enemy patrols operating to the west of the RCT's assembly area.

Due to the absence of the enemy along the entire front, the Eighth Army commander scheduled a large reconnaissance in force - Operation Thunderbolt. Regimental units began moving by foot toward the line of departure prior to daylight on the 25th. The 4th Battalion (GEF) and the 3rd Battalion crossed the line of departure at 0730 hours. The operation progressed smoothly with the only resistance being the very difficult terrain. Strong combat patrols swept the entire area, and the sector was secure by 2230 hours. All battalions went into a tight perimeter defense in view of the extended frontages, and artillery and heavy mortars were registered on all logical approaches to the positions. The units settled down to await the enemy's expected reaction to this bold thrust - 20 miles deep in enemy territory. Ambushes were established in each battalion area in an attempt to capture enemy prisoners. Despite the fact that the adjacent regiment to the west came under heavy attack during the night, there was no attack against the 7th Cavalry's positions.

Bryant Moore's IX Corps attacked in concert with I Corps on the morning of Jan. 25th. The attack was spearheaded by the 1st Cavalry Division. Although Hap Gay still was present in Korea, his replacement, Charlie Palmer, conducted these operations.

Palmer, nicknamed Charlie Dog for his initials, was a rough, tough, demanding commander and strict disciplinarian. His first orders to his men were explicit and detailed. All bayonets were to be "well-sharpened." Any man found without a steel helmet would be punished. All outer garments (overcoats, jackets) were to be buttoned up at all times. No "foreign weapons" were to be utilized. All men on guard were to be "alert at all times" or suffer dire consequences. The Army historian explained: *"The command greatly needed something to symbolize the birth of a new spirit. Restoration of the bayonet, and a dramatizing of that action, was at one with the simple message given to the troops: 'The job is to kill Chinese.' Once men could be persuaded that those in other units were deliberately seeking hand-to-hand contest with the enemy, they would begin to feel themselves equal to the overall task. There can be no question about the efficacy of this magic in the particular situation: It WORKED!"*

During the early morning hours of Jan. 26th,

Attacking with the support of tanks from the 70th Tank Battalion. (U.S. Army photo)

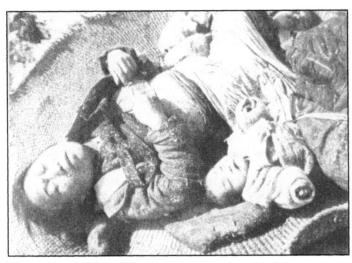

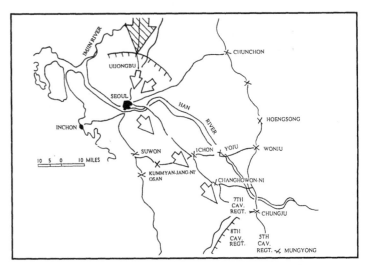

Thousands of refugees perished during the severe cold weather of 1950-51. Here a Korean mother and her two children, found frozen in a ditch at Osan, February 1951. (Irwin Tress-NPI, UPI)

In the face of an overwhelming New Year's Eve attack against Seoul, United Nations Forces withdrew behind the Han River early in January 1951. The 1st Cavalry Division set up defensive positions in the vicinity of Chugju, south-east of Seoul.

Roads were always clogged with refugees. (Courtesy of Bob Mauger)

one ambush party of the 1st Battalion was overrun by an enemy force that attacked from the rear. The ambush personnel retreated into a perimeter of their battalion after losing two killed, three wounded and one missing in action. Considerable blood in the area indicated the enemy patrol suffered heavy casualties; however, all apparently were evacuated by the enemy.

At approximately 0830 hours, the Regimental Combat Team was given the mission of attacking into the 8th Cavalry zone to get behind the resistance holding up their 2nd Battalion. The 2nd Battalion, 7th Cavalry, was given this mission and moved by motor to the vicinity of Ochonni, closing into the detrucking area at 1200 hours. The unit moved into position immediately and

began the attack at 1400 hours. Hills 364, 421 and 367 were seized without resistance, thus outflanking the enemy holding up the 8th Cavalry. As part of this maneuver, the 1st Battalion seized Hill 419 to protect the east flank of the 2nd Battalion.

The 4th Battalion (GEF) sent two platoon-sized combat patrols forward to the high ground where they engaged an enemy battalion. The patrols withdrew at 1700 hours after inflicting an estimated 20 enemy casualties with small arms fire, plus an undetermined number by directing artillery fire and air strikes. the 4th Battalion (GEF) patrols suffered three killed and three wounded.

Ambushes were established during the night of Jan. 26th-27th along the entire front, but all failed to make contact with the enemy. At daylight on the 27th, combat patrols were given the mission to find and inflict maximum losses on the enemy by making full use of supporting artillery and air. Patrols from the 4th Battalion (GEF) accomplished their mission with particularly outstanding results as they directed artillery fire that killed an estimated 250 to 350 enemy without the loss of a single man.

During the night of Jan. 28th-29th, beginning at 2225 hours, the 1st Battalion perimeter came under heavy attack by an enemy battalion from the 335th Regiment, 38th Chinese Communist Army. This attack originated north of Nagong-ni and struck to the south and southeast. The battalion outpost line was driven in and the perimeter defenses penetrated as fierce close-in fighting raged throughout the night. All available artillery and mortar fires were placed in support of the defense, and air strikes were made by night intruder B-26s directed by flare aircraft. The 4th Battalion (GEF) was ordered to move into counterattack and blocking positions to support the 1st Battalion. One company of the 4th Battalion (GEF) participated in a counterattack with tank under control of the 1st Battalion Commander.

During the early morning hours of the 29th, a number of changes were made in the disposition of Company C, 70th Tank Battalion, in order to reinforce the regiment's west flank. Following the repulse of the enemy attack during the previous night, the tank units reverted to their normal

attachments. Two platoons of the 2nd Battalion were moved to the rear area as security for the regimental supply point. The 2nd Battalion ambush, located west of Ochon-ni, was forced to withdraw by two enemy platoons at 0130 hours; however, by 0335 hours, all enemy attacks had been beaten off. Patrols of the 1st Battalion reached Hills 641 and 614 during the day, but on the return to their area they were engaged by the enemy on these same hills.

The 3rd Battalion patrols encountered small groups of the enemy manning observation posts who withdrew upon approach of the friendly patrol, while another 3rd Battalion patrol encountered an enemy company on Hill 632. Daylight clearing patrols from the 1st Battalion counted 48 enemy dead within their perimeter from the skirmish during the previous night. It was evident that the 1st Battalion had accounted for additional dead and wounded from the amount of blood and equipment in the area surrounding their perimeter; however, the enemy again had removed the casualties that occurred outside the battalion's perimeter.

At 0400 hours on Jan. 30th, the 4th Battalion (GEF) came under heavy attack by a Chinese Communist Regiment of 3,000 supported by mortars, which was attempting to seize Hill 381. Fierce and bitter fighting raged throughout the night, and three times the enemy reached the crest of Hill 381 only to be driven off by the ferocious counterattacks of the brave Greek company holding the top of the hill. The fighting on this hill - hand-to-hand with grenades, rifle butts and bayonets - saw many personal examples of heroism as the tenacious Greek soldiers entered their first major action as part of the United Nations Forces. The hilltop on which they fought was vital to the security of the regiment, and its seizure by the enemy would have allowed him to cut off and surround the 1st Battalion. The four square yards, constituting the peak of Hill 381, were covered with 15 enemy dead who had reached the top only to die by the bayonets, knives and rifle butts of the courageous Greek soldiers. Those who ran out of ammunition fought with their bare hands to retain the important hill. Lt. Col. D. Arbouzis, the 4th Battalion (GEF) commander, estimated the enemy lost 800 killed, and the blood that covered the hillside was mute evidence of the terrific struggle and the high casualties that the enemy had paid in their unsuccessful efforts to seize this vital terrain feature. The 4th Battalion (GEF) had established their fighting reputation in Korea and had taken their rightful place among the best of the GARRYOWENs.

The enemy withdrew at approximately 0430 hours, leaving only the dead that lay within the 4th Battalion's positions on the pinnacle of Hill 381. Three prisoners were taken, all of whom were mortally wounded; however, before their death, interrogation revealed that the entire 334th Regiment, 38th Chinese Communist Army, had taken part in the abortive attack on Hill 381. As dawn arrived, the dead and wounded of the 4th Battalion (GEF) began the long journey down the precarious mountain trails, and ammunition, food and water was carried forward on the backs of native carriers. Casualties had been heavy during the close-in fighting, but the enemy had paid 20-to-1 and had failed in his attack. Throughout the attack, the 4th Battalion (GEF) was supported by artillery and heavy mortar fires, and by the machine gun fire of the 1st Battalion to their north. However, due to the precarious terrain, movement of reserves into the area during the night was not possible.

During the period of the attack on the 4th Battalion (GEF), an enemy combat patrol, estimated at company strength, engaged the perimeter defenses of the 2nd Battalion. It is believed that this enemy unit was sent forward to recover bodies, as many were removed that had been killed in the attack of the previous night. This attack also terminated at approximately 0430 hours.

During the day of the 30th, a Company B patrol was surrounded in the vicinity of Hill 641 but was rescued by other elements of the 1st Battalion, and approximately 150 casualties were inflicted on the enemy. The 3rd Battalion began an assault of Hill 641 following movement to their new area but later withdrew to establish a night perimeter defense. In view of the possibility of another enemy attack during the forthcoming night, the 2nd and 4th Battalions continued reorganization and improvement of their defensive perimeters during the day.

On Jan. 31st, units were ordered to execute strong combat patrols in their zone with the exception of the 4th Battalion (GEF). The 1st Battalion probed enemy positions to the north and northeast, the 2nd Battalion sent strong combat patrols to Hill 614, and the 3rd Battalion sent patrols to Hill 641. All engaged the enemy and inflicted losses with artillery in accordance with their reconnaissance in force missions. Based on the information gathered by the 2nd and 3rd Battalion patrols, a coordinated regimental attack utilizing maximum artillery and tank fires was planned. Units were notified and necessary preparations were made to execute this attack on the following morning.

During the night, Sgt. Sanders, of the I&R platoon, was shot through the lower left arm while investigating a suspicious person behind the regimental headquarters. This was the fourth time this courageous soldier had been wounded. The I&R platoon cleared the area, but the sniper escaped, and the night passed without further incident.

Heavy artillery support fire at night. (U.S. Army Photo)

Shell torn earth within a fierce battle. (U.S. Army Photo)

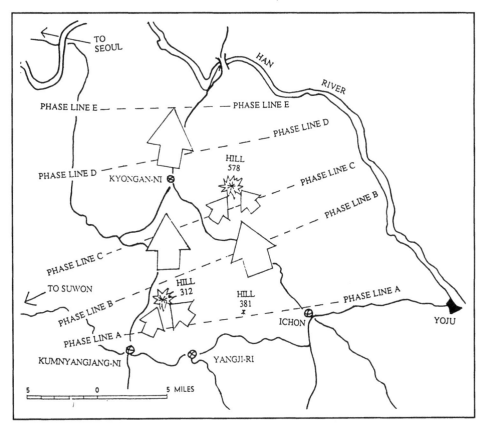

When the Chinese failed to follow up their all-out attack on Seoul, the Eighth Army began probing northward again. On 25 January, in the IX Corps sector, the 1st Cav. undertook a reconnaissance in force. Due to the absence of large-scale enemy resistance, this soon developed into a limited offensive which carried methodically northward across a series of phase line (A-E) until the Division was relieved in mid-February.

Clockwise from the top: General Charles D. Palmer receiving his second star from General Bryant E. Moore, Commanding General of IX Corps. General Palmer then became Commanding Officer of the 1st Cavalry Division, February 1951. (U.S. Army Photo) — L to R General Matt Ridgway, Commander, Eighth Army; Major General Charles Palmer, Commander 1st Cavalry Division; Colonel William Harris, Commander, 7th Cavalry; Colonel John Daskalopoules, Commander Greek Battalion, attached to the 7th Cavalry. Feb. 23, 1951. (Army Photo) — The Greek Expeditionary Forces were attached to the 7th Cav. Reg. as the 4th Bn. on Dec. 19, 1951. (Courtesy Col. Frank Griepp) — The Greek Expeditionary Forces were disciplined and tough soldiers. (Army Photo) — Refugee being searched and screened for safe passage. (Courtesy of Bob Mauger)

CHAPTER VIII
COUNTERATTACK

A planned regimental attack on Hills 641 and 614 was delayed by a heavy fog from 1000 hours to approximately 1100 hours on Feb. 1st. The fog also forced the cancellation of a planned bombing strike with 1,000-pound bombs against the strong points on the crest of the hill mass. This same fog, however, provided excellent concealment for the positioning of Battery B, 77th Field Artillery Battalion, three sections of 155mm howitzers from the 96th Field Artillery Battalion, and 13 tanks from Company C, 70th Tank Battalion - the direct support units for the regiment. Extensive preparatory fires were fired on the ridges by the artillery an tanks at point-blank range in conjunction with other supporting weapons.

Advancing to the line of departure under heavy fog, the lead elements of the 2nd and 3rd Battalions began the assault against the commanding terrain. At about 1215 hours, the fog lifted above the 600 meter line and intensive close support fires were placed in front of the advancing troops by the direct-firing artillery and tanks. Targets spotted by front line commanders were relayed promptly by radio to the tanks waiting in the valley below. The tanks in turn eliminated such targets as machine gun nests, or marked area targets with smoke rounds for the artillery whose ammunition supply was considerably less than that of the tanks. These close-in fires were best executed by the light tanks due to their extreme accuracy in this situation where visibility was limited.

A secondary attack launched by the 1st Battalion against Hill 268 also utilized tanks in direct support of the attacking troopers. The intensity and terrifying nature of this accurate tank fire resulted in securing the objective with a minimum of casualties.

On the following day, all units moved forward in their zone, with the 1st Battalion encountering resistance just north of Konjuam-ni from an estimated enemy platoon with automatic weapons. The 4th Battalion (GEF) encountered resistance in the vicinity of Hill 512. The 2nd Battalion went into a rest and recuperation area at Ochon-ni while the 3rd Battalion (minus) assumed responsibility for Hills 641, 614 and 225. The remainder of the 3rd Battalion was held in reserve at Nogong-ni.

At 0315 hours on Feb. 3rd, a night patrol of the Regimental I&R Platoon was taken under fire and withdrew into friendly lines, and in the early morning hours, the 1st Battalion executed a coordinated attack to seize Hills 231, 402 and the high ground beyond. Despite stiff resistance from frontal and flanking fires, Company A succeeded in clearing the forward slopes of Hill 231 as Company C seized the approaches to Hill 402. However, both units became pinned down, and Company B was passed through Company C. Following an intense artillery preparation, Company B was able to advance to within assaulting distance of Hill 402, and after close-in infantry fighting, seized the objective. Due to the great distances between units, the 3rd Battalion was passed through Company A to occupy Hill 231, and Company A reverted to the 1st Battalion's control. The 3rd Battalion, less Company I and Headquarters Company, established a perimeter defense on Hill 231 after engaging the enemy on the high ground northeast of this hill. The 1st Battalion established a perimeter defense on Hill 402. The remainder of the 3rd Battalion blocked the road and valley entrance to the Regimental Combat Team area at Konjuam-ni.

Meanwhile, the 2nd Battalion had attacked at 0700 hours on Feb. 3rd, passing through the 4th Battalion (GEF). Company E assaulted Hill 481 while Company F assaulted Hill 512. Company E then relieved Company F on Hill 512, and the battalion went into a perimeter defense at Ungdong. The fight on this position was bitter and marked by the extreme cooperation between the infantry and the close air support. The concealed enemy waited in ambush on the towering heights until the attacking elements of the 2nd Battalion approached within grenade range below them. These ambush tactics were discovered by hovering Mosquito aircraft. One of the outstanding examples of close air support in this action occurred when an F51 aircraft came in at tree-top level through blistering small arms and machine gun fire to land a napalm bomb on the key position within 50 yards of our own assault troops. This close support made it possible for the 2nd Battalion to secure their objective. The dogged tenacity and fighting spirit of the 2nd Battalion troopers were essential elements in holding these positions against three successive counterattacks, and at the end of the day's fighting, 105 enemy dead were counted on the position.

February would see the departure of the Commander of the First Cavalry Division. From the book, "The Forgotten War," author Clay Blair wrote: *"During early February at the First Cavalry Division, Ridgway reaffirmed his decision that Hap Gay should be relieved of command. Originally Ridgway had planned for Babe Bryan to relieve Gay, but since the command crisis at the 24th Division was the more urgent, he postponed the relief of Gay to follow that of Barr and Church. Happily, he found a suitable replacement for Gay within the First Cavalry staff; the tough-minded artillery chief, Charlie Palmer, who could gradually take over from Gay without a public clamor.*

Charlie Palmer was a 'Ridgway man' in every sense of the phrase. Ridgway had known Palmer since his early days at West Point. As Ted Brooks' chief of staff in the 2nd Armored Division, Palmer had fought close by Ridgway in Normandy. Inasmuch as the First Cavalry ADC, Frank Allen, was seven years senior to Palmer and not, in Ridgway's opinion, a qualified candidate for divisional command, Ridgway decided to send him home as well. He would be replaced by West Pointer (1923) Elwyn D. Post, 51, then commanding an administrative district in Japan."

Regimental positions were consolidated during the next two days and on the evening of Feb. 5th, the night reconnaissance patrols from the 3rd Battalion, which had departed from their area at approximately 2100 hours, reached the village of Haktong-ni. Their mission was to verify the presence of a large number of enemy troops reported to be in this village. By 2400 hours, the patrol penetrated through the enemy lines into the town and reported that many Chinese troops were in the town and the surrounding hills. The enemy troops could be heard singing, laughing and talking in apparent celebration of the Chinese New Year. This information was reported by radio; however, the enemy intercepted the transmission and soon began moving to surround the patrol. The patrol sent in a hurried radio message that the enemy was outflanking them, that they would withdraw, and that the artillery should immediately place a Battalion TOT concentration was fired and resulted in heavy enemy casualties according to civilian refugees interrogated on the following morning.

The patrol escaped without casualties and returned through the 3rd Battalion's lines, as Company L came under a heavy attack on their left flank from small arms and 60mm mortar fire. This attack may have been interrupted by the patrol action; however, the direction and strength of the attack, and the fact that it was later found that the enemy had pack animals carrying supplies and ammunition indicated that he had planned to stage a major attack. This attack on Company L's position followed a feint attack from the north. The fighting was severe and close-in and, in spite of supporting artillery and heavy mortar fire, the enemy overran two of Company L's forward positions. By 0350 hours, the entire company was engaged in the intense hand-to-hand fighting with Chinese troops.

During this action, 1st Lt. Pierre C. Chrissis distinguished himself above and beyond the call of duty by heroically fighting the area guard action for his platoon when they withdrew at the last possible moment as an artillery concentration was placed on the enemy, which had overrun his position. In this action, Lt. Chrissis fought the Chinese with his carbine until he ran out of ammunition, and then with his bare hands until he was mortally wounded by an enemy who shot him in the side as he battled on the high ground. One of his men came forward under fire and moved him to a position of safety; however, these efforts were to no avail, and this gallant officer died. Inspired by the heroic example of Lt. Chrissis, the men fought on, counterattacked, forced the enemy back and recaptured their position.

During this attack, a platoon of tanks from Company C, Tank Battalion, attached to a platoon of Company L, fired approximately 80 rounds into the flank and assembly area of the attacking Chinese forces. The dogged resistance of Company L coupled with the excellent tank support and the accurate direct fire of the tank cannon finally drove the enemy back, and they withdrew on signal of a red flare at 0430 hours under artillery and mortar fire.

During the action, Company B was ordered to the vicinity of the 3rd Battalion command post to be prepared to assist in the defense of Hill 231. As dawn broke on the morning of Feb. 6th, air strikes were placed on the enemy positions to add further to the casualties he had suffered during the early morning hours.

The 2nd Battalion moved out at 0830 hours on the morning of the 6th, and seized the high ground without contact. A patrol consisting of one platoon of tanks and a platoon from Company E advanced to the village of Tawsong-myong-ni where they received small arms fire. Patrols from the 3rd Battalion cleared the area in the immediate vicinity of the Company L engagement during the remainder of the day.

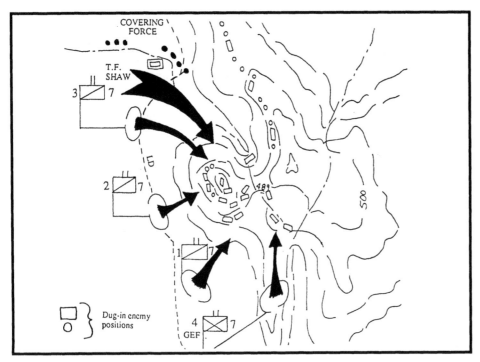

7th Cavalry attack against Hill 578-12-13 February 1951.

The 1st Company of the 4th Battalion (GEF) established blocking positions behind the 3rd Battalion at 0005 hours; however, there was no enemy contact during the early morning hours of Feb. 7th. The remainder of the 4th Battalion (GEF) moved out of their assembly area to relieve the 3rd Battalion at 0800 hours.

At 0855 hours on Feb. 7th, the 2nd Battalion attacked and seized Hill 243. Patrols from the 2nd Battalion encountered enemy troops heavily reinforced with machine guns.

The 4th Battalion (GEF) engaged an estimated two enemy companies strongly reinforced with automatic weapons above Hill 402. Due to the precarious nature of the terrain and the fact that there was no room for maneuver, the enemy - using reverse slope tactics - was able to stop the advance of the 4th Battalion (GEF).

All units broke contact with the enemy between 1500 and 1600 hours, and closed into tight perimeter defenses for the night. The 3rd Battalion occupied the reserve blocking positions of the 1st Battalion, which went into a rest and recuperation area in Nogan-ni. The 19th ROK Regiment relieved the 5th Infantry Regiment on our right flank, and contact was established with this new unit. There was no further enemy contact prior to midnight on Feb. 7th.

At 0150 hours on Feb. 8th, an estimated 20 enemy troops were heard digging in front of Company G's position. The company outpost was withdrawn, 60mm mortar fire directed on the enemy, and the outpost was returned. At approximately 0200, the I&R Platoon sighted a 16-man enemy patrol in front of the 2nd Battalion area. The I&R Platoon held their ground, and as the enemy patrol began to surround them, the I&R Platoon opened fire, wounding two of the enemy.

The 1st Battalion departed from Nogan-ni and relieved the 3rd Battalion, which moved into a rest and recuperation area in the vicinity of Kung-pyong-ni. The 2nd Battalion sent out a number of strong combat patrols, which received heavy automatic weapons and small arms fire and

at 1600 hours, the battalion returned to a tight perimeter defensive position for the night.

The 4th Battalion (GEF) attempted to take the objective on Hill 402, which it had reached on the previous day, by first softening it with repeated air strikes, artillery and mortar barrages. The lead company pushed forward aggressively, and its lead platoon reached the first objective only to be driven back by a strong counterattack from the reverse slope of the hill. Again, artillery and mortar fire were placed on the hill, and again the company attacked, seized the objective and was driven back. This was repeated a third time, and again the lead unit was driven back to its original positions. The battalion was ordered to hold up the attack until the following day and retired into a tight perimeter defense position.

All units prepared for a coordinated attack on Feb. 9th to seize the objectives and to position themselves for an enveloping attack on Hill 578.

A night attack was planned by the 2nd Battalion for the early morning hours of Feb. 9th. Beginning at 0330 hours, units of the battalion began assembling for this attack. Illuminous radium buttons were fastened on the back of webbed belts to identify officers and non-commissioned officers, thereby furnishing a means of recognition and reorganization. All personnel went through briefings during the daylight hours of Feb. 8th, and late that evening small villages at the base of the objective were set afire to be used as reference points by the assaulting units during the night attack. Platoons from Companies F and G secured their assembly areas at the base of Hill 202 at about 0440 hours, and upon report that these areas had been cleared of enemy, the companies moved out in the attack. There were no further reports until Company G came under small arms and automatic weapons fire at 0550 hours when the company overran a Chinese outpost and one Chinese ran toward the top of the hill screaming the alarm. The company immediately came under heavy fire from three

machine guns on top of the ridge and the flanks, and were forced to withdraw fighting a rearguard action.

On the other hand, Company F gained their initial objective by 0600 hours without making enemy contact; however, when daylight broke, Company F became engaged in a machine gun duel at about 75-yards range. The fire fight continued throughout the day with the 2nd Battalion elements being supported by direct tank cannon fire. Company G was reorganized and committed on the west flank of Company F, and by 1400 hours had gained the southern end of Hill 202. Company G then moved up, cleared the area and dug in on the west slope of the hill. As darkness fell, Companies F and G buttoned up for the night. At 2330 hours, Company F received a heavy counterattack and was forced to withdraw from their position through Company G. Both units then were withdrawn since the enemy now occupied the dominating ground on Hill 202. Plans were made to pass the 3rd Battalion through the 2nd Battalion to take Hill 202 on the following day and for the 2nd Battalion to revert to regimental reserve.

During the day, the 1st Company of the 4th Battalion (GEF) again assaulted dominating terrain about 1,500 yards north of Hill 202, using flame throwers, grenades and bayonets. They again took the knoll that had been taken three times on the previous day, but again the enemy counterattacked in strength and forced the lead platoon to withdraw.

The 1st Battalion, led by Company C and followed by Company B, moved out at 0800 hours on Feb. 10th to seize Hill 227. The remainder of the battalion remained in position. The lead companies moved steadily forward without opposition until 1000 hours when heavy automatic weapons and small arms fire was received from an estimated reinforced enemy company on the objective. All available mortar and artillery fires, plus the fire power of supporting tanks, were placed on the position and the advance slowly continued. By 1125 hours, the companies had driven the enemy from the crest of Hill 227 but were unable to remain on the hill due to heavy machine gun fire from the reverse slopes.

At 0720 hours on the 10th, the 3rd Battalion began moving from its position to attack the high ground in their zone. Company I, the lead unit, advanced from the valley under cover of artillery and mortar fires with additional protection provided by an air strike on the objective. Enemy small arms and automatic weapons fire was encountered, but this resistance was overcome as the battalion pushed aggressively against an estimated enemy battalion. The objective was secured at 1425 hours, and Company I conducted a sweeping operation of the ridge. The enemy dead counted on the ridge totaled 200.

An air strike in addition to an artillery and mortar barrage placed on the objective provided a prelude to the attack of the 4th Battalion (GEF) at 0900 hours. In the vicious exchange of small arms and automatic weapons fire, and by closing with the enemy in hand-to-hand combat, the 1st Company succeeded in securing the top of the mountain at 1515 hours. Approximately 200 enemy were observed on the northern slopes of Hill 271. Tanks supporting the 1st Battalion shifted their fires to this target and the enemy fled north.

The 1st Company continued to clear the ridge of the objective, and by 1545 hours two squads of the company had reached the northern end, despite sporadic small arms fire from the north and northeast. At 1730 hours, the 1st and 3rd companies repulsed an enemy counterattack of platoon strength and the battalion closed in a perimeter defense for the night.

At 0900 hours on Feb. 11th, Companies A and B moved out of the 1st Battalion's perimeter. Company B had advanced about 1,000 yards by 1020 hours when enemy fires were received from Hill 206, and from the western slopes of Hill 578. Fifteen minutes later the company was forced to withdraw due to a friendly airstrike, which was very close to the company's positions. By 1110 hours, Company B had advanced to the second ridge leading to Hill 578, and Company A was advancing from the west without enemy contact. By 1255 hours, the 1st Battalion had secured the ridges, and the enemy was fleeing toward Hill 578. All available fire power, artillery, mortars, tank cannons and machine guns, was placed on the enemy in his retreat. Although small arms fire was received sporadically, the battalion closed into the perimeter at 1705 hours.

Company E moved out at 0700 hours to lead the 2nd Battalion's attack, and by 0755 hours was engaged in a sharp fire fight with the enemy on Hill 229. Company E had advanced up Hill 229 by 0840 hours when the attack was delayed for ammunition resupply. At 1055, Companies F and G were in a position to aid Company E. At 1125 hours, Company G began to attack Hill 227 and captured this objective by 1340 hours. By 1350 hours, the enemy started to withdraw to the vicinity of Hill 152 and were taken under small arms, automatic weapons, artillery, heavy mortar, tank cannon and machine gun fire with excellent results. The enemy force was estimated at battalion strength. After conducting sweeping operations, the battalion closed into a perimeter defense at 1700 hours.

A patrol from Company K led by Master Sgt. Aron Cook reconnoitered Hill 178 without enemy contact and returned to the 3rd Battalion position at 1237 hours. The battalion closed into its perimeter defense at 1700 hours.

A patrol from the 4th Battalion (GEF) moved out of the battalion perimeter at 0930, and by 1300 hours, had reached a point 600 yards south of Hill 489. In the course of the operation, the patrol met a small enemy group of three, which was killed. This small enemy group was armed with one heavy machine gun, one light mortar and one light machine gun. Many discarded weapons were found along the patrol route and were collected by the patrol, and at 1700 hours the patrol withdrew into the battalion perimeter without casualties.

In furtherance of the 7th Cavalry Regiment's mission, in conjunction with the Eighth Army's reconnaissance in force, it became necessary to seize Hill 578, a key terrain feature in the regimental zone strongly defended by the enemy. Plans and preparations for this operation were initiated on Feb. 12th when an attempt was made to surround the hill and force its capitulation by utilization of maximum air and artillery fires coupled with strong combat patrols probing from all sides. The attempt to surround the hill, however, was frustrated by additional enemy defenses in depth, which were located north of the town of Magam-ni. The enemy manning these defenses north of Hill mass 578 prevented the 3rd Battalion from moving in rear of the hill by accurate, heavy mortar fire. Thus it became necessary to seize the hill by a coordinated regimental attack.

The initial planning for this coordinated attack began during the afternoon of Feb. 12th. The commanders of the 2nd and 3rd Battalions who were to make the main effort under the tentative plan formulated by the regiment, met with the regimental operations office and their own battalion operations officers in the zone of the 3rd Battalion where excellent observation of the enemy position was available.

Contemplated objectives were pointed out to both commanders on the ground and zones of responsibility were agreed upon. It was tentatively agreed that the very crest of the hill mass would be assigned to the 2nd Battalion alone and that certain key features north of the crest would be assigned to the 3rd Battalion. This decision was necessary in view of the length of the ridge line proper as opposed to the area covered by the hill mass itself. On request of the 2nd Battalion commander, and with concurrence of the 3rd Battalion commander, the tentative objective that had been selected for the 3rd Battalion, which was the first dominating knoll below the main ridge line, was moved approximately 250 yards further north of the slope to another knoll. This change was made due to certain problems of artillery fire coordination, which would have been presented due to the close proximity of the objectives originally selected. Both battalion commanders discussed their planned routes of approach to the hill mass and the contemplated deployment of their units with the regimental operations officer. Both commanders were assured that maximum use of available fire power would be made in support of the operation, and that secondary attack by the 1st and 4th Battalions designed to exploit the seizure of the ridge had been planned. These commanders also were advised that an air preparation would be requested on the objective area.

In view of the necessity for coordination, planning, reconnaissance and rest for the personnel to be involved, it was determined that operations would commence on Feb. 14th, rather than on Feb. 13th. This also would provide a 24-hour period for softening up the objective area by artillery fire and air strikes. Discussion of the most suitable time to cross the line of departure also was made. It was estimated that the problem of movement to the ridge line itself and the closing of attacking elements on the ridge line would take from two and a half to three hours even if there were no enemy on the hill. Both commanders agreed that from the standpoint of the attacking infantry battalions, 0900 hours was the most desirable "H" hour. This hour provided:

1. Sufficient time for organization and deployment of the attacking forces during daylight hours.

2. Sufficient time after crossing the line of departure to reach the objective and, under favorable conditions, to seize and organize it prior to darkness.

0900 hours was tentatively agreed upon as "H" hour and, there being no further matters for discussion, the conference broke up - speeded by three enemy 60mm mortar rounds, which landed in the near vicinity of the group.

The plan for this attack included an attack from the west by the 2nd Battalion to seize the crest of the ridge, coordinated with an attack by the 3rd Battalion from the northwest to seize the northern portion of the hill mass and to bring flanking fire on the enemy's rear positions from

Observation Post on Hill 427, observing a returning friendly patrol, on March 7, 1951. (Courtesy of Col. Frank Griepp)

Colonel "Wild Bill" Harris, Commander 7th Cavalry Regiment, addressing the non-commissioned officers of the 3rd Battalion, on March 22, 1951. (Courtesy of Col. Frank Griepp)

F-80 Shooting Star, note napalm bombs. (U.S. Army Photo)

F-84 Thunderjet, note napalm bombs. (U.S. Army Photo)

A Chinese attack at night with blazing gunfire and flares. (Warren Lee-UPI)

the north. This main effort of the regiment was to be followed by an exploitation attack of the 1st and 4th Battalions to cover the eastern portion of the hill mass. These battalions also were to assist by diversionary fires against enemy positions on the southern and eastern ridges leading to Hill 578.

A request was made at this time for the following:

1. An additional supporting artillery battalion.

2. An additional company of tanks.

3. A 20-minute air preparation of napalm and 1,000-pound bombs on the crest of the ridge.

4. An air-smoking mission on the high ground north of Mugam-ni.

5. An air strike on the peak of Hill 578 every 30 minutes after 0900 hours until called for on other targets.

Although an additional direct support artillery battalion could not be attached, all Division Artillery did support the operation. Further, an additional tank company could not be made

available, but the Reconnaissance Platoon, 70th Tank Battalion, was attached to the regiment.

The 1st and 4th Battalions, as well as the artillery, heavy mortars, tanks, engineers and regimental staff, were advised of the tentative attack plans. The artillery and heavy mortar company, in particular, were given instructions to intensify their fire on the night of Feb. 12th-13th and until the actual preparation for the attack on Feb. 14th. The tactical air control party also was briefed on the tentative attack plans and all available air strike forces were scheduled to attack the crest of the ridge line and other known enemy targets on the hill mass.

During the night of Feb. 12th-13th, the 77th Field Artillery Battalion, supported by other units of division artillery, fired a number of TOT concentrations on the objective area. In conjunction with these TOT concentrations, a series of "Surrender Now" broadcasts in the 3rd Battalion area were made over a loudspeaker system. These broadcasts by the regular U.S. team were augmented by a Chinese lieutenant colonel captured

in the 5th Cavalry area who urged the enemy to surrender. Three prisoners surrendered on Feb. 13th as a result of these broadcasts and the morale of a great many other enemy troops was undermined according to prisoners captured in later fighting.

On the morning of Feb. 13th, a meeting was arranged with the Division G-3 and the S-3 of the 8th Cavalry Regiment on the northwest. Prior to departure, the operations officer and commanders of the various units were called in and the verbal orders covering the operation were given, including the extensive fire support plan. This program initially called for increasing and intensifying fires against Hill mass 578 on Feb. 13th-14th. On Feb. 14th, preplanned concentrations on the forward slope of 578 were to be fired from 0700 hours to 0830 hours on known and suspected enemy locations. An intensive concentration of time fire and VT fuse was to be placed in a 400-yard square area. This second concentration by heavy mortars was designed to:

1. Catch the enemy in the open on the

objective after giving him time to get up out of his emplacements.

2. Cover those draws immediately behind the principal objective, which could not be reached by the artillery.

This period from 0830 to 0850 was set aside for an air preparation of napalm and 1,000-pound bombs on the top of the ridge line. In view of previous experiences with preplanned air strikes, the artillery was advised to be prepared to continue their fires during the 0830 to 0850 period in the event the air strikes did not arrive or were late. The artillery also was directed to be prepared to smoke the top of Hill 578 and the high ground north of Mugam-ni. A request also had been made to smoke the high ground north of Mugamni with aircraft.

Three final steps were taken in the fire support plan. One provided that the artillery would fire one round every five seconds into the artillery concentration area (which was fired from 0850 to 0900) to begin at 0900 hours. These rounds were designed to prevent the enemy from reinforcing, moving his reserves or manning his positions at the top of the ridge, and to be lifted on request of either of the leading company commanders. In addition, the 1st and 4th Battalions were directed to furnish support fire on the south and eastern portions of Hill 578 with their own organic mortars. The third step was the complete use of Company C, 70th Tank Battalion, for direct supporting fire. Two platoons of tanks were attached to the 2nd Battalion for direct tank fire support of the assaulting units, and one platoon of tanks was attached to each of the 3rd and 1st Battalions for the same purpose. In addition to the direct support of the assaulting units, these tanks were positioned to expedite seizure of the ridge by taking any retreating enemy under fire.

Further exploitation of the operation was planned through organization of Task Force Shaw. Task Force Shaw initially included the two platoons of tanks supporting the 2nd Battalion whose fires would be masked as the 2nd Battalion seized

their objective. No infantry protection with the tanks was considered necessary as the 3rd Battalion could watch over the tanks from their positions. This task force was to move out as the assault unit moved on to their objective areas and was to proceed north through the village of Mugam-ni to a position in rear of Hill mass 578 to direct fire into the reverse slopes. The Reconnaissance Platoon of the 70th Tank Battalion also was attached to Task Force Shaw to assist in its exploitation mission.

On request of the 1st Battalion commander, the original attack plans were modified to provide for the seizure of a small peak immediately north of the 1st Battalion's position, which dominated that area and was strongly held by the enemy. This ground was known as the "Ice Cream Cone."

During the night of Feb. 13th-14th, the 3rd Battalion S-2's radio intercepted a Chinese broadcast that indicated that a heavy attack also was being planned by the enemy. However, the location of the enemy attacking forces cold not be determined. As a result of some of these intercepts, units of the 7th Cavalry were on an alert status for most of the night. The enemy force actually attacked in the 8th Cavalry area and elements of the 8th Cavalry were engaged until well after daylight. As a result of this action, the 8th Cavalry was forced to clear enemy groups from its zone and could not stage its diversionary attack against the high ground on the northwest of Mugam-ni. It then was necessary to rearrange the regimental plan by placing one section of tanks, formerly supporting the 2nd Battalion, plus the tank Reconnaissance Platoon in positions on the northern flank of the 3rd Battalion to cover and protect this area during the attack.

The regimental commander and his mobile command group, consisting of the operation officer, artillery liaison officer, TACP, heavy mortar liaison officer, tank liaison officer, a number of radiomen, and an additional officer from the S-3 Section plus a journal clerk, moved to the regimental observation post (OP) beginning at 0630.

The regimental OP had been selected and prepared in advance in a location from which the leading elements of the 1st, 2nd and 3rd Battalions could be observed. Both wire and radio communications were available from his OP to all units as well as to Division headquarters.

The initial artillery preparation went off as planned, beginning at 0700 hours on Feb. 14th and consisted primarily of time fire and VT fire over the forward slope of the hill mass, coupled with sporadic intense concentrations on suspected troop areas on the reverse slope. At approximately 0820 hours, the regiment was notified that aircraft would not be available since all aircraft in the Army zone had been shifted to support the X corps due to a major enemy attack in that sector. The artillery was notified to continue its preparation up to H-10 minutes as a substitute for the planned air preparation.

The lack of napalm preparation later was to prove an extremely vital factor in this attack. It is believed that had napalm been available, the hill would have been much easier to seize due to the concentration and type of enemy defenses on the top of the ridge.

The leading elements of Company K, 3rd Battalion crossed the line of departure at 0900 hours. Company G of the 2nd Battalion crossed the line of departure on time but halted for nearly 20 minutes in a village at the base of Hill 578 to reorganize prior to continuing up the hill.

Pineapple aircraft operating in the area began to report enemy mortar positions and camouflaged supplies. These enemy targets were taken under fire by the artillery, directed by both T6 (Mosquito) aircraft and by the Pineapple aircraft. At 0934 hours, two enemy soldiers were seen running down the reverse slope of Hill 578. This was the first indication that the enemy was aware that our infantry forces had actually begun the attack. It was possible that the intense artillery concentration had destroyed the enemy's wire and radio communication. By 0940 hours, tank screening forces of one section of tanks plus the

Major General Hobart Gay salutes the 1st Cavalry Division as he prepares to depart Korea in February 1951. (U.S. Army Photo)

Lt. Colonel John W. Callaway, Commander, 2nd Battalion, 7th Cavalry, discusses with General of the Army Douglas MacArthur, about the tactical situation north of Chipyong, Korea 1951. (U.S. Army Photo)

Reconnaissance Platoon of the 70th Tank Battalion arrived in position on the north flank of the 3rd Battalion and began firing against known enemy positions on the high ground north of Mugam-ni. Pineapple aircraft reported five more enemy soldiers moving on a trail on the reverse side of Hill 578 at 0942 and they also were taken under fire. At 1005 hours, sporadic small arms fire was received by Company K, and from this point forward mortar and small arms fire increased in intensity.

At 1120 hours, the 1st battalion, having waited until the enemy was "stirring" on the "Ice Cream Cone," began their attack with heavy mortar, small arms and automatic weapons fire.

At 1123 hours, Company G began receiving white phosphorus rounds, and at 1155 hours Company K was held up in its advance by an estimated enemy company with automatic weapons and small arms fire. At 1202 hours, both Companies I and K were receiving extremely heavy mortar fire, and a number of reports of enemy "recoilless rifle" fire was received. This fire later proved to be from 2.36-inch rocket launchers that were being used as anti-personnel weapons.

At 1210 hours, Pineapple aircraft located two more mortars that were taken under artillery fire. Tanks screening the 3rd Battalion's left flank began receiving heavy mortar fire at 1225 hours. At 1325 hours, a report was received that Company K had reached its objective and was receiving heavy small arms and automatic weapons fire. Company L, which was following in the trace of Company K, dispatched one platoon to the right of Company K and above the objective area. This platoon succeeded in getting above and behind the enemy forces defending the area.

Suddenly finding themselves surrounded, 14 of the enemy surrendered, and the rest were killed. During this action, there also were numerous occasions when enemy soldiers would continue to fight until every round had been fired and then raise their arms to surrender. At 1340 hours, Pineapple aircraft reported approximately 40 enemy moving east on the road out of Mugam-ni apparently to reinforce the enemy positions on Hill 578.

By 1345 hours, both of the attacking companies of the two leading battalions were in their assault positions. Company K already had secured its objective, and Company G was within 50 yards of the peak of Hill 578. However, this last 50 yards was an almost vertical, rock-faced cliff. The 1st and 4th Battalions were ordered to begin a coordinated attack. At 1400 hours, Pineapple aircraft reported 15 enemy lying in ambush at a distance of only 15 feet immediately behind a portion of the ridge that Company G was approaching. Company G troops were met by a shower of grenades from the enemy troops and machine guns on both flanks opened up and forced the leading elements of the 2nd Battalion to withdraw approximately 25 yards. Since this was the most critical point of the operation, a request was made for an air strike on the peak of the hill. Company G and the enemy battled along the ridge line using hand grenades and light mortars. The 3rd Battalion was directed to move Company K south to support the 2nd Battalion. Company K had an extremely difficult time in seizing this objective, which was strongly defended. This objective turned out to be the center of communications for the hill mass defense and included the enemy regimental command post (CP), one battalion CP and several company CPs.

This CP area was particularly well-defended, a[nd] many enemy were killed in this area. This fig[ht] made it necessary to pass Company L throu[gh] Company K to continue the momentum of t[he] attack at 1445 hours.

At 1440 hours, Task Force Shaw was o[r]dered to proceed on its mission, and the tan[ks] began moving out to their initial assembly are[a]. The 4th Battalion (GEF) reported that their lea[d] elements, the 2nd Company, had moved out a[t] 1445 hours. By 1505, they were receiving heav[y] fire from Hill 489. A further report was received that the hill on their east flank, which had been reportedly captured by the South Korean forces, was still in enemy hands and that the position of Hill 489 would be untenable until the ground to the east was secure. The 4th Battalion was ordered to block in their forward positions and to take the enemy positions to their immediate front under fire until the dominating ground on the east could be secured by the Koreans.

At 1525 hours, Task Force Shaw reported that the road west of Magam-ni had been mined and that the tanks had backed up and blown the mines out of the road with their tank cannon and proceeded on their mission. The Task Force fired into the town of Magam-ni proper but apparently all supplies, ammunition and enemy troops had been removed. Leading elements of Task Force Shaw moved to a point several hundred yards beyond Magam-ni until the road became a trail.

A round became lodged in the chamber of one of the tank guns, and one of the crew got out in front of the tank with a rammer to dislodge the shell. In so doing, he was wounded by mortar fire that had been falling sporadically in and around the tanks. The wounded man was placed on one of the tanks and evacuated to the 3rd Battalion

The sheer ridges and the crest of Hill 578, contained many enemy machine gun positions. In the foreground, troopers of Company F, 2nd Bn., 7th Cavalry, take a breather. (Courtesy of Suey Lee)

L to R: 1st Lt. Jim Gorman, Captain Harold Gray C/O, 1st Lt. John Potts and 1st Lt. Tom Kilduff, of Company F, 2nd Bn., 7th Cavalry. Hongchon Valley March 1951. (Courtesy of Suey Lee)

Dead Chinese soldier, still smoldering from napalm bomb. (U.S. Army Photo)

Hill 578 was devastated by air strikes and artillery fire. February 1951. Courtesy of Suey Lee)

1st Cavalry Division trooper looking at dead Chinese soldier who was carrying an American novel, "Died in the Wool". (U.S. Army Photo)

L to R: Corporals Seebold and Suey Lee of the 3rd Platoon, Co.F, 2nd Bn., 7th Cavalry, look over two dead Chinese on Hill 578 in February 1951. Enemy soldiers were probably killed by artillery or air strikes. (Courtesy of Suey Lee)

Aid Station while the remainder of the Task Force continued to engage the enemy.

Elements of the 1st Battalion were heavily engaged in their objective area, and Company B was stopped on the approaches to the objective. The 1st Battalion commander immediately committed elements of Company C around both flanks and pushed his attack successfully in overrunning the objective. Despite the difficult terrain, considerable enemy casualties were inflicted, a number of enemy supplies were captured, and the objective of the 1st Battalion was secured by 1600 hours.

As of 1600 hours, the leading elements of the 2nd Battalion still were maneuvering on the top of the ridge and still were heavily engaged with the enemy. Company L continued its move up the slope followed by Company K under heavy enemy fire. In its attempt to outflank the enemy on the reverse slope, Company L ran into an enemy strong point and became engaged in an intense grenade fight as well as by enemy machine gun and mortar fire, and by 1730 hours was pinned down. Elements of the 2nd Battalion continued to move and maneuver, with the enemy "looking down their throat," in an attempt to outflank and overrun the enemy positions. The 2nd Battalion had received a number of casualties from mortar fire from the top of the hill and was in an extremely exposed position. At 1735, Lt. Col. John W.

Callaway, the commanding officer, 2nd Battalion, who had moved up the hill to the vicinity of the assault company, reported that the battalion's position was entenable, and requested permission to withdraw, reorganize and begin the attack the next day; however, he was directed to storm the hill regardless of the costs and to capture the objective. The 3rd Battalion also was notified of these orders, and Company L was placed under operational control of the 2nd Battalion pending seizure of the hill and until daylight the next morning.

Fighting continued throughout the night. The 2nd Battalion commander who had gone personally to the scene of action to direct his battalion, maneuvered Company F to the right; however, they were pinned down by fire and driven back. He then committed Company E to the left of Company G and contacted Company L, which had reached the crest of the north and was firing into the northeastern portion of the reverse side of Hill 578. It was impossible for Company L to fire into the southeast portion of the hill due to the terrain, which consisted of two half-moon formations on the reverse slope of the hill. The enemy's strongest reinforcements were in the southeastern area. The Chinese had placed five machine gun pill-box-type emplacements on the hill, which had excellent fields of fire and were able to sweep the entire area with cross fire. Company G then made an unsuccessful attempt to maneuver a 75mm recoil-

less rifle into position to destroy these machine guns.

A flame thrower operator from Company G finally pushed forward and destroyed the machine gun position on the extreme northern flank. Shortly thereafter, the operator was driven back by enemy hand grenades. However, this enabled later capture of this end of the ridge by the 2nd Battalion.

Reports from prisoners captured during the daylight fighting indicated, as of 2045 hours, that there were approximately 20 enemy troops manning the topographical crest of the ridge. However, enemy troops in position behind the crest totaled one battalion plus two platoons. These enemy reserves successfully counterattacked each time the 2nd Battalion's forces succeeded in moving up on the ridge.

In addition to grenades, small arms and automatic weapons, the enemy made excellent use of his mortars, and of the 2.36-inch rocket launchers as a direct fire anti-personnel weapon.

At 2330 hours, the 2nd Battalion reported that Company E, which had been committed on the left flank of Company G finally had overrun the top of the ridge on the extreme northern portion of the position and had destroyed two machine gun positions.

Three additional enemy machine guns still were in position and operating, and both Compa-

Troopers of the 3rd Platoon, Co. F, 2nd Bn., 7th Cavalry, on Hill 578, in February 1951. (Courtesy of Suey Lee)

Tank Support from the 70th Tank Battalion, attached to the 7th Cavalry. (Courtesy of Bob Mauger)

P.F.C. Arthur Hunter, Company G, 2nd Bn., 7th Cavalry, bringing in Chinese prisoners on February 27, 1951, during Operation Killer.

Litter team with the difficult task of getting wounded off of the hill. (U.S. Army Photo)

nies E and L were pinned down by the fire from these guns. When the regiment suggested by radio that marching fire be used, the reply was: "There is no room to march." and "Every man here is pinned flat to the ground by a solid sheet of machine gun fire."

Upon establishing contact with Company E, Company K, which had been supporting Company L, was ordered back to reinforce the 3rd Battalion perimeter at the foot of the hill mass. This perimeter was in an extremely exposed position due to the enemy's capability to counterattack from the north.

At 0025 hours, enemy resistance was slackening, and another attempt was made to push over the ridge. 60mm mortars were used effectively against the enemy by the leading companies, as Company L fired 300 rounds from one mortar tube alone. By 0100 hours, all elements of the 2nd Battalion still were engaged in fire fights and had not overrun the ridge, and at 0125 hours, approximately 150 to 200 enemy still were on top of the ridge line.

Company F continued to maneuver to the right flank to get behind the enemy, while Com-

pany E held the high ground that it had gained. During the period 0400 to 0600 hours, the 2nd Battalion again assaulted the enemy positions, but was hit by a strong counterattack of approximately 50 enemy in a fanatic attempt to drive them off the position before daylight. However, this effort was unsuccessful and proved to be the enemy's last desperate counterattack effort.

When the counterattack was first reported, air support was urgently requested from Division. Pineapple aircraft arrived almost immediately, and fighters were directed against the rear slope of the hill. By 0725 hours, Company E had seized an additional portion of the ridge.

Task Force Shaw was ordered to move out at 0735 hours to exploit the reverse slope of the hill. The 4th Battalion was ordered to move to an assembly area in the vicinity of the 2nd Battalion CP at the base of the hill and to be prepared to relieve the 2nd Battalion upon their seizure of the objective. The air controller reported that a number of the enemy were withdrawing at 0845 hours, and Task Force Shaw was directed to take these enemy troops under direct tank fire.

By 0900, the 2nd Battalion reported that the

enemy was in flight and that the objective had been seized by hand-to-hand fighting. All companies of the 2nd Battalion and Company L organized perimeters on the ridge line and immediately sent out sweeping patrols to clear the area in the vicinity of the objective and the approaches thereto. The 1st Battalion was directed to send a sweeping patrol up from the south to the crest of 578. This action completed the capture of Hill 578 at a cost of 16 killed and 137 wounded - primarily from Companies B, E, G, K and L.

Following the successful attack on Hill 578, platoon-size patrols cleared the approaches and slopes to the hill and the 27th Infantry Regiment began relieving the regiment during the morning hours of February 15th. This relief continued throughout the day, and the 27th Infantry Regiment was in position at 1700 hours while the 7th Cavalry Regiment went into a temporary assembly area. The exhausted troopers settled down for a much needed rest, and the night passed without enemy contact. However, an enemy aircraft dropped a series of bombs at 2007 hours, which injured three men from the 27th Infantry's 1st Battalion, and six more bombs were dropped at

2024 hours killing one and injuring four. These bombs were dropped around the town of Longianni by enemy long-range bombers of the B-26 type that were operated so as to appear to be friendly aircraft. At 0800 hours on Feb. 16th, the regiment began arriving at an assembly area northwest of Chang-kow-ni, and by 1420 hours, all units had closed into the new assembly area.

At 1350 hours, the 4th Battalion (GEF) was ordered to furnish two squads with an officer in charge to provide security for Hill 679 and the high ground to the north. At 1650 hours, information was received that typhus was discovered in the 1st Battalion area. The 1st Battalion was ordered to move to a new area on Feb. 17th and further ordered to place the village off limits with guards around it. This action apparently was effective as no typhus cases were reported in the regiment.

The regiment continued rest and recuperation in its assembly area during the remainder of the month of February, and was in Division reserve on Feb. 22nd when the Eighth Army's "Operation Killer" began.

As a result of the regiment's action during this phase of the Korean War, the following letter was received:

HEADQUARTERS 1ST CAVALRY DIVISION

Office of the Commanding General
APO 201
17 February 1951

SUBJECT: Commendation
TO: Commanding Officer
7th Cavalry Regiment, APO 201

Through you, I wish to commend all elements of the command which constituted the Seventh Regimental Combat Team during the period of offensive action from 24 January 1951 to 15 February 1951.

During this period of three weeks your command pressed continuous offensive action in which it was necessary to overcome not only a stubbornly resistive enemy, but also many difficulties of terrain. This action was climaxed by an outstanding display of determination, leadership, courage and endurance in the successful assault of the determinedly held Hill 578.

The magnificent showing of the members of your command during this action under your leadership and guidance, was representative of that courage, ability and will to do which symbolizes the high traditions which have made American soldiery always successful in the ultimate.

/s/ Charles D. Palmer
CHARLES D. PALMER
Major General USA
Commanding

On March 1st, the regiment remained in Division reserve and patrolled the rear area. Contact was maintained with the 27th British Commonwealth Brigade. One man from Company A stepped on an enemy anti-personnel mine at 2330 hours while moving up to his OP and was killed. From this date forward, enemy mine activity markedly increased in the Korean War.

The regiment replaced the 5th Cavalry Regiment on the line south of Yondu-ri on March 2nd. The 4th Battalion (GEF) went into position by 0800 hours, the 1st Battalion by 1030 hours, the 2nd Battalion by 1200 hours. The 3rd Battalion remained in reserve and completed their move by 1125 hours.

During the movement into position, the 4th Battalion (GEF) received a number of casualties from enemy mortar fire. The commander of the 2nd Battalion, 5th Cavalry was killed by an enemy mortar round as he left his command post following the relief of his battalion. Both the 5th Cavalry and the 7th Cavalry units were harassed constantly by heavy mortar and 75mm artillery fire during the relief.

At 1955 hours, an estimated 20-man enemy patrol attacked an OP of Company N, 4th Battalion (GEF). Enemy casualties were unknown but estimated to be heavy, and Company N lost one killed. Following contact, the enemy withdrew to the north and was taken under artillery fire. Due to the gap in the line between the 7th and 8th Cavalry Regiments on the southwest, the I&R Platoon was placed in a pass above the regimental CP area, which was close to the enemy lines in that sector. At 2355 hours, an enemy aircraft dropped flares in the 2nd Battalion's sector as the battalion engaged enemy patrols.

Enemy activity increased early on March 3rd when the 1st Battalion was attacked by an estimated enemy platoon at 0500 hours. Unfortunately, the area that became engaged was in a Company C platoon sector where, earlier in the morning, the assistant platoon sergeant, three squad leaders and six other men were lost in a hand-grenade accident. Without this leadership,

L to R: Lt. Colonel Charles Hallden, Commander, 3rd Battalion (after Lynch); Lt. Colonel John W. Callaway, Commander, 2nd Battalion; Colonel William A. "Wild Bill" Harris, Commander, 7th Cavalry Regiment. (Photo Courtesy of Ed Daily)

After General MacArthur, General Matt Ridgway became commander-in-Chief of the UN Forces. With pearl handled pistol is General James A. VanFleet, April 1951. (U.S. Army Photo)

Colonel William A. "Wild Bill" Harris, standing in front of his command jeep with the saddle mounted on the hood and adorned with the GARRYOWEN crest. Note that he is holding a captured Chinese horn. (U.S. Army Photo)

Tank Task Force of the 70th Tank Bn., and 3rd Platoon, Company F, 2nd Bn., 7th Cavalry. Hongchon Valley, March 1951. (Courtesy of Suey Lee)

Enemy contact and withdrawal of Tank Task Force of 70th Tank Bn., and 3rd Platoon, Company F, 2nd Bn., 7th Cavalry. Hongchon Valley, March 1951. (Suey Lee)

the platoon became disorganized during the attack and lost contact with the remainder of the company. The enemy used small arms, automatic weapons and some 60mm mortar fire in this attack, and the platoon was forced to pull back from its positions. They were reorganized, ordered back and reoccupied these positions prior to 0600 hours, but lost one killed and three wounded. At 0130 hours, six rounds of 60mm mortar fire fell in the Company C area. At about the same time, an OP of Company B received enemy small arms and automatic weapons fire. At approximately 0235 hours, an OP of Company A observed 50 to 60 enemy on Hill 235 and directed artillery fire on them. Seven rounds of 60mm mortar fire were received in the vicinity of the 1st Battalion's roadblock, and the OP of Company B received small arms and automatic weapons fire at the same time.

Beginning at 0800 hours, all battalions in the line sent patrols forward to locate the enemy's positions. Patrols of the 4th Battalion (GEF) received heavy automatic weapons fire from Yondu-ri and the high ground and villages adjacent thereto. Company C patrols received small arms and automatic weapons fire from Hill 300 and directed tank and artillery fire against these positions. As darkness fell, the enemy began probing patrols against the regiments positions, and at 2000 hours, a small patrol attacked the left flank of company F with hand grenades but withdrew under heavy fire. Another enemy group began moving around the Company F right flank, and mortars and artillery were placed on them. At 2010 hours, Company A patrols heard Chinese voices and directed artillery in that area, and an enemy force of about 200 was reported at 2045 hours to the front of Companies A and C. At the same time, Company B reported approximately 20 enemy troops had made contact with their patrols and were engaged and driven off. At 2200 hours, the 4th Battalion (GEF) began using a propaganda loudspeaker placed in defilade in an effort to get enemy troops to surrender, but attracted only enemy machine gun fire in return. They located the enemy machine gun positions,

took them under mortar fire and silenced the enemy guns.

At approximately 2230 hours, trip flares and grenade booby traps placed in front of Company C were exploded, six rounds of enemy artillery were received, and at 2355 hours, they were attacked by an estimated enemy platoon. Contact was broken at 0125 hours on March 4th without losses to our troops.

At 0045 hours, Company K of the reserve battalion was placed on a 30-minute alert because of an attack on Company C. However, this alert later was lifted as it became evident that the enemy action was not a major effort. Radar-controlled B-26s conducted air strikes throughout the night, and patrols were active during the daylight hours of March 4th. These patrols received 81mm mortar, small arms and machine gun fire and a tank attached to the 4th Battalion (GEF) hit a land mine. The 4th Battalion (GEF) patrol received small arms and automatic weapons fire from Hill 273, which was north of their objective.

At 2255 hours, Company O, 4th Battalion (GEF), was attacked by an enemy patrol, which later broke contact and withdrew to the north. At 2330 hours, a small enemy patrol attacked Company E's OP with grenades and also was driven off. An enemy group of approximately two platoons was sighted moving west across the Company E front and taken under artillery and mortar fire.

At 0800 hours on March 5th, two Chinese prisoners surrendered to the 4th Battalion (GEF), as a result of the propaganda broadcast of March 3rd, and 1st Battalion patrols captured two more prisoners.

At 0800 hours on March 8th, the regiment began a major attack as a part of the Eighth Army's operation "Ripper." The regiment's attack included an assault by the 1st Battalion on the high ground west of Yondu-ri, Hills 273 and 341; as the 4th Battalion (GEF) attacked the high ground northeast of Yondu-ri, including Hills 326 and 443. An armored task force - Task Force Laloge - moved up the Hyongchong-Yondu-ri

highway to support the attack on the right and left. Both attacks were made against extremely heavy resistance, including 120mm, 81mm and 60mm mortar fire in addition to 75mm artillery, small arms and automatic weapons fire. By 1210 hours, the 1st Battalion had secured Hill 273 and was moving forward to attack Hill 341, which they secured at 1400 hours.

Contact with the enemy was made again at 0010 hours on March 8th, when Company A reported approximately 25 enemy troops at the base of their hill, and three rounds of 76mm fire were received in their positions. At 0830 hours, the regiment began the attack in continuation of the previous day when Task Force Laloge secured their initial objective after taking the enemy positions under direct tank fire. Patrols from Company C reinforced with one platoon of tanks engaged the enemy on Hill 328 with artillery and mortar fire after receiving small arms and automatic fire from the enemy position on the high ground to the north and east. Tank and artillery fire was placed on the located enemy positions with good results as the 2nd Battalion prepared for an attack on Hill 285 the following day.

The battalions continued the attack at 0700 hours on the 9th. Company E secured Hill 285 by 0910 hours after overcoming light small arms and automatic weapons fire, and continued their attack to seize Hill 451, driving off an estimated enemy platoon to the north. The 3rd Battalion, maneuvering from the west, moved against light resistance across the hill mass, including Hills 389 and 409. By 1440 hours, both the 2nd and 3rd Battalions had dispatched platoon screening patrols to the north over Phase Line Albany. At 1600 hours, these patrols received heavy automatic weapons fire and mortar fire from an estimated enemy battalion and some artillery fire from Hill 345. The regiment moved up in strength behind the patrols after experiencing congested traffic conditions in the pass area along line Albany.

At 0730 hours March 10th, the regiment again moved out in a continuation of the attack as part of operation "Ripper." The 2nd Battalion

The call for "medic" as Corporal O'Neil of the 3rd Platoon, Company F, 2nd Bn., 7th Cavalry was Killed in Action. Hongchon Valley, March 1951. (Suey Lee)

Troopers of the 3rd Platoon, Company F, 2nd Battalion, 7th Cavalry, in the Hongchon Valley, March 1951. Platoon Leader was 1st Lt. Jim Gorman. (Courtesy of Suey Lee)

attacked Hill 554 with Companies E and G. This position was defended by an enemy battalion and both companies received heavy mortar, small arms, and automatic weapons fire. Patrols from the 4th Battalion (GEF) supported the attack by directing tank fire on the west flank of the hill mass, resulting in the destruction of several small enemy groups. The hill mass was secured by 1400 hours, and patrols moved out to clear the slopes.

At 0734 hours, Companies K and L moved to Hills 345 and 445 where they received a heavy volume of 120mm mortar and 76mm artillery fire. Company K finally was able to seize Hill 345; however, the attack of Company L against Hill 445 was unsuccessful despite a number of artillery and air strikes, and the 3rd Battalion closed in a tight perimeter at the base of their objective as darkness fell.

The 4th Battalion (GEF) patrolled aggressively in its zone moving out at 0730 hours. After overcoming machine gun, small arms and other automatic weapons fire, the battalion seized Hill 293, the high ground immediately north of Yonduri and an area adjacent to the town itself. Enemy fire from the northeast of the town continued to sweep Yondu-ri and prevented the engineers from clearing mines in that area so that tanks could pass through the town. One tank from Company C, 70th Tank Battalion, struck a mine and was disabled temporarily, and supporting patrols of the 4th Battalion (GEF) continued to receive machine gun, artillery and mortar fire during the early part of the evening.

At 0730 hours on March 11th, the regiment resumed the attack, utilizing patrols to develop enemy positions to the front. A Company N patrol, 4th Battalion (GEF) received intense small arms and heavy weapons fire from enemy positions on the hill occupied by the company at 1330 hours. Company P engaged an estimated reinforced enemy platoon on Hill 332 after receiving heavy small arms and automatic weapons fire but seized the hill by 1130 hours and captured one prisoner.

Company K attacked at 0730 hours and

immediately received small arms and mortar fire from the vicinity of Hill 561. At 1230 hours, Company K had reached the northern slopes of Hill 345 and routed an enemy platoon killing six and wounding 12. At 0730 hours, a Company L platoon departed for Hill 445, but by 1335 hours, they could not advance further due to the intense small arms and automatic weapons fire.

Company F captured two prisoners during a patrol action at 1020 hours but did not encounter heavy resistance. Contact was made with the 27th British Commonwealth Brigade on the right. By 1230 hours, the road to the mountain pass immediately north of the village of Yandongwon-ni had been cleared of mines, and Task Force McDonald, consisting of Company B, 70th Tank Battalion and Company E, attacked astride the road to the north. The Task Force received small arms and automatic weapons fire, finally was stopped by mines and forced to return by 1630 hours.

During the month of March 1951, Sgt. Thomas E. Randell, forward observer, Heavy Mortar Company, remembers a combat mission, and he wrote:

"One bright sunny afternoon, Company F, under the command of Capt. Gray, had been ordered to attack and occupy a hill directly to our front. My unit was to give 4.2 mortar support during the initial attack. The hill was defended by well dug-in Chinese infantry, and Capt. Gray had requested an air strike to precede our ground assault.

Capt. Gray explained to me that if the combat aircraft could not be over the target by 1600 hours, he had requested that they abort the mission. Our ground assault would begin at that time without air support.

We waited until 1600 hours, and we kept scanning the sky for aircraft, but none appeared. So Company F went forward with their planned assault, and soon began routing Chinese from their fortified positions.

Then suddenly overhead, two F-51s with Australian insignia and markings appeared above us, and they began swooping in low over the hill.

Capt. Gray was furious and stood up waving his arms in an attempt to wave them off. We quickly spread our florescent banner out on the hill to signify that we were friendly troops. On their second run, however, they came in strafing, rocketing and bombing. Company F was caught in a dilemma and was halfway up the hill in taking their objective. Then they came at us again, repeating the same grizzly performance. For some reason, they climbed to 1,000 feet, wiggled their wings and headed south.

Company F sustained numerous casualties. However, the hill was taken and secured prior to darkness. To our surprise, as we looked at the enemy occupied hill to our immediate front, we could see that the Chinese had spread out a huge florescent banner!"

Task Force Laloge, consisting of two platoons of tanks from Company C, 70th Tank Battalion, attacked up the stream bed running northwest from the village of Yangdogwon-ni, but at 1230 hours, they also were stopped by the impassable terrain.

A regimental attack was ordered for March 12th to seize the ridge line in the western part of the zone, which constituted the only portion of Line Albany in the regimental sector that had not been cleared. The attack began at 0700 hours by a platoon from Company B, which reached objective 73 without enemy contact. The 1st Battalion continued to attack from Objective 73 to Objective 74 and received small arms and automatic weapons fire from the west. Objective 74 was taken only after fierce hand-to-hand, grenade and bayonet fighting on the part of Company B. Following seizure of Objective 74, Company C moved through Company B to attack toward Objective 75 in the 3rd Battalion sector. The action of the 1st Battalion in securing these dominating features of the ridge was an outstanding example of aggressive infantry small unit actions.

Concurrent with the above actions, platoon-sized patrols of the 2nd Battalion had secured Hill 447. Task Force O'Neil, consisting of Company A, 70th Tank Battalion reinforced, was committed through the pass leading through this hill mass and reached a point some 800 yards north of the pass by 1150 hours.

Company I attacked at 0930 hours to seize Objective 75 but met heavy resistance from positions on the objective as well as from the approaches thereto. Numerous artillery and air strikes were placed on the positions, and heavy casualties were inflicted as the enemy moved from one position on the ridge to another. Finally, at 1455 hours, Company C, having been committed from Objective 74 in the 1st Battalion's zone along the ridge from the east, assaulted and seized Objective 75. Company I moved up through Company C from the south to continue the attack and swung west against Objective 76, which was seized by 1435 hours. Enemy machine gun fire, however, continued to be received in the northwest area, and Company I remained on Objective 76 to provide fire support while Company L passed through them to seize objectives 77 and 77A, which dominated the ridge line in this area. At the close of the day, Objective 77 had been secured, but 77A still was under heavy enemy fire. Objective 77 was not tenable as a result of

this fire and was abandoned prior to darkness.

The 4th Battalion (GEF), which attacked at 0700 hours, reached their objective without enemy contact and advanced to the northeast to seize the ridge line in their sector.

The 3rd Battalion attacked at 0700 hours on March 13th to secure Objective 77A. This objective was in the 8th Cavalry Regiment's sector; however, it dominated the ridge line on which the 7th Cavalry units were located. Company L reoccupied Objective 77 by 0835 hours against moderate enemy resistance, but as the attack continued on Objective 77A, the company received intense small arms, mortar and automatic weapons fire from an estimated two enemy companies. Artillery fire and air strikes were placed on the enemy defenses but these efforts met limited success due to the strongly entrenched bunker-type positions that the enemy had prepared. By 1030 hours, Company I had secured Hill 540 with a combat patrol and then occupied the hill with the remainder of the company. Objective 77A again was taken under attack at 1410 hours from the east with Company L. Despite intense and bitter fighting, including numerous

air and artillery strikes, the objective was not taken. The enemy, inside his strongly reinforced pill boxes, apparently was safe from anything except direct hits.

At dusk, the 3rd Battalion still was attacking Objective 77A. At 1725 hours, an enemy column of approximately 700 troops in a column of two's, covering a distance of about 2,000 yards, started moving toward Objective 77A along the ridge from the north. This enemy column was attacked by artillery TOT concentrations as well as by air strikes. Three separate times, the enemy attempted to reorganize the column, and each time, they were taken under fire with artillery (VT fuse) and heavy mortars. This resulted in the complete defeat of the enemy force and caused casualties estimated at 400 killed and 200 wounded. As the remainder of this enemy group ran in wild disorder to the northwest, the artillery continued to pound them. The die-hard enemy forces an Objective 77A continued to hold however, and at 1830 hours, the 3rd Battalion was forced to break contact and returned to Objective 76.

At 0800 hours on the 14th, the regiment continued its attack to the north. Objective 77A was abandoned by the enemy during the night following the attacks of the previous day, and elements of the 6th ROK Division relieved the western elements of the 3rd Battalion. The regiment moved forward with the 1st Battalion on the right and the 4th Battalion (GEF) on the left, and reached Phase Line Baker without further enemy contact.

The 2nd Battalion, 7th Cavalry, was under the operational control of the 5th Cavalry regiment throughout the period.

During the general advance of the IX Corps toward Phase Line Buffalo, the 7th Cavalry Regiment was given the mission of attacking and securing Hill mass 655. This mountain, and the outlying mountains to the east (Hills 325 and 320) blocked any advance north of the Hongchon River in the regimental zone. The following describes the action of the 4th Battalion (GEF) and the 1st Battalion, the two assault battalions, in their preparation for and in the attack on Hill mass 655.

Hill mass 655 dominated the regimental zone as well as that of the 6th ROK Division on the west. In order to assault this hill mass and the

L to R: 2nd Lt. Edward L. Daily, Leader 1st Platoon, Company H, 2nd Bn., 7th Cavalry, Corporals Barnes, Buckley and E. Thomas. Digging defensive positions of Phase Line Benton, March 31, 1951. (Courtesy of Margie Thomas)

Combat Screening Patrol from the 2nd Battalion, 7th Cavalry in the Hongchon Valley, March 1951. (Courtesy of Bob Mauger)

L to R: The 70th Tank Bn., was attached to the 7th Cavalry Regiment. Crewmen on tank were, Davis, Donnley, Mury, Ritchie and Anderson. Note painted tiger on front of tank. (Courtesy of Ashley Anderson)

Some roads were almost impassable. (U.S. Army Photo)

Attacking with the support of tanks from the 70th Tank Battalion. (U.S. Army Photo)

major ridge line immediately north of Hill 655, it first was necessary to seize a bridgehead over the Hongchon River to provide a means for moving supplies, supporting weapons and ammunition within range of the operation by way of the Hongchon River valley, as there were no supply roads or trails into the area. It thus was decided to divide the assault on Hill 655 into two phases: The first phase to seize Hills 325 and 320, and the second phase to be a continuation of the attack to outflank and seize Hill mass 655.

On March 15th, a combat patrol from Company O, 4th Battalion (GEF), while reconnoitering for a crossing of the Hongchon River, received heavy small arms, machine gun and mortar fire from the south slope of Hill 325. Air reconnaissance revealed that there were many dug-in positions and other evidence of enemy activity on Hill 655 and the adjacent hills and ridges to the east, particularly Hills 325 and 320.

In order to determine the enemy locations and strength, patrols were ordered to Hills 325 and 320 by the 4th Battalion (GEF) and 1st Battalion respectively on March 16th. Company P sent a platoon-sized patrol toward Hill 325, which encountered heavy small arms, machine gun and mortar fire from enemy positions located on the ridge leading to the hill mass from the southeast. Mortar and artillery fire and air strikes were placed on the enemy, but the patrol was unable to advance against the heavy enemy resistance. The patrol repulsed a 30-man enemy counterattack and was subsequently ordered to withdraw.

A platoon-sized patrol from Company A was sent across the Hongchon River toward Hill 320 on the same day. This patrol reached a point 50 yards from the top of their objective when they received heavy small arms and automatic weapons fire. The patrol reported that it had located eight enemy machine guns on Hill 320 and had withdrawn in order to place artillery fire on this positions. Fire was adjusted with good results, but the patrol was unable to advance and also was ordered to withdraw.

As plans were issued for the attack on Hill 655, all indications pointed toward a hard fight ahead for the regiment. The enemy strength in the Hill 655-Hill 325-Hill 320 area was estimated to be approximately one regiment. Hills 325 and

Sharp Shooter from the 2nd Battalion, 7th Cavalry, name unknown. (Courtesy of Ed Daily)

320 had to be attacked simultaneously since the positions were mutually supporting and dominated the Hongchon River valley. Possession of the objectives was essential therefore in order to move supplies and ammunition forward to support the attack on Hill mass 655. The enemy was well-entrenched and tenaciously defended his underground positions, which were covered with several layers of logs and connected by trenches.

The plan to seize Hill 655 was:

Phase I - the 4th Battalion (GEF) and the 1st

Battalion were to attack at 0730 hours on March 17th to secure the bridgehead across the Hongchon River. The 4th Battalion (GEF) to seize Hill 325 and to be prepared to continue the attack to Hill 655. The 1st Battalion to secure Hills 320 and 349.

Phase II - the 2nd Battalion was to be prepared to pass through the eastern portion of the 1st Battalion and continue the attack upon seizure of the other bridgehead.

The 3rd Battalion was to be in regimental

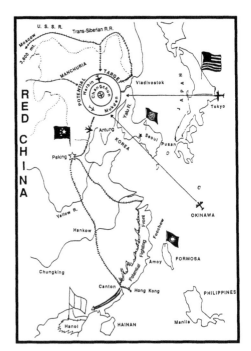

MacArthur's plan, although never stated in detail, is shown above. It would include: 1)bombing Manchurian airfields on which enemy planes are now massis; 2)blockading the coast of China; 3)bombing Chinese supply centers; 4)helping the Chinese Nationalist to build up anti-Communist resistance in South China. These actions, together with and advance by the United Nation Forces in Korea, might endanger the Chines Red regime, forcing them to end the war. Truman, however, feared that attacking the Chinese anywhere outside the Korean peninsula would provoke the Russians into entering the war.

reserve and to support the attack with 81mm mortar fire, heavy machine gun and fire and 75mm recoilless rifle fire on the southern slopes of Hill mass 655.

An intense artillery and mortar preparation was to be placed on the objective area during the night of March 16th-17th, and a general artillery preparation to be fired prior to and after H-hour. Air strikes were requested for March 17th with the first strike to begin at 0715 hours.

At 0800 hours on March 17th, after an artillery and air strike preparation on Hill 325, Company O of the 4th Battalion (GEF) crossed the Hongchon River 2-1/2 miles from their objective. The company received enemy fire at 0830 hours from Hill 325 and from the east side of Hill 655, and immediately deployed into an attack formation. At 0930 hours, the company commander was wounded by machine gun fire, and the executive officer assumed command of the company. The advance of the company was slow and methodical. The enemy positions were so well-prepared that they had to be individually neutralized with bayonets and hand grenades. The 4th Platoon, Company C, 70th Tank Battalion, attached to the 4th Battalion (GEF) provided outstanding support to the assault elements, advancing over terrain ordinarily considered impassable for tanks, overrunning and caving-in enemy emplacements and firing direct 76mm tank fire into enemy machine gun positions at ranges of 25 to 60 yards.

After seizure of a strategically located peak by the 4th Battalion (GEF), the enemy staged a counterattack, which was repulsed by the tenacious Greek soldiers with grenades and bayonets resulting in many enemy casualties. The battalion inched forward against an enemy that refused to give ground; however, the gallant Greeks did not falter and continued toward their objective - Hill 325. The enemy was at his strongest on the peak just south of Hill 325 where he had reinforced his position and stubbornly defended it. For three hours, the 4th Battalion (GEF) forces attacked and maneuvered, and finally after exceptionally close support by the artillery, heavy mortars, tanks, air support, 60mm and 81mm mortars, they fixed bayonets and charged. After fierce and brutal hand-to-hand combat with grenades and bayonets, fighting amidst the fierce traditional Greek battle cries of "Aera" mixed with shouts of "GARRYOWEN," the gallant battalion drove the enemy from the hill. The enemy regrouped his forces and immediately initiated a 100-man counterattack but were met again by Greek bayonet and repulsed. The fanatic enemy attacked a second and third time, determined to retake the strategic high ground, but with grim determination to hold their objective, the 4th Battalion (GEF) met each attack with the bayonet and repulsed each enemy thrust infliction increasingly heavier casualties on the Chinese Communist Forces. The peak and ridge were secured, the remainder of the enemy withdrew, the enemy's defense of the Hongchon River line was broken, Hill 655 was threatened from the east by our forces, and at 1600 hours, Hill 325 was secured without further opposition.

Company N then moved into position behind Company O, prepared to defend the newly

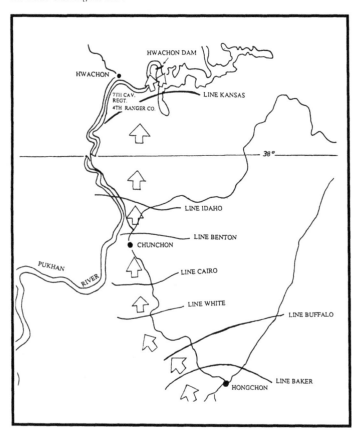

Commencing on 7 March, Cavalry units drove northeast to the Hongchon area, then turned north and continued through Chunchon to line Kansas, north of the 38th parallel. On 11 April elements of the 7th Cav. Regt. and the 4th Ranger Co. pushed on to the Hwachon reservoir. Their initial assualt on the enemy defenses was successful, but they wree soon pinned down and received orders to pull back.

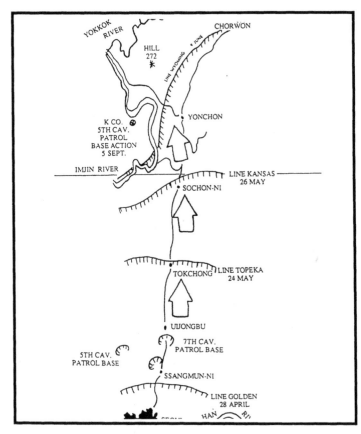

The Chinese spring offensive got under way of 22 April, and the 1st Cav. Div. was soon committed along line Golden in the defense of Seoul. When the Red drive had been stopped, United Nations forces began probing northward. During the latter part of May and early June, the Cavalry jumped off and pushed ahead to line Wyoming, which was to be its main line of resistance until October 1951.

won ground and to continue the attack on Hill 655 the following day. Company P was used as a base of fire, from a strategically located ridge line south of the Hongchon River running parallel to the ridge line leading to Hill 325. The following day, Company N advanced and secured their objective without enemy opposition and the Greek national flag waved proudly on Hill 655. The mission of the 4th Battalion (GEF) was accomplished with only one killed and six wounded. Enemy casualties were 187 dead and an estimated 300 wounded.

While the above action was taking place on March 17th, Company A had crossed the line of departure at 0730 hours and proceeded up the southeast ridge leading to Hill 320. By 0845 hours, the company's leading elements reported that they were receiving small arms and automatic weapons fire from Hill 349. 75mm recoilless rifles, 81mm mortars and heavy machine guns were employed to give close support and assistance to Company A's advance on the objective, and by 1135 hours, Company A, following closely behind the supporting fire, had advanced steadily against the intense small arms and automatic weapons fire, driven the enemy from his prepared positions and secured the first peak on Hill 320. However, the company was unable to advance further against the continuous sheet of small arms and automatic weapons fire delivered from a second peak about 100 yards to the west.

At 1430 hours, the enemy - estimated to be a company - on the high ground in front of Company A was reinforced and launched aggressive counterattacks on the flanks of the company's positions. The company was low on ammunition and awaited resupply when this occurred, and although heavy artillery and mortar concentrations were placed on the enemy he continued his counterattacks. The quick-thinking company commander redistributed the remaining ammunition and immediately launched a counterattack of his own. The Company A troopers, yelling, "GARRYOWEN," charged with bayonets and killed and dispersed the enemy. The momentum of Company A's attack carried them across the entire ridge, which constituted Hill 320. One platoon advanced down the southwest ridge of the hill, engaged a platoon of enemy, and killed 19 and took 12 prisoners in a fierce bayonet charge. The total enemy casualties on Hill 320 was 96 counted dead, 14 prisoners and an estimated 200 wounded. As Company A reorganized and established defensive positions, the remaining enemy fled to the north in confusion with all available artillery and mortar fire following them and inflicting additional casualties.

At 1500 hours, Company C was ordered to pass through Company A and to continue the attack to seize Hill 349; however, the enemy had been defeated so soundly that the hill was secured without opposition by 1700 hours.

The regiment continued the attack at 0755 hours on the 18th and advanced rapidly. This rapid advance was due to the successful action of the 1st and 4th (GEF) Battalions on the preceding day, which had broken enemy resistance along the entire Hill mass 655. Two rounds of enemy mortar fire received at 2115 hours was the only enemy resistance during the day, and

plans were made for the 8th Cavalry Regiment to relieve the 7th Cavalry Regiment following seizure of the next phase line by the 7th Cavalry.

The 2nd and 3rd Battalions attacked at 0700 hours on March 19th. At 1010 hours, Company G received light automatic weapons and small arms fire, and by 1230 hours, the 2nd Battalion had secured Phase Line Red - the next phase line. Patrols from Company G continued on through the phase line but received automatic weapons and small arms fire. The 3rd Battalion continued forward, clearing the phase line in its zone without enemy resistance and the relief of the 7th Cavalry was completed by 1700 hours. The 2nd and 3rd Battalions assembled in their assigned areas and went into division reserve near Hongchon. During the day, the 1st and 4th (GEF) Battalions and the regimental trains moved into Division reserve areas south and west of Hongchon.

On March 22nd, the 1st Battalion was ordered to Chunchon to organize a base of operations from which patrols would operate to contact the enemy, and to serve as a covering force for the remainder of the First Cavalry Division then establishing defensive positions south of Chunchon. This force was called Task Force Exploit and operated directly under Division control. The Task Force - commanded by Maj. Lucian Croft - was composed of the 1st Battalion, 7th Cavalry Regiment; Company C, 70th Tank Battalion; 16th Reconnaissance Company; the Reconnaissance Platoon, 70th Tank Battalion; 16th Reconnaissance Company; the Reconnaissance Platoon, 70th Tank Battalion; and the 1st Platoon of the Regimental Heavy Mortar Company. Supporting artillery consisted of the 77th Field Artillery Battalion; the 82nd Field Artillery Battalion; the 92nd Field Artillery Battalion; and one battery of the 17th Field Artillery Battalion.

During the period March 22nd to 25th, Task Force Exploit conducted several tank reinforced patrols deep into enemy territory. Separate patrols led by 1st Lt. S. T. Rhodes, 16th Reconnaissance Company and Capt. Anthony Martino of Company A, 7th Cavalry, were particularly successful. After three days of constant patrolling, Task Force Exploit was relieved by the 3rd Battalion, 8th Cavalry Regiment, having inflicted 250 casualties on the enemy with a loss to the Task Force of only one killed and eight wounded.

On March 25th, the regiment relieved the 5th Cavalry Regiment along Phase Line Cairo and accepted responsibility for the zone at 1330 hours. Patrols from the 2nd and 3rd Battalions reached the Soyang River but returned at the end of the day without having made contact with the enemy.

On the following day, the regiment continued to patrol in its zone against light enemy opposition, as enemy forces continued their withdrawal northward.

The 4th Battalion (GEF), remained in regimental reserve on March 26th to celebrate Greek Independence Day with a parade, review and other festivities. The celebration was attended by Lt. Gen. Matthew Ridgway, Eighth Army Commander; Lt. Gen. William M Hoge, IX Corps Commander; and Maj. Gen. C. D. Palmer, Commanding General of the First Cavalry Division. Other distinguished guests included Maj. Gen. Athanasios Dascarolis, Greek liaison officer to

the Far East Command; Col. John Daskslopoulos, Commander, Greek Expeditionary Force; Lt. Col. D. Arbouzis, 4th Battalion (GEF) Commander; and other invited dignitaries. The celebration was high-lighted by a presentation of awards to members of the Greek Battalion and addresses commemorating Greek Independence Day. First Cavalry Division shoulder patches were presented to all members of the 4th Battalion (GEF) as Greek and American friendship was greatly enhanced during the festivities of the day.

The following address was delivered by Maj. Gen. A.G. Dascarolis during the ceremony:

"The commander of the fighting Greek Battalion and the Commander of the Greek ground forces in Korea in their orders to their unit praised the history and significance of our Independence Day.

Now, permit me, the senior Greek officer and the representative of Greece in the Far East, to express to you in a few words neither the fighting spirit nor the skill in the art of waging war of the Greek Expeditionary Forces, for that purpose you are more qualified than I, but to express to you the feeling of those Greek officers and men, your comrades in battle in this war against Communism in Korea.

All of us understand that our mission here in Korea is double; first of all, to remain worthy of what is expected from us by the Greek people living up to the traditions of Greece; and second, to accomplish our mission according to your orders, as our superiors here in Korea.

All the Greek soldiers fighting under your command are not a select group among the Greek forces but are a small unit of the Regular Greek Armed Forces, with the natural and acquired characteristics of the Hellenic people.

We do not know if you gave much thought in attaching the Battalion to the 1st Cavalry Division and to the 7th Cavalry Regiment, the famous GARRYOWEN, but we feel that you have captured 1,000 Greek hearts by doing so, and the leaders who win the hearts of soldiers can realize miracles and wonders.

As soldiers, we will do our best so that one day to hope that the future officers and men of the 7th Cavalry Regiment will remember in their songs our names as in the verse:

'Look at Cameron and O'Brien Sgt. Flynn
With a smile they're fighting, dying Sgt. Flynn
Though not one will be alive
Still their spirits will survive
To sing the name and fame of dear old GARRYOWEN.'

Greece through its long life 3,000 years ago respecting the noble traditions and the human dignity looks at all the facts in all their bleakness and nakedness with a manly optimism and dares to hope and remain alive."

At 0900 hours on March 27th, the 4th Battalion (GEF) relieved the 1st Battalion in place. A 1st Battalion patrol became engaged in an action, which resulted in one soldier seriously wounded. The 2nd Battalion patrols received 60mm mortar, small arms and automatic weapons fire from enemy positions until they broke and withdrew. The 3rd Battalion dispatched two patrols to the same area as those of the preceding day; however, upon reaching the area, the patrol found that the enemy had withdrawn.

During the remainder of March, the regiment continued to advance and occupied defensive positions on Phase Line Benton with the only minor enemy contact on Hill 610.

Patrols of platoon-size reinforced with tanks were dispatched on April 1st across the Soyang River. These patrols had the combined mission of developing enemy positions and inflicting maximum enemy casualties.

On April 2nd, the 2nd and 4th (GEF) Battalions established bridgeheads across the Soyang River without enemy contact and continued the attack the following day. The 2nd Battalion was head up by an enemy force entrenched on Hill 785. However, this objective was captured on April 4th without opposition. The 2nd Battalion also seized Hill 621 and continued patrolling to the north.

The 1st and 3rd Battalions relieved the 2nd and 4th (GEF) Battalions on April 5th and continued the attack. Enemy resistance was slight until April 7th, when the 3rd Battalion was halted momentarily on Hill 878 by a small enemy force and the sheer rock cliffs of the hill. Hill 878 was seized on April 8th, and the 1st Battalion then directed artillery fire with excellent results against an enemy battalion located in the vicinity of the village of Yuchon-ni.

On April 10th, the First Cavalry Division, except the 7th Cavalry Regiment, was placed in IX Corps reserve. The 7th Cavalry Regiment was given one final mission - the capture of the Hwachon dam and reservoir.

West of the town of Hwachon, the Pukhan River turns suddenly north and then sharply back to the south just below the town. The dam, built on the curve where the river flows northward, backs the water up to the south and east, forming the Hwachon reservoir. On April 8th, the enemy had opened the flood-gates of the dam, causing a rise in the Pukhan River, thus threatening to cut off friendly forces, which had crossed the river further to the south. The regiment's mission before joining the rest of the Division in reserve was to capture the enemy stronghold around the dam and prevent further flooding of the river.

The regiment's rapid advance over the rugged terrain during the preceding few days had placed them in an area where it was impossible for vehicles larger than a one-quarter-ton jeep to travel due to the poor roads. The direct support artillery (105mm Howitzers) could not provide support since the regiment was beyond their range, and medium artillery (155mm Howitzers) could furnish support only by firing at their maximum range.

On April 10th, the 2nd Battalion was given the mission of capturing the knife-like ridge bounded by the Pukhan River on the west and the Hwachon reservoir on the east. The battalion advance against the stubborn defense of an estimated two enemy companies over the extremely rugged terrain. By nightfall, they had reached a point approximately 1,000 yards south of Pukhan dam, facing a well dug-in reinforced enemy.

Since the area between the river the reservoir was limited, additional units could not be committed to reinforce the 2nd Battalion's attack, and it became evident that additional forces would be required to take the objective. Plans therefore were made for an amphibious operation across the reservoir to the northeast in an effort to outflank the enemy holding up the advance of the 2nd Battalion and to capture the dam.

Emergency calls were made for assault boats and motors to be brought up from the rear, and the Air Force was requested to paradrop life rafts. Since the roads would not permit the passage of trucks, five assault boats and motors finally were shuttled forward by jeep and trailer. Upon arrival, it was found that only three motors would run and an emergency call was sent to all units for a motorboat mechanic - a skill almost as hard to find as horseshoer on the Korean peninsula.

Also to arrive at the south shore of the reservoir were infantry reinforcements from Company I, 3rd Battalion, 7th Cavalry Regiment and the 4th Ranger Company commanded by Capt. Dorsey B. Anderson. To further support the attack on the dam, the following equipment was received from the 8th Engineer Combat Battalion: 35 assault boats, 20 outboard motors, 245 paddles, 160 life preservers, one demolition kit with detonators, 50 electric caps, 400 feet of primer cord, 386 pounds of TNT, 100 non-electric caps, 500 feet of time fuse, 45 fuse lighters and 20 adapters.

At 0345 hours on April 11th, the 4th Ranger Company - attached for the operation - and Company I, 7th Cavalry, began an amphibious operation to outflank the enemy in front of the 2nd Battalion. The landing was made without incident on the north side of the reservoir. The Ranger Company received small arms and automatic weapons fire as they secured the first objective, but at 1330 hours, both companies received a vicious counterattack from an estimated enemy battalion.

Meanwhile, the 2nd Battalion again had launched an attack down the narrow neck of land between the Pukhan River and the reservoir but could not dislodge the enemy from his positions. The 1st Battalion attempted a diversionary attack across the river to the west but could not force a crossing or even find a suitable site for one by the end of the day.

Without sufficient artillery support, the regiment could not advance against the determined enemy and was ordered to withdraw. The 4th Ranger Company and Company I were withdrawn by boat during the late afternoon of April 11th, and the withdrawal was completed by 0135 hours on April 12th after both companies had suffered severe casualties. Killed in action during this combat operation were two company commanders from the 2nd Battalion; Capt. Harold Gray, Commander, Company F and 1st Lt. Richard Gerrish, Commander, Company H.

The following is an account of the action of the Hwanch'on Reservoir during April 10th-12th, from Col. (then Lt. Col.) John W. Callaway, Battalion Commander, 2nd Battalion, 7th Cavalry Regiment.

"As stated previously, this description of the operations in connection with Hwach'on Reservoir Dam represents my personal recollections as the commander of the 2nd Battalion, 7th Cavalry Regiment. This operation was selected because it was unusual and demonstrates how some small mistakes can be costly.

This operation began on April 10, 1951, with the battalion conducting a reconnaissance in force toward the Hwanch'on Reservoir some 10 miles away. Initially, the enemy resistance was not that bad in the extremely rugged terrain. As a matter of fact, the terrain was such that it was impossible for vehicles to keep up. Companies F and G led the reconnaissance with E Company in reserve. I and my radio operator accompanied Company G. Shortly after noon, we reached the reservoir and Company G followed a road northward along the bank of the lake. We soon were able to see the Hwanch'on Reservoir Dam. There

Forward elements of the 2nd Bn., 7th Cavalry at Hwach'on Reservoir on April 10, 1951. (Courtesy of Suey Lee)

Air strikes using napalm bombs hit enemy positions at Hwach'on Reservoir on April 11, 1951. (Courtesy of Suey Lee)

Extremely sharp and razor-like ridges existed within the Hwach'on reservoir. April 11, 1951. (Courtesy of Suey Lee)

The Hwach'on Reservoir Power house, along the Pukhan River. April 10, 1951. (Courtesy of Suey Lee)

was no enemy activity in front of Company G. At this time, a message was received from an excited radio operator that F Company had been ambushed and that medics and stretchers were urgently needed. I took the radio from my operator and asked to speak to Capt. Gray, the F Company commander. After a moment, the company radio operator replied that Capt. Gray had been killed. I asked if any other officers were in the vicinity. The answer was negative. I told the company radio operator to locate the company executive officer and have him taken charge of the company, and I would join the company shortly. I ordered Companies G and E to halt, go into defensive positions and await further orders. According to the coordinates give me, Company F was about 700 yards west of my location. The terrain was extremely rugged, but I felt I could reach the Company within an hour. After going over a number of rugged ridges, I realized that the coordinates furnished to me were incorrect. I had no choice but to continue to the west to locate the company. Finally, after an hour and a half, I located the company. To my amazement, there were only two casualties - Capt. Gray and the lead point man both were killed. I then gave instructions to the executive officer to go into defensive positions and await further instructions.

By the time I reached the ridge overlooking the reservoir, it was around 1700 hours. I saw that the gates on the Hwach'on Reservoir Dam were being opened. As I studied the terrain toward the dam, I could see that the peninsula formed by the reservoir and the Pukhan River on the west was about 300 yards wide with a knife ridge up its center. This peninsula was wide enough for only one company to attack. As I was sitting on this OP, my S-3 came up with a strange message from higher headquarters. It read: 'Take the Hwach'on Reservoir Dam if possible, but don't get hurt.'

G Company was selected to make the attack up the peninsula the following morning. Unfortunately, we had out-distanced our 105mm direct support artillery.

The following day, my artillery forward observer spent the day trying to zero in any heavy artillery that was available from the division 155mm howitzers or Corps artillery. Because of

the extreme range involved and the rugged terrain, the forward observer was never able to adjust the artillery fire, so we were without this critical support. My request for air strikes was denied because of the low ceiling. The only crew support weapons we had were our machine gun, mortars and one 75mm recoilless weapon on a jeep that Maj. Mel Chandler had managed to winch over a mountain to get to us.

Capt. Moses, the G Company commander, used one of his platoons and his supporting weapons to lay down a base of fire. Using the limited width of the peninsula, he tried to maneuver his other platoons around the flanks of the enemy on the ridge. The enemy had every avenue covered and was well dug-in. I joined Company G in hopes that my presence might make a difference. It became clear that the enemy defenses were too strong and that we would receive too many casualties if we attempted to storm the enemy positions. With no air or artillery support and limited maneuver room, the dam could not be taken by going up to the peninsula in daylight.

Col. Harris was advised of the situation and decided to obtain some pontoon motor boats to cross the lake the following morning and attack the enemy from that direction. During the first day, there had been no enemy artillery or mortar fire. Because of this, I and other members of my staff exposed ourselves on the Observation Post overlooking the action of Company G as it attacked the enemy up the peninsula. Suddenly, an enemy artillery shell landed a few feet of us on the OP. I was knocked off my feet but was not hurt. I began to check the others near me. Only my heavy weapons company commander, Lt. Richard Gerrish, had been hit. He was killed instantly. Two of my company commanders had been killed in this operation!

My plan for the following morning was to have E Company conduct a night attack. I ordered the attack to commence at 0400 hours because I wanted to seize the objective just before daylight so that our troops could defend against a counterattack during daylight hours. For some reason, the attack did not take place at 0400 hours. As a matter of fact it was daylight before the lead platoon crossed the line of departure. The enemy was awake and could see our troops approaching. The enemy opened fire, and E Com-

pany was able to do no better than G Company the day before. Company I and the 4th Ranger Company attached to the 7th Cavalry Regiment crossed the reservoir in boats and landed without opposition; however, after moving a short distance toward the day, the two companies ran into heavy enemy fire and were forced to withdraw.

Lt. John Matthews' platoon of Company G was ordered to provide security for the battalion CP. The platoon had moved along the road some 500 yards south of the peninsula when suddenly without warning an enemy mortar round landed on the platoon, killing several of its members. These types of deaths don't make sense since the enemy mortar fire in this area had been practically non-existent.

We were unable to seize the Hwach'on Reservoir Dam. We withdrew and joined the division in reserve position some miles to the south.

As I recall this operation, I wonder what would have happened if rather than halting G Company, I had continued with the G Company toward the dam the first afternoon of the operation. We had surprised the enemy as evidence by his opening the dam gates. I am convinced that with air and artillery support, we could have taken the Hwach'on Reservoir Dam. I also believe that if E Company had attacked at night as ordered, the company could have seized a foothold on the ridge along the peninsula and assisted Company I and the 4th Ranger Company in taking the dam."

From the book, "Rangers in Korea," author Robert Black wrote:

"In the high mountains near the city of Hwach'on is one of the largest reservoirs in Korea, extending over 13 square miles, with an estimated capacity of 19,140,000,000 cubic feet of water. The dam is a straight-line overflow type, 275 feet high, with a spillway 826 feet long. There are 18 spillway gates, and an identical number of penstocks at the base to run the dynamos for electrical power. When the gates are closed, they contain up to 32 feet of water above the spillway.

There was more chill than warmth in the early April winds, but the melt of the winter snows would soon be at hand. The waters of an uncontrolled river would flow swift and deep, fords would become impassable, and bridges could be washed out. The Hwach'on dam held at bay the

95

Air strikes bombing the Hwach'on Reservoir dam. The dam actually contained eighteen sluice gates.

Pukhan River - and the dam was in the hands of the Communists.

While the dam was a problem, it did not appear to be a First Cavalry Division problem. The division, attacking north, was scheduled to be relieved by the 1st Marine Division on April 10. Relief would be at phase-line "Kansas" about 4,000 yards south of the Hwach' on dam.

Intelligence reports on the dam were ominous. Aerial observers reported that the spillway gates were close to their maximum extent, and only a trickle of water was being released. Local civilians said the water level of the river below the dam was well below normal. If the enemy planned to bring the water behind the dam to its maximum height, then suddenly open the gates and release it, the effect could seriously hinder operations of IX Corps. A 10- to 12-foot rise of water would occur in the Pukhan and Han rivers, bridges would be washed away, low areas flooded and corps units separated from each other. Eighth Army Engineers doubted the Chinese capability to destroy the dam by demolitions, and it is likely that neither side wished to do this. The Hwach' on reservoir and dam had been built to provide water and electric power to the city of Seoul; to the victor would go the prize.

Though the dam was too valuable to be destroyed, Gen. Ridgeway and Maj. Gen. William Hoge, commanding general of IX Corps, felt that some action must be taken to eliminate the threat of flooding. Gen. Hoge thought a raid was in order, an operation that would last but a few hours. After closing the floodgates, the machinery would be blasted. While leaving the dam intact, the threat would be removed.

Gen. Hoge felt the 4th Ranger Company was the unit to perform the mission and ordered the First Cavalry Division to begin making plans. The 4th Rangers moved from Taegu on April 4 and reached First Cavalry Division headquarters the morning of April 6. At 1905 hours on April 8, Hoge informed Gen. Ridgeway, who approved the Hwachon dam mission but ordered that it be done without a large number of casualties.

The Chinese also had reviewed their options. The night of April 8, two squads of Chinese soldiers and five Koreans who worked at the dam began to open the floodgates. A rush of water sped away. Between April 9 and 11 all of the five bridges that spanned the Pukhan and Han rivers were at one time disconnected and inoperable or washed out. Still fortune smiled on the U.N. Forces. The central power system was not operating, and only two of the 18 gates were raised completely; two were raised three-quarters of the way, and six opened only slightly. For some reason - perhaps because it took 10 hours to raise on gate manually - the Chinese did not open the remaining gates.

The action of the Chinese demonstrated that they could turn the water on and off at will. Spurred by concern over this fact, Gen. Hoge ordered the First Cavalry Division to move immediately against the dam. Caught up in preparation for the relief of his division, Maj. Gen. Charles Palmer, commanding general of the First Cavalry Division, gave vague instruction to the 7th Cavalry Regiment. The 7th felt Division wanted the dam seized because it 'would be nice to do so,' though preparations for relief were the highest priority.

Capt. Dorsey B. Anderson, company commander of the 4th Rangers, had been informed on April 7 by Lt. Col. Carlson (G-3, First Cavalry Division) that the Rangers would be given the job of making the dam inoperable.

On April 8, Anderson had accompanied Maj. Wilson, commander of the 8th Engineer Combat Battalion, to the Chong-pyong dam, as the machinery there was believed to be similar to that of the Hwach'on dam. The officers decided the floodgates could be made inoperable by destroying the cogs on the powerwheel that controlled them.

On April 9, Capt.. Anderson made an aerial reconnaissance. Below the wing of the light aircraft, some 6,000 meters west of the city of Hwach'on, in terrain so steep the map contour lines crowded one upon the other, lay the reser-

voir that contained the waters of Pukhan River. Before the river could pursue its meandering course southward, it was rudely thrust north then west by a thumb-like projection of land some 5,000 meters long. Thus, the spillway of the dam faced north, with the dam laying on an east-west axis.

An attacking force moving north up the thumb to reach the west end of the dam would find their approach channeled into an inverted V, some 600 meters wide at the base. The defense had reason to be inspired: with water at their back and flanks, they were hemmed in.

Anderson saw the difficulties in attacking up the thumb, but there was a daring alternative - one Anderson believed in. If assault boats were used, the Rangers could embark under cover of darkness from land at the eastern base of the thumb, cross 1,100 meters of open water and land on the Tonchon-ni peninsula about 1,000 meters south of the east edge of the dam. Surprise was critical, and this outer offered a chance of getting to the dam before the enemy was aware of the Ranger presence. Anderson's reconnaissance was interrupted by a message saying that an attack was underway to seize the dam and that the 4th Rangers were involved. He hurriedly rejoined the company.

The 2nd Battalion, 7th Cavalry, was in the attack, moving northward up the thumb of land, and the 4th Rangers followed, ready to pass through and close or destroy the floodgates. Rapid progress was made against light resistance until the battalion reached an east-west road at the narrow base of the thumb. Here they came under heavy fire from well-constructed and mutually supporting pillboxes. Simultaneously, enemy machine gun and mortar fire was received from the high ground west of the Pukhan River. The battalion attempted to maneuver to flank the enemy position but was unable to penetrate the defense.

Again, there was uncertainty about the mission. The 2nd Battalion was told to prepare for relief at the same time it was told to advance - and to do so without getting cut up and without withdrawing unless necessary. Night was coming on, so the battalion requested permission to continue the attack in the morning. Permission was granted.

The attack kicked off at 0730 the morning of April 10. The weather was bad, so there was no air support. Once more, enemy fire broke up the attack. Casualties in the battalion were six killed and 27 wounded, most by mortar fire.

At 1000 hours that day, Gen. Hoge visited the First Cavalry Division and found units moving rearward to Army reserve. As Hoge reviewed the situation, his anger grew. In blunt and direct language, he told Gen. Palmer to make a 'bona fide' attempt to take the dam. The mission would be completed before the First Cavalry Division was relieved.

With a clear sense of purpose, the 7th Cavalry Regiment discontinued relief planning and geared up to attack the dam. The plan was to have the 2nd Battalion continue its attack north of the thumb of land toward the west end of the dam. The attack would be made prior to dawn on April 11. The 1st Battalion would make a diversionary attack on the high ground to the west of the Pukhan River in order to draw off the heavy flanking fire the 2nd Battalion had been receiving. The 4th Rangers would embark in assault boats under cover of darkness, cross the reservoir, and land on the peninsula east of the dam, as Capt. Anderson had envisioned. The 3rd Battalion meanwhile would be prepared to assist either the 2nd Battalion or the Rangers.

American fighter-bombers had worked over Chinese positions with napalm; these fires and a grass fire in the Greek Battalion area created a heavy smoke that obscured visibility.

By nightfall on April 10, the attack had encountered enormous problems. The terrain was so difficult that four-wheel-drive jeeps could not use their light trailers when bringing ammunition forward. The engineers of the First Cavalry already had departed to go into Army Reserve. The 105mm howitzers, the workhorse of the artillery, could not be brought forward close enough to support the operation. Only the 155mm howitzers and 8-inch guns, with their slower rate of fire, could provide support. There were no assault boats or outboard motors or engineers to operate them, yet the operation had to be done that night.

Frantic efforts were begun to improve trails and locate boats and motors. Volunteers were summoned to operate boats; smoke pots, generators and life preservers were requested; air-sea aircraft were requested to drop power launches; artillery and air priority were requested and air-smoke missions planned for. The effort by the division staff was Herculean, but division resources were scattered, bad weather precluded air support, and time was running out.

A 2200 hours, Capt. Anderson was summoned to a meeting of the regimental staff and battalion commanders. Anderson knew he would be required to do something with the dam; just what was not yet clear. He had been told first to destroy the dam machinery, then was told his mission would be to seize the dam. The latest instruction was to destroy the dam mechanism if the Rangers could not hold the high ground east of the dam. Anderson had briefed his officers of the courses of action. Throughout the afternoon of April 10 the Rangers were preparing demolitions, organizing into team, and rehearsing. They were prepared to carry out any of the missions.

The regimental staff briefed the gathering. S-2 (Intelligence) said that enemy forces were believed to be a regiment with one battalion on the high ground west of the river, another on the thumb of land, and a third on the peninsula east of the dam. (Later information reported that the 115th Communist Chinese Forces (CCF) Division was dug in throughout the zone.) The S-3 said that the Ranger covering party would embark at 0230 hours to seize the landing site; the remainder of the company would cross at 0330, and 2nd Battalion would begin its attack at 0400, assisted by the 1st Battalion's diversion. Nine engineer assault boats were available, as were six motors, of which only two worked.

By 2300 hours, the instructions were issued. Anderson still had to move his company from their defensive positions in the 2nd Battalion area to the embarkation site. The move was begun under the direction of the company executive officer Lt. John S. Warren. Anderson briefed his leaders on his plan.

The assault boats could carry a maximum of 12 men. Lt. Michael Healey, 3rd platoon leader, would lead his 1st squad as a 'killer' element armed with knives, hand axes, grenades, pistols and carbines. This group would secure the landing site while a team from another squad would carry and place demolitions. The remainder of the platoon would carry sniper and automatic rifles and machine guns plus Ranger field-expedient rifle grenades (60mm mortar shells rigged to fire from a grenade launcher on M-1 rifles). This group would provide close support to the killer and demolition teams.

The 2nd platoon, company headquarters, and attachments would follow the 3rd platoon to shore. A 21-man machine gun section from Company M, 7th Cavalry, 81mm and heavy mortar forward observers and their radio operators, plus an artillery forward observer party, were attached. Due to the shortage of assault boats, the 1st platoon would have to be carried over in a second lift. Lt. Warren would come with the last group and serve as beach master organizing the landing site for resupply and evacuation.

The 410-pound boats would be paddled across; motors would not be used until the enemy was aware of the landing force, or until daylight, whichever came first.

The 2nd Battalion moved to attack at 0400 on April 11. Delayed by the need to move into position, the Rangers did not embark until 0345 hours. The quiet blackness of night and soft sound of water lapping at the shore were made eerie as a gray, clammy fog mixed with smoke crept stealthily across the surface of the water. Visibility was extremely limited, and navigation would have to be by compass; a 28-degree azimuth had been plotted for the voyage. The men entered the boats, unbuckling web gear and slinging bandoleers on one shoulder so that equipment could be shed easily should the boat overturn. Assault-boat crossing was a part of Ranger training, and the men adjusted to the paddles quickly.

The crossing and landing were successful,

with Lt. Healey and his men reaching shore at 0420 and securing the landing site. Capt. Anderson, the 2nd platoon, and attachments arrived, their boats grounding lightly on the rocky shore. Sgt. Goolsby hung as a landing marker a purple light that could only be seen from the water. Moving quickly, the Rangers began to climb through a cold, sleeting rain, toward a hill some 500 meters north designated as Objective 79.

The hill was occupied by a squad of Chinese who, apparently mistaking the climbing Rangers for their own forces, stood in the first light of dawn and waved and shouted to the men. The Rangers waved back and continued climbing. The Rangers had closed to within 100 meters when the enemy discovered their mistake and opened fire with a machine gun. The first burst of fire killed the radio man for the 81mm mortars forward observers and wounded Sgt. Williams of the Rangers four times in the leg. Sgt. Goolsby and the aid man immediately went to Williams' assistance.

The hill was barren, without trees or ditches, and the Rangers had to use fire and movement to close. Another enemy machine gun opened up from the right front and enemy snipers engaged from the left. The 3rd platoon's 57mm recoilless rifle knocked out the machine gun on the right but could not locate the one on the left. Lt. Healey and the two lead scouts flanked the gun position, assaulted with grenades and small arms and killed the machine gun crew. The rest of the enemy retreated. Around 0615 the Rangers were in possession of the hill, but their presence was known to the Chinese, and they were some 600 meters short of the east edge of the dam.

To the west, the 2nd Battalion was stalled, unable to penetrate Chinese defenses that included reinforced concrete pillboxes. The 1st Battalion's diversionary attack also was unsuccessful. Anderson now was faced with a dilemma. His 1st platoon had not yet landed, and its boats were receiving heavy fire from machine guns and

American and United Nations troops recently captured, begin their long journey into North Korea and to the Prisoner of War camps. Many would end up in Death Valley, where hundreds would die from starvation and exposure to the extreme cold weather conditions. (Chinese People's Committee for World Peace)

mortars. There was high ground to his immediate front (designated Objective 77), but to attack there would expose his forces to a flank attack from a hill to his left (designated Objective 80). Anderson was convinced that if he moved forward, reinforcements would not be able to land and those on shore would be cut off from the beach. He sent a patrol to keep watch on Objective 80.

On the other side of the reservoir 20 additional boats now were available with 10 motors (none of which worked). One of the two working motors had expired; there were now 29 boats and one motor. Four boats were disabled by enemy fire, which became increasingly heavy, forcing men to paddle in a roundabout manner to reach the beach.

Between 0600 and 0700, Lt. James L. Johnson's 1st platoon had paddled to reach the landing site. Sgt. Goolsby, who was waiting on shore with the wounded Sgt. Williams, guided them to land. Goolsby then placed Williams in a boat and joined the disembarking platoon to guide them to the remainder of the company.

The 1st platoon came up the hill about 0815 and immediately was dispatched by Anderson to seize Objective 80. The platoon came under heavy fire from its front, tried to flank the objective and received fire from the front, right and rear. The Chinese mortar fire was galling, and attempts to respond were not effective. The Greek Battalion was providing supporting 81mm mortar fire. In communication between them and the American forward observer, accuracy was lost. At about 1330, under heavy Chinese mortar fire, the 1st platoon was hit by an enemy counterattack of 50 to 60 men. Anderson sent two squads of the 3rd platoon to assist, and the attack was repelled. Sgts. Wilcoxson and Anglin and Cpls. Chada and Braxel distinguished themselves in this action, Chada cradling an A-6 machine gun in his arms and firing into the Chinese. The 1st platoon (reinforced) then returned to Objective 79 and tied in on the left flank of the company. The 2nd platoon was in the center, company headquarters and a 3rd platoon squad on the right.

The Chinese may have made this attack as a diversion to draw the Rangers off from the point of their main thrust. In any case, the Chinese were reinforcing - sending men across the dam to face the Rangers from the north and from the west.

Some men of the 1st Cavalry arrived with water-cooled machine guns, which they set up to the left of the 2nd platoon. The Rangers were spread along the crest with a man about every 12 feet. Across the way, the Chinese began bobbing up and down, trying to draw automatic weapons fire and pinpoint the positions of these weapons. The Rangers did not take the bait; instead a Ranger riflemen promptly killed one of the Chinese and the rest decided to stay low.

In the afternoon, firing picked up slowly, growing increasingly heavy, and at approximately 1415 hours, 300 to 400 Chinese launched a screaming, bugle-blowing charge on the positions of the company headquarters, the 2nd platoon, and the almost-vacated 3rd platoon area. Sgt. Goolsby, who had left the 1st platoon when there were no casualties to treat, saw the Chinese coming toward company headquarters and gave warning.

The Chinese made no attempt to use terrain or covering fire; theirs was a headlong banzai charge by a mass of men, terrifying in its ferocity. Due to depressed ground to their front, the Rangers had to stand up, exposed against the skyline, to pour fire into the close-packed advancing bodies. In the 2nd platoon area, BAR men, Forbes and Sanchez, moved across the crest and down the hill past a water drainage ditch to get better firing positions. Forbes had fired six magazines into the massed Chinese when he heard men screaming for him to get back on line. Stuffing empty magazines in his pockets, Forbes ran back up the hill. As he crossed the drainage ditch he felt two sharp blows in his lower body. He saw Ranger Cyril Tritz stand up and fire a carbine directly at him. The bullets were intended for, and killed, a Chinese soldier who had shot Forbes from a few feet behind - one of a number of Chinese coming up the ditch. Forbes made it over the crest, where his wounds were treated by aid-man Leonard Koops. Lt. Forney, the artillery F.O. from the First Cavalry, and the 4.2-inch mortar observer called down accurate fire to within 75 meters of the Rangers, but the Chinese came on into machine guns, rifles and carbines until, finally, the Rangers were using pistols. Capt. Anderson, Sgt. Schroeer (the communications sergeant) and the six men in the company headquarters position fired for 15 minutes, stopping only to reload.

Elsewhere on the line, Cpl. Angarano was hit, his arm almost severed. Goolsby pulled Angarano to cover, treated him for shock and tried to inject albumen, but Angarano's veins had collapse, and he died from loss of blood. Pvt. Young, a BAR man, was hit in the head, convulsed and died. Ammunition was taken from the dead and redistributed. Squad leader, Ken Robinson, doled out five to six rounds per man, telling them, 'Don't use it all on one man.'

The number of wounded began to increase. Sgt. Carbonel and Pvts. Sanchez and Bauer were wounded seriously; Rangers Blacketter, Tackach, Williams, Gustafson, Capone, Ackley, Dillan, McClellan, Tritz, Bigelow, Gibson, Lopes, Anglin, Pinckney, Heffernan, Chada, Wilcoxson, Holohan and Golden were struck. Among the worst hit was Cpl. Ligon, who was shot in the stomach. He would die of wounds the following day. During the height of the battle, few of the casualties could be evacuated, and even many of the wounded fought.

The furious attack lasted for 30 to 45 minutes before the Chinese were beaten off. More than 100 enemy dead lay to the front of the Ranger positions. The 2nd platoon had been slowly driven from position. As they began to withdraw, Lt. Waterbury, the platoon leader, was confused by a grenade explosion and in a state of shock. The bulk of the platoon then destroyed its 57mm recoilless rifle, took its machine guns and weapons and withdrew to the beach. At Anderson's position, there was one-half box of machine gun ammunition remaining and an average of 16 rounds per M-1 rifle and 30 rounds per carbine - no grenades remained. He attempted to cover the 2nd platoon position with the 3rd squad of the 3rd platoon, but the enemy had the location under enfilade fire. The continuing rain and fog prevented air support.

When Anderson's position was no longer supportable, he radioed Regiment for permission to withdraw, and 7th Cavalry replied that Company I was landing on the beach and would join

him on position, bringing ammunition. Anderson was then to take his combined force and attack Objective 80. The 7th Cavalry Regiment was prepared to ferry additional forces over the reservoir to build up the attack force. At about 1630, as Anderson was preparing to carry out his instructions, he received orders to cancel the attack and return to the landing site. Company I would cover the withdrawal.

Gen. Hoge had wanted a quick, surgical operation, but this now was turning into a situation that could require the commitment of a large number of troops. 'Bring them back,' he ordered.

There was anger on the hill - the Rangers had beaten off the Chinese, Company I was ashore, and other units were in position to cross - but Capt. Anderson could only shrug his shoulders in resignation; the orders were clear. Covered by Company I, which fought off another Chinese attack, the Rangers disembarked, followed by Company I. At 0126 hours on April 12, the last American reached the point from where the operation had begun. Material to support the attack now was arriving in quantity.

The Hwach'on dam loomed large. Like the gates of Rome were to Hannibal, to the 4th Rangers and the 7th Cavalry the dam always would be 'so close and yet so far.'"

Relief of the regiment was effected at 0800 hours on the 12th by elements of the Korean Marine Corps, and the regiment moved to positions in Army reserve northeast of Seoul. The period from April 12th to 21st was spent in the maintenance of equipment, in rest and rehabilitation of troops, and in training.

During this period, President Truman relieved Gen. MacArthur of all his commands and replaced him with Gen. Matt Ridgeway on April 11. Lt. Gen. James A. Van Fleet was dispatched posthaste from Washington, D.C., to take command of the 8th Army and attached forces. He arrived and assumed command on April 14.

After a series of public utterances over national policy and military strategy, Gen. MacArthur addressed the joint session of Congress on April 19. The historian continued: In conclusion, MacArthur spoke the deeply moving words that brought tears and were most remembered and quoted:

"I am closing my 52 years of military service. When I joined the Army, even before the turn of the century, it was the fulfillment of all my boyish hopes and dreams. The world has turned over many times since I took the oath on the Plain at West Point, and the hopes and dreams have long since vanished, but I still remember the refrain of one of the most popular barrack ballads of that day, which proclaimed most proudly that old soldiers never die; they just fade away.

And, like the old soldier of that ballad, I now close my military career and just fade away, an old soldier who tried to do his duty as God gave him the light to see that duty. Good-bye."

President Truman and Dean Acheson were contemptuous of the speech. The president saltily characterized it as 'nothing but a bunch of bull shit.' Acheson dismissed it as 'demagogic' and 'more than somewhat pathetic.' The president - and perhaps Acheson - believed that once all the hullabaloo died down, people would see what he was.

They were sadly mistaken. The MacArthur

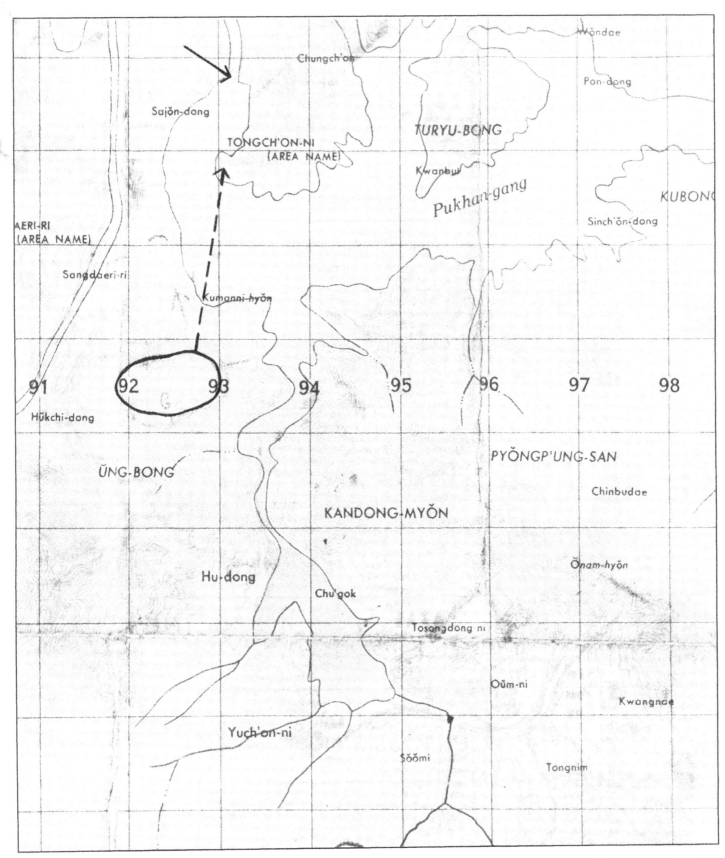

Actual map of the Hwach'on Reservior, April 10, 1951. The circle shows the general location of 2nd Battalion, 7th Cavalry Regiment. Dotted line shows direction of the assault by the 4th Rangers and Co. "I", 7th Cavalry Regiment on the Hwach'on Dam, indicated by the top arrow. (Courtesy of Bob "Snuffy" Gray)

address to Congress was probably the most important political event of the Korean War.

By that time, the American people were sick of the war in Korea. What seemingly had begun as a fairly simple military task had turned into a nightmare. Nearly 70,000 American casualties had been incurred. It was galling that the war apparently could not be 'won,' that after nearly a year of fight, friends and enemies were again back on a line at the 38th Parallel. There were no mass protests or marches, no campus riots, no burning of draft cars, but there was deep and widespread dissatisfaction.

On April 21, the regiment was alerted for possible employment in the reconnaissance parties were sent to reconnoiter these sectors on April 22nd and continued until April 26, when the 7th Cavalry Regiment was placed under operation control of the 3rd Infantry Division in the Uijongbu sector.

Clockwise from the top: Major General Charles D. Palmer, Commander, 1st Cavalry Division, visiting the 7th Cavalry Command Post on April 15, 1951. (Courtesy of Col. Frank Griepp) — Lt. S. Alevizakos, (GEF), Platoon Leader of 3rd Platoon, Company P, on combat patrol crossing of 38th Parallel, in the Spring of 1951. (Courtesy of Col. (Ret) S. Alevizakos) — 1st Lt. David Hughes, Company K, 7th Cavalry, is riding a captured Chinese Communist Cavalry horse. (U.S. Army Photo) — 2nd Lt. Robert Early, 3rd Platoon Leader, Co.H and 1st Lt. Richard Tobin, Co. Commander, Co.H, in 1951. (Courtesy of Ed Daily) — L to R Col. William A. Harris, Commander 7th Cavalry Regiment, talks with former prisoners of Chinese Communists, Capt. Carroll D. Harrod, 49th Field Artillery, 7th Inf. Div., and 1st Lt. Wilbur R. Webster, Battery D, 82nd AAA Bn., 2nd Div., after being rescued by the 7th Cavalry regiment on March 12, 1951. (U.S. Army Photo) — Sgt. 1/c Ralph Bernotas, 3rd platoon of Company F, 2nd Bn., 7th Cavalry, in Hongchon Valley in the Spring of 1951. (Courtesy of Suey Lee)

CHAPTER IX
CHINESE SPRING OFFENSIVE

The long-expected Chinese Communist offensive was launched by the light of a full moon in the early evening hours of April 22nd when three Chinese Communist armies attacked the United Nations forces following four hours of artillery bombardment. The initial attack, a secondary one, was made against the 6th ROK Division in the Namdae River valley south of Kumhwa. The 6th ROK Division was driven back, creating a gap in the line between the U.S. 24th Infantry and the 1st Marine Divisions.

The main enemy attack was launched about midnight on the same date when Chinese Communist infantrymen forded the waist-deep Imjin River, drove the 1st ROK Division back and cut the Seoul-Kaesong highway on April 26th. This outflanked the city of Uijongbu, and the U.S. 3rd Infantry Division was withdrawn to positions four miles north of the outskirts of Seoul, while the ROK troops withdrew down the road to Munsan-ni.

The regiment moved to an assembly area north and west of Uijongbu without enemy contact and relieved the 65th Infantry Regiment on April 27th.

Company B received an attack at 1735 hours, which succeeded in isolating one platoon. This platoon was ordered to dig in and hold for the night, and the line was restored by 0930 hours on April 28th. At 0530 hours on April 28th, Companies B and C came under attacks from an estimated enemy battalion. Despite foggy weather, which limited visibility to 25 feet, the enemy force was driven off; however, these companies continued to receive sporadic attacks throughout the morning.

As the regiment withdrew to an assembly area in Seoul, the 1st Battalion received a heavy volume of small arms and automatic weapons fire, but the skillful coordination of supporting fire by the battalion commander and his command group effected the successful withdrawal of the battalion. The remaining units in the regiment completed the withdrawal without incident.

On April 29th, reconnaissance of counterattack routes and of traffic arteries in the Seoul Metropolitan area were conducted by all units. Construction of permanent-type defenses began in the regimental sector during the first three days of May, as defensive positions were prepared along the northern approaches to Seoul. Civilians entering the Seoul area were screened by the 1st and 3rd Battalions. The regimental and battalion commanders made an air reconnaissance of the regiment's zone of responsibility.

The eight days of combat between April 22nd-30th, 1951, known as the CCF Spring Offensive, proved to be the biggest single battle of the Korean War. During it, Eighth Army had suffered some reverses. It had been forced off its positions on the 38th Parallel, had ceded about 35 miles of real estate, had sustained about 7,000 casualties. It had lost the Gloucester Battalion and another 40 howitzers. No one was proud of this withdrawal, which at times had been messy; nor did UN soldiers clearly understand that it had

been planned fully. Morale slumped. GIs began ridiculing the conflict as a "yo-yo war" without end.

Yet in reality, the battle was another magnificent victory for 8th Army. Although not always executed perfectly - war seldom is perfect - the withdrawal had repulsed and savaged the CCF's greatest offensive, inflicting 70,000 casualties and had denied the enemy his primary objective, Seoul. Beyond that, the battle must have caused grave concern in Peking. It demonstrated that in order to throw 8th Army out of Korea - if it could be done at all - the CCF would require a massive new, possibly prohibitive commitment of manpower. Even so, Peking gave no hint that it was interested in negotiations. It was, in fact, planned yet another massive offensive.

A task force consisting of the 7th Cavalry Regiment reinforced with artillery, tanks and engineers was organized to establish a patrol base in the vicinity of Uijongbu, approximately six miles north of the main U.N. line and to contact the enemy with strong combat patrols. This operation began on May 7th and continued to May 20th.

From the book, "The Forgotten War," author Clay Blair wrote: *"In the 1st Cavalry Division, Charlie Palmer, holding on Line Lincoln astride the Uijongbu road, sent the 7th Cavalry, newly commanded by Dan Gilmer, to man the division's OPLR. Gilmer went up the road to Uijongbu, assisted by Hawkins' 64th Tank Battalion from I Corps reserve.*

On this, his first combat mission, Dan Gilmer came across as a less than heroic character and an officer who showed little concern for the welfare of his men. 'He was a brilliant staff officer,' a contemporary remembered, 'but as a commander, he didn't have it.' His men accused him of sandbagging his own CP first, protecting it with 'about 50 miles of barbed wire.' They said he issued thoughtless orders, such as, 'Captain, I want you to take that hill within 15 minutes,' and often countermanded or nullified such orders with conflicting orders. He equipped his command jeep with a .50-caliber machine gun ringmount and drove around standing up inside it, a practice the men thought was the 'silliest thing you ever saw' and which led to a derisive nickname, 'Ringmount Gilmer' or 'Ringmount Dan.' "

The patrol base was established without incident, as three battalions formed a tight perimeter in this area, while the 4th Battalion (GEF) was assigned the mission of forming a perimeter around the supporting artillery units located to the rear. The area was prepared for defense by laying barbed wire, setting trip flares and booby traps, constructing gun positions and the registration of artillery and mortar fire. Tank patrols were dispatched to the north of Uijongbu, and infantry patrols were dispatched to clear the adjoining ridges. All patrols returned to the perimeter during he night.

In an effort to maintain enemy contact, tank-infantry patrols were dispatched in a 9,000 meter area ranging from west to east from the patrol base during the period. On May 5th, a Company K patrol surrounded 15 enemy troops in a house, killing six and taking three prisoners. Another patrol from Company K found 10 Chinese pack horses northwest of Uijongbu. The horses were

brought to the company area, pack saddles were obtained from some unknown source, and the horses used to great advantage to transport supplies up the rugged mountains to the front line troops. It was estimated that these 10 small, rugged, long-haired Manchurian ponies could carry supplies equivalent to 80 Korean bearers in half the time. Lacking transportation and forage for the animals when the unit moved to its next location, the ponies were turned over to the relieving unit; so, the cavalry had horses once again - even if momentarily.

As tank-infantry patrols probed areas 6,000 meters north of Uijongbu, artillery units were moved forward to positions that better enabled them to render supporting fires. A provisional battalion - commanded by Lt. Col. John W. Callaway - was formed to provide security for the artillery units.

On May 6th, a patrol from the 2nd Battalion found a Philippine Army soldier who had been captured by the Chinese. He was taken to the regimental collecting station where he was given medical treatment. Patrols from the 2nd Battalion located a large number of enemy troops on Hill 337 and directed air strikes, artillery and mortar fire on the positions. These patrols also directed tank and artillery fire on enemy positions. These patrols also directed tank and artillery fire on enemy positions located on Hill 146 and directed air strikes on enemy positions in the valley between Hills 158 and 213.

During the period May 9th-10th, enemy resistance was concentrated on Hills 361, 158 and 213. Enemy positions on these hills were attacked repeatedly by air strikes, artillery and mortars. On May 9th, the air observer located 500 to 600 enemy troops in the open, and the tactical controller reported 1,500 to 2,000 enemy troops moving north of Uijongbu. Numerous air strikes were placed on these enemy groups with excellent results. On May 15th, 15 American prisoners were freed by a tank-reinforced 1st Battalion patrol and brought to the regimental collecting station and given medical treatment.

Operations for the period May 4th-20th accounted for the capture of 187 prisoners. Counted enemy casualties were 383 dead and 40 wounded, and the enemy was estimated to have suffered an additional 1,100 dead and 1,691 wounded.

On May 18th, the regiment began a withdrawal to positions 1,000 meters south of Uijongbu and was ordered into Division reserve north of Seoul on May 22nd. The 7th Cavalry Regiment relieved the 5th Cavalry Regiment at 0800 hours on May 24th along the front approximately 20 miles north and east of Seoul. Patrolling activities were resumed and continued to the end of the month. Counted enemy casualties during the period May 20th to 31st were two enemy dead with an additional estimated 215 dead and 257 wounded. Twenty-six prisoners were captured.

On June 1st, the regiment remained in positions along the front line without enemy contact. A full field inspection of clothing and equipment was ordered held all units. The following day, the regiment moved forward where an outposts line was established and patrols captured five prisoners.

The regiment began an attack to the north in its zone on June 3rd as the 2nd Battalion advanced 5,000 yards against heavy small arms and

Crossing over the Pukhan River on a pontoon bridge, south of the Hwach'on Reservoir on April 15, 1951. (Courtesy of Frank Griepp)

7th Cavalry jeeps crossing small river near Phase Line Wyoming, on May 31, 1951. (Courtesy of Col. Frank Griepp)

automatic weapons fire. This attack was continued until Phase Line Wyoming was reached on June 9th. As the regiment moved forward, enemy resistance became increasingly stronger as he used greater amounts of mortar, artillery, small arms and automatic weapons fire.

Upon occupation of Phase Line Wyoming on June 9th, intensive efforts were made to consolidate positions. Tactical wire was laid and patrols were dispatched to develop enemy positions in front of the regimental sector along Line Wyoming. An increasing number of casualties, both in personnel and equipment, were sustained during the next few days as a result of enemy mines, and tank-infantry patrols continued to search out the enemy to the front.

An advance patrol base, approximately 12 miles in front of Line Wyoming, was established by the 2nd Battalion on June 15th. The patrol base was established by the 2nd Battalion on June 15th. The patrol base was established to permit extended patrol activities in an effort to maintain contact with the main enemy force that had withdrawn almost 15 miles from Line Wyoming.

Task Force Croft was organized on June 23rd to proceed on the following day to To-San to destroy enemy personnel, equipment, supplies, and gun positions. A review attended by Maj. Gen. Charles D. Palmer, 1st Cavalry Division Commander was held on June 25th in commemoration of the 75th Anniversary of the Battle of the Little Big Horn. Another task force ranged 12,000 yards in advance of friendly lines on June 28th in an attempt to locate the enemy forces, which continued to withdraw northward, and to avoid contact.

Enemy resistance appeared to diminish during the latter part of June. The success of the regiment's attack from June 3rd to 9th and the vigorous patrol action could well have accounted for this decrease in enemy activity. Additionally, casualties inflicted on the enemy during the period were as follows: *Counted:* Killed, 729; Wounded, 1; Prisoners captured 251; *Estimated:* Killed, 1,286; Wounded, 1,810.

The regiment's casualties for June totaled 25 killed and 290 wounded.

On July 1st, the 7th Cavalry Regiment continued to occupy defensive positions along Line Wyoming. Two patrol bases were established forward of the main line against light enemy resistance. The 1st Battalion, reinforced with one platoon of heavy mortars, established one base and a reinforced company of the 3rd Battalion established the other base. The patrol bases permitted the regiment to maintain closer contact with the enemy and thus inflict a greater number of casualties.

Extensive patrols into enemy territory to capture prisoners, inflict maximum casualties, and destroy enemy equipment, were conducted during the period July 1st to 15th. Enemy casualties during this period were: 86 counted and 263 estimated killed; 217 estimated wounded and nine prisoners. On July 6th, the 2nd Battalion relieved the 1st Battalion on their patrol base. The next day, a 3rd Battalion patrol was engaged by about 60 enemy trying to outflank them, and the fight developed into hand-to-hand combat. The friendly patrol suffered only two wounded while the enemy's casualties were estimated at 25 killed and 10 wounded. The increased use of night patrolling and night ambushes was emphasized.

On July 9th, all officers reconnoitered positions on Line Kansas - a defense line along the 38th Parallel, which had been under preparation since mid June. On July 12th, the 3rd Battalion relieved the 2nd Battalion at their patrol base. The 2nd Battalion then took the position occupied by the 1st Battalion on Line Wyoming with the 1st Battalion moving to occupy the 3rd Battalion's sector. The frequent reliefs among units of the regiment were made to maintain combat efficiency due to enemy inactivity along the Wyoming Line - the main line of resistance - and to permit necessary reorganization of positions. In so shifting, each battalion was positioned in a sector, which they had prepared for defense - the sector they were most familiar with, and the one they would be required to defend if attacked.

It should be borne in mind that during this period the entire regiment - with the exception of

approximately four officers - consisted of all new personnel. The experienced combat veterans who had been with the regiment since the beginning of the Korean War either had become casualties or rotated from Korea. Rotation of the remaining experienced personnel had taken place during the short period of two months and left the once combat-wise regiment with all new officers, non-commissioned officers and troopers - most of whom were inexperienced in combat. It was therefore necessary to devote considerable time to training activities, and in many respects, it was indeed fortunate that the enemy cooperated by remaining inactive.

Due to the rotation of personnel, the 1st Cavalry Division would see the departure of its most courageous and experienced leadership. The Commander, Charles D. Palmer, was rotated and went on (like his brother, Williston) to four stars. Cols. Peter Clainos and James Lynch were transferred previously to other units. Clainos received a command in the 8th Cavalry, and Lynch went to I Corps G-3 section. Lynch would rise to one-star general before retirement. Billy (Wild Bill) Harris, Commander of the crack 7th Cavalry Regiment, departed in April and rose to two stars. John W. Callaway, Commander, 2nd Battalion, 7th Cavalry Regiment, was rotated in July and retired a full Colonel in 1971. Crusty Marcel Crombez of the 5th Cavalry Regiment and then the oldest regimental commander in Korea (50 years old) remained at his post until July. Having the distinction of commanding a regiment in Korea longer than any other officer, Crombez got one star before retirement in 1956. Bob Blanchard, Commander, 8th Cavalry Regiment, also was rotated in July and went on to one star. Dan Gilmer continued to command the crack 7th Cavalry Regiment for several more months until he was forced out by an inspector general's investigation. He retired in 1962, still a colonel.

Peace talks began on July 10th between the United Nations Command and the Communist Forces. On July 14th, the 2nd Battalion - under command of Maj. M.C. Chandler - was selected from among all other Eighth Army units as the

Honor Guard for the Peace Camp at Munsan-ni where the United Nations peace delegates were quartered. The 2nd Battalion was placed under the operational control of the Eighth Army for this duty.

On July 16th, the regiment was relieved along the Wyoming Line by the 24th Infantry Regiment, and the 1st, 3rd and 4th (GEF) Battalions moved to Line Kansas in Division reserve. Company C and one platoon of Company B were attached to the 8th Cavalry in their sector of Line Wyoming.

The 1st, 3rd and 4th (GEF) Battalions returned to Line Wyoming, relieving the 24th Infantry Regiment, on Aug. 1st. Reinforced platoon and squad-size patrols were sent out to the north from the 1st and 4th (GEF) Battalions. The 1st Battalion relieved elements of the Turkish Brigade and extended their boundaries to join the 3rd Infantry Division on the right.

The 3rd Battalion departed on their mission to capture Hill 487 on Aug. 5th, but due to high water and swollen streams, supplies and support units could not be moved forward and the mission was canceled. On Aug. 7th, the 3rd Battalion began their attack in front of Line Wyoming, utilizing closely coordinated artillery and air strikes. This attack was made by Company I against an estimated two enemy companies. Company I received intense small arms and automatic weapons fire from the top of Hill 487. By nightfall, the company was 150 yards from the hilltop and dug-in for the night. One platoon of the 1st Battalion was attached to Company I to assist in repulsing an expected counterattack during the night. At 0100 hours on Aug. 8th, the company received a 15-minute attack accompanies by 105mm artillery and 82mm and 120mm mortar fire. This attack was repulsed, but they again were attacked by an estimated enemy platoon stronger than the preceding attack.

Company L was passed through Company I to attack Hill 487 the following morning and was engaged in a heavy fire fight from three sides. Due to the poor visibility, Company L was forced to withdraw into a perimeter with Company I and sent out contacting patrols to Hill 487 and vicinity to locate the source of enemy fire. Visibility, due to heavy fog and rain, was reduced to zero and in view of an expected heavy counterattack, all units of the 3rd Battalion were ordered back to their former positions on the main line of resistance. The heavy rains during the past week had flooded all streams, and units were notified that mines had washed out and extreme caution was to be taken in crossing fords and streams.

On Aug. 9th, planes with loud speakers flew over Hills 477 and 487, telling the enemy to surrender or die. On Aug. 11th, the 2nd Battalion returned from the Peace Camp and returned to regimental control. Two enlisted men from the 24th Infantry Regiment walked into the 4th Battalion (GEF) area having been prisoners of the Chinese for 35 days. They stated that they had received indoctrination by the Chinese but were well treated.

On Aug. 16th, the 2nd Battalion relieved the 1st Battalion on their position on Line Wyoming and the 1st Battalion moved into Division reserve.

On Aug. 19th, the 3rd Battalion launched another attack on Hill 487 with limited success. The enemy emplacements were extremely well dug-in with heavy overhead cover and were situated on commanding terrain. Two further the attack would have resulted in an undue number of casualties. Therefore, the troops were ordered to return to their reserve positions on Line Wyoming. The 4th Battalion (GEF) was relieved by the 3rd Battalion on Aug. 20th, and moved into a reserve position.

On Aug. 22nd, 472 enlisted men and 34 officers were rotated from the 4th Battalion (GEF) to their homeland - the first rotation from this gallant Greek Battalion, which had fought so bravely as an integral part of GARRYOWEN.

On Aug. 28th, the 2nd Battalion was relieved on Line Wyoming by elements of the 15th Infantry Regiment and moved to new positions on the line. On the following day, all battalions prepared positions on the new main line of resistance - a forward relocation of Line Wyoming.

Bugler playing church call at the 7th Cavalry Command Post, north of Chunchon, April 8, 1951. (Courtesy of Col. Frank Griepp)

Major General Charles D. Palmer, Commander, 1st Cavalry Division, presenting Silver Star Medal to Captain Crawford "Buck" Buchanan, 2nd Bn., 7th Cavalry Regiment. To his left are Sergeants McMahan and Eddie Mohair. (Courtesy of "Buck" Buchanan)

Farewell Ceremony to the departure of Colonel "Wild Bill" Harris, in April 1951. (Courtesy of Col. Frank Griepp)

Clockwise from the top: These enemy soldiers are from the last effort by a North Korean Army unit to fight against the U.N. Forces, in April 1951. The North Korean Army had been completely destroyed. (Courtesy of Col. (Ret) S. Alevizakos, GEF) — Major General William M. Hoge, Commander IX Corps, decorates Lt. Colonel D. Arbouzis, Commander 4th Battalion (GEF), and other officers of the Greek Battalion, attached to the 7th Cavalry, April 1951. (United Nations photo) — 7th Cavalry Regiment assisting the evacuation of refugees (women, children & old men), during the Chinese Spring Offensive, in April 1951. (Courtesy of Col. Frank Griepp) — Troopers of Company B, 7th Cavalry, move up to attack Chinese Communist positions near Chipyong, Korea, Febrary 1951. Note sniper scope on rifle of soldier on the left. (U.S. Army Photo)

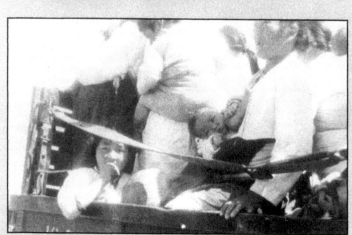

Counter-clockwise from the bottom: Mountainous Korea was the worst place to fight a war. (U.S. Army Photo) — Wounded 7th Cavalry trooper being evacuated by a medical helicopter, on May 28, 1951. The use of helicopters were very limited because of the high mountains of Korea. (Courtesy of Col. Frank Griepp) — 7th Cavalry 2 1/2 ton truck crossing a partially constructed bridge, near Uijongbu. (U.S. Army Photo) — 7th Cavalry 1/4 ton jeep, which is stuck in the mud. The severe winter of 1950-51 brought many hardships to the American and United Nations troops. (U.S. Army Photo) — Medical helicopter leaving with wounded troopers of the 7th Cavalry, on May 28, 1951. Please note on each side the two capsules with caps, which contain the wounded. (Courtesy of Col. Frank Griepp) — L to R Captain Crawford "Buck" Buchanan and Captain Herman K. Vester, Commander, Headquarters Company, 2nd Battalion, 7th Cavalry Regiment, February 1951. (Courtesy of Crawford Buchanan.)

CHAPTER X
IRON TRIANGLE

During September, the 7th Cavalry Regiment established defensive positions along the new Wyoming Line and extensively patrolled to the northwest of the regimental sector.

Company G established a company-size patrol base on Hill 339, well out in front of the regiment, in order to send patrols deeper into enemy territory and at the same time keep the patrols within range of supporting weapons.

Company C relieved Company G on Hill 339 on Sept. 5th and was there only one day, when at approximately 2200 hours on Sept. 6th, the company was attacked from the west, north and south by an estimated reinforced enemy company. The enemy gained the element of surprise, and with the numerically superior force drove Company C from Hill 339 with heavy losses of equipment and the complete disorganization of the unit. Platoon-size outposts on Hills 321 and 343 were not subjected to the attack and offered a line of departure for the heavily reinforced company of the 2nd Battalion, which recaptured Hill 339 during the early morning hours of Sept. 7th.

The remainder of the regiment occupied and organized their defensive positions along the adjusted Line Wyoming on Sept. 6th. This adjustment was made to provide better fields of grazing fire for all weapons.

On Sept. 9th, Company I established a reinforced company-size patrol base 1,000 yards forward of the regiment's line. This patrol base unit was replaced by Company F on Sept. 13th.

The 2nd Battalion was relieved of responsibility on Line Wyoming on Sept. 17th by the 1st Battalion of the 8th Cavalry Regiment. At this time, Company F rejoined the 2nd Battalion in an assembly area behind the main line of resistance. A new patrol base was established by Company B on Hill 265. The 2nd Battalion then moved to a forward assembly area on Sept. 18th with Company G proceeding to the high ground 1,500 yards northwest of the regimental sector. the remainder of the 2nd Battalion was moved immediately to reinforce Company G and to establish a battalion-size patrol base on the following day.

The 16th Reconnaissance Company was attached to the 7th Cavalry Regiment on Sept. 20th, and moved to a blocking position that was later shifted on Sept. 24th to effect a physical tie-in with the 65th Infantry Regiment, on the regiment's right flank.

Activities until Sept. 22nd consisted of preparing defensive positions along the adjusted Wyoming Line and extensive patrol activity. These patrols resulted in skirmishes with squad and company-size enemy units on key terrain features in the regimental sector.

On Sept. 21st, Company B rejoined the 1st Battalion on the line, and the 3rd Battalion moved to a second battalion-size patrol base on Hills 321 and 339. The 1st Battalion subsequently was attached to the 8th Cavalry Regiment, and the 7th Cavalry Regiment was relieved of responsibility along Line Wyoming on Sept. 24th when the 4th Battalion (GEF) was moved to a patrol base on Hill 343. Probing attacks against the regimental forward elements increased in severity until Sept.

28th when a reinforced enemy battalion attacked Company K.

The enemy struck the 3rd Battalion from the northwest, west and south, making two penetrations in the 3rd Battalion's perimeter. The Company K men remained in position and fought off a well-planned enemy attack. The enemy had small groups equipped with wire cutters to isolate the company communications net, to break through and attack friendly elements from the rear, and others to destroy supporting weapons. The four-hour attack was repulsed successfully, resulting in 77 counted enemy dead and an estimated 600 enemy wounded. The regiment's casualties were eight killed, 18 wounded and three missing in action.

The 1st Battalion reverted to regimental control on Sept. 28th and moved into the positions of the 16th Reconnaissance Company.

The enemy suffered heavy casualties as a result of the regiment's aggressive patrolling and maximum use of supporting weapons throughout the month of September. However, the enemy had employed an increasingly greater number of mortar and artillery weapons resulting in a corresponding increase in the regiment's casualties.

Operations for the month of October were highlighted by Operation Commando, a coordinated I Corps attack against the most carefully prepared enemy defensive positions and the largest enemy build-ups yet experienced by the 8th Army in Korea. The 7th Cavalry Regiment broke through the enemy's prepared winter line in three places after two weeks of the bloodiest fighting in the history of the regiment.

The enemy's front line, which had taken him four months to prepare, was supported by reserve unit and the heaviest artillery and mortar concentration encountered in a year of fighting in Korea. the enemy was deployed in depth on commanding terrain, which was defended by heavily reinforced fresh units of the Chinese Communist Forces who frequently staged fanatical battalion-size counterattacks. The enemy had prior knowledge of the regiment's attack and had replaced their 140th Division with the fresh 139th Division 24 to 48 hours prior to the attack. The entire 139th Division and one regiment of the 141st Division opposed the 7th Cavalry on its front on Oct. 3rd when the attack began.

The enemy defense was supported by rockets, artillery fire ranging to 150mm in size, self-propelled direct fire weapons, and the heaviest concentrations of light, medium and heavy mortars.

Oct. 1st found the 1st Battalion deployed on the regiment's right flank, and the 2nd 3rd and 4th (GEF) Battalions on patrol bases forward of Line Wyoming.

After 2400 hours on Oct. 2nd, the 2nd, 3rd and 4th (GEF) Battalions moved platoons out to secure the line of departure for the forthcoming attack to secure Line Jamestown - the objective of Operation Commando. Aggressive patrolling by the regiment previous to the attack had succeeded in pushing the enemy outpost system in, and complete tactical surprise was gained when the attack began from this forward line of departure. The 1st Battalion conducted a feint attack on the right flank before dark and moved with great secrecy under cover of darkness of the regimental left flank to the vicinity of Hill 339, to act jointly as left flank security and the regimental reserve.

At 0600 hours on Oct. 3rd, the regiment attacked as the I Corps spearheading main effort in Operation Commando. By 0800 hours, all elements were engaged heavily with the enemy on three initial objectives.

The 2nd Battalion, Company G leading, attacked objective Bourbon - Hill 418 - following up the intense mortar and artillery preparation. Company F attacked the left portion of Bourbon, an unnumbered hill 500 yards southwest of Hill 418. Advancing while under very heavy mortar and artillery fire, the companies became heavily engaged with a determined enemy on the peaks and ridge lines. Intense automatic weapons fire over bare terrain inflicted many casualties before close contact was gained. At 0945 hours, Company G assaulted the peak and stormed through a rain of grenades and mortar fire to take the hill at 1010 hours by closely following a rolling artillery barrage. The enemy launched a swift counterattack and called deadly mortar fire in on the hill to hamper the reinforcement of Company G. The company fought back and placed a maximum of supporting fire on the reverse slopes, but the enemy, using unlimited grenades, pushed the thin line of defenders off the peak at 1030 hours. Company F came under interlocking machine gun fire and an equally intense barrage of grenades and were able to gain only a toe hold on their objective. As soon as Company G reformed, and with Company E moving up to assist, they assaulted again. The fire support of tanks, 75mm recoilless rifles, and flame throwers were called in, and the troops gained and lost the hill five times before late afternoon. At 1720 hours, the elements of the 2nd Battalion were ordered into a night perimeter. The battalion had suffered 170 casualties from the deadly enemy fire and heavy barrages of mortars, grenades and artillery.

The 4th Battalion (GEF), Company N leading, began their attack on objective Scotch after intense preparatory and close support machine gun fires. Company O provided a base of fire from the high ground on the line of departure. This gallant battalion gained two peaks close to the top, but were repulsed at 0820 hours by an overwhelming force. After quick reorganization and upon increasing the size of the attack with all platoons of Company N, and the fire support of Company P, they assaulted again, reaching the trenches near the crest where a fierce bayonet, grenade and rifle-butt fight raged until 0920 when Company P also was committed. At 1015, the two companies were engaged on a 200-yard area on the hill top. The enemy immediately reinforced their units and counterattacked the 4th Battalion (GEF) which, by this time, was forced to use enemy weapons and ammunition. By 1500 hours, they had occupied all of objective Scotch but were under heavy attack and intense mortar fire. This battalion then had to withdraw to the left of the 2nd Battalion after suffering approximately 130 casualties.

The 3rd Battalion, with Company I attacking objective Rye on the right, received heavy mortar fire immediately upon crossing the line of departure. Company K stormed the pointed peak of objective Rye at 0655 hours and gained the top by the sheer impetus of their assault. In the attempt to reorganize, all riflemen on the peak became casualties from continuous mortar fire, which was called in by the enemy - still deep in their bunkers on the objective. Machine gun fire swept the attackers from both flanks, a swift counterattack was launched, and the hill was retaken by the enemy at 0720 hours. Company I ran into four concealed machine guns and was unable to close with the enemy across flat ground for most of the day. Tanks attempted to move in and overrun the machine guns but encountered a dense mine field across the road, and deep rice paddy mud restricted movement in the valley. Artillery and tanks took the deeply entrenched weapons under fire. Company L was committed to assist Company K on objective Rye, but only after a third fierce assault with grenades and bayonet were they able to gain the top. Company A was attached to the 3rd Battalion and placed behind Company K to support the attack by fire. Company M's 75mm recoilless rifles fired on bunkers at 300 yards range, and tanks fired from the valley at 500 yards range with little telling effect against the massive bunkers. Company L stopped a counterattack on objective Rye at 1600 hours, but the battalion was withdrawn into night positions at the base of the objective to reorganize, as Companies K and L had suffered 60 casualties.

The 1st Battalion, securing the regimental left flank, committed Company B on Hill 300. Company B moved their 1st Platoon forward under heavy bombardment of 60mm, 81mm mortar and 105mm artillery, and managed to reach the first crest of Hill 300 where they came under intense machine gun and small arms fire. Under severe counterattack, this platoon managed to hold for 50 minutes and upon being reinforced, they pressed their attack to the top of Hill 300, inflicting terrible casualties against the determined superior enemy. Company B held their position and repulsed strong enemy counterattacks supported by severe artillery bombardments. After suffering heavy casualties, Company B again was attacked by an overwhelming force and forced to withdraw at 1530 hours under cover of friendly artillery fire. The 1st Battalion occupied a strong position on Hill 339 for the remainder of the night.

At the end of the first day, it was apparent that the enemy was putting up a most determined defense. Heavy artillery fell in counter-battery fire far to the rear of the action. Air strikes were placed on objectives Scotch, Bourbon and Hill 347 before dark, and objective Scotch was bombed after dark by B-26s armed with 500-pound bombs.

On Oct. 4th, the company objectives became battalion objectives, and preparations were increased as large amounts of ammunition were carried forward. Quadruple mounted .50-caliber machine guns were used as bases of fire.

The 1st Battalion, from its position on Hill 339, launched a coordinated attack on Hill 300 with Companies A and C. Company C attacked from the east with Company A attacking from the north. After a furious battle under constant mortar and artillery bombardment, and after the hill top changed hands three times, the enemy strong hold finally crumbled under the strong attack of the determined troopers of the 1st Battalion. At 1300 hours, Company B moved down Hill 339 and joined the battalion perimeter with Companies A and C on Hill 300.

The 2nd Battalion, Companies E and F leading, attacked the left peak of objective Bourbon at daylight, and the assault was pressed all morning in the face of withering enemy fire. Heavy concentrations of supporting fire were placed on bunkers and trenches, but the positions could not be reduced by fire alone. The infantry had to assault into the well-placed interlocking fires time and time again receiving heavy casualties. At 1400 hours, all remaining rifle elements of Companies E, F and G were consolidated and the force, totaling 60 men, secured the hill.

The 1st Battalion, 8th Cavalry Regiment, under the operational control of the 7th Cavalry, moved into the 2nd Battalion perimeter at 0130 hours. The fresh battalion prepared to attack the peak of Hill 418 at daylight the following day.

The 3rd Battalion attacked objective Rye with three companies abreast under cover of smoke and after a heavy artillery preparation. Again, the top was within grasp by noon when the superior enemy reserves and planned defensive fires beat back the attacking forces. Eighty casualties were suffered before breaking contact at 1300 hours. A four-hour barrage of heavy mortar fire was placed on objective Rye throughout the afternoon while artillery engaged point targets. Supporting tanks closed to within a range of 150 yards to fire, but the enemy trenches were too deep and too well-concealed in the folds of the terrain to be easily reduced.

The 4th Battalion (GEF), after a half day of heavy firing with all caliber weapons against objective Scotch, committed Company O at 1400 hours. A severe hand-to-hand battle was waged within the trenches for four hours, but the heavy interdiction by the enemy mortars and continuing counterattack from within the hill itself, over entrenched routes of access, prevented the complete seizure of the objective. The assault elements were forced to withdraw at 1700 hours.

During the night of Oct. 4th and 5th, the 1st Battalion's positions were probed by the enemy, and by 0245 hours all companies on Hill 300 were heavily engaged from the south, west and north. Refusing to give ground, the 1st Battalion savagely defended their position until 0330 hours

Preparing to move out from trench positions. (U.S. Army Photo)

Fix bayonets and prepare to attack. (U.S. Army Photo)

High dug in position with a .30 caliber light machine gun. (U.S. Army Photo)

An attacking rifle squad with fixed bayonets. (U.S. Army Photo)

Many hills in Korea looked like "Bloody Ridge." (U.S. Army Photo)

Chinese soldier captured, in August 1951. (Courtesy of Col. (Ret) S. Alevizakos, GEF)

with small arms, grenades and artillery. Maintaining their position under severe mortar bombardment, the battalion again came under attack at 0605 hours, and by 0820 hours all companies were heavily engaged. By 1020 hours, the defeated foe was forced to withdraw, leaving scores of his dead littering the hillside.

On Oct. 5th, the regiment secured all three assigned objectives, but only after one last vicious battle by the 3rd Battalion. The 3rd Battalion sent out patrols at 0700 toward objective Rye and developed the enemy resistance. Fire was placed on enemy bunkers throughout the day. A 155mm self-propelled gun took a position on the Hyonjo Pass and at a range of 2,000 yards, by direct fire, reduced the enemy positions. The battalion was ordered into the attack at 1715 and by a furious assault in the twilight and darkness, gained the peaks and occupied them. By daylight the following morning, all of objective Rye was secured, 20 prisoners taken, and 44 enemy dead were counted in one 50-yard square area.

Objective Bourbon was taken without resistance due to the tremendous casualties inflicted on the enemy during the previous two days of fighting. The enemy withdrew under cover of darkness from Hill 418, and a prisoner disclosed that they had abandoned Hill 477, a similar objective in the adjacent 3rd Infantry Division's sector. The commanding officer of the 15th Infantry was notified that Hill 477 had been abandoned by the enemy, and his two

poised battalions occupied their objective without resistance.

The 4th Battalion (GEF) pounded objective Scotch again until 1400 hours with artillery, mortar, recoilless weapons, tanks and air strikes. Company O moved out rapidly and rushed to the peak with fixed bayonets to seize it at 1530 hours. Resisting enemy were cleared from their positions, and five prisoners were taken from the isolated bunkers. The remainder of the battalion moved up to consolidate the objective and sent a strong patrol to Hill 334 furthering the successful penetration of the defense line. Great numbers of enemy dead were found on the hill. Bunkers three levels deep were revealed on the objective, with cover consisting of 16 to 30 feet of logs, rock and dirt.

After objectives Bourbon, Scotch and Rye fell to the 7th Cavalry Regiment, the Division boundary changed on the right flank, narrowing the regimental sector to exclude Hill 418, Hill 334 and Hill 313 (the right portion of Scotch).

The 1st Battalion held the left flank against repeated counterattacks, probes and heavy bombardments during the night of Oct. 5th and 6th. At 0110 hours, Company C again was forced to defend their position against the savage attack of the enemy and repeatedly repulsed attack after attack with the support of mortars and artillery fire, and illuminating artillery flares. The attack persisted throughout the night with the enemy constantly reinforcing and committing his troops

until the attack had reached battalion strength. Company C stood their ground and forced the enemy to withdraw at 0635 hours, inflicting heavy casualties on the attacker.

On Oct. 6th, the 2nd, 3rd and 4th (GEF) Battalions patrolled aggressively in their sectors and prepared for a renewal of the attack.

The 1st Battalion fought fiercely throughout the day against long-range fire from the south and the counterattacking enemy from the west. The strong enemy force counterattacked from the west but finally was contained with the assistance of air support and artillery fire. At 1500 hours, the 1st Battalion launched another attack, but immediately upon leaving their positions, they came under a hail of enemy small arms fire. Savagely fighting for every foot of ground, and although suffering heavy casualties, Company A advanced under a rolling barrage, which terminated into a screaming assault and secured the hill.

On the night of Oct. 6th, the 7th Cavalry was deep in the heart of the enemy defense line and the enemy resistance became reckless and fanatical as he shifted his reserves to oppose the 1st Battalion on the left, the 3rd Battalion on the right, and to hold tenaciously to the wooded ridge between the two battalions. The 4th Battalion (GEF) was designated to capture that ridge and was relieved on objective Scotch in order to attack between the 1st and 3rd Battalion.

The morning of the 7th found the 1st Battalion still firmly entrenched in enemy territory, maintaining its position after having fought savage counterattacks throughout the night, which inflicted more than 100 casualties on the enemy.

On Oct. 7th, the 3rd Battalion launched a maximum effort attack against objective Harris, a denuded hill top where one battalion of enemy defended the cap of the hill in an area 100 yards square, and where 250 enemy dead were left behind after the battle. The attack began at 0600 hours, and after three separate attacks by all three rifle companies of the 3rd Battalion against the perimeter, the hill was secured at 1435 hours. It was discovered that an enemy division command post was located on this hill. During the morning, 129 prisoners were taken and 100 enemy dead were counted within a 50-yard area on the hill top, while the 3rd Battalion suffered 71 casualties.

Line Jamestown had been reached and secured on the right and in the center of the 7th Cavalry Regimental sector. The 2nd Battalion, 8th Cavalry Regiment, relieved the 3rd Battalion, 7th Cavalry, at 0130 hours on Oct. 8th, and the 3rd Battalion went into regimental reserve for 24 hours.

The 4th Battalion (GEF), having been relieved on objective Scotch, passed behind the 3rd Battalion on objective Rye, and attacked at 0600 hours to secure the high ground between objectives Rye and Hill 300. This point of terrain became important as the 1st and 3rd Battalions drove deeper into enemy positions since it commanded the ridge-line between objectives Rye and Hill 300. The enemy hastily assembled and counterattacked from points along this ridge, but the 4th Battalion (GEF) attacked the enemy wherever he was found, assaulting, clearing and reducing positions all day, until ordered into a night perimeter at 1840 hours. This action, although not seizing any major terrain feature, inflicted heavy casualties on the enemy and reduced their potential to attack the adjacent battalions.

The 2nd Battalion, having moved to the regiment's left flank, occupied Hill 300 while the 1st Battalion continued the attack toward, and to the north of, Hill 287. The 2nd Battalion then attacked to the southwest against the enemy on two peaks with tiered emplacements, which had delayed the advance of the 5th Cavalry Regiment. The objectives were, in fact, due south of Hill 300, which afforded the enemy opportunities to launch counterattacks from many points of the compass. After a day of heavy fighting against resurgent enemy artillery and mortar barrages, and frequent strong counterattacks by fresh reserves from the west, the 2nd Battalion broke contact to form a perimeter defense for the night.

At daylight on Oct. 8th, the 2nd Battalion continued the attack toward the southwest but was engaged quickly by the enemy who was determined to hold their ground. The daylight hours were consumed by attack and counterattack, barrages and counter-barrages, until twilight. The enemy defended aggressively but received heavy casualties from the well-observed fire.

The backbone of the enemy defensive line of the regimental left flank showed sign of snapping as enemy heavy caliber fire was increased to compensate for their terrible attrition.

The 1st Battalion, at 0900 hours, against violent resistance, took the dominating unnumbered hill overlooking Hill 287. The battalion became a deep salient into the enemy line - a threat the enemy was determined to remove.

At 0045 hours on Oct. 9th, the enemy unleashed a devastating barrage of mortars, rockets and artillery, followed by a two-battalion mass attack on the battered 1st Battalion. The 1st Battalion was ordered to withdraw into a tight perimeter and to hold. After one hour of savage fighting, the furiously attacking enemy had driven

North Korean Prisoner of War Camp #5, Pyoktong, North Korea. Located on the Yalu River. Many prisoners that died were buried in the adjacent hills.

This town was Uijongbu. It was completely destroyed by the U.N. forces and this photo was take in June 1951. (Courtesy of Col. Frank Griepp)

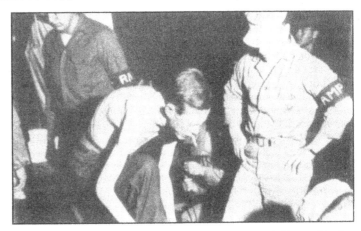

Emaciated and Wounded American Soldier receiving new clothing at Freedom Village, Panmunjom. (U.S. Army Photo)

American field-grade officers in a North Korean POW camp. (Eastfoto)

Turkish soldiers in a North Korean POW camp. They were tough and their record proved it. (Eastfoto)

in a portion of Company B. A fast-moving, slashing attack was unleashed by the yelling troopers from Company A. who quickly restored the Company B sector, and the situation began to improve. Throughout this period, Company C was engaged heavily but stubbornly held their ground. Although this savage attack had continued for almost seven hours, this battered battalion managed to retain its position, despite the fact that at times both the enemy and the GARRYOWENs shared the same trenches.

During this period, Richard Applegate of United Press was assigned to the First Cavalry Division on Oct. 9, 1951. He wrote in the headlines of Stars and Stripes on this date, the following: "Cav 'Revenges' Custer's Stand - Bloody Hand-to-Hand Fight Nets Peak." In the newspaper Special Edition, he wrote:

"The 3rd Battalion of the 7th Cavalry Regiment of the First Cavalry Division made up for its defeat at Custer's Last Stand Sunday by storming 'Bloody Baldy' mountain in a hand-to-hand grenade charge.

Four times the 3rd Battalion got to the top of the sparsely wooded peak only to be hurled back down by fanatical Chinese resistance. Early Sunday afternoon, a fifth charge took the hill.

From a forward observation post on the ridge-line two miles away I watched the final assault through powerful binoculars. It was one of the most impressive infantry charges I have seen in several years of covering war.

Come with me into the forward observation post, hacked-out of the rock and dirt and overlooking the valley below and 'Bloody Baldy' in the distance.

In the cave-like post with us are Capt. Marvin Rottenberg of Columbia, S.C., and Lt. Robert B. Easter of West Medford, Mass.

Each is busy with glasses and telephones, relaying what is going on before our eyes to intelligence in the rear. On our left, through the smoke-blackened pine trees and shattered underbrush - this hill too was taken only a short time ago - is a rising peak where a battle has been going on for two days. It, too, is under attack as are several minor peaks jutting out of the valley in the foreground, but 'Bloody Baldy' is straight ahead.

Through the big glasses, we can see American men forming up on the higher slopes of this peak, their green combat clothes barely perceptible as they crouch behind ridges, boulders and bomb craters. There is continual smoke on the peak, both from our artillery and mortars and from the hand grenades the Chinese are lobbing down on their tormentors.

It looks as though only a handful of men are in the attack, but we know better. The air is quivering and shaking from the big American guns feeling for the Chinese.

The Chinese are dug in so deeply on the crest of the hill that heavy artillery has failed to shake them. They lob hand grenades down the hill like popcorn, but this fifth assault is going on anyway.

We can see the American men break from cover and race up the hill, spread out in skirmish line. Some stumble as they run up the steep hill, but all go on. There is a perfect hail of enemy grenades, kicking up brown dust as they explode. One grenade goes off, apparently in the very middle of a cavalry group of about six, but when the dust had cleared all six are still on their feet although they have spread out more.

This assault grinds to a stop in the face of the murderous storm of grenades, mortars and burp guns. We can hear the sharp rip of the burps from here, cutting like a whine into the heavier pound of machine guns and the thuds of mortars.

The Americans crouch where they can throughout the assault. Six men start to work their way around a finger leading up to a huge Chinese bunker at the very top. They are moving in what seems to be suicidal bunchiness but the men know what they are doing. They are moving upright and as Chinese grenades come down on them they dash to the right or left to escape the explosion but they keep going.

When within range, they start pitching their own fragmentation grenades up the slope, the heavy black smoke showing which are American and which are Chinese grenades. Two of the men are within 10 yards of the Chinese trenches on the top, dodging back and forth but pitching grenades like baseballs.

The two men - I learned later from one of our wounded who had been there that it was the platoon sergeant and a private leading the assault - are pushed back several times.

It looked as though the six or seven men who are all alone out in front of the attack were about to get killed - you can't go on dodging grenades forever - but now we can see other American soldiers creeping up the ridge to the right, stealthily and steadily working their way up for the break.

There is a great gout of mingled brown smoke from the Chinese grenades coming down and black smoke of American grenades going up. The six men at the left are joined by about 20 coming up from the right. Apparently there are Americans on the far side of the slope also for some black puffs are too far back to have come from any of the men we can see from here.

The artillery has stopped because our men are too close. The last great charge carries the Americans to the top, and we can see infantrymen leap into the Red trenches, firing their rifles and carbines down into the trenches and bunkers and throwing grenades into the holes.

We have been told that some of these bunkers are three stories down with logs and dirt on top up to 12 feet thick. There are men dying up there on the peak but most of them are Chinese.

The American assault has taken 50 prisoners, killed an unknown number of enemy, and taken another Korean hill for the United Nations autumn offensive.

Now the wounded and the dead are being brought back down the murderously steep 'Bloody Baldy' and the 3rd Battalion of the 7th Cavalry, the same outfit that was with Custer on the Little Big Horn, has earned a new star for its crown. The 3rd Battalion now is being relieved as the cold, clear Korean day comes to an end."

Also on Oct. 9, 1951, Cpl. Wayne Klein of the Pacific Stars and Stripes had an article on Headquarters 8th Army. The headlines were: "Infantrymen Grab Enemy Position North of Yonchon After Four Futile Efforts." In the newspaper story, he wrote:

"Under murderous enemy fire, the 3rd Battalion of the 7th Cavalry Regiment in marching fire stormed straight up a scraggly hill north of Yonchon Sunday tossing grenades into each Red bunker on the way and securing the objective at 3 p.m.

Pvt. Tim Adams, Stars and Stripes staffer covering the western front, said the battalion futilely assaulted the mortar-topped hill four times. In the final drive, Adams said, the Cavalrymen marched abreast straight up the hill with their weapons blazing.

Northwest of Yonchon, the 1st Battalion of the GARRYOWEN 7th Regiment secured another bare peak high ground objective against heavy enemy resistance. After securing the hill, they were under vigorous Red fire from the north, northwest and south.

On another hill secured by the regiment, the cavalrymen took 50 POWs, the largest bag of Chinese Communists in months.

American and other United Nation troops who are slashing the Reds off hills in the western front battle area faced some of the heaviest Communist gunfire of the Korean war.

In one area north northwest of Yonchon Sunday, the Reds were said to have hurled 4,000 rounds of artillery and mortar fire at the attacking Allies."

At 0239 on Oct.. 12th, Companies A and B came under attack, and by 0300 hours the entire 1st Battalion was attacked simultaneously, disrupting all communications. Under a wall of intense mortar and artillery fire, followed closely by a grenade-throwing fanatical enemy battalion, the enemy finally overran two companies of the 1st Battalion and forced them from their most advanced positions back to the dominating hill overlooking Hill 287. The 1st Battalion, 8th Cavalry, under the operational control of the 7th Cavalry, then relieved the 1st Battalion on this dominating position. The 1st Battalion, 7th Cavalry, then moved to Division reserve and remained there until Oct. 25th.

The 4th Battalion (GEF), after having cleared the ridge between objectives Rye and Hill 300 by aggressive combat patrolling and attack, passed to the operational control of the 8th Cavalry on Oct. 11th. It then consolidated and patrolled from Line Jamestown under 8th Cavalry control when the 7th Cavalry went into Division reserve on Oct. 21st.

Oct. 13th saw the end of the attack phase for the 7th Cavalry except for the attack on Hill 200 by the 2nd Battalion, 5th Cavalry - then under the operational control of the 7th Cavalry - and for the night attack on Oct. 28th by the 1st Battalion, 7th Cavalry, on Hill 199, which the 5th Cavalry had been unable to secure for a patrol base.

During the first 10 days of the attack, the 7th Cavalry took all objectives assigned. It fought successfully against four enemy regiments and inflicted 65 enemy casualties per hour for an unrelenting 10 days. Only the fighting heart and the GARRYOWEN spirit maintained the aggressive attitude of the riflemen against the great odds of terrain and massive enemy numbers. Only magnificent leadership held units intact after the heavy casualties and continuous enemy barbardment. No line company was out of the attack for more than 48 hours at any time during the offensive, while the enemy exploiting his depth of manpower at night, replaced his shattered elements as fast as possible. In one 24-hour period, 3,300 rounds of enemy artillery fire fell in the regimental sector. Resupply was over long foot routes that were continually subjected to heavy artillery and mortar fires.

The supporting 77th Field Artillery Battalion fired 89,781 rounds of 105mm ammunition in 15 days in support of the regiment - exceeding on two days any known previous World War II record.

Every unit in the regiment exerted maximum effort to defeat the enemy decisively. Every available man in the regiment was moved for-

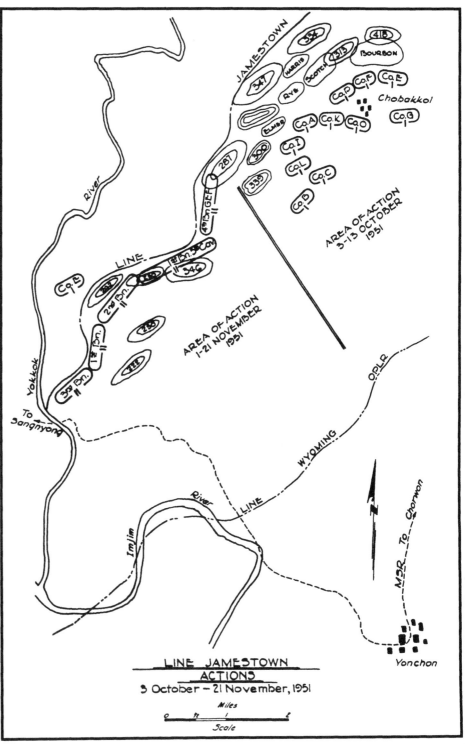

LINE JAMESTOWN
ACTIONS
3 October – 21 November, 1951

Miles

Scale

1st Cavalry Division Commander with 7th Cavalry Regimental Staff. L to R: Lt. Col. Charles Hallden, Commander 3rd Bn.; Lt. Col. D. Arbouzis, Commander 4th Bn., (GEF); Maj. Gen. Charles D. Palmer, Commander 1st Cav. Div.; Col. Dan Gilmer, Commander 7th Cavalry Regiment; Lt. Col. Lucian Croft, Commander 1st Bn.; Lt. Col. DeLancy, Commander 77th Field Artillery Bn.; Lt. Col William Cochrane, Regimental Executive Officer. (U.S. Army Photo)

ward to act as a rifleman until the rear area personnel were reduced by two-thirds of its authorized strength.

The regiment, less the 4th Battalion (GEF), went into Division reserve on Oct. 21st, and after a short period of reorganization and training, replaced the 5th Cavalry Regiment, again bringing all units of the 7th Cavalry on the line.

The enemy had suffered 2,501 killed (with an estimated 616 additional killed), an estimated 8,787 wounded, and 210 prisoners from the 7th Cavalry Regiment's attack to and including Line Jamestown. The enemy, however, had increasingly large amounts of mortar and artillery weapons at his disposal, and the use of these weapons was a major factor in the increase of the regiment's casualties, which amounted to 175 killed, 1,110 wounded and 70 missing during the operation.

The 1st, 2nd and 3rd Battalions remained on Line Jamestown improving defensive positions and patrolling aggressively during the first part of November. The 4th Battalion (GEF) returned to regimental control on Nov. 1st.

From the book, "The Forgotten War," author Clay Blair wrote: *"The next major operation took place on Eighth Army's left flank. Called Commando, it was carried out by I Corps, now commanded by W. "Iron Mike" O'Daniel, 57, the legendary commander of the 3rd Division in World War II. The strategic aim of Commando was to keep "unrelenting" pressure on the enemy; the tactical aim was to push the U.N. line about six miles northwest from Wyoming to Jamestown, in order to keep CCF artillery fire off the Seoul-Chorwon-Kumhwa railroad, which was being developed into a primary supply line behind that sector of the front. Five reinforced divisions would participate, left to right: the ROK 1st, the newly created British Commonwealth Division (commanded by A.J.H. Cassels), the 1st Cavalry, Shorty Soule's 3rd Division, and the 25th Division of Bill Hoge's IX Corps.*

Operation Commando commenced on Oct. 3. The right- and left-flank forces in I Corps advanced to the new line without undue hardship or casualties, but in the center the 1st Cavalry Division, now commanded by West Pointer (1952) Thomas L. Harrold, 49, ran up into the dug-in CCF 47th Army, which was determined not to yield an inch. Ghastly fighting like that on Bloody and Heartbreak ridges took place on or near hills dominated by Old Baldy."

It took about 16 days of hard, bloody fighting for the 1st Cavalry Division to advance six miles to Line Jamestown. During this period, practically the entire division was engaged. The four division artillery battalions fired an astonishing 380,856 rounds. I Corps incurred about 4,000 casualties, about 2,900 of which were in the First Cavalry. The historian described the carnage:

"The 1st Cavalry Division was engaged almost constantly in the most bitter fighting of the entire Korean campaign. The effort required in driving an entire Chinese Army from an excellent defensive line was so great as to almost defy description. One of the regiments, 7th Cavalry, reported that fully two-thirds of its rear area personnel had been sent up to front line units to fill the gaps left by an unprecedented number of casualties. Survivors of companies joined with remaining fragments of other companies to return and assault again the positions that had previously all but wiped them out. This maximum, around-the-clock exertion extended to every unit and every man in the division.

After the 1st Cavalry finally had reached Line Jamestown, the I Corps commander, 'Iron Mike' O'Daniel, issued orders for the corps to hold that line and dig in. There would be no more major offensives. As the British historian wrote: 'Future operations would be confined to those necessary to maintain existing positions.' One month later, the battered 1st Cavalry was withdrawn from Korea and returned to Japan, replaced by the 45th (Oklahoma National Guard) Division, which had arrived in Japan the previous spring. Having originally embarked for an amphibious landing and mopping-up operations at Inchon, which had been expected to take no longer than about six weeks, the 1st Cavalry Division had spent 16 terrible months in Korea."

During the period Nov. 1st through Nov. 21st, the enemy forces opposing the regiment consisted of three regiments of the 47th Chinese Communist Army. On the western flank of the regiment's line, the enemy's line of defense was anchored along the east bank of the Imjin River, south of the Yokkok River junction. An enemy battalion occupied Hill 222 and the hill mass to the south. From this point, defensive positions along the Yokkok River, running northeast, were manned by an enemy battalion with an estimated two companies from a fourth regiment occupying Hill 168 and the ridge-line west of Hill 287. One enemy battalion occupied and prepared defensive positions northwest of the Yokkok River in the vicinity of Hill 214, and an entire regiment remained in reserve northwest of Sang-nyong, preparing for and executing special missions against the 7th Cavalry Regiment.

At the beginning of November, positions occupied by the enemy forces were prepared partially along a secondary line since his main line positions had been penetrated during Operation Commando. Improvement, extension and winterization of these positions continued throughout the month. This defense consisted primarily of organized and prepared key terrain features with the intervening ground lightly held by small outposts. Maximum advantage was taken of the natural obstacle afforded by the Yokkok River. Strategic approaches and crossing of this river were strongly defended as well as the main road running northwest along the east bank of the Imjin River.

It is estimated that the 139th Chinese Communist Division, opposing the 7th Cavalry Regiment during November, was 29 percent under strength initially, due to the heavy casualties suffered during Operation Commando. Enemy front-line troops were bolstered by the assignment of service and rear echelon personnel from Division and Army. Toward the middle of November, it is believed that a sufficient number of replacements were received to bring the Division back to full strength. There was no appreciable deterioration of enemy morale as a result of the high attrition and previously suffered as evidence by the tenacious and fanatical defense of key positions against our patrol activity. There was, on the other hand, no aggressive counteraction taken against our patrols, thus indicating the sole mission of defense of the strategic terrain.

On Nov. 4th, an estimated enemy battalion successfully attacked the regiment's positions on Hill 200. This enemy battalion departed its reserve area in the vicinity of Sangnyong on the night of Nov. 3rd, and after crossing the Yokkok River, moved into an assembly area on the reserve slope of Hill 222. Preceded by a 30-minute concentration of artillery, mortar and rocket fire, during which an estimated 2,000 rounds fell on the regiment's positions, the attack was launched prior to midnight on Nov. 4th from the west and northwest with the main effort exerted from the northwest. After some of the regiment's positions had been overrun, enemy carrying parties were dispatched to collect and evacuate equipment and the attacking elements were relieved by an unknown unit, estimated to be of company size, whose mission was the defense of the hill.

Hill 200 was recaptured by the 1st Battalion at 1745 hours on Nov. 5th. Early on Nov. 6th, the enemy launched a regimental-size attack against the hill with two battalions attacking abreast. Again the main effort came from the northwest, with a secondary attack exerted against the opposite flank from the west and southwest. Concentrated artillery, mortar and rocket fire was employed prior to and during the attack. During the following five hours, continuous, deadly pressure was applied against the 1st Battalion, and by dawn on Nov. 6th, the 1st Battalion was forced to withdraw, and the enemy forces secured the hill for the second time. The enemy attacking elements moved off the hill, evacuated their dead and wounded, and collected captured equipment, and left a token force estimated to be a platoon size to defend the ground.

On Nov. 7th, the 2nd Battalion recaptured Hill 200, meeting light resistance from the token force defending the ground. For the remainder of the month while the regiment occupied these positions, enemy activity was restricted to squad and platoon-size raids in this area. It is believed that the enemy's mission in these attacks was to capture equipment and inflict maximum casualties.

The pattern of the enemy's attack reflected the use of reserve elements, passing through front line units, to launch the assault in fanatical, ferocious, "Banzai" charges supported by artillery, mortar and rocket concentrations. Leading elements of the attacking forces were armed with bangalore torpedoes and explosives to breach protective wire forward of the regiment's positions. The enemy effectively massed his artillery and mortar fire, inflicting heavy casualties and damaging front line positions prior to the assault. During the 48-hour period Nov. 5th and 6th, an estimated 8,000 rounds of concentrated artillery, mortar and rocket fire fell into the regiment's positions. Throughout the remainder of the period from Nov. 7th to 21st, 200 to 500 rounds per day were employed by the enemy against front line troops, the major portion being harassing fires with defensive fires employed against patrols. Large amounts of tank and self-propelled gun fire was used and as many as 37 enemy artillery pieces were sighted each day. Normally, the direct-fire guns were fired from positions in defilade, and moved to alternate of supplemental positions after firing 12 to 15 rounds during daylight hours.

The main road along the east bank of the Imjin River was lined heavily, in some cases with box mines planted two or three deep. Tank traps were dug at critical points, and antitank defensive positions were prepared to cover these with fire, which effectively denied access to this route.

Total casualties inflicted upon the enemy during the period Nov. 1st to 21st by the 7th Cavalry Regiment were 171 counted dead, seven counted wounded, 11 prisoners and an estimated 403 killed and 310 wounded. The regiment suffered 23 killed, 303 wounded and 161 missing for the same period.

At 1102 hours on Nov. 21st, the 7th Cavalry Regiment passed to the operational control of the 3rd Infantry Division, reverted to Division reserve and moved to new positions. In this location, the regiment conducted intensive training for the remainder of the month of November.

The 4th Battalion (GEF), which since their entry into the Korean War had been part of the GARRYOWENs, were transferred to the 3rd Infantry Division.

The month of December began with the regiment under the operational control of the 3rd Infantry Division in a reserve area. They conducted training until Dec. 15th. On Dec. 16th, the regiment reverted to 1st Cavalry Division control.

On Dec. 17th, the entire regiment moved by rail from Yonchon to Inchon and the following day boarded the USS Picksway, USS Henrico, USS Meniffee, and the USS Epping Forest for the return trip to Japan. The regiment landed at Muroran, Hokkaido, Japan, on Dec. 22nd, boarded trains for Camp Crawford and remained there throughout the remainder of the month of December.

Prior to the departure from Korea, an advance party of the 7th Cavalry Regiment was sent to Camp Crawford, where they assumed responsibility for the property of the 179th Infantry, 45th Infantry Division. At the same time, advance details of the 179th Infantry arrived in Korea and assumed responsibility for the property of the 7th Cavalry. Only personal baggage and one 2-1/2-ton kitchen truck per company

were retained and moved with the regiment. These trucks were transported aboard the USS Epping Forest. Equipment and personnel were lightered aboard the ships in the roadstead at Inchon and debarked at the wharves in Muroran, Japan.

The remainder of December was spent in reorganizing, limited training and by observing the holiday season at Camp Crawford.

Thus, the regiment ended the year after 17 months of continuous combat in the Korean War under every possible condition. It was indeed a different regiment that returned than the poorly equipped, undermanned, but proud regiment that had left the shores of Japan 17 months before on a mission that was expected to take at the most three months.

1952

The new year began with the regiment stationed at Camp Crawford, Japan. Immediately after the holiday season, a 17-week intensive training cycle was initiated with emphasis on cold weather training, including over-snow mobility, training in Arctic survival, skiing and snowshoeing.

New hopes for peace were brought forth when Washington, D.C. introduced the doctrine of voluntary repatriation into the negotiations in January 1952, but the Communists launched a vicious and massive propaganda attack against the United States, in which POWs held by them and the U.N. became victim or instruments. This campaign consisted of three cunning and interrelated elements:

*Germ warfare: On Feb. 2, 1952, Soviet Ambassador to the U.N., Jacob Malik, accused the United States of employing bullets filled with "toxic gases" in Korea. Later that month, picking up and expanding this theme, Peking and Pyongyang and Communist organs worldwide charged that United States airmen and artillerymen had dropped and fired bacteria-infected insects and shellfish (beetles, lice, ticks, rats, fleas, clams, et cetera) into North Korea. To substantiate these claims, the Communists created faked "exhibits," inaugurated a massive inoculation program, and finally, by torture and threats, forced two

United Nations Delegation at Kaesong. L to R: General Craigie, USAF; General Yup, ROK I Corps; Vice Admiral Joy, Far East Naval Commander; General Hodes, Eighth Army; Rear Admiral Burke, U.S. Navy. (U.S. Army Photo)

General Mark W. Clark, Far East Commander, signs the Korean Armistice Agreement on July 27, 1953, after two years of negotiation, during which hundreds of thousands of men were killed and wounded in continued hostilities. (U.S.Navy Photo)

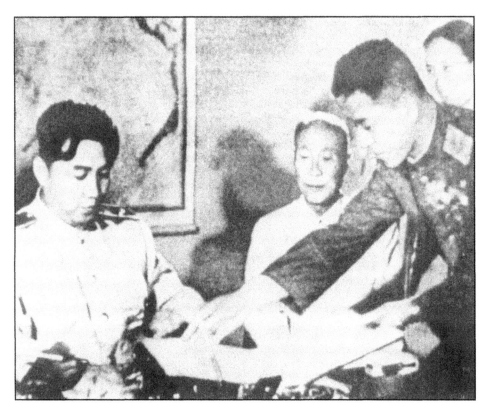

North Korean Premier Kim Il Sung prepares to sign Armistice document handed to him July 27, 1953, by General Nam Il, head of the Communist delegation at Panmunjom. (Eastfoto)

young Air Force POWs (and later, a senior Marine Corps pilot and 35 other Air Force pilots) to "confess" on film, on tape and in press interviews that they indeed had been part of a huge United States germ warfare conspiracy. This wholly fabricated propaganda attack, supported by Communist-manipulated "demonstrations" all over the world, was astonishingly successful; Washington's slow-footed and righteous denials were not.

*Brainwashing: Simultaneously with the germ warfare campaign, the Communists launched an "indoctrination" program of U.N. POWs, designed to turn them against the West and even refuse repatriation. The program included not physical torture, but rather a form of mental torture: endless repetition of Communist slogans, phrases and ideas and the exploitation of grievance, especially among black POWs. Although no POWs were directly threatened with grave harm or death, they knew that thousands of U.N. POWs earlier had been tortured and murdered, and partly as a result of this knowledge, this Communist campaign (which came to be known as "brainwashing") also was astoundingly successful. Postwar studies were to show that only about 12 percent of American POWs (Bill Dean among them) "actively and consistently" resisted the program. The majority "cooperated in indoctrination and interrogation sessions in a passive sort of way, although there was a tendency to refuse to say anything obviously traitorous." Nonetheless, many U.N. POWs signed "peace petitions" and similar pro-Communist testimonials, which were distributed in the West. Ultimately, 21 Americans and one Briton were to refuse repatriation.

*POW riots: Beginning in early 1952, the Communists allowed trained agents to be captured as POWs. These agents were instructed to organize the hard-core Communist POWs and foment riots and other disturbances inside U.N. POW compounds on the island of Koje and elsewhere, for the purpose of incurring U.N. punitive countermeasures, which the Communists then could exploit. Per plan, "riots" in U.N. POW compounds occurred on Feb. 18th and March 13, 1952. In attempting to quell these riots, U.N. guards fired into the POWs, killing 89 and wounding 166. Having cunningly staged these incidents, the Communists then denounced the U.N. worldwide for "barbarous massacres" and "atrocities."

Athletics were stressed throughout the year. On Feb. 23rd, the regimental basketball team won the Division Championship, and on March 2nd, won the XVI Corps championship at Camp Shimmelphenning. The basketball team then went on to win the All Japan Tactical Troop Championship by defeating the 19th Infantry Regimental team to end the season with 32 wins against no losses.

During the early morning hours of March 30th, a fire broke out in the regimental headquarters. Before the post fire department could be summoned, the wooden frame building was in flames and the guard personnel in the building were lucky to escape alive. Through the heroic efforts of Master Sgt. Glenn Bigler, the Regimental Sergeant Major, the Regimental Colors were saved. All other records, trophies and historical items were destroyed.

Peace negotiations continued to be stalemated with riots and other disturbances inside U.N. POW compounds on the island of Koje. After the Communists had broken off the talks on April 28, 1952, the POW "riots" intensified. On May 12th, during one spectacular riot at Koje, Communists seized the American POW camp commander, Brig. Gen. Francis T. Dodd, who, in

an attempt to negotiate with the rioters, got too close. The POWs "tried" Dodd and sentenced him to death. In an effort to save his own life, Dodd signed a document, agreeing to cease immediately the "barbarous behavior, insults, torture . . . (and) mass murdering" of POWs by U.N. guns, germs, poison gas and atomic weapons and to halt the screening of POWs for the purpose of complying with the U.N.'s "illegal and unreasonable" voluntary repatriation program. Sent to Koje to free Dodd by military force if necessary, the new I Corps chief of staff, Brig. Gen. Charles F. Colson, decided against using force and signed a document that he believed would gain Dodd's freedom. Colson conceded that numerous POWs had been killed and wounded by U.N. guards and that he would do all within his power "to eliminate further violence and bloodshed." He guaranteed "humane treatment" for U.N. POWs and agreed that there would be "no more forcible screening of any remaining POWs in this camp." Dodd got out, but the Communists exploited the two documents as further "proof" of U.N. "atrocities," humiliating the United States and Eighth Army and raising serious questions worldwide over the validity of the voluntary repatriation doctrine.

During the month of April, a two-day Regimental and Division Command Post Exercise was held. During the period May 20th to 23rd, the regiment moved by motor to Camp Chitose for airlift problems. All three battalions were airlifted and returned to participate in a river crossing problem as the combined arms phase of training began.

In May, the Regimental Leadership School graduated the first class of 34 troopers.

Operation Seahorse - an Amphibious Landing Exercise - was conducted during the period June 16th to 19th with all members of the regimental and battalion staffs participating.

Review ceremonies were held on July 4th at Camp Crawford for Maj. Gen. Thomas L. Harrold, departing 1st Cavalry Division Commander. Gen. Harrold served as the Regimental Personnel Adjutant as a Second Lieutenant in the 7th Cavalry Regiment during the period 1926-1927.

On Aug. 16, the regimental baseball team won the Division championship, and on the 27th won the XVI Corps Championship.

During the period Sept. 2nd to 6th, Regimental Combat Team tests were conducted by XVI Corps. On Sept. 8th, the Regimental Tank Company was activated.

On Oct. 3rd, the 1st Cavalry Division held a review at Camp Chitose II. This was the first review in which all units of the Division had participated since their return from Korea.

In December, the regiment again was called for service in Korea. An advance party departed for Korea on the 3rd for the purpose of preparing for the relief of the 8th Cavalry Regiment - then performing guard duties around the port city of Pusan and guarding the prisoner of war camps on the Island of Koje-do. The regiment sailed from Pusan, Korea, on the 15th. Upon arrival, the 3rd Battalion, with the 29th Anti-aircraft artillery Battalion attached, performed guard duties with the Prisoner of War Command on the island of Koje-do. The mission of the remainder of the regiment, with the 77th Field Artillery Battalion attached, was:

1st Battalion - performed port security in the Pusan area.

2nd Battalion - furnished security guard for the Headquarters, Korean Communications Zone, and performed train guard duty along the Pusan-Taegu railway, which was subjected to frequent attacks by guerrillas.

Heavy Mortar Company - performed security guard duty for the United Nations Civil Affairs Headquarters.

1953

The new year found the regiment, and its attachments, widely scattered in Korea, continuing guard and security duties generally in the Pusan area and the small islands off the southern coast of Korea as follows:

Regimental Headquarters - Tongnae Annex Area

1st Battalion - Pusan (Daisan School) Area

2nd Battalion less Company E - Taegu (Camp Walker)

3rd Battalion - Koju-do Island

Company E - Taejon

77th Field Artillery - Ichon-ni

On Jan. 15th, Company E was selected as the Honor Guard for Gen. Mark W. Clark, Commander in Chief, Far East, at Taegu, Korea.

On Feb. 1st, an advance party departed for Hokkaido, Japan, and on Feb. 15th, the regiment was replaced in Korea by the 5th Cavalry Regiment, and departed for Japan, arriving at Otaru on the 19th.

After settling in their quarters at Camp Crawford, Hokkaido, Japan, the regiment began a winter training program on March 2nd.

On March 20th, the Regimental Tank Company was returned to Regimental control, as it had been attached to the 70th Tank Battalion for training since October.

On March 23rd, more than 700 replacements, including 500 Puerto Rican personnel, were received. This large number of replacements forced the cancellation of the winter training program and the basic unit training cycle again was started in the regiment. Another factor that caused the cancellation of the winter training program was the unusual winter weather - a complete lack of snow in northern Japan.

Notwithstanding stepped-up fighting all along the truce line, the swap of sick and wounded POWs, called "Little Switch," started on April 20th and continued to May 3rd. Governed by elaborate security measures, this extraordinary operation was accomplished without notable incident. The U.N. turned over a total of 6,670 POWs: 5,194 NKPA, 1,030 CCF, and 446 civilian internees. In return, the U.N. received a total of 684 POWs: 471 ROKs, 149 Americans, 32 Britons, 15 Turks and 17 other U.N. personnel.

Having brought Syngman Rhee into line and resolved all other outstanding issues, the senior delegates met at Panmunjom at 10 a.m. on July 27th. In a cold, wordless ceremony, witnessed by Western and Communist journalists and photographers, Gens. Harrison and Nam Il each signed nine copies of the armistice. As set forth by its terms, 12 hours later, at 10 p.m., the guns fell silent along the front, and the war in Korea was over. In the days following, the final exchange of POWs, called "Big Switch," proceeded. The Communists returned a total of 12,773 U.N. prisoners, including 3,597 Americans (Bill Dean among them), 7,862 ROKs, 945 British (mostly Gloucesters), 229 Turks and 140 others. The U.N. returned a total of 75,823 Communist prisoners, including 70,183 of the NKPA and 5,640 of the CCF.

Of the many generals' sons serving in the Korean War, Don Faith and James A. Van Fleet Jr., were the only ones killed in action. After completing 105 FEAF bombing missions, Hap Gay's son, Hobart R., Jr., was killed in an aircraft accident in August 1952. Al Gruenther's son, Richard, had been wounded severely in northeast Korea. Mark Clark's son, William, who rose to executive of the 9th Infantry, was wounded three times. The last time, in October 1951, on Heartbreak Ridge, he was hurt so severely that he was ultimately forced to retire. The sons of the 2nd Division ADC George Stewart and Eighth Army engineer Pat Strong were wounded and physically disabled, respectively and medically evacuated.

From Oct. 16th to 29th, the regiment participated in afloat and landing phases of amphibious training at Chigasaki Beach.

During December, the regiment completed the XVI Corps Tests.

The Demilitarized Zone was established in the vicinity of the last battle lines near the 38th Parallel, which barely differed from demarcation that had separated North and South Korea before hostilities broke out in 1950. But the opposing forces did not simply pack up and go home. An uneasy truce had been signed, and a powerful United Nations presence would be required for years to come.

The 7th Cavalry Regiment is the patriarch of the modern Army's organizational family. The modern pentomic units scattered worldwide that bear the name "7th Cavalry," have inherited a proud 126-year-old military history. Throughout these years, GARRYOWEN has been synonymous with esprit de corps throughout the military profession. Today's modern Army 7th Cavalry troopers are the custodians of this esprit resulting from these years of service to Regiment and Nation.

During the Vietnam War, the 7th Cavalry was called upon to meet a new concept in warfare and tactical doctrines in the use of helicopters, which opened the way to a bold, new role in combat for the Regiment.

These crack "Skytroopers," as a new Cavalry with an old spirit but young at heart, would fight heroically with determination to destroy the Communist enemy in Vietnam. Many bitter and vicious battles were hard-fought and won, creating another new chapter in the history of the 7th Cavalry Regiment and the United States Army.

Then, in August 1990, the 7th Cavalry was alerted for quick deployment to Saudi Arabia for Operation Desert Shield. Again answering the call of their nation, it was a period of intense activity to meet their new task. This time to stop the oppressive enemy army of Saddam Hussein and to restore freedom to the country of Kuwait.

It was a new generation of American soldiers who were highly trained and skilled to do their jobs efficiently, with the best military weaponry in the world. In Operation Desert Storm, the 7th Cavalry used tactics by probing and jabbing with fast lightly armored Bradley and Cobra vehicles against enemy positions in Iraq. This would make way and guide the MIAI tanks of the First Cavalry Division into battle.

The Persian Gulf War soon was over and the freedom of a small country preserved. Once again, it showed the world that aggression will not be tolerated. Within the Army organization, the 7th Cavalry exemplified that it always will be ready to fight, any time, any where and win. Furthermore, our nation demands it, and our freedom depends on it. GARRYOWEN . . .

Enemy Delegation L to R: General Fang; General Hua, Chinese Army; General Nam Il, delegate for the Communists; General Lee Sang Cho and General Chang Pyong San, North Korean Army. (U.S. Army Photo)

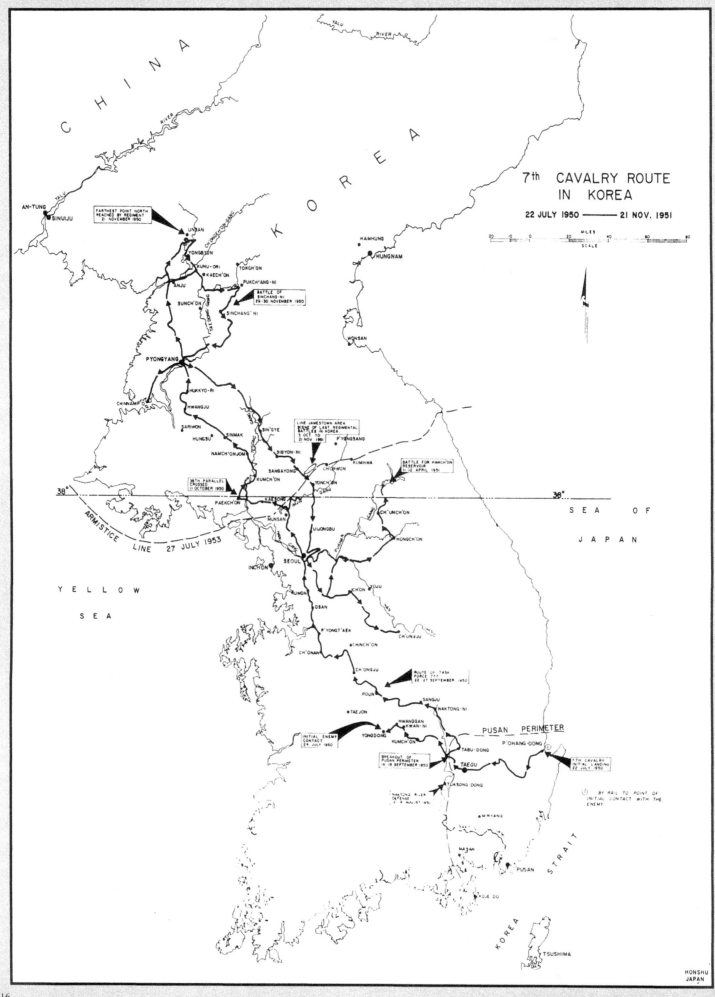

7th CAVALRY ROUTE
IN KOREA

22 JULY 1950 ——————— 21 NOV. 1951

CAMPAIGNS FOUGHT BY
THE 7TH U.S. CAVALRY

Indian War Campaigns
Comanches
Little Big Horn
Nez Perces
Pine Ridge
Montana 1873
Dakota 1874

Mexican Expedition Campaigns
Mexico 1916-1917

World War II Campaigns
New Guinea
Bismarck Archipelago
(With Arrowhead Device)
Leyte (With Arrowhead Device)
Luzon

Korean War Campaigns
UN Defensive
UN Offensive
CCF Intevention
First UN Counteroffensive
CCF Spring Offensive
UN Summer/Fall Offensive
Second Korean Winter
Third Korean Winter

Vietnam Campaigns
Defense
Counteroffensive
Counteroffensive, Phase II
Counteroffensive, Phase III
TET Counteroffensive
Counteroffensive, Phase IV
Counteroffensive, Phase V
Counteroffensive, Phase VI
TET 69/Counteroffensive
Summer/Fall 1969
Winter/Spring 1970
Sanctuary Counteroffensive
Counteroffensive Phase VII
Consolidation I
Consolidation II
Cease-fire

DECORATIONS OF THE 7TH U.S. CAVALRY
Presidential Unit Citation (Army), Streamer Embroidered <u>Antipolo, Luzon</u>
Philippine Presidential Unit Citation, Streamer Embroidered <u>17 October 1944 through 4 July 1945</u>
Presidential Unit Citation (Army), Streamer Embroidered <u>Yonchon, Korea</u>
Presidential Unit Citation (Army), Streamer Embroidered <u>Pusan, Korea</u>
Republic of Korea Presidential Unit Citation, Streamer Embroidered <u>Waegwan-Gaegu</u>
Republic of Korea Presidential Unit Citation, Streamer Embroidered <u>Korea</u>
Chryssoun Arition Andrias (Bravery Gold Medal of Greece), Streamer Embroidered <u>Korea</u>
Presidential Unit Citation (Army), Streamer Embroidered <u>Pleiku Province</u>
Valorious Unit Award, Streamer Embroidered <u>Fish Hook</u>
Valorious Unit Award, Streamer Embroidered <u>Quang Tin Province</u>
Valorious Unit Award, Streamer Embroidered <u>Defense of Saudi Arabia</u>
Valorious Unit Award, Streamer Embroidered <u>Liberation and Defense of Kuwait</u>

Acts of Valor
THE MEDAL OF HONOR
The Korean War
1950 - 1953

Number of medals: 131

AIR FORCE: 4   ARMY: 78   MARINES: 42   NAVY: 7

*Awarded Posthumously

AIR FORCE
*Davis, Maj. George A., Jr. (Sinuiju-Yalu River Area)
*Loring, Maj. Charles J., Jr. (Sniper Ridge, N. Korea)
*Sebille, Maj. Louis J. (Ianchang)
*Walmsley, Capt. John S., Jr. (Yangdok)

ARMY
Adams, Sfc. Stanley T. (Sesim-ni)
*Barker, Pvt. Charles H. (Sokkogae)
*Bennett, Pfc. Emory L. (Sobangsan)
Bleak, Sgt. David B. (Minari-gol)
*Brittin, Sfc. Nelson V. (Yonggong-ni)
*Brown, Pfc. Melvin I. (Kasan)
Burke, 1st Lt. Lloyd L. (Chong-dong)
*Burris, Sfc. Tony K. (Mundung-ni)
*Charlton, Sgt. Cornelius H. (Chipo-ri)
*Collier, Cpl. Gilbert G. (Tutayon)
*Collier, Cpl. John W. (Chindong-ni)
*Coursen, 1st Lt. Samuel S. (Kaesong)
*Craig, Cpl. Gordon M. (Kasan)
Crump, Cpl. Jerry K. (Chorwon)
Dean, Maj. Gen. William F. (Taejon)
*Desiderio, Capt. Reginald B. (Ipsok)
Dodd, 2nd Lt. Carl H (Subuk)
*Duke, Sfc. Ray E. (Mugok)
*Edwards, Sfc. Junior D. (Changbong-ni)
*Essebagger, Cpl. John, Jr. (Popsudong)
*Faith, Lt. Col. Don C., Jr. (Hagaru-ri)
*George, Pfc. Charles (Songnae-dong)
*Gilliland, Pfc. Charles L. (Tongmang-ni)
*Goodblood, Cpl. Clair (Popsydong)
*Hammond, Cpl. Lester, Jr. (Kumwha)
*Handrich, MSgt. Melvin O. (Sobuk San Mtn)
*Hanson, Pfc. Jack G. (Pachi-dong)
*Hartell, 1st Lt., Lee R. (Kobangsan-ni)
Harvey, Capt. Raymond (Taemi-Dong)
*Henry, 1st Lt. Frederick F. (Am-Dong)
Hernandez, Cpl. Rodolfo P. (Wontong-ni)
Ingman, Cpl. Einar H., Jr. (Maltari)
*Jecelin, Sgt. William R. (Saga)
*Jordan, Pfc. Mack A. (Kumsong)
*Kanell, Pvt. Billie G. (Pyongyang)
*Kaufman, Sfc. Loren R. (Yongsan)
*Knight, Pfc. Noah O. (Kowang-San)
Kouma, Sfc. Ernest R. (Agok)
*Krzyzowski, Capt. Edward C. (Tondul)
*Kyle, 2nd Lt. Darwin K. (Kamil-ni)
Lee, MSgt. Hubert L. (Ip-o-ri)
*Libby, Sgt. George D. (Taejon)
*Long, Sgt. Charles R. (Hoeng-song)
*Lyell, Cpl. William F. (Chup'a-ri)
*McGovern, 1st Lt. Robert M. (Kamyangjan-ni)
*Martinez, Cpl. Benito (Satae-ni)
*Mendonca, Sgt. Leroy A. (Chich-on)
Millett, Capt. Lewis L. (Soam-ni)

Miyamura, Cpl. Hiroshi H. (Taejon-ni)
Mize, Sgt. Ola L. (Surang-ni)
*Moyer, Sfc. Donald R. (Seoul)
*Ouellette, Pfc Joseph R. (Yongsan)
*Page, Lt. Col. John U.D. (Chosin Reservoir)
*Pendleton, Cpl. Charles F. (Choo Gung-Dong)
*Piliaau, Pfc. Herbert K. (Pia-ri)
Pittman, Sgt. John A. (Kujang-dong)
*Pomeroy, Pfc. Ralph E. (Kumhwa)
*Porter, Sgt. Donn F. (Mundung-ni)
*Red Cloud, Cpl. Mitchell, Jr. (Chonghyon)
Rodriguez, Pfc. Joseph C. (Munye-ri)
Rosser, Cpl. Ronald E. (Ponggili)
*Schoonover, Cpl. Dan D. (Sokkogae)
Schowalter, 1st Lt. Edward R., Jr. (Kumhwa)
*Shea, 1st Lt. Richard T., Jr. (Sokkogae)
*Sitman, Sfc. William S. (Chipyong-ni)
*Smith, Pfc. David M. (Yongsan)
*Speicher, Cpl. Clifton T. (Minari-gol)
Stone, 1st Lt. James L. (Sokkogae)
*Story, Pfc. Luther H. (Agok)
*Sudut, 2nd Lt. Jerome A. (Kumhwa)
*Thompson, Pfc. William (Haman)
*Turner, Sfc. Charles W. (Yongsan)
*Watkins, MSgt. Travis E. (Yongsan)
West, Pfc. Ernest E. (Sataeri)
Wilson, MSgt. Benjamin F. (Hwach'on-Myon)
*Wilson, Pfc. Richard G. (Opari)
*Womack, Pfc. Bryant H. (Sokso-ri)
*Young, Pfc. Robert H. (Kaesong)

MARINES
*Abrell, Cpl. Charles G. (Hangnyong)
Barber, Capt. William E. (Chosin Reservoir)
*Baugh, Pfc. William B. (Koto-ri ro Hagaru-ri)
Cafferata, Pvt. Hector A., Jr. (Chosin Reservoir)
*Champagne, Cpl. David B. (Korea)
*Christianson, Pfc. Stanley (Seoul)
Commiskey, 2nd Lt. Henry A., Sr. (Yongdungp'o)
*Davenport, Cpl. Jack A. (Songnae-Dong)
Davis, Lt. Col. Raymond G. (Hagaru-ri)
Dewey, Cpl. Duane E. (Panmunjon)
*Garcia, Pfc. Fernando, L. (Korea)
*Gomez, Pfc. Edward (Hill 749)
*Guillen, SSgt. Ambrosio (Songuch-on)
*Johnson, Sgt. James E. (Yudam-ni)
*Kelly, Pfc. John D. (Korea)
*Kelso, Pfc. Jack W. (Korea)
Kennemore, SSgt. Robert S. (Yudam-ni)
*Littleton, Pfc. Herbert A. (Chungchon)
*Lopez, 1st Lt. Baldomero (Inchon)
McLaughlin, Pfc. ALford L. (Korea)
*Matthews, Sgt. Daniel P. (Vegas Hill)
*Mausert, Sgt. Frederick W., III (Songnap-yong)
*Mitchell, 1st Lt. Frank N. (Hansan-ni)
*Monegan, Pfc. Walter C., Jr. (Sosa-ri)
*Moreland, Pfc. Whitt L. (Kwagch'i-dong)
Murphy, 2nd Lt. Raymond G. (Korea)
Myers, Maj. Reginald R. (Hagaru-ri)
*Obregon, Pfc. Eugene A. (Seoul)
O'Brien, 2nd Lt. George H., Jr. (Korea)
*Phillips, Cpl. Lee H. (Korea)
*Poynter, Sgt. James I. (Sudong)
*Ramer, 2nd Lt. George H. (Korea)
*Reem, 2nd Lt. Robert D. (Chinhung-ni)
*Shuck, SSgt. William E., Jr. (Korea)
Simanek, Pfc. Robert E. (Korea)
Sitter, Capt. Carl L. (Hagaru-ri)
*Skinner, 2nd Lt. Sherrod E., Jr. (Korea)
Van Winkle, SSgt. Archie (Sudong)
*Vittori, Cpl. Joseph (Hill 749)
*Watkins, SSgt. Lewis G. (Korea)
Wilson, TSgt. Harold E. (Korea)
*Windrich, SSgt. William G. (Yudam-ni)

NAVY
*Benford, Hospital Corpsman 3d Class Edward C. (Korea)
Charette, Hospital Corpsman 3d Class William R. (Korea)
*Dewert, Hospital Corpsman Richard D. (Korea)
*Hammond, Hospital Corpsman Francis C. (Korea)
Hudner, Lt. (j.g.) Thomas J., Jr. (Chosin Reservoir)
*Kilmer, Hospital Corpsman John E. (Korea)
*Koelsch, Lt. (j.g.) John K. (North Korea)

The following statistical data concerning numbers captured, repatriated and still alive was reported by the American Ex-Prisoners of War on Jan. 1, 1989:

KOREAN CONFLICT (a/b)

	Total	Army	Navy	Marine	Air Force
Captured and interned	7,140	6,656	35	225	224
Died While POW	2,701	2,662	4	31	4
Returned to U.S. Military Control	4,418	3,973	31	194	220
Refused Repatriation	21	21	—	—	—
Alive on Jan. 1, 1982	3,770	3,390	26	166	188
Alive on Jan. 1, 1989	3,394	3,050	22	151	171

a) This data indicates status through Nov. 4, 1951. As of that date, 24 still were missing. By Sept. 15, 1955, 15 of these men had been released and the other nine were declared dead.
b) Does not include 81 Navy personnel who were involved in the Pueblo incident.

UNITED NATIONS CASUALTIES IN THE KOREAN WAR

Along with American servicemen and women, medical units from Sweden and India, and allied combat continguents from the countries listed below, were the "First United Nations Army." All of these countries responded to the U.N. appeal to support the Republic of Korea in confronting Communist aggression. We honor them in their commitment to the cause of freedom.

Country	Dead	Wounded	Missing	Captured	Total
Austria	291	1,240	39	21	1,591
Belgium	97	350	5	1	453
Luxembourg					
Canada	291	1,072	65	12	1,396
Columbia	140	452	65	29	686
Ethiopia	120	536			656
France	288	818	18	11	1,135
Great Britain	710	2,278	1,263	766	5,017
Greece	169	543	2	1	715
Netherlands	111	589	4		704
New Zealand	34	80		1	115
Phillipines	92	299	57	40	488
South Africa	20		16	6	42
Thailand	114	794	5		913
Turkey	717	2,246	107	219	3,349
United States	54,246	103,284	8,177	2,000	172,707
Korea (Military & Non-military)	392,000	230,000	330,000	85,000	1,037,000

Source: World Almanac & Korean Overseas Information Service

The Korean War showed that a multinational army can function effectively in spite of differences in language and military doctrine.

CHAPLAINS WHO DIED IN THE LINE OF DUTY DURING THE KOREAN CAMPAIGN

Lawrence F. Brunnert	*Robert M. Crane
Wayne H. Burdue	Hermann G. Felthoelter
James W. Conner	Kenneth C. Hyslop
Francis X. Coppens	**Emil J. Kapaun
Leo P. Craig	Bryron D. Lee

Samuel R. Simpson

*Episcopal Chaplain Robert M. Crane was the last U.S. Army Chaplin to be killed in action in Korea, while serving with the 40th Infantry Division.
**Died as a prisoner of war in the North Korean prison camp.

Department of the Army
Washington 25, D.C., 4 June, 1951

GENERAL ORDERS
NO. 35

REPUBLIC OF KOREA PRESIDENTIAL UNIT CITATION
GENERAL   Section I
LIST OF UNITS AND CITATIONS Section II

I. GENERAL - 1. Confirmation - The following list of units of the United States Army to which the Republic of Korea Presidential Unit Citation has been awarded by the Republic of Korea, together with citations therefor, is confirmed in accordance with current regulations.

II. LIST OF UNITS

1st CAVALRY DIVISION (Inf)
****

7th Cav Regiment (Inf)

REPUBLIC OF KOREA PRESIDENT UNIT CITATION awarded by citation dated 29 September 1950, by Syngman Rhee, President of the Republic of Korea, for outstanding and heroic performance of duty on the field of battle during the period 16 August 1950, to 26 September 1950, inclusive, with citation as follows:

For the defense of Taegu and Waegwan-Taegu axis of the enemy's advance from 16 August 1950, to 25 August 1950, and from 5 September to 15 September 1950, against determined and repeated enemy attack; and for its destruction of these same forces in the Waegwan area from 16 to 21 September and for its subsequent pursuit and destruction of the enemy from Waegwan to its juncture with the U.S. 7th Div north of Osan on 26 September 1950. This marked and brilliant performance of duty by each individual member of the 1st Cav Div of the U.S. Army is in accord with the highest traditions of the military service.
****

By Order of The Secretary of the Army:
J. LAWTON COLLINS
Chief of Staff, United States Army

Official:

Wm. E. Bergin
Major General, USA
Acting the Adjutant General

REPUBLIC OF KOREA PRESIDENTIAL UNIT CITATION - The Republic of Korea Presidential Unit Citation, which was awarded by the Republic of Korea to the following units of the United States Army, is confirmed in accordance with AR 220-315:
****

Infantry Units
7th Regimental Combat Team (less)
Heavy Tank Company, 7th United
States Cavalry Regiment(Infantry),
and Company B, 8th Engineer Combat (Battalion)
****

REPUBLIC OF KOREA PRESIDENTIAL UNIT CITATION awarded by citation dated 1 October, 1953 by Syngman Rhee, President of the Republic of Korea, for exceptionally meritorious service to the Republic of Korea during the period 11 July, 1952, through 1 October, 1953, with citation as follows:

The Korean Communications Zone was activated on 11 July, 1952, and assigned the mission of completely or partially supporting all friendly forces in Korea. The tremendous difficulties encountered in assuming responsibilities of such magnitude were overcome through planning and sound leadership. In spite of language barriers, personnel of the Korean Communications zone contributed to the harmonious placing into operation a comprehensive economic aid and relief program for the Republic of Korea. This monumental task involved the supervision and control of the major ports, transportation and communication facilities, and coordination with United Nations Korea Reconstruction Agency. Under the supervision of the Korean Communications Zone, millions of dollars of economic aid, supplies and equipment were furnished to thousands of Korean people afflicted by the ravages of war. Critical materials were furnished for family housing, hospitals and welfare institutions. The establishment of a Foreign Language Institute in Pusan proved to be a distinct contribution toward the rehabilitation of education facilities. Realizing that the people of Korea were confronted with a critical shortage of medical doctors because of reduced teaching staffs in the medical schools, the Korean Communications Zone, with exceptional ingenuity and resourcefulness, organized a teaching assistance program that resulted in the improvement and expansion of medical education in Korea. Through the joint effort of Koreans and Korean Communications Zone personnel, an aggressive program was developed to rehabilitate electric power facilities which contributed immeasurably to the health, comfort and welfare of the civilian population. The people of the Republic of Korea will remember with profound gratitude the services rendered by the personnel of the Korean Communications Zone whose performance and devotion to duty are in keeping with the highest traditions of the military service.
****

By Order of The Secretary of the Army:
M.B. RIDGWAY
General, United States Army,
Chief of Staff

Official:

Wm. E. Bergin
Major General, United States Army,
The Adjutant General

DEPARTMENT OF THE ARMY
Washington 25, D.C., 5 March, 1952

GENERAL ORDERS
NO. 74

DISTINGUISHED UNIT CITATION - Citation of Units, Section I

MERITORIOUS UNIT COMMENDATION - Awards, Section II

1. DISTINGUISHED UNIT CITATION As authorized by Executive Order 9396 (Sec. I, WD Bul. 22, 1943), superseding Executive Order 9075 (Sec. III, WD Bul. II, 1942), citation of the following units in the general orders indicated is confirmed in accordance with AR 220-315 in the name of the President of the United States as public evidence of deserved honor and distinction. The citation reads as follows:

The 1st Battalion, 7th Cavalry, 1st Cavalry Division, and the following attached units:
1st Platoon, Medical Company, 7th Cavalry;
2d Platoon, Heavy Mortar Company, 7th Cavalry;
3d Platoon, Heavy Mortar Company, 7th Cavalry (2d Award);
Company C, 70th Tank Battalion (2d Award for 2d and 3d Platoons only);
77th Field Artillery Battalion (2d Award for Battery C only);are cited for outstanding performance of duty and extraordinary heroism in action against the enemy in the vicinity of Yonchon, Korea, during the period 3 to 12 October 1951. On 3 October, this battalion was assigned the critically important mission of protecting the left flank of the regimental sector, supporting an attack by the 3d Battalion, and preparing to launch an assault through the positions secured by the 3d Battalion to capture strategic objectives farther north. In order to accomplish their primary mission, several intermediate objectives had to be seized by the personnel of this battalion, although the heights to be taken were protected by heavy concentrations of enemy artillery, mortars and automatic weapons. The friendly troops moved indomitably through the intense hostile fire and launched repeated, determined attacks in an effort to dislodge the foe from the strategic slopes. After several days of bitter fighting, the friendly force secured the commanding hills and immediately set about to organize effective defensive perimeters. The fanatical enemy quickly launched a large-scale counter-attack. This assault was repulsed at great cost to the hostile force, but, obsessed with the idea of regaining the vital ground they had lost, the enemy troops attacked again and again. Fifteen separate assaults were launched by the enemy and each was met with the utmost aggressiveness by the friendly troops, who held their positions tenaciously although forced to go without food, water and sleep. In the valiant defense of their sector, the members of this battalion killed approximately 800 of the enemy, wounded approximately 1,500 and captured 60. As a result of this action, one enemy regiment was completely decimated and two more were depleted to such an extent that it was necessary for the hostile force to replace them with reserve units. The 1st Battalion, 7th Cavalry, 1st Cavalry Division, with its attached units, displayed such superlative effectiveness in accomplishing its mission under extremely hazardous and difficult conditions as to set it apart and above other units participating in the action.

The extraordinary heroism, magnificent fighting spirit and esprit de corps exhibited by the members of this battalion reflect the greatest credit on themselves and are in keeping with the most esteemed traditions of the military service. (General Orders 328, Headquarters, Eighth United States Army, Korea, 23 June 1952).

By Order of The Secretary of the Army:
J. Lawton Collins
Chief of Staff, United States Army

Official:

WM. E. BERGIN
Major General, USA
The Adjutant General

THIRD BATTALION:

DEPARTMENT OF THE ARMY
Washington 25, D.C., 31 March, 1952

GENERAL ORDERS
NO. 33

DISTINGUISHED UNIT CITATION - Citation of Units, Section I

MERITORIOUS UNIT COMMENDATION - Awards, Section II

1. DISTINGUISHED UNIT CITATION - As Authorized by Executive Order 9396 (Sec. I, WD Bul. 1943), superseding Executive Order 9075 (sec. III, WD Bul. II, 1942), citation of the following units in the general orders indicated are confirmed in accordance with AR 260-15 in the name of the President of the United States as public evidence of deserved honor and distinction. The citations read as follows:

1. The 3d Battalion, 7th Cavalry Regiment, 1st Cavalry Division, is cited for outstanding performance of duty and extraordinary heroism in action against the enemy in the vicinity of Taegu, Korea, on 12 September, 1950. On that date, the 3d Battalion was assigned the mission of capturing Hill mass 314 which was held by a numerically superior enemy force. At this time, the enemy was exerting a determined effort to capture Taegu, the temporary capital of the Republic of Korea and Hill mass 314 was a vital point of departing for the hostile troops in pressing their drive on this city. The battalion used frontal assault tactics against the strongly defended hill positions and by unrelenting and sustained attacks, drove up the steep approaches to the crest of the hill, breaking the resistance of two enemy battalions and inflicting approximately 900 casualties on the hostile force. After securing the crest of the hill, the battalion then delivered flanking fire on adjacent ridges and hills which enabled other friendly units to take their objectives. Upon securing its objectives, the battalion found large quantities of ammunition and equipment abandoned by the fleeing enemy. Although the 3d Battalion suffered more than 200 casualties in less than three hours of fighting, it nevertheless captured an enemy position which had withstood three previous attacks of battalion-size strength. The accomplishment of this mission by the 3d Battalion in a minimum time enabled the United Nations Forces to hold the perimeter surrounding Taegu and forced the enemy to relinquish its grip on several other key hill masses. Providing a setting from which the United Nations Forces eventually launched their offensive. The 3d Battalion displayed such gallantry, determination and esprit de corps in accomplishing its mission under extremely difficult and hazardous

conditions as to set it apart and above other units participating in the action. The great skill, indomitable courage, and aggressiveness exhibited by all members of the 3d Battalion, 7th Cavalry Regiment, 1st Cavalry Division, throughout this action reflect great credit on themselves and are in keeping with the highest traditions of the military service. (General Orders 770, Headquarters, Eighth United States Army, Korea, 15 October 1951)

****

By Order of the Secretary of the Army:
J. LAWTON COLLINS
Chief of Staff, United States Army

Official:

WM. E. BERGIN
Major General
The Adjutant General

THIRD BATTALION:
EXTRACT
****
DEPARTMENT OF THE ARMY
Washington 25, D.C., 8 April, 1952

GENERAL ORDERS
NO. 35
DISTINGUISHED UNIT CITATION - Citation of Units, Section I

MERITORIOUS UNIT COMMENDATION - Awards, Section II

1. DISTINGUISHED UNIT CITATION - As authorized by Executive Order 9396 (Section 1, WD Bul. 22, 1943), superseding Executive Order 9075 (Sec. III, WD Bul. II, 1942), citation of the following units in the general orders indicated is confirmed in accordance with AR 260-15 in the name of the President of the United States as public evidence of deserved honor and distinction. The citations read as follows:

****

2. The 3d Battalion (second award), 7th Cavalry Regiment, 1st Cavalry Division, and the following attached units:

2d Platoon, Company C, 70th Heavy Tank Battalion;
3d Platoon, Company C, 70th Heavy Tank Battalion;
3d Platoon, Heavy Mortar Company, 7th Cavalry Regiment;
Intelligence and Reconnaissance Platoon, 7th Cavalry Regiment;
2d Platoon, Company B, 8th Engineer Combat Battalion;
Battery C, 77th Field Artillery Battalion;
339th Radio Team, 13th Signal Company;
3d Platoon Medical Company, 7th Cavalry Regiment;

are cited for outstanding performance of duty and extraordinary heroism in action against the enemy on the road northward through Ch'ongju, Korea, subsequent to breaking out of the Pusan Perimeter, during the period 21 to 27 September 1950. On 21 September, the 3d Battalion and attached units were assigned the mission of driving north to make contact with friendly forces moving south from Inchon. In order to carry out its task, the battalion was forced to fight its way through elements of three North Korean divisions. As a result of their courageous spirit and unshakable determination, the friendly troops met the hostile forces in a number of decisive engagements and inflicted extremely heavy personnel and equipment losses. Through swift and effective tactical moves, the battalion was able to stab through 137 miles of enemy territory, thus effecting an irreparable split in the main body of the hostile army opposing the United Nations Forces and thereby setting the stage for the ultimate defeat of the North Korean People's Army. The operation conducted was at all times with the utmost aggressiveness, gallantry and esprit de corps and is deserving of emulation in all future campaigns. The 3d Battalion and its attached units displayed such unsurpassed individual and collective bravery in accomplishing their mission under extremely difficult and hazardous conditions as to set them apart and above other units participating in the action. The extraordinary heroism exhibited by all members of the 3d Battalion, 7th Cavalry Regiment, 1st Cavalry Division, and its attached units reflects great credit on themselves and upholds the most esteemed traditions of the military service of the United States. (General Orders 87, Headquarters, Eighth United States Army, Korea, 10 February 1952)

****

By Order of the Secretary of the Army:
J. LAWTON COLLINS
Chief of Staff, U.S. Army

Official:

WM. E. BERGIN
Major General, U.S. Army
The Adjutant General

FOURTH BATTALION:

EXTRACT
****
DEPARTMENT OF THE ARMY
Washington 25, D.C., 8 April, 1952

GENERAL ORDERS
NO. 35

****

5. The Greek Expeditionary Forces Battalion, United Nations Forces in Korea, is cited for outstanding performance of duty and extraordinary heroism in action against the enemy in the vicinity of Sonbyok, Korea, during the period 3 to 10 October 1951. While attached to the 7th Cavalry Regiment, 1st Cav. Div., the Greek Expeditionary Forces Battalion was assigned the mission of seizing and securing an area of vital strategic importance from a numerically superior hostile force. After an intense friendly artillery barrage, the Greek Expeditionary Forces Battalion moved forward aggressively toward their objective. Their route of attack led them across a wide expanse of exposed terrain and leading elements were subjected to a heavy volume of mortar and artillery fire from the well-entrenched and heavily armed enemy. Undeterred by the intense fire, the friendly force continued to advance until they reached the base of the enemy-held hills. Three times they charged up the steep slopes toward the hostile positions, constantly closing with the enemy in savage hand-to-hand combat, but they were repeatedly forced to withdraw because of the overwhelming number of enemy troops which they faced. After manifesting a superb disposition to overcome all opposition during a three-day period of the most bitter and violent fighting, the Greek Expeditionary Forces Battalion forced the enemy not only to relinquish valuable terrain, but also to commit their primary defense force as well as many of their reserve troops in resisting the unrelenting pressure of the friendly force. This action enabled the friendly flanking units to launch a series of attacks which drove the hostile troops from their positions with heavy casualties. With their first objective secured, the Greek Expeditionary Forces Battalion continued to advance until they were halted by fanatical enemy troops occupying a commanding ridge. Once again, the courageous members of this battalion launched a series of assaults up the rugged slopes direct into the devastating column of fire directed against them by the well-entrenched enemy. Displaying unsurpassed tenacity, they reached the hostile emplacements and, in the bitter battle which ensued, vast numbers of the enemy were killed and wounded and finally forced to abandon their positions. The routed enemy force left behind large scores of ammunition and weapons in their haste to reach safety from the unrelenting fury of the Greek Expeditionary Forces Battalion. The steadfast determination and selfless heroism displayed by the members of the battalion throughout this action earned them the deep respect and admiration of all those with whom they served. The Greek Expeditionary Forces Battalion displayed such gallantry, devotion to duty, and esprit de corps in accomplishing its mission under extremely difficult and hazardous conditions as to set it apart and above other units participating in the action (GO 16, Hqs 8th US Army, Korea, 7 January 1952)

****

By Order of the Secretary of the Army:
J. LAWTON COLLINS
Chief of Staff, U.S. Army

Official:

WM. E. BERGIN
Major General, USA
The Adjutant General

EXTRACT
****
DEPARTMENT OF THE ARMY
Washington 25, D.C., 2 February, 1956

GENERAL ORDERS
NO. 2

BRAVERY GOLD MEDAL OF GREECE. The Bravery Gold Medal of Greece (Chryssoun Sristion Andrias) which was awarded by Paul, The King of Greece, in accordance with Royal Order dated 15 June 1955, is confirmed in accordance with AR 220-315.
No device is authorized to be worn for this award.
The citations are as follows:

1st Cavalry Division:
****
7th Cavalry Regiment

In accordance with the Royal Order dated 15 June, 1955, CHRYSSOUN ARISTION ANDRIAS (BRAVERY GOLD MEDAL) is awarded to the Colors of the 1st Cavalry Division, U.S. Army, because, during the long period of war in Korea, the above unit positioned with the Greek Expeditionary Forces, with which the latter was assigned, took part in hard-fought battles in which the fluidity and the maneuvers experienced by the American and Greek soldiers who, falling together in the field of honor, won battles and succeeded the final victory, defending their colors and the Freedom of Humanity.

****

(AG 200.62 (13 Jan 56)
By Order of Wilber M. Brucker, Secretary of the Army:
MAXWELL D. TAYLOR
General, United States Army
Chief of Staff

Official:

JOHN A. KLEIN
Major General, United States Army
The Adjutant General

To The Long Gray Line
United States Military Academy - West Point

The Korean War was a young man's war. The West Point Class of 1949 saw 21 of its graduates killed in Korea. A shocking fourteen were married and seven were bachelors (Five additional Air Force graduates of '49 were killed in training). Furthermore, the class of 1950 saw 18 killed in action, or died of wounds. An additional 10 casualties were caused by Korean non-battle, Air Force U.S., and auto accidents. Many died less than six months after graduation. All these men served as lieutenants, most of them were as infantry platoon leaders, and they were therefore the most expendable of soldiers.

GLOSSARY OF PRINCIPLE WEAPONS

During the Korean War, all combatants chose to fight largely with surplus weapons from World War II. The United States made innovations and great improvements in logistical techniques, cold-weather clothing and medical services. However, no startling developments, either in weaponry or tactics, came out of the conflict. One of the only new developments was the use of helicopters for reconnaissance, transport and evacuation on a large scale, and the employment of the jet aircraft in combat. The most modern jet at that particular time was the F-86 Sabre, which was thrown into the aerial war when the Communist forces introduced a first-rate aircraft, the MIG-15, as a field test.

Although newer series of weapons, radios and vehicles were developed and available on both sides, the entire course of the Korean War remained of World War II vintage. Also withheld were the use of nuclear weapons. One great weakness at the beginning was caused by the failure of the United States to procure modern weaponry for ground warfare following World War II. However, the Communist forces had followed the same course by employing only old or obsolescent weaponry.

The principal infantry weapons used in the Korean War were the following, and the majority of which now are obsolete. (Exception for British issue to Commonwealth forces.)

U.S. RIFLE CALIBER .30 M-1 (Garand): The basic shoulder weapon of the United States, ROK and many other U.N. rifle regiments. A vintage of the mid-1930s, it was gas-operated and semiautomatic, fired an 8-round clip, and weighed 9.5 pounds, 10.5 with bayonet. Its effective range was about 500 yards, and its rate of fire up to approximately 30 rounds per minute.

U.S. CARBINE CALIBER .30: Produced as both semiautomatic and full-automatic weapon, it fired a lighter bullet than the M-1 Rifle, with correspondingly less range, accuracy and killing power. Fitted with a 15-round magazine, or 30-round or so-called "banana magazine"; gas-operated, it was carried principally by company-grade officers, NCOs, clerks and the like. Weight, 6 pounds. Developed during World War II from Garand principle.

PISTOL, CALIBER .45 M-1911 A-1: The standard United States side arm, a large semiautomatic pistol, with great stopping power and an effective range of some 25 yards. Developed and issued prior to World War I, it was carried by field-grade officers, signal linemen, gun crews, tankers and men whose duties or other burdens precluded carrying of rifle or carbine.

BROWNING AUTOMATIC RIFLE, or BAR: Firing the same cartridge as the Rifle, M-1, either semi- or fully automatic, the BAR could be operated either as a shoulder weapon or from a bipod. With a rate of fire of almost 500 rounds per minute, it was the principal automatic weapon of the rifle companies, one or more being issued to each rifle squad. Weight 16 pounds, it was developed from Browning's principle during World War I.

U.S. MACHINE-GUN, CALIBER .30, M-1919 A-4 (light machine- gun, or LMB): An air-cooled, 32 pounds fully automatic machine-gun, with bipod and shoulder rest; recoil-operated on the Browning principle, capable of sustained fire of 450-500 rounds per minute. Firing the same cartridge as the Rifle, M-1 and BAR, it was the infantry platoon machine-gun. Developed in World War I.

U.S. MACHINE-GUN, CALIBER .30, M-1917 A-1 (Heavy Machine-Gun, or HMG): A heavier version of the above, water-cooled and tripod mounted, and thus capable of both a greater, longer and more accurate rate of fire. Issued to the Weapons Company of the infantry battalion. There were approximately 500 machine-guns of both types in the U.S. infantry division.

U.S. MACHINE-GUN, CALIBER .50, BROWNING: Weighing 82 pounds, this large-caliber machine-gun was mounted on trucks, tanks and other vehicles, and not carried into close infantry combat. Air-cooled, but with a heavy barrel, the .50-caliber machine-gun fired approximately 575 rounds per minute, to a range of 2,000 yards. Approximately 350 scattered throughout the infantry division.

ROCKET LAUNCHER, 3.5-INCH OR 2.36-INCH (Bazooka): Rocket launchers, developed during World War II, fire a hollow-shaped charge capable of penetrating thick armor plate. The 3.5, which replaced the obsolete 2.36 in 1950, weighing 15 pounds and firing an 8.5 pound charge. There were some 600 bazookas in the Korean infantry division. Characterized by a large and distinct backblast, the aluminum tube generally was not effective beyond 75 yards against medium armor. Widely issued as infantry antitank weapon.

THE 57MM, 75MM AND 105MM RECOILLESS RIFLES: Infantry-carried artillery. They developed high blast from escaping gases on discharge, but no recoil, as with howitzers or cannon. The obsolescent 57mm could be shoulder-fired, while the newer and heavier guns were crew-served, firing from tripods. Effective against infantry and fortifications, such as bunkers, they fire regularly shells with a flat trajectory over long ranges. The 105mm was developed during Korea.

INFANTRY MORTARS, 60MM, 81MM, 4.2-INCH: Mortars primarily are antipersonnel weapons, consisting of simple, sealed-breech tubes and base plates, which throw high explosive shells at a high angle, capable of reaching into valleys, trenches and into defilade impervious to direct fire. The 60mm mortars were carried into position with the rifle companies; the 81mm's were handled by the weapons companies, and the 4.2-inch fired by a special mortar company within the regiment. The 81mm, with an effective range of 4,000 yards, to 1,800 for the 60mm, weighs more than 100 pounds and is not easily transportable in rough terrain by foot troops. The 4.2-inch, virtually an artillery weapon, is normally vehicle mounted.

THE QUAD .50: This was a half-tracked vehicle of World War II vintage, mounting four .50 machine-guns capable of being fired as a unit. Developed as an anti-aircraft weapon, with the advent of fast jet craft, it became an antipersonnel weapon capable of hurling an immense amount of fire into hillsides and valleys against advancing infantry, or of throwing long-range harassing small-arms fire against enemy routes by night. Firing as many as 100,000 rounds per day, the Quad .50 could go over hills like a vacuum clear, sucking them devoid of life.

THE DUAL 40: Also developed as an AA weapon, the Dual 40 was a fully tracked vehicle with a tank-like silhouette mounting twin Bofors 40mm anti-aircraft automatic cannon. It also was used to support the infantry line, in the same manner as the Quad .50.

THE ARTILLERY WEAPONS: During Korean operations, the standard U.S. artillery of World War II, the 105mm, 155mm, and 8-inch howitzers and rifles were employed in tremendous quantity. Developments were made in directions, spotting, and radar-sensing. Toward the end of the conflict, Korea was primarily an artillery war, with both sides dug in and cannonading each other rather than employing maneuver.

ARMOR: At the onset of the fighting, to its tremendous disadvantage, the United States had no tank in the Far East capable of engaging the obsolescent Russian T-34. The light M-24, primarily a reconnaissance vehicle with thin armor plate and light 75mm cannon, was augmented during August and September 1950, with various U.S. interim model medium tanks, such as the M-26 Pershing, mounting a 90mm gun. Gradually, the old M4A3E8, the World War II workhorse, the Sherman, fitted a newer high-velocity 76mm gun, became the principal Korea battle tank. It had a high silhouette, light tremor, and an inadequate gun, but it was more maneuverable in the alternately steep and boggy Korean terrain than more modern tanks, such as the heavy-armor, heavy-gun British Centurion III. Failure to mass produce a good main battle tank was one of the Army's principal weaknesses during the period; the concentration was more on seeking an effective antitank weapon than relying on the more expensive tank itself.

THE COMMUNIST NATIONS

Throughout the fighting, the enemy was adept at capturing and employing U.S. weapons and equipment. During the first 90 days, the North Korean People's Army secured enough equipment from ROK and U.S. division to outfit several of their own; and the Chinese Communist Forces, on entrance, were in many cases equipped with U.S. arms shipped to the Nationalist Government both during and after World War II, all of which had fallen into Communist hands. The Chinese (as the ROKs) also had a considerable quantity of surrendered Japanese arms and ammunition, from rifles to field guns. The principal source of armament for both North Koreans and Chinese, however, was Soviet Russia. Just as the United States provided 90 percent of all munitions used in the United Nations forces, the Russians designed, mass-produced and delivered the bulk of all Communist weapons.

As with American arms, the majority of Russian equipment was of World War II vintage.

Russian weaponry, as Russian equipment in general, has one marked characteristic: It is extremely rugged, of the simplest design consistent with efficiency and very easy to maintain, making it in many cases more suitable for the equipping of peasant armies than the more sophisticated U.S. arms. Despite its simplicity and lack of refinement, it was good.

INFANTRY RIFLES. The Communist forces were equipped with a miscellany of shoulder weapons, from the Russian 7.62mm turbine, a bolt-action rifle of 1944 vintage, to Japanese 7.7mm Imperial Army rifles, taken by the Soviets from the Kwantung Army in 1945 and turned over to the CCF. The tendency in Communist armies had been to discard the rifle in favor of the submachine-gun, less accurate, but able to throw much higher plume of fire in the hands of unskilled personnel.

THE SUBMACHINE-GUN 7.62MM PSh41 (Burp Gun): Designed during World War II, the PPSh 41 submachine-gun indicated the Soviet belief that highly accurate small arms were wasted in the hands of ground troops, while a large volume of fire was a requisite. Cheap to make, simple to operate and thoroughly dependable under any battlefield conditions, the Soviet submachine-gun was the best of its class during World War II. Fired either full or semiautomatic, it held a magazine of 72 rounds, with a cyclic rate of 100 per minute. Inaccurate except at close ranges. Toward the end of the war, Chinese infantry carried submachine-guns or grenades almost exclusively while on the offensive.

THE TOKAREV 7.62MM SEMIAUTOMATIC RIFLE: This rifle, fitted with flash hider and bipod, served a purpose similar to that of the U.S. BAR.

THE DEGTYAREV 14.5MM ANTITANK RIFLE, PTRD-19411: This extremely long, ungainly weapon was designed against armor of the early World War II type. With the advent of thicker plate, it became an antivehicular rifle, and was used for long-range sniping against personnel. Each NKPA division carried 36 of these, called by Americans the "elephant" or "buffalo" gun.

THE MACHINE-GUNS: Several varieties of light machine-guns were used by the NKPA and CCF, together with the Coryunov heavy machine-gun, which was wheel-mounted. Russian machine-guns generally were 7.62mm, an excellent military cartridge.

THE MORTARS: While as with other arms, a miscellany of calibers and types of found in Communist armies, the standard Russian make predominated. Because of its ready transportability by hand and its cheapness of manufacture, the mortar was a favorite weapon of both the NKPA and CCF. An NKPA regiment contained six 120mm mortars; each of its three battalions has nine 82mm's; and the smaller 61mm was found at company level. The smaller Soviet mortars had an added advantage of being able to fire U.S. 60mm and 81mm mortar ammunition, of which the Communists captured great stores. The American tubes, unfortunately, could not reciprocate. Other infantry support weapons, such as rocket launchers and recoilless rifles, were not standard enemy issue; they were employed only when captured.

ARTILLERY: The artillery support of NKPA and CCF divisions closely followed that of the World War II Soviet division, though initially the CCF left most of its heavy artillery behind on crossing the Yalu. A division contained 12 122mm howitzers, 24 76mm field guns, 12 SU-76mm self-propelled guns on the T-34 chasis, and 12 45mm antitank guns. In addition, each of the division's three regiments had four organic 76mm howitzers. The 122mm rifle also was furnished by the Soviets. With the exception of a few Japanese pieces, Communist artillery was Soviet-made and during the later stages of the fighting appeared in quantities reminiscent of the Soviet massed artillery used in front of Berlin in 1945. Larger, long-range artillery, such as the 152mm gun, were used sparingly, in contrast with U.S. employment of medium artillery (155mm) in great quantities; the CCF had a marked reluctance to fire on targets they could not observe.

ARMOR: The Russian T-34/85, the Soviet main battle tank of World War II, which appeared in final form during the winter of 1943-1944,

remained the Communist battle tank throughout. The T-34, weighing 35 tons and capable of 34 miles per hour, had excellent traction and was admirably suited to the terrain of Korea, where heavier American tanks such as the Patton, found rough going. The T-34, mounting an 85mm gun and two 7.62mm machine-guns, was considered by the Soviets an obsolescent tank in 1950. Their heavier, more modern tanks, such as the Josef Stalin III, were never furnished to satellite or auxiliary armies. In the first weeks, 150 T-34s, spearheading the NKPA attack, raised havoc with both ROK and U.S. forces. Later, both preponderance of American armor and air power reduced Communist armor to a minor role; it was concealed carefully and hoarded, and rarely employed.

Since both combatants tended to use old and obsolescent armament - such as the T-34/85 and the Sherman M4A3E8, or the 1944 7.62mm rifle and the pre-World War II M-1 - no comparison of weaponry is particularly significant or valid in the Korean War. In general, Communist equipment proved adequate, and in its class comparable in performance to American.

"You can stop firin' — It sez here that no UN troops are in contact with the enemy!"

(Cartoons courtesy of Ed Daily, from the Stars and Stripes Newspaper, 1950 - 1951)

"What's That, Reveille?"

"Poor Guy, Hell! He's Just Comin' Back From R&R Leave."

ROSTER OF THE 7TH U.S. CAVALRY

Abbey, John P.
Abell, Richard
Abshear, James R. "Jim"
Ackerman, Richard R.
Adamcazk, Bernard
Adams, Russell E.
Adams, Warren E.
Adams, William A.
Albrecht, Jeffry L.
Alcon, David
Alevizakos, Spyridon
Alexander, William
Alicea, Robert
Alicea, Ronald H.
Allen, John P.
Allen, Louis
Allen, Roy E.
Allison, Benjamin W.
Allison, John E.
Almy, Frank H.
Alva, Jose "Joe"
Alvarez-Perez, Wilfredo
Ammons, Terry
Anderson, Ashley C.
Anderson, James A.
Anderson, Joe E.
Anderson, Robert J.
Anderson, Robert V.
Anderson, Jr., Robert P.
Apple, James D.
Applegate, James H. "Jim"
Arbasetti, Robert "Bob"
Arendt, Orville R.
Arnoldt, Robert P.

Back, James Daniel
Back, Wendy Mae
Baer, Ralph
Bafs, Carl J.
Bagdasarian, Douglas G. D.
Baker, William E.
Balicki, Robert R.
Balish, Thomas A.
Ball, Jesse B.
Ballard, Jr., Henry E.
Bamesberger, John G.
Banko, III, Stephen T.
Bannister, Harold R.
Barber, Junio-Omar
Barca, Joseph S.
Bartlett, Perry
Barton, John H.
Beard, John Richard
Bearden, Hall
Beck, Bill
Becker, Virgil H.
Bell, Edwin
Bell, Urcel L.
Benn, Edmond B.
Bentley, Jr., Mack
Benton, Ronald H.

Bents, Reinhold A.
Berberich, James G.
Berendsen, Henry E.
Berge, Gregory S.
Bernotas, Ralph G.
Berube, George E.
Bess, Buy F.
Birkel, Jr., Anthony A.
Blanc, Harold
Blanc, William
Blessing, Dennis D.
Blockhus, Christopher L.
Bloss, Robert W.
Blume, William F.
Blumenauer, Roy C.
Bly, Darald G.
Bodnar, Mike
Bohlender, Otto R.
Boland, John F.
Boldt, Glenn M.
Bollinger, Royal D.
Bondurant, Edward R.
Bookwalter, Thomas E.
Bosse, Donald John
Boudurant, Mildred C.
Bouterse, Robert A.
Bower, Robert J.
Bowman, Arnold Jimmy
Bowman, Perry A.
Bowman, Robert
Boyd, Margaret Ann
Boyd, Richard T.
Boyd, Thomas E.
Boyle, Jr., Richard A.
Bradbury, Richard E.
Bradley, Thomas E.
Bragg, Ernest C.
Braunstein, Ralph E.
Breen, Joseph B.
Bremer, Charles L. "Chuck"
Brennan, Donna L.
Brennan, MD, Michael
Briley, William H.
Brister, Alan A.
Britton, Richard T. "Dick"
Brookover, Jesse
Brooks, Paul E.
Brostrom, Gerhard
Browning, IV, John W.
Bruner, Sr, Vincent G.
Buchanan, Crawford
Buck, Paul Ray
Bugher, James D.
Buhr, Herman H.
Bumgarner, Glen G.
Burditt, Elijah F.
Burnett, Thomas R.
Burns, Billy D.

Burton, Jonathan R.
Burton, Joseph J.
Busho, Sr., Waylen G.
Butler, Joseph C.
Butler, Sir H. Nathaniel
Byron, Milton

Cable, Rick
Caffey, Robert I.
Calabrese, Dennis J.
Calhoun, Guy R.
Callaway, John W.
Campbell, Donald D.
Cangro, Peter V.
Canorro, Warren W.
Caper, Lamont
Carlson, Donald T.
Carnahan, Douglas E.
Carney, Clarence A.
Carroll, John
Carroll, Robert M.
Cash, John A.
Cauley, John E.
Chacon, Joseph L.
Chafin, Bobby D.
Chance, Rayford E. "Ray"
Chandler, Vera
Chaney, Jr., Leroy
Chatham, Mary Lou
Childs, Norman R.
Childs, W. F. "Jack"
Chirchill, Richard S.
Christensen, Kurt A.
Cisson, Kenneth
Clainos, Peter D.
Clair, Alfred B.
Clancy, Daniel
Clark, Harold J.
Clark, John P.
Calrk, Orval D.
Clarke, Timothy M.
Clear, Charles C.
Cloeter, John J.
Clutts, Robert E.
Coblentz, Richard L.
Cochran, Bill D.
Cochren, Rowland E.
Coiner, Benjamin W.
Cole, Peter C.
Collins, William T.
Comer, James C.
Conlon, Robert
Conlon, Jr., John J.
Connors, Lawrence E.
Conrow, Kevin S.
Cook, Robert W.
Cooper, Robert M.
Copeland, Everett L.
Copello, C.L.
Copulos, George A.
Cordero, Jr., Mauricio F.
Cordon, Steven C.
Cotterell, Jr., John
Couch, Jack L.

Court, James V. "Jim"
Cox, Robert E. "Bob"
Cox, Jr., Daniel J.
Creamer, George T.
Creazzo, Dominick
Crist, Junior E. "Edward"
Crocker, John R.
Cross, Jr., Joseph H.
Crowley, James F.
Culley, Harriet
Cullings, Donavan A.
Cumbow, Elliott R.
Cummings, James F.
Cummings, Michael L.
Curram, James W. "Jim"
Cyr, Michael P.

Daily, Edward L.
Daly, James E.
Daly, James R.
Daly, John E.
Dandy, Kevin M.
Dandy, Matthew W.
Daniel, Marvin C.
Dashner, Jr., Charles A.
Daugherty, Francis "Pancho"
Daujatas, Donald
Davidson, David S.
Davie, Robert M. "Bob"
Davis, Charles M.
Davis, Claude L.
Davis, Jr., James C.
DeMaine, John
Deal, Dennis J.
Deal, Stephen Robert
DeFino, Frank
Dehart, Bill
DeLao, Robert
Della Ripa, John
Dempewolf, Vincent M.
Dempsey, Philip
Dennigan, James J.
Detty, Raymond M.
Dewitt, Allen E.
Deyoe, William A.
Diaz, Justo M.
Dillon, Dana B. "Horse"
Doerner, John August
Doherty, John C.
Donnelly, David A.
Donnelly, Donald R.
Dover, Thomas
Dowd, John J.
Dowell, Richard K.
Down, Donald D.
Dunaway, Robert L.
Dunkleberger, Jonathan K.
Dunlow, Garry
Duranty, Edward T.

Dutram, John H.
Duty, Chirls S. "Charly"
Duve, Fred A.
Dyson, Johnie M.
Early, Earl
Eason, Emory Allen
Eastham, Kenneth G.
Eckert, Michael G.
Edens, Jackie C.
Edwards, Shawn M.
Edwards, Woodrow P.
Elkins, James
Elliott, Sara
Ellis, Ester H.
Elmore, Pearlie L. "Lee"
Ernst, Louis
Erwin, Ira "Ike"
Etts, Larry Eugene
Etts, Sandra Jean
Eubanks, Hal D.
Evans, Thomas J.

Fahrnow, Erwin D.
Fairly, Kenneth W.
Fallon, Joseph E.
Fantino, Sam P.
Farrell, James E. "Jim"
Farrell, Joseph James
Farrelly, Peter T.
Faulkner, Wayne
Fels, Eugene
Ferguson, Denver C.
Ferraro, Ron
Ferwerda, Merle
Fewell, Anthony A.
Fillmore, C. Mike
Fillmore, Margaret
Finch, Ellen R.
Finley, Allison R.
Fischer, Clifford O.
Fisher, Joe M.
Fitch, Robert K.
Fitzgerald, William T.
Flanders, Sherman C.
Flesch, Joseph E.
Flick, Jack R.
Flierl, Leroy H.
Flynn, Ronald B.
Foley, Thomas C.
Fonder, Russell C.
Ford, Buford W.
Fowler, Robert A.
Fox, Allen G.
Fox, Victor L.
Francioni, George F.
Frank, Jr., Timothy Jay
French, Michael L.
Frisbie, Robert
Frost, MD, Lawrence A.
Fry, William D.
Fullam, Edward R.
Fuller, Thomas W.

Funderburk, Earl F.

Gaborsky, Jr., Joseph
Galloway, Joseph L.
Galloway, Roger
Game, Henry Erio
Gange, Joseph G.
Gargis, Paul
Garrett, Jerry
Garvin, James E.
Garza, Homer Miguel
Gast, Gerald L.
Gavin, Martin T.
Gehling, Duane W.
Gemelli, Bernard N. "Barry"
Genz, Marilyn
Goeghegan, Camille
Gerrits, Paul
Gersten, Roy
Getman, Paul L.
Gibbs, Lyle R.
Gibson, Robert E. "Bob"
Giedeman, Gregory W.
Gigandet, Francis V.
Gilbert, Lawrence R.
Gilreath, Larry M.
Girard, Terrance P.
Gish, Frank D.
Glasco, Anthony D.
Glass, Charles R.
Glass, Rexford L.
Glowdowski, Conrad "Duke"
Glover, Reece M.
Glowiak, Raymond P. "Ray"
Godfrey, James T.
Gonzalez, Enrique G. "Hank"
Gooden, James H.
Goodrich, Horace Gideon
Goodwin, Lynn R. H.
Gottesman, Harold
Gourley, Daniel F.
Graham, Arlene M.
Graham, Chong Suk Lee
Graml, Otto A.
Graumann, Otto G.
Gray, Carolyn J.
Gray, Earl G. "Gene"
Gray, Millard G.
Gray, Robert C. "Snuffy"
Green, Jesse L.
Green, William E.
Greenway, Thomas J.
Gregory, Melvin L.
Greiner, John W.
Griebel, Ronald J. "Ron"
Griepp, Frank R.
Griffin, Robert L.
Griffiths, Don
Grimbsy, Roger

Groft, Edward S.	Houf, Thomas A.	Kinney, Michael L.	Mack, Theodore	Mehl, Louis S. "Lou"	Nemetsky, Howard A.
Grohowski, Jerry	Hough, Robert M.	Kinser, Todd J.	MacMillan, IV, William D.	Melander, Robert J.	Newhouse, Gregory
Guarnieri, Jr., Albert	Houston, William E.	Klein, Alfred A.	Madigan, James C.	Melano, Frank M.	Ngiralmau, Godwin S.
Guffey, Paul D.	Howard, John R.	Klincke, Gunther	Mancini, Daniel P.	Menard, William E.	Nichols, Claude V.
Guyer, Kenny	Howden, John M.	Klincke, Matilda	Mapp, Bill	Mercer, William R. "Bill"	Niemeyer, Walter A.
Gwin, Jr., S. Lawrence	Howell, Robert M.	Kluever, E. Kent	Mapson, Betty	Merchant, Richard "Dick"	Niles, David P.
Hackett, James F. "Jim"	Howley, Carlos W.	Kluever, Patty	Marancik, Andrew G.	Metrando, Andrew J. "Doc"	Niles, Guy Richard
Haight, Sherman P.	Hughes, Richard G.	Kofman, Edmunde	Mariotti, Peter J. "Pete"	Meyer, John J.	Nonweiler, Gregory P.
Hale, Stephen D.	Hughes, Thomas Edward	Konek, John B.	Marks, Frank L.	Meyers, Christopher Shawn	Norman, Donald W.
Hall, Dillard R.	Hughes, Thomas M.	Korry, Julius	Marm, Walter "Joe"	Meyers, David E.	Norris, Billie P.
Hall, Ibby	Hume, Mark	Kosinski, John E.	Martin, Calvin	Meyers, John C.	Norris, Else R.
Hall, James W.	Hume, Shannon S.	Krachinski, Roger W.	Martin, Lewis	Miceli, Carmen S.	Norris, Roland E.
Hall, Kerry D.	Hunt, George L.	Kral, Daniel R.	Martin, Randall D.	Migut, Ronald J.	
Hamberger, Charles D.	Hunt, Henry C.	Krampien, Robert F.	Martin, Robert "Bob"	Millar, Tim	O'Brien, John
Hanell, John C.	Hunter, Art	Kreischer, William H. "Bill"	Martinez, Jose J.	Miller, Dall H.	O'Dea, Milton L. "Mike"
Hanlen, Don F.	Hunter, Sheryl D.	Kruske, Richard T.	Martinez, Robert V.	Miller, Frank L.	O'Donnell, Robert
Hanson, Douglas G.	Huritt, Thomas Leroy	Krysik, John	Maruhnich, John	Miller, Frederick E.	Oakes, Gary A.
Hardy, Douglas C.	Hutson, Frank Lee	Kuykendall, Anthony	Massey, Gary L.	Miller, Paul V.	Odems, Paul
Hargrove, Lawrence E.	Hyde, Charles V.	Kvidt, Reuben D.	Masterson, Michael J.	Miller, Robert E.	Oden, Charles B.
Harman, Charles W.			Matichak, William	Milliner, William K.	Ogden, Lawrence J.
Harris, James	Ingley, Stephen J.	Lacey, Richard S.	Mattes, Charles W.	Millis, Michael Edward	Olivier, George A.
Harris, Ralph N.	Inka, Dennis	Lacey, William J.	Matthews, John A.	Milum, Hank	Oneal, Lewis John
Harris, Thomas Pressley		Lacey, Sr., William J.	Matthews, John D.	Miner, Norval M.	Oresick, Andrew
Harry, Curtis E.	Jackson, Bobby J.	Lajeunesse, Robert W. "Bob"	Matthias, Henry N.	Minnick, Walter D.	Ortiz, Guillermo C.
Hartin, Thomas E.	Jackson, George "Bob"	Lajoie, Daniel G.	Mauger, Robert N.	Mione, Saluatore	Ortiz, Nelson
Haskell, John "Jack"	Jackson, MD, John M.	Landis, Tim	Maxwell, M. Donald	Mitchell, Charles F.	Osborn, George M.
Hasson, Alain Victor M.	Jacobson, Lyle W.	Langevin, Joseph	Maybury, Richard E.	Mitchell, Jr., Tommie L.	Osterby, Norman R.
Hatch, Gardner	Jerome, Roy W.	Larsen, Clifford "Swede"	Mayer, Christopher T.	Mohr, Jerry A.	Osterby, Peggy
Hatfield, Emsley	Johns, Barbara	Larson, Bobby D.	Mayse, Jack h.	Molloy, E. A. "Mike"	Ouellette, Robert P.
Hawksby, Richard	Johnson, Dale N.	Larson, Rorik W.	Mazza, Emilio A.	Montean, Carl R.	Owen, Joseph K.
Hayes, Douglas	Johnson, Delores	Larson, Todd A.	McAleer, Charles A.	Montgomery, William	
Hazen, Robert D.	Johnson, Elmer R.	Lasater, R. C.	McAnnany, Joseph "Joe"	Mooney, Wm. T. "Bill"	Paine, Cletus L.
Hedges, L. Wesley	Johnson, Gregory W.	Laws, Bill R.	McBride, Jack E.	Moore, Curtis G.	Palmer, Fred L.
Hedley, William	Johnson, Harlen	Leary, Michael C.	McBride, Norman L. "Doc"	Moore, Gary L.	Parker, Larry B.
Heis, June	Johnson, Kenneth D.	Lee, Edgar J.	McBroom, Richard C.	Moore, Harold G. "Hal"	Parkinson, George T.
Heismann, Steven H.	Johnson, Robert D.	Lee, Jesse F.	McCamley, John	Moore, James R.	Parle, John J.
Heiter, James A. "Tony"	Johnson, Jr., Shirley J.	Lee, W. Suey	McCarey, Edward J.	Moore, William F.	Parton, Joey N.
Heltsley, Nancy Bernice	Johnston, E. Bruce	Lehigh, Laura C.	McClung, Jr., William	Moran, Ray J.	Passos, Connie
Henry, Larry P.	Johnston, Robert J.	Lemmons, Elzie G. W.	McClure, James A.	Moreland, H. Boyd	Passos, Ignacio "Nash"
Herman, Jeffrey B.	Jones, Alzalkie C.	Lenon, Helen	McClure, Robert M.	Morelli, James	Paterson, Steven J.
Hernandez, Andrew M.	Jones, Robert D.	Lenon, Jr., James E.	McComas, Clyde W. "Mac"	Morgan, Robert Dwight	Patterson, Howard D.
Hernandez, Cesar A.	Jordan, Dwight E.	Lent, Thomas D.	McComber, Alex T.	Morton, Richard L.	Pauley, Sr., Henry John
Herren, John D.	Julian, Casey H.	Lewis, Ernest R. "Ray"	McCray, Catherine	Moseley, Robert G.	Paulsen, James G.
Herrmann, Fred		Lewis, George	McDonald, Robert E.	Mote, Robert G.	Peardon, Robert E.
Hickey, Pennell "Joe"	Kahrs, Jr., Donald H.	Lewis, Robert D.	McDonald, Jr., George J.	Mrochek, Jeffry A.	Pellerito, Andrew P. "Andy"
Hill, Carl M.	Karhohs, Fred E.	Lippincott, John C.	McElhannon, Paul	Murphy, Charles U.	Pelot, Marguerite
Hill, Jacque	Kaufman, David X.	Lippincott, Kevin A.	McIlroy, David A.	Murphy, George N.	Pelot, Mell S.
Hillegas, Samuel R. "Richard"	Kazantzas, Peter T.	Litle, Jr., Robert F. "Bob"	McKee, Mark	Murphy, Isaac	Pennison, Forrest J.
Hindman, John T.	Keane, Patrick J.	Little Big Horn Association	McKenzie, James A.	Murphy, Jim	Perales, Frank J.
Hines, Sr., Woodrow N.	Keck, Dennis	Litton, James "Larry"	McKeon, Thomas L.	Murphy, Thomas L.	Perkins, James D. "David"
Hobbs, Michael C.	Keeton, Douglas W.	Long, Thomas R.	McKinley, Russell "Russ"	Myers, Charles W.	Perozek, Charles J.
Hoffman, Christopher	Kelley, Donna Kay	Lorris, Nicholas G.	McKinney, John J.	Myres, Jacob C.	Peterson, Merle J.
Hoffman, William H.	Kennemore, Jr., Charles M.	Lovell, William C. "Bill"	McKnight, Thomas L.		Peyser, Daniel B.
Hogans, Darius N.	Kerecz, James J.	Lowry, James M. "Jim"	McKown, William N. "Bill"	Nacke, Albert	Phillips, Christopher L.
Holland, Theron	Kesterson, William J.	Lucas, Jennifer	McManus, Francis W.	Nadal, II, Ramon A. "Tony"	Phillips, Herbert D.
Hollingworth, Roy	Kiernan, John P.	Lucero, Richard L.	McNancy, Phillip J.	Nardi, Patrick	Phillips, Ronald W.
Holtsberry, Russell J.	Kieslar, John D.	Ludke, Tammy J.	McQuistion, Jeffrey D.	Natale, Gil	Pickett, Earl E.
Horn, Charles R. "Chuck"	Kietzman, Gerald R.	Lutz, Roger	Meeker, Jeffrey L.	Neill, Marion C.	Pignatona, George
Horn, Roland E.	Kilduff, Thomas C.	Lynd, Allyn David		Nelson, Charles W.	Piscal, Richard G.
Hoskins, Jr., Clayton	Kincaid, Charles E. "Bob"			Nelson, Tommy A.	Pittman, Donald R.
	Kinder, Robert E.	Mac Farland, Donald J.		Nemec, Alice	Plaisance, Jr., Ecton J.
	King, C.	Mace, Herman A.			Pless, Paul E.
	King, Daniel J. W.				
	King, Jr., Charles F.				
	Kinler, Robert R.				
	Kinnard, Harry W. O.				

Plumley, Basil L.
Poley, Clinton
Pomeroy, William B.
Pool, James C.
Porche, Stanley E.
Post, Alton G.
Potts, John O.
Pressgraves, Donald C.
Preslan, Robert S. "Bob"
Pujals, Enrique V.

Rabchenia, Nick J.
Raisner, Walter T.
Ramirez, John M.
Ramsey, Alberta
Ramsey, Willie L.
Randazzo, George
Randel, Jr., Herbert R.
Randell, Thomas E.
Ransome, John G.
Ransmussen, Michael R.
Reed, Brian L.
Reed, Cliff V.
Reeves, Scott E.
Reigle, Kenneth
Rescorla, Richard
Reyes, Roy C.
Reynolds, Pamela
Rhea, Samuel G.
Richard, Emile
Richards, Jerry R.
Richardson, Eva
Richardson, Francis H. "Frank"
Richardson, Harold E.
Richardson, Robert D.
Richardson, William A.
Riley, Linda
Rivera, Mary T.
Roberts, Kaylon E.
Roberts, William H.
Roberts, Sr., Charles R.
Robey, James E.
Robinson, Dan
Robinson, J. Paul
Robinson, John B.
Rodgers, Martin A. "Marty"
Rodriguez, Jose N.
Rodriqueg, Jr., Sebastain
Rolf, Oliver E.
Rosado, Ed
Rose, James K.
Rosinski, Sr., Adam J.
Ross, Billy R.
Ross, Donald S.
Ross, Mary A.
Ross, Nadean
Roth, Pauline S.
Rottenberg, Marvin
Roulhac, Jerome L.
Rourke, MD., John C.

Rowley, Ada Ruth
Rowley, Glenn W.
Royan, MD, E. H.
Rozanski, Gordon P.
Rudel, Karen Metsker
Ruffin, Donald C.
Rulon, Hurley
Runnion, Lewis R.
Runyon, Myron D.
Rupert, Robert B.
Russ, Marion T.
Russell, Robert G.
Ryan, Frank L.
Ryland, Richard C.
Rylant, Timothy M.
Sack, Thomas A.
Sagerhorn, James
Saldana, Rafael
Sales, James M.
Samaniego, Jr., Pedro "Pete"
Sammons, Kenneth R.
Sammons, Robert B.
Sandidge, Donovan B.
Sanford, M. Daniel
Santry, Robert M.
Savoie, Phil
Schaaff, Fred
Schild, James "Jim"
Schleusner, C. R.
Schlieve, Gregory A.
Schmitz, Charles R.
Schoelch, Frank F.
Schrank, Walter C.
Schwietert, Clinton L.
Screws, Eldon D.
Sebranek, David C.
Selber, Eric A.
Self, Jimmy R.
Selley, Harold V.
Serge, Michael L.
Serri, Domenico P.
Setelin, John I.
Severson, Gordon J.
Sewak, Steven Michael
Shackelford, Ray
Shannon, Robert A.
Sharp, Stephen E.
Sharp, Walter L.
Sheldon. Harrison W. "Bill"
Shields, Richard J.
Shingler, John
Shipman, Charles C.
Shirah, James L.
Short, Lawrence J.
Shutt, Don "Doc"
Silber, II, Carl H.
Simmeth, Jr., Harry G.
Simmons, Milton E.
Simpson, Darrell D.
Sinegar, James M.
Singer, Nena
Sisson, Robert D.
Skal, Carl E.
Sleeis, Ronald G.
Smith, Barton M.
Smith, Dwight

Smith, Jack P.
Smith, James C.
Smith, James R.
Smith, John P. "Jack"
Smith, Joseph M.
Smith, Leo B.
Smith, Raymond J.
Smith, Timothy J.
Smith, Toni
Smith, William D.
Smolik, Vincent Wm.
Snow, Jr., Tommy A.
Snyder, John H.
Sowder, Jo
Sparrow, Stephen P.
Spriggs, Montie F.
St. Martin, Robert D.
Stahl, Earnest L.
Stallman, Donald L.
Stanley, Jr., Arthur J.
Stanton, Billy
Stausmire, John W.
Steffen, Jan P.
Stern, Roy
Stevens, Sr., Fred
Stewart, Billy
Stewart, William J.
Sticken, Robert J.
Stockton, Carlos J. "Jay"
Stoker, Sr., Carl E.
Stokes, Sr., William
Stone, Jt, Thomas W.
Stone, Jr., Willie W.
Stopper, Larry E.
Stoutland, Fredrick A.
Streeter, William T.
Stripling, Carrol D.
Stump, Vallie H.
Sugdinis, Joel E.
Sulcer, James R.
Sullivan, Bradley C.
Sullivan, Kenneth G.
Sunde, Eiven
Swain, Richard A.
Swan, William H. "Bill"
Sweet, Clarence A.
Swoyer, David L.

Talavera, III, Jose M-Toso
Tallau, Howard G.
Talley, Jack H.
Tapia, Peter Genaro
Tardiff, Chris
tasker, Kenneth Rodger
Tavean, IV, Horatio Sprague
Templeton, Robert L.
Terrell, Jr., Ernest P.
Thoele, Evelyn
Thomas, John W.
Thompson, James W.
Thompson, Jr., William R.
Thorn, Thomas H.
Tilelli, Jeanne M.
Tilelli, John
Tilelli, Margaret A.

Toborg, Robert H. "Bob"
Tompkins, William R.
Torres, Jr., Frank G.
Toskas, Anthony L.
Towles, Robert L.
Trefry, Jr., Paul I.
Trevino, Hector L.
Trevion, Noe S.
Trout, Jr., Donald F.
Trowbridge, Jr., Gordon P.
Tucker, Frank
Tucker, Terry L.
Turner, Dave
Tuzzolino, Paul L.
Tyree, Elzie

Umpherville, Kenneth R.

Valane, Peter "Pete"
Vallier, Emry A.
Valliere, Ronald B.
Van Dyke, Sherman M.
Vassalotti, Michael J.
Velarde, Mike A.
Villacres, Edward J.
Visor, MD., Rick L.
Viveros, Thomas J.
Von Ruedgisch, Margarete
Vosmeir, Leonard F. "Bud"
Votaw. E. L. "Chip"

Wagner, William D.
Wagnild, Edward
Walker, Jr., Robert E.
Walks Over Ice, Loreen
Wallace, Owen C.
Wallace, William C.
Wallenius, John W.
Walsh, William J.
Ward, Daniel G.
Ward, Greg
Ward, Richard J.
Wares, Jr., William M.
Watkins, William D.
Webster, Albert A.
Weichmann, Jack
Weinstein, Stanley A.
Welch, Charles Alfred
Welch, Dean A.
Wenger, Craig W.
Werner, Jr., Floyd S.
Wernsing, Merrill
Wertman, Millard W.
Wessels, Jr., Herman J.
West, Gene
West, Robert D.
West, William W.
White, Richard
White, William J.
Wickham, Jr., John A.
Widener, Larry E.

Wigant, Harold M.
Wiley, William T.
Willen, Charles J.
Williams, Herman D.
Williams, Howard M.
Williams, John R.
Williams, Nevin R. "Pete"
Williams, II, Nevin R.
Williamson, Barry L.
Wilson, James A.
Wilson, Robert J.
Wilson, Jr., David E.
Wiltshire, Clifford R. "Bucky"
Wing, Jr., Franklin F.
Winter, Peter J.
Witte, Peter N.
Wolfe, Robert H.
Wood, James P.
Woodall, Harold L.
Woodley, Clinton A.
Woodrow, William W.
Woods, William J.
Wyosnick, Kathleen Cronan

Young. Chester D. "Chet"
Younger, Edwin Wm.
Youts, Jr., Robert B.

Zadell, Joe
Zallen, Jerald D. "Jack"
Zanoni, Scott A.
Zapata, Maurilio
Zent, Larry D.
Zent, Lillian
Zook, Phillip Martin

No Address

Abram, Timothy L.
Anderson, Mark A.
Armstrong, Edward Cross
Benton, Michael D.
Boles, Jr., Gorden Bennie
Brauer, Billy R.
Brosius, Tim
Bullington, Billy N.
Campbell, James
Chase, Al
Chewey, Pat
Coco, Rick
Cooke, James D.
Corti, Christopher
David, Rodney B.
Dennis, Michael L.
Doran, Robert E. "Bob"
Dougherty, John M.
English, Lance
Floyd, David B.
Foster, Leland C.
Frix, Robert S.
Glenn, Michael B.
Gregory, Robyn M.
Griffin, Charles E.

Grisius, John
Grocott, Karl J.
Halladay-Pierce, Virginia G.
Harris, Charles M.
Herrera, Jr., Gilberto A.
Hill, Thomas
Hudson, George
Hurd, Steven E.
Hyatt, Scott W.
Illing, Thomas R.
Kenche, Ronald
Lukes, Frank J.
Mateyka, Charles A.
Mattes, James
McFetridge, C. Don
Mumby, Rodger L.
Palmer, Jackson F. "Jack"
Reid, Fredrick D.
Reinhart, Richard C.
Riley, James C.
Roberson, James O.
Schneider, James
Schooner, Raymond J.
Schull, Robert F.
Sexton, Rhonda
Sheean, Daniel
Short, Ted
Siegreen, Richard L.
Smith, Arlo C.
Smythe, John A.
Spalding, Tom W.
Stevens, Randall R.
Sutton, Charles K.
Swahn, John
Tavean, V, Hiratio S.
Thompson, Angelo L.
Thompson, III, Jamie Campbell
Valenti, Peter J.
Williams, James D.
Ysais, Felix E.

Deceased 7th Cavalry Members

Coffman, Allen
Croy, Noel L.
Culley, Frank
Cumberland, James
Curran, Jr., Glen E. "Slim"
Down, Edna R.
Jean, William W.
Lahue, William H.
Lane, John R. "Bob"
Lenihan, Timothy N.
Lucas, Velmer R.
McGraw, Grover C.
McKee, Clarence C.
Moore, Robert
Morrison, Claude B. "Mick"
Nye, George J.
Paolone, Ernest E.
Starkey, J. M.
Stowe, Jack
Tobin, Richard E.
Zent, Jack A.

ACKNOWLEDGEMENTS

I wish to express my personal debt to Colonel John W. Callaway (Ret.), for his individual encouragement and support to write this book. And to his lovely wife, Mrs. Lynn Callaway, for her understanding and confidence in the undertaking of the book project; I give both my most humble thanks.

A special thanks to those individuals who assisted the author along the way and the support that was expressed by those members of the 7th U.S. Cavalry and 1st Cavalry Division Associations. And especially to those former officers and enlisted troopers of the 7th Cavalry Regiment, Korean War 1950-51, to whom I am particularly indebted to all of them, my deepest thanks and appreciation. I realize that I cannot thank each one separately, then it is with hope that this book will serve as their reward.

Special Recognition

General Matthew B. Ridgway (Ret.), U.S. Army; to one of the Army's finest generals, former Commander-in-Chief of the United Nations Forces during the Korean War.

General Charles D. Palmer (Ret.), U.S. Army; to an excellent general who always was tough-minded with a fighting stance and former 1st Cavalry Division Commander, during the Korean War 1950-51.

Lieutenant General Harold "Hal" Moore (Ret.), U.S. Army; thanks for your continued loyalty to the 7th U.S. Cavalry and 1st Cavalry Division Associations; and for the support of this book project.

Colonel Robert F. Litle, Jr. (Ret.), U.S. Army; former 2nd Battalion Commander (Vietnam), 7th Cavalry Regiment, 1st Cavalry Division; presently Executive Director, 1st Cavalry Division Association. Thanks for your continued support, Col. Bob.

Lieutenant Colonel Mell S. Pelot (Ret.), U.S. Army; former officer of the Medical Company assigned to the 2nd Battalion, 7th Cavalry Regiment, Korea 1951. And to his lovely wife, Marguerite, for their dedication and loyalty to the 7th U.S. Cavalry and 1st Cavalry Division Associations, and for the support of this book project.

Dr. John C. Rourke, former Captain and Battalion Surgeon, 2nd Battalion, 7th Cavalry Regiment, 1st Cavalry Division, 1950-51; for his devotion to duty in attempting to save the lives of the wounded under some of the most critical and overwhelming odds.

Major John "Jack" Haskell (Ret.), U.S. Army; former officer 545th Military Police Company and who had the only hobby horse in the 1st Cavalry Division during the Korean War 1950-51. Thanks, Jack, for your continued support of the 7th Cavalry and 1st Cavalry Division Associations and for the support of this book.

Mrs. Vera Chandler (widow of Lt. Col. Melbourne C. Chandler); for permitting the author to use invaluable material from the book, "Of GARRYOWEN In Glory"; and Associate Member of the 7th U.S. Cavalry Association. I extend my most sincere thanks and appreciation.

James Chandler (son of Melbourne C. Chandler); his wife, Suzanne, and son, Christopher. Thanks, Jim, for your continued support.

Kathleen Cronan Wyosnick; thanks for your devotion and dedication to the Korean War Veterans of America, and to the 7th U.S. Cavalry Chapter, Korean War Veterans 1950-53. Again, our many thanks of appreciation.

Patti Harris, a special thanks in the computer work and processing of many notes and manuscript.

Fred and Lois Carlen of Carlen's Free-lance Photography; thanks for the excellent photo service.

To all former GARRYOWEN officers, non-commissioned officers and enlisted men who served during the Korean War 1950-51; I salute all of you! Their names are not listed due to the limited space in this book. (Refer to the roster of the 7th U.S. Cavalry Association in this book.)

In Memory

In memory of Douglas MacArthur, General of the Army, U.S. Army; former Allied Supreme Commander, Far East Command.

In memory of William H. Harris, Major General, U.S. Army; former Regimental Commander, 7th Cavalry Regiment, 1st Cavalry Division, 1950-51.

In memory of Melbourne C. Chandler, Lt. Colonel, U.S. Army; former Executive Officer and Battalion Commander (after Callaway), 2nd Battalion, 7th Cavalry Regiment, 1st Cavalry Division. He was the author of the military book, "Of GARRYOWEN In Glory," and insofar as it is known today, this book is the only history covering the entire life of the 7th U.S. Cavalry from its origination on July 28, 1866, through the year 1957.

In memory of all of those GARRYOWEN officers, non-commissioned officers and enlisted men of the 7th Cavalry Regiment 1950-53, who served with relentless courage and dauntless bravery and who made the supreme sacrifice - their names are not listed due to space limits. This book, however, is a tribute to them and their families.

In Recognition

Greek Expeditionary Forces (GEF), 4th Battalion
8th Engineers Combat Battalion
70th Tank Battalion
61st Field Artillery
77th Field Artillery
82nd Field Artillery
99th Field Artillery
15th Medical Company
4.2 Heavy Mortar Company, 7th Cavalry Regiment
16th Reconnaissance Company
27th Ordinance Company
15th Quartermaster Company
15th Replacement Company
5th Cavalry Regiment
7th Cavalry Regiment
8th Cavalry Regiment
13th Signal Company
92nd AAA Battalion
545th Military Police Company
1st Cavalry Division Association
7th United States Cavalry Association

My thoughts and love

To all my immediate family and relatives and especially to my grandsons, Eddie III and Patrick, and my granddaughter, Julie.

Edward L. Daily
Clarksville, TN

FRIENDS AND REMEMBRANCES

SOURCES

The 1st Cavalry Division
Korea, June 1950 - January 1952
Albert Love Enterprises, publishers
Atlanta, Ga.

At War in Korea (1985 edition)
George Forty, author
Bonanza Books, Publishers
Distributed by Crown Publishers, Inc.
225 Park Avenue South
New York, N.Y. 10003

The Korean War - History and Tactics
David Rees, Consultant Editor
Cresent Books, Publishers
Distributed by Crown Publishers, Inc.
225 Park Avenue South
New York, N.Y. 10003

South to the Naktong - North to the Yalu
Roy E. Appleman, author

United States Army in the Korean War
Office of the Chief of Military History
Department of the Army
Washington, D.C.

Korea, 1950
Copyright 1952 by Orlando Ward
The Chief of Military History
Department of the Army
Washington, D.C.

Korea, 1951-53
By John Miller, Jr., Owen Jr. Carroll, Major
U.S. Army and Margaret E. Tackley
The Chief of Military History
Department of the Army
Washington, D.C.
This Kind of War
By T.R. Fehrenbach, author 1963
The Macmillian Company
New York, N.Y.

The Forgotten War
Clay Blair, author
Times Books, a division of Random House of
Canada Limited,
Toronto

General MacArthurs' Address to Congress
Joint Session of Congress, April 19, 1951
National Research Bureau Inc.
Chicago, Ill.

Rangers In Korea
Robert W. Black, author
Published by Ballantine Books
Division of Random House, Inc.
New York, N.Y.

Of GARRYOWEN in Glory
Lt. Col. Melbourne C. Chandler, author
The Turnpike Press
Annandale, Va.

Black Market
National Archives
Eighth Army HQ Command Reports
"Narrative of Operations" and
"War Diary G-3 Section"
(Hereafter Command Report, monthly)
File no. RG407
7th Cavalry Regiment, Command Reports
1st Cavalry Division, File no. L88-3380-
RJW
Richard Boylan
Assistant Chief
Military Field Branch
Military Archives Division
Washington, D.C. 20409

Legacy of the 7th U.S. Cavalry, in Korea
Edward L. Daily, author
Turner Publishing Company
P.O. Box 3101
Paducah, Ky. 42002-3101